John Foster Dulles and the
Diplomacy of the Cold War

John Foster Dulles and the Diplomacy of the Cold War

Edited by Richard H. Immerman

PRINCETON UNIVERSITY PRESS

PRINCETON, NEW JERSEY

Library of Congress Cataloging-in-Publication Data

John Foster Dulles and the diplomacy of the Cold War / edited by Richard H.
Immerman.

   p.   cm.
   Includes index.
   ISBN 0-691-04765-0
   1. Dulles, John Foster, 1888–1959.   2. United States—Foreign relations—1953–
1961.   3. Cold war.   I. Immerman, Richard H.
E748.D868J64   1989
973.921′092—dc20   89-34975

Publication of this book has been aided by the Whitney Darrow Fund
of Princeton University Press

This book has been composed in Linotron Baskerville

Princeton University Press books are printed on acid-free paper,
and meet the guidelines for permanence and durability of the
Committee on Production Guidelines for Book Longevity of the
Council on Library Resources

Printed in the United States of America by Princeton University Press,
Princeton, New Jersey
10 9 8 7 6 5 4 3 2 1

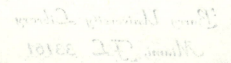

TO NANCY BRESSLER

For her incalculable contribution to the study of John Foster Dulles

Contents

Acknowledgments

This book contains revised papers initially presented to the "John Foster Dulles Centennial Conference: The Challenge of Leadership in International Affairs," held at Princeton University's Woodrow Wilson School of Public and International Affairs February 25–27, 1988. Convened precisely one hundred years after Dulles's birth, the conference would not have been possible without the generous support of the Henry Luce Foundation, the Konrad-Adenauer-Stiftung, the governments of Austria and the Republic of China, and the Woodrow Wilson School. The former secretary of state's many family members, friends, and colleagues, who made up the sponsoring committee of the John Foster Dulles Program for the Study of Leadership in International Affairs, warrant a special note of thanks. The committee's membership is too large to list, but particular mention must be made of the contributions of Gerard C. Smith, its executive chairman, and Eleanor Lansing Dulles, its guiding spirit and most indefatigable worker.

Conference participants included an unusual blend of scholars, practitioners, and Dulles acquaintances. Consequently, those who presented papers benefited from an array of expert commentaries. The contributors to this book therefore would like collectively to thank Robert Amory, Tapley Bennett, Robert Bowie, Henry Brandon, Herbert Brownell, Hodding Carter, C. Douglas Dillon, D. David Eisenhower, Alan Emory, Robert Fearey, Andrew Goodpaster, John Hanes, U. Alexis Johnson, George Kennan, Phyllis Macomber, William Macomber, Ross Mark, David Newsom, Warren Rogers, Gerard Smith, David Waters, and Burke Wilkinson. The authors also gratefully acknowledge the insights offered by the scores of scholars who took part in the concluding "roundtable" on contemporary implications and future research.

Dean Donald E. Stokes and Assistant Dean Ingrid W. Reed, both of the Woodrow Wilson School, gave unstintingly of their time and energy, and Fred I. Greenstein, the conference chairman, demonstrated the true meaning of leadership. Janice Finney and Amy Valis provided indispensable secretarial and organizational skills, and Agnes Pearson somehow managed to hold everything together. Jayne Bialkowski typed and retyped the manuscript, while Helen Gregutt applied her editorial skills to countless instances of fractured syntax and dangling participles. The breadth of Thomas Banchoff's research assistance was remarkable. At the Eisenhower Library, Martin Teasley and David Haight went out of their way to run down "lost" citations; as usual Nancy Bressler, of Princeton University's Seeley G. Mudd Library, responded to my every request, no matter how big or small. I also want to thank Sanford Thatcher of Princeton University Press, Kevin Ahern, my copyeditor, and Waldo Heinrichs and Stephen Ambrose, the two referees. Their nitpicks as well as probing critiques contributed to a much-improved manuscript.

Personally I received financial support from an SSRC/MacArthur Foundation Fellowship in International Peace and Security Studies. More importantly, I received emotional support from Marion and Tyler. They sacrificed a lot for this book but will receive none of the credit. They deserve more than they will ever know.

Key to Primary Sources and Abbreviations

These frequently cited primary materials are referred to by the following abbreviations. Although the collections and series will be abbreviated, folder titles will not and will be denoted by quotation marks.

AWD   Ann Whitman Diary—in AWF.

AWF   Dwight D. Eisenhower Papers of the President of the United States, 1953–1961. This collection is known as the Ann Whitman File, named after Eisenhower's personal secretary who organized the documents at Gettysburg. It is divided into various series, which are cited separately in this list.

CAB   Documents of the Cabinet—in PRO.

CS   Chronological Series—in DPEL.

DG   *Documents on Germany, 1944–1985*.

DHS   Dulles–Herter Series—in AWF.

DPEL   John Foster Dulles Papers, 1951–1959. These papers derive primarily from Dulles's tenure as secretary of state. They are on deposit at the Dwight D. Eisenhower Library, Abilene, Kansas; copies are also available at the Seeley G. Mudd Library, Princeton University. The collection is divided into various series, which are cited separately in this list.

DPP   John Foster Dulles Papers, 1888–1959. These are Dulles's personal papers that cover his entire public career. Located only at the Mudd Library in Princeton, they do not include those files under the regulations of the Department of State.

DSB   *Department of State Bulletin.*

DSRG   Department of State General Records, followed by the record group number. The State Department's central file, this collection is available at the National Archives, Washington, D.C.

EDS   Eisenhower Diary Series–in AWF.

FO   Documents of the Foreign Office—in PRO.

FR   *Foreign Relations of the United States*, followed by the year. Compiled by the Office of the Historian, U.S. Department of State, these volumes constitute the official record of U.S. foreign policy. The following volumes, all published by the Government Printing Office in Washington, D.C., are cited in many of the chapters in this book.

FR, 1945, 2: *The Conference of Berlin (The Potsdam Conference)* (1960)

FR, 1948, 2: *Germany and Austria* (1973)

FR, 1948, 6: *The Far East and Australia* (1974)

FR, 1948, 9: *The Western Hemisphere* (1972)

FR, 1949, 7: *The Far East and Australia* (pt. 1, 1975; pt. 2, 1976)

FR, 1950, 6: *East Asia and the Pacific* (1976)

FR, 1951, 6: *Asia and the Pacific* (1977)

FR, 1952–1954, 1: *General: Economic and Political Matters* (1983)

FR, 1952–1954, 2: *National Security* (1984)

FR, 1952–1954, 4: *The American Republics* (1983)

FR, 1952–1954, 5: *Western European Security* (1983)

FR, 1952–1954, 6: *Western Europe and Canada* (1986)

FR, 1952–1954, 7: *Germany and Austria* (1978)

FR, 1952–1954, 12: *East Asia and the Pacific* (pt. 1, 1984; pt. 2, 1987)

FR, 1952–1954, 13: *Indochina* (1982)

FR, 1952–1954, 14: *China and Japan* (1985)

FR, 1952–1954, 15: *Korea* (1984)

FR, 1952–1954, 16: *The Geneva Conference* (1981)

FR, 1955–1957, 2: *China* (1986)

FR, 1955–1957, 3: *China* (1986)

FR, 1955–1957, 4: *Western European Security and Integration* (1986)

FR, 1955–1957, 6: *American Republics: Multilateral; Mexico; Caribbean* (1987)

FR, 1955–1957, 7: *American Republics: Central and South America* (1987)

GCMS   General Correspondence and Memoranda Series—in DPEL.

IS   International Series—in AWF.

JCSRG   Records of the U.S. Joint Chiefs of Staff, followed by the record group number. Available at the National Archives, Washington, D.C.

JFDOHC   John Foster Dulles Oral History Collection. Available at the John Foster Dulles Diplomatic and Mudd Libraries, Princeton University.

NSCS	National Security Council Series—in AWF.
PD	Personal Diary (in part independent of AWF)—in AWF.
PREM	Documents of the Prime Minister—in PRO.
PRO	British government documents located in the Public Record Office, London. They are classified by departments, which are cited separately in this list.
SFRC	Documents of the Senate Foreign Relations Committee.
SPS	Speech Series—in AWF.
SS	Subject Series—in DPEL.
TTS	Telephone Transcript Series—in DPEL.
WHMS	White House Memoranda Series—in DPEL.
WHOF	White House Official File. A component of the Central File, which is the largest collection in the Eisenhower Library.
WHOSANSA	White House Office of the Special Assistant for National Security Affairs, 1952–1961. The records of Robert Cutler, Dillon Anderson, and Gordon Gray. Available at the Eisenhower Library.
WHOSS	White House Office of the Staff Secretary, 1952–1961. The records of Paul T. Carroll, Andrew J. Goodpaster, L. Arthur Minnich, and Christopher H. Russell. Available at the Eisenhower Library.

Additional published and unpublished primary material will be cited in full where appropriate.

John Foster Dulles and the
Diplomacy of the Cold War

Introduction

Richard H. Immerman

THOMAS DEWEY once described John Foster Dulles as "no ordinary mortal" when it came to understanding and conducting international relations.[1] Dwight D. Eisenhower was not that effusive, but he did confide in his private diary that "[t]here is probably no one in the world who has the technical competence of Foster Dulles in the diplomatic field."[2] To the president, Dulles was "well-informed" and deserving of "his reputation as a 'wise' man"; he was "a dedicated and tireless individual" who "passionately believes in the United States, in the dignity of man, and in moral values."[3] In 1953 Eisenhower's was the consensus view. Most informed Americans considered his designation of Dulles as the administration's chief diplomatist to be a foregone conclusion, and only 4 percent of those polled in April 1953 on their "attitudes toward the secretary of state" registered a negative response.[4]

Yet even before cancer robbed Dulles of his last years in office (he died in 1959), he had come to personify the shortcomings of America's affairs of state, the symbol of misguided and mismanaged foreign policy.[5] In a large part he owed his declining popularity to his public image, that of a Presbyterian moralist ever ready—and eager—to do battle with the devil: that is, the communists. Dulles's countless speeches and writings frequently included sterile and simplistic notions that, far from sounding innocent, were interpreted as naive, alarmist, and dangerous. To this day his rhetoric haunts his reputation. "[B]ecause of his dangerous tendency toward overstatement,"

[1] Quoted in Hans Morgenthau, "John Foster Dulles," in Norman Graebner, ed., *An Uncertain Tradition: American Secretaries of State in the Twentieth Century* (New York, 1961), 302.

[2] Entry for January 10, 1956, in Robert Ferrell, ed., *The Eisenhower Diaries* (New York, 1981), 306.

[3] Entry for May 14, 1953, in Ferrell, ed., *The Eisenhower Diaries*, 237.

[4] H. Schuyler Foster, *Activism Replaces Isolationism: U.S. Public Attitudes 1940–1975* (Washington, 1983), 131. Of those polled, 36 percent were not prepared to provide an opinion.

[5] For a cogent critique see Norman Graebner, *The New Isolationism: A Study in Politics and Foreign Policy since 1950* (New York, 1956), 90–93, 184.

Dulles, according to a recent survey of historians, ranks among the five worst secretaries of state in America's history.[6]

Dulles would have been disappointed with his standing. He was sensitive to the criticism of his contemporaries, but hoped that his image would improve with the passage of time. "It's too early to tell [how I will go down in history]," he confided to his personal assistant not long before his death. "The returns aren't in, and the returns won't be in for another twenty-five years, for anybody to make an objective assessment of my role as secretary of state. That's comforting for me in many ways."[7] It has now been more than twenty-five years, and the returns still are not in.[8] The centennial of Dulles's birth on February 25, 1888, nevertheless, marked an appropriate occasion for attempting such an assessment, or more accurately, an archivally based reassessment. This book is a start in that direction.

No secretary of state could have avoided all the international and domestic minefields that characterized the turbulent years of the cold war. Dulles, however, had created a climate of expectation and apprehension that demanded he make nary a misstep. In 1952, as the prime architect of and spokesman for the Republicans' foreign policy platform, he had dismissed the Truman–Acheson program as "negative, futile and immoral."[9] In a much-publicized *Life* article he had proposed to replace these "treadmill policies" with a "policy of boldness." Specifically Dulles had proclaimed the need to seize the initiative from the communists by making it *"publicly known that it* [the United States] *wants and expects liberation to occur."* At the same time America had to develop the will and organize the means *"to retaliate instantly against open aggression by Red armies, so that, if it occurred anywhere, we could and would strike back where it hurts, by means of our own choosing."*[10]

From the standpoint of Dulles's public image it was bad enough that the popular abbreviation for this last clause became "massive retaliation," which provided grist for the mills of the secretary of state's

[6] David L. Porter, "The Ten Best Secretaries of State and the Five Worst," in William Pederson and Ann McLaurin, eds., *The Rating Game in American Politics* (New York, 1987), 90.

[7] William Macomber commentary, February 25, 1988, the John Foster Dulles Centennial Conference, Princeton University. Verbatim transcripts of all the conference sessions are available at the Seeley G. Mudd Manuscript Library, Princeton University.

[8] For a still informative perspective see Ole Holsti, "Will the Real Dulles Please Stand Up?" *International Journal* 30 (Winter 1974–1975): 34–44.

[9] Kirk Porter and Donald Johnson, comps., *National Party Platforms, 1840–1964* (Urbana, 1966), 499.

[10] John Foster Dulles, "A Policy of Boldness," *Life* (May 19, 1952): 146, 151, 154. Italics in original.

critics on both the left and the right. What added insult to injury was the perceptibly vast discrepancy between the rhetoric and the reality. Americans undoubtedly were relieved that the United States did not retaliate massively when it confronted the communists over Dien Bien Phu, or Quemoy-Matsu, or Berlin. Still, they came increasingly to suspect Dulles of being a paper tiger, and an irresponsibly hypo-critical one. After all, to boast about nuclear duels at the brink seemed the height of recklessness, strained allied relations, and threatened to erode America's credibility.[11] How often could Dulles rattle his nuclear saber before the enemy stopped taking his warnings seriously?[12] And as for the other component of his policy of boldness, liberation or "rollback," the administration's inability—or unwilling-ness—to liberate captive peoples, epitomized by what transpired in East Germany in 1953 and Hungary in 1956, reinforced the percep-tion that Dulles promised more than he could deliver. He had led Americans to believe that their security required a victory in the cold war and that he would produce one. In the event, they were not even sure that he could guarantee a draw.

No one likes to be criticized, let alone vilified and ridiculed, as Dul-les often was. He was a proud man, an ambitious man, acutely sensi-tive to public opinion and concerned about his place in history. That he made surprisingly little effort to improve his public image or per-sona was unquestionably due in part to his definition of his respon-sibilities to the nation and the president. As long as his policies en-gendered the necessary public and congressional support, he was satisfied.[13] He "never believed in decision-making by Gallup Poll," in the words of one former associate.[14] Yet Dulles's apparently thick skin was also due to his personality and philosophy. He was supremely self-confident; some would say arrogant and self-righteous. He never doubted the wisdom of his policies, nor their moral rectitude. More-over, since his days as a student of Henri Bergson in Paris, he had accepted change as the law of life—the dynamic triumphs over the static—a principle that applied equally to individuals and nations. It

[11] Dulles's association with "brinkmanship" stems from James Shepley, "How Dulles Averted War," *Life* (January 15, 1956): 70–72+.

[12] See Henry Kissinger, *Nuclear Weapons and Foreign Policy* (New York, 1957), and, more generally, Thomas Schelling, *Arms and Influence* (New Haven, 1966).

[13] For evidence that Dulles carefully monitored public support for his policies, see Dulles to the U.S. Delegation (in Geneva), May 24, 1954, *FR, 1952–1954*, 16:911–12. The State Department's internal analyses of public opinion have been collected in Fos-ter, *Activism Replaces Isolationism*. On Dulles and Congress see Anna Kasten Nelson, "John Foster Dulles and the Bipartisan Congress," *Political Science Quarterly* 102 (Spring 1987): 43–64.

[14] Richard Nixon interview, JFDOHC.

stood to reason, therefore, that as time passed he, and his policies, would be vindicated. In Dulles's opinion such had been the fate of Woodrow Wilson, whose experience left an indelible impression on Dulles's worldview.

In one fundamental respect, historical perspective has already begun to alter the common wisdom. Although Eisenhower's tenure has been labeled the "time of the great postponement," and commentators continue to apply the epithet "inertia" to the 1950s,[15] historians have progressively recognized that the years during which Dulles presided over the State Department were remarkably complex, dynamic, and, yes, exciting. These years confronted the United States with an extraordinary set of problems, challenges, and opportunities which, in their totality, represent a pivotal period in the evolution of U.S. foreign policy and the international system. Not only did the 1950s witness advances in thermonuclear technology and delivery capabilities that forced statesmen to rethink the very definition of national security, but these innovations required the integration of nuclear weapons into strategic policy despite the incontrovertible conclusion that their rational employment was an oxymoron.[16] All the while, moreover, the global environment was punctuated by the increasingly volatile situation between the two Chinas; by the irrevocable challenge that the Third World posed for the traditional order; and by the intensification of ideological competition that threatened to erode further the systemic sources of stability on which escape from the nuclear apocalypse appeared to depend.

In a large part because many scholars no longer perceive the Eisenhower years as bland and uninstructive, the 1950s have become the subject of many innovative and imaginative investigations. Predictably, assessments of the Eisenhower presidency (particulary regarding its conduct of foreign affairs) have undergone a remarkable transformation over the past decade. Of course, subsequent developments contributed to this historiographic revolution. In contrast to the Kennedyesque ideal of the 1960s, in the post-Vietnam, poststagflation era, Eisenhower's restraint and penny-pinching ways appeared more positive. "A generation of historians and political scientists, bred in the progressive tradition, have applied an activist

[15] For example, see John Patrick Diggins, *The Proud Decades: America in War and Peace, 1941–1960* (New York, 1988), 122–53. William Shannon coined the "time of the great postponement" in "Eisenhower as President," *Commentary* 26 (November 1958): 390–98.

[16] The dilemma inherent in this "nuclear revolution" is anticipated in Bernard Brodie, *The Absolute Weapon* (New York, 1946). See also Michael Mandelbaum, *The Nuclear Revolution* (New York, 1981).

standard to Ike's negative record and have found it wanting," explained one noted writer. "Yet in the aftermath of Vietnam, it can be argued that a President who avoids hasty military action and refrains from extensive involvement in the internal affairs of other nations deserves praise rather than scorn."[17]

From a less subjective standpoint, nevertheless, this transformation owes much to academia's propensity to follow the trail of the archives. Through the middle of the 1970s, historians of Eisenhower's foreign and national security policies had no alternative other than to rely on the public record, the "official file" of documents, and Dulles's personal papers at Princeton. The acquisition by the Eisenhower Library of the massive "Whitman File" demonstrated that these sources were both incomplete and misleading.[18] Scholars trekked to Abilene, Kansas, in search of new material and insights. Soon the opening of complementary collections in Britain, France, West Germany, and elsewhere permitted researchers to broaden their data base. The resultant outpouring of literature seriously challenged the interpretation that the administration's immature attitude toward nuclear weapons, its moral absolutism, and its courtship of its party's right wing produced strategic and diplomatic paralysis. The revisionist wisdom holds quite the opposite. It portrays Eisenhower avoiding the grief suffered by his successors by conducting policy with a deft, perceptive, and remarkably sensitive touch. Definitive assessments will require further research and additional time. The ferment already aroused, however, is intellectually stimulating.[19]

---

[17] Robert Divine, *Eisenhower and the Cold War* (New York, 1981), 154.

[18] Eisenhower's presidential papers (the so-called "Whitman File") include his correspondence, memoranda of conversations and meetings, diary entries, telephone conversation transcripts, and other revealing documents. Used by Eisenhower when preparing his memoirs, they were first made available at the Eisenhower Library in 1975. For a full description see the library's 1988 publication, *Historical Materials in the Dwight D. Eisenhower Library.*

[19] For reviews of the revisionist literature, both pro and con, see Vincent DeSantis, "Eisenhower Revisionism," *Review of Politics* 38 (April 1976): 190–207; Gary Reichard, "Eisenhower as President: The Changing View," *South Atlantic Quarterly* 77 (Summer 1979): 265–81; Mary McAuliffe, "Commentary: Eisenhower, the President," *Journal of American History* 68 (December 1981): 625–32; Arthur M. Schlesinger, Jr., "The Ike Age Revisited," *Reviews in American History* 11 (March 1983): 1–11; Robert McMahon, "Eisenhower and Third World Nationalism: A Critique of the Revisionists," *Political Science Quarterly* 101 (Centennial Year 1886–1986): 453–73; Anthony James Joes, "Eisenhower Revisionism and American Politics," in Joann P. Krieg, ed., *Dwight D. Eisenhower: Soldier, President, Statesman* (Westport, Conn., 1987), 283–96; and Robert Burk, "Eisenhower Revisionism Revisited: Reflections on Eisenhower Scholarship," *Historian* 50 (February 1988): 196–209. A major recent study that bucks this trend is Piers Brendon, *Ike: His Life and Times* (New York, 1986). Suggestive of the current dominance of

Dulles would have found this phenomenon gratifying, albeit not surprising. In fact, as if to pique scholars' intrinsically revisionist interests, he took extraordinary measures to ensure that his records would be widely available.[20] Ironically, however, there has yet to be a focused reassessment of Dulles and his diplomacy based on the new archives. He is still saddled with his low rating.[21] To a certain extent this apparent paradox is to be expected. Eisenhower had long been underestimated, and the largest collection of documents that became available were his papers. Because they surprised researchers by revealing a man so at odds with the Herblock caricature, he naturally attracted the most attention.[22] But in terms of foreign policy an added dimension is involved. Congruent with their image of a cerebrally and temperamentally ill-equipped president who reigned rather than ruled, the initial commentators on the Eisenhower presidency took it as an article of faith that Dulles designed and orchestrated foreign policy. The old saw that he "carried the State Department in his hat" was the view put forth by the administration's memoirists and echoed by both journalists and historians, frequently to exonerate the beloved Eisenhower from what they considered the Republicans' excesses.[23] Yet the new archives suggest that the perception that Eisenhower, to cite one distinguished authority, "trusted Dulles so completely and admired his ability as Secretary of State so unreservedly that he gave him, for all practical purposes, a free hand to conduct the foreign policy of the United States as he saw fit," is a gross oversimplification.[24] Even the partially opened documentary record available a decade ago led me to conclude that by "using this new material in combination with the extant but often overlooked

revisionism, Brendon's biography has received relatively little scholarly attention. See Bernard Sternsher, "Two Views of Eisenhower: Robert A. Divine and Piers Brendon," *Psychohistory Review* (forthcoming).

[20] Richard Immerman, "Diplomatic Dialings: The John Foster Dulles Telephone Transcripts," *Newsletter of the Society for Historians of American Foreign Relations* 14 (March 1983): 1–15.

[21] Eisenhower's ranking, on the other hand, has risen dramatically. See R. Gordon Hoxie, "Eisenhower and the Rating Game," in Pederson and McLaurin, eds., *The Rating Game*, 388–99.

[22] See in particular Fred Greenstein, *The Hidden-Hand Presidency: Eisenhower as Leader* (New York, 1982).

[23] In addition to Graebner, *The New Isolationism*, and the sources listed in notes 47–49 below, see Sherman Adams, *Firsthand Report: The Story of the Eisenhower Administration* (New York, 1961); Emmet Hughes, *The Ordeal of Power: A Political Memoir of the Eisenhower Years* (New York, 1963); Richard Rovere, *Affairs of State: The Eisenhower Years* (New York, 1956); Marquis Childs, *Eisenhower: Captive Hero: A Critical Study of the General and the President* (New York, 1958).

[24] Morgenthau, "Dulles," 302.

sources . . . the current scholar can determine that the standard view of Dwight Eisenhower on the leading strings of John Foster Dulles is highly problematic."[25]

Pointedly entitled "Eisenhower and Dulles: Who Made the Decisions?" my article broke limited historiographic ground when published in 1979; others soon took the reinterpretation much farther. As Eisenhower's stock rose, Dulles's fell, especially in terms of responsibility. Whereas the initial revisionism accented the consultation and interchange between president and secretary of state, later studies left the impression that Dulles functioned primarily as a sounding board—or a rubber stamp. He did little more than carry out Eisenhower's directives and take the heat that they generated. "What the documents show . . . is how completely Eisenhower dominated events," wrote the author of the president's most comprehensive biography in 1984. "The truth was that Eisenhower, not Dulles, made the policy, as anyone who knew anything about the inner workings of the Eisenhower Administration realized."[26]

Accordingly, the initial spate of studies of Dulles's diplomacy was replaced by studies of Eisenhower's diplomacy.[27] Historians and political scientists relegated the secretary of state's participation, most dramatically with regard to conceptualization, to a subordinate role. This book seeks a more balanced interpretation. Consequently, though the authors fill a lacuna by using the new archives to flesh out Dulles's ideas and input, readers should not interpret this focus to mean that they reject the emerging paradigm that places Eisenhower at the center of the foreign and national security policy machinery. The president did retain control of policy- and decision-making. But Dulles was an integral actor in the sphere of formulation as well as implementation. Eisenhower did not dominate Dulles any more than we once thought the reverse true. Moreover, because their levels of interest and expertise differed, their contributions to different policy issues and areas varied. On some occasions Dulles took the lead; on others it was Eisenhower. They were in a real sense a team.[28]

The need for an archivally based reassessment of Dulles is evident. This is the purpose of these chapters; but the book does not purport to be definitive. Dulles, once thought to be transparent and one-

[25] Richard Immerman, "Eisenhower and Dulles: Who Made the Decisions?" *Political Psychology* 1 (Autumn 1979): 21.

[26] Stephen Ambrose, *Eisenhower.* Vol. 2: *The President* (New York, 1984), 10, 442.

[27] For a representative sampling, see Richard Melanson and David Mayers, eds., *Reevaluating Eisenhower: American Foreign Policy in the Fifties* (Urbana, 1987).

[28] See in particular C. Douglas Dillon's prepared remarks, "Remembering the Eisenhower–Dulles Relationship," February 25, 1988, Dulles Centennial Conference.

dimensional, has proven to be an extremely elusive subject. An inherent problem is that the contemporary observations and early commentaries suffer from more than incomplete data and misperception. It is axiomatic that all historical writing reflects current values and trends. But in Dulles's case motivated biases—interpretations conditioned by affect—exert a profound influence. Because of Eisenhower's leadership style, Dulles's powerful personality, and the advent of the television age, the secretary of state achieved unprecedented notoriety. His commanding presence and peripatetic activities were the stuff of legends; he was too "large" to reduce to paper, David Eisenhower explained.[29]

More to the point, Dulles simply was disliked. "Indeed, it would be difficult to think of an American Secretary of State who was less beloved during his term of office than Dulles," read the introduction to one assessment in the 1960s.[30] In part this was because he was not well known. For such a highly visible personality Dulles was incongruously shy and reserved, much more comfortable at home playing backgammon with his wife, Janet, than at social gatherings. The "inner" John Foster Dulles who looked forward to his dog's greeting every evening, or who came to his office on a cold Saturday to check the temperature of his aquarium's water, or who playfully teased his secretaries, bore little resemblance to the "outer" Dulles. In public he displayed none of the humor, warmth, or sensitivity that he did in private. Rather, he projected an austere, impersonal demeanor, as if he were both unconcerned with and ignorant of the human dimension of those with whom he had contact. The inescapable comparisons to the amiable Eisenhower made Dulles's personality appear that much less attractive. "I like Ike," Americans and foreigners were fond of saying, even as they criticized the president's policies. "Dull, Duller, Dulles" was their put-down of his secretary of state.[31]

The root cause for Dulles's failure to engender affection ran deeper than his inability to be "one of the guys" or his practically reclusive private side. To much of the public, and for that matter to

[29] David Eisenhower commentary, February 25, 1988, Dulles Centennial Conference.

[30] Gordon Craig, "John Foster Dulles and American Statecraft," in Craig, *War, Politics, and Diplomacy: Selected Essays* (New York, 1966), 262.

[31] In addition to Immerman, "Eisenhower and Dulles," the biographies cited in these notes, and the John Foster Dulles Oral History Collection, for assessments of Dulles's personality see the transcript of the session entitled "The Qualities of Leadership: An Appreciation of John Foster Dulles," Dulles Centennial Conference. Over the years I have profited from many interviews with Dulles's family, friends, and associates, particularly Robert Bowie, Eleanor Lansing Dulles, John Hanes, William and Phyllis Bernau Macomber, and Herman Phleger.

many domestic and foreign officials, he was more than impersonal and distant. He was virtually an Old Testament figure. When Dulles spoke he seemed to lecture, to pontificate such that he alienated if not antagonized many of his listeners.[32] His ethnocentrism grated on the nerves even of Americans; his frequent references to God and the flag grew tiresome. "He [Dulles] is not particularly persuasive in presentation," Eisenhower himself conceded at the outset of his administration, "and, at times, seems to have a curious lack of understanding as to how his words and manner may affect another personality."[33] The president later complained about Dulles's "practice of becoming a sort of international prosecuting attorney." He recommended that the secretary stress American positives, not dwell on Soviet negatives.[34]

Compounding the problem, Dulles was not a dynamic speaker, and the press looked particularly hard for a catchy phrase or slip of the tongue that would make good copy. Thus, for example, it highlighted "agonizing reappraisal," headlined his misstatement over Goa, and came up with "massive retaliation" and "brinkmanship." The result was a battle of words, a battle fought over nuance, emphasis, and context. The secretary's incessant efforts to explain, defend, and exhort provided both sides with ammunition. Dulles "rattled ideas as he rattled weaponry," one representative of the 1950s press remembered. "From the time he stalked down the aisle of the departmental auditorium it was an adversary relationship," recalled another.[35]

Because of his personality traits and idiosyncracies, journalists, congressmen, foreign leaders, and other opinion makers were loathe to give Dulles the benefit of the doubt. Politics also exerted a heavy influence. As the Republican trustee of bipartisan foreign policy turned point man during the 1952 campaign, Dulles became the bête-noire of the Democrats. Once in office his attentiveness to his party's right wing, which enveloped Joseph McCarthy, fueled the Democrats' fire further. They widely interpreted Dulles's admonition to his department personnel about "positive loyalty" as a slur on their patriotism and hence condemned the purges from Foggy Bottom as politically motivated as well as morally reprehensible. "As ye [sow], so

---

[32] For an illustration of how this trait affected those who wrote about Dulles, including scholars, see Herman Finer, *Dulles over Suez: The Theory and Practice of His Diplomacy* (Chicago, 1964).

[33] Entry for May 14, 1953, in Ferrell, ed., *The Eisenhower Diaries*, 237.

[34] Entry for January 24, 1958, AWD, "January, 1958 (1)," AWF.

[35] Ross Mark and Burke Wilkinson commentaries, February 26, 1988, Dulles Centennial Conference.

shall ye reap, and believe me, you have so sown and so you reap," Hubert Humphrey warned Dulles angrily.[36] The Democrats sought revenge at every opportunity, which during the turbulent 1950s was not infrequently.

The Republican defense of Dulles was far from universal. Despite the coincidence of viewpoints on many issues, the right wing never totally or unreservedly embraced their party's foreign policy spokesman. Dulles's ambition to head the Department of State was itself reason for concern. Why would a loyal American seek such extensive contact with foreigners? Perhaps the answer could be found with Dulles's many friends and associates among the Eastern establishment, including at one time Alger Hiss. The secretary's active opposition to the Bricker Amendment exacerbated these suspicions; so did his complicity in the "Geneva Munich" of 1954. Many conservatives lost confidence completely once Dulles exercised restraint when it came to massive retaliation, and when his professions of support for liberation proved hollow. From both these perspectives the 1956 Hungarian uprising provided an object lesson. The United States should have used force to support the rebels, Barry Goldwater remarked unequivocally. "If the United States had fulfilled its duty to Hungary in this way, Hungary would be a free country today."[37] On one matter, then, Goldwaterites and the Democrats agreed. They attributed Dulles's faults as much to his character as to his judgment. He was morally bankrupt.

Because Dulles stirred up strong emotions, the analyst must approach each piece of evidence with extreme care. Subjective judgments pervade the contemporary record and much of the derivative scholarship. Another impediment to reaching confident conclusions is the recent revelation that Eisenhower used Dulles as a "lightning rod," as someone who would attract criticism, thereby shielding the president and providing him with a greater degree of flexibility. Distinguishing Dulles's true beliefs from trial balloons and orchestrated obfuscations can prove frustrating, if not impossible.[38]

Dulles's legal training complicates the task further. "[I]f you gave him his premises, he would get you with his conclusions," General Andrew Goodpaster said of the logic of Dulles's mind and the power of his exposition.[39] Yet few public figures have been more adept at

---

[36] Quoted in George Herring and Richard Immerman, "Eisenhower, Dulles, and Dienbienphu: 'The Day We Didn't Go to War' Revisited," *Journal of American History* 71 (September 1984): 352.

[37] Quoted in Craig, "Dulles," 263.

[38] Greenstein, *Hidden-Hand Presidency*, 87–91.

[39] Andrew Goodpaster commentary, February 26, 1988, Dulles Centennial Conference.

hiding behind qualifications, caveats, or loopholes. At press conferences and congressional hearings, not even the most persistent inquisitor could pin him down.[40] The opening of the hundreds of thousands of pages of documentation, while revealing much of the above, has not always provided satisfactory answers, and it has raised additional questions. Without adequate knowledge of the context in which a remark was made, or a memorandum written, an archival fragment can prove misleading. In addition, because the nature of the documents is so varied—reflecting different times and different audiences—discrepancies and contradictions abound. The scholar must sift through all the evidence, weighing it according to ill-defined criteria in order to determine which is more persuasive and representative.

Making matters worse still, notwithstanding the wealth of material now in the public domain, much remains classified. In addition to highly sensitive or confidential select documents, entire series or record groups are unavailable. Not only must researchers await declassification of the documents covering the last years of Dulles's life. The review process that must precede the opening of files pertaining to the operations of the National Security Council (NSC) Planning Board, or Dulles's own Policy Planning Staff, has not yet begun. Considering the prominent role Eisenhower and Dulles assigned to these organs in the policymaking process, the absence of these data is a severe handicap.[41] As will be seen, almost all the chapters in this book draw heavily on memoranda of NSC meetings, and they lead to some startling reinterpretations. The position papers, background discussions, briefings, and similar records are potentially more valuable.

The declassification of these records will not remove all obstacles. Eisenhower held numerous off-the-record meetings with his key advisors. He especially liked to meet with Dulles informally, often over drinks late in the day. These tête-à-têtes must have produced revealing exchanges that influenced the more formal NSC and cabinet deliberations. No minutes were taken. Nor do we know what Dulles discussed when he and his brother Allen, director of the Central Intelligence Agency (CIA), dined regularly at sister Eleanor's home on Sundays. In fact, because the administration focused heavily on covert operations, countless conversations took place behind permanently closed doors.[42]

[40] Ross Mark commentary, February 26, 1988, Dulles Centennial Conference.

[41] See Anna Kasten Nelson, "The 'Top of the Policy Hill': President Eisenhower and the National Security Council," *Diplomatic History* 7 (Fall 1983): 307–26.

[42] Richard Immerman, *The CIA in Guatemala: The Foreign Policy of Intervention* (Austin, 1982), 133–34.

The wide range of papers available at the Eisenhower Library, Princeton University, the National Archives, Britain's Public Record Office, and other repositories does compensate. Regardless of the delays and foibles of the declassification process, the analyst has unparalleled access to the Eisenhower administration's thought processes. But the more we learn about Dulles, the more difficult it is to arrive at a comprehensive profile. As mentioned, Dulles made a point of opening up his record in office. But as was also mentioned, he diligently guarded his private side. Consistent with this behavior, unlike Eisenhower, Dulles kept no diary, nor did he write reflective, introspective letters. Therefore one must search extensively for even cryptic clues concerning his core beliefs and deepest values, his personal and national objectives, and his innermost fears as well as joys. Intangibles that may have influenced his perceptions and recommendations, such as his deteriorating health or extracurricular activities, are exceptionally hard to uncover. But they are important. Dulles the secretary of state cannot be separated from Dulles the man.

Nor can Dulles the secretary of state be separated from the times during which he held office. Even as these years were critically important, so were they frightening and confusing, and this ambience poses challenges for the historian. Empathizing with the world of a former policymaker is a daunting task. How easy it is to take a "presentist" perspective, treating the rush of history as if it conformed to a preordained script. How easy it is to lose track of the great number of issues that crowd the State Department chief's calendar, or to fail to appreciate the speed and depth of the changes he must assimilate. All secretaries of state bear this burden, but in Dulles's case it was particularly acute. Whether one maintains that the turning point came in 1947 or 1950,[43] Dulles undeniably inherited a foreign policy agenda unlike that of any of his predecessors. It is hardly an exaggeration to use the term "revolution" to describe the impact of the Truman Doctrine, Marshall Plan, North Atlantic Treaty Organization, fall of China, Korean War, and so much more on America's global relations. And this drama unfolded at a time when the United States was at peace. These events, which heavily influenced Eisenhower's election ("I will go to Korea" electrified the nation),[44] would have paled in significance had there been the global war that many deemed inevitable. As some contemporaries argued, in light of its

[43] For the dispute see John Lewis Gaddis, "Was the Truman Doctrine a Real Turning Point?" *Foreign Affairs* 52 (July 1974): 386–402; and Melvyn Leffler, "Was 1947 a Turning Point in American Foreign Policy?" Peter B. Lewis Lecture, Princeton University, 1987.

[44] For the origins and reactions to the speech see Hughes, *Ordeal of Power*, 29–33.

technological superiority, America might have survived a nuclear conflagration;[45] but at the cost of its values and way of life, not to mention millions of citizens. Hence at the same time Eisenhower instructed his national security managers to devise a new strategy for the nuclear age, he conceded that "the only thing worse than losing a global war was winning one."[46] Thus Dulles had to plan and implement policies designed to win a war without fighting one.

In appraising Dulles's performance, historians must consider the magnitude of his unprecedented responsibility and consider the circumstances under which the secretary had to operate. Dulles's share of the blame for the 1950s making a mockery of the adage "politics stop at the water's edge" must not desensitize historians to the ordeals he experienced. We must not ignore his conviction that the political complexion of Congress required that he try to avoid locking horns with Joseph McCarthy, particularly as Dulles felt vulnerable because of his erstwhile association with Alger Hiss.[47]

Yet the internal obtacles Dulles confronted were not as formidable as the external ones. Subscribing to the theory that the dynamic prevails over the static did not make it easier for him to recognize, keep pace with, and react to the momentous changes that characterized the international order. How was he to predict the shifting strategic balance and implications of the arms race, evaluate the ramifications of Stalin's death, or assess the political and economic fortunes of America's European allies? Where could Dulles look for guidance when formulating U.S. policy toward two Chinas, an occupied Austria, and a divided Korea, Germany, and soon Vietnam? How constraining would be the entanglements that derived from peacetime alliances, and, from the opposite perspective, could the North Atlantic Treaty Organization (NATO) serve as a model for other regional security pacts? Was the UN a viable institution for protecting U.S. interests as well as maintaining peace? The secretary of state had neither a clear precedent nor solid intelligence to draw on.

Many of the questions confounding Dulles were more amorphous. The upheavals in the colonial and less developed areas of the globe were gathering momentum. Throughout Asia, the Middle East, Africa, and the Pacific, formerly mute colonies and dependencies were demanding louder voices in determining their futures. With the United States suddenly a global power in a military as well as economic and ideological sense, the administration would have to delin-

---

[45] Herman Kahn, *On Thermonuclear War* (Princeton, 1960).

[46] Memorandum by the Special Assistant to the President for National Security Affairs (Cutler), July 16, 1953, *FR, 1952–1954*, 2:397.

[47] Immerman, "Eisenhower and Dulles," 34.

eate and establish priorities for its interests. What criteria it would use had yet to be decided. Dulles found himself listening to anticolonial cries with one ear and those of Washington's major allies with the other. It seemed but yesterday that the British, or the French, or the Dutch, or other traditional powers were expected to deal with any difficulties that arose in the Third World. Now America was being thrust into the maelstrom, and into what many considered a no-win situation. To earn the allegiance of the international underclass without jeopardizing that of its allies was frequently tantamount to squaring the circle. Even in Latin America, where multilateral concerns were of less consequence, the financial requisites of a good neighbor policy proved irreconcilable with the costs of hemispheric military containment, especially to an administration committed to a balanced budget.

The chapters in this book, represent a collective effort to analyze and evaluate Dulles's response to these and other problems. To do so each contributor has tried to define the environment in which policy was made in the 1950s as Dulles did, to see the world through his eyes and thereby determine the bases on which he made choices. Only in this manner can the secretary be judged according to what he knew, or should have known, then—not by what we know now. In reaching this judgment, moreover, Dulles's experiences, predispositions, beliefs, and values are additional factors in the equation. None of the authors has ventured into the field of psychohistory, nor attempted anything like constructing an operational code. For a variety of reasons previous analysts of Dulles have considered him a rich subject for these methodologies, but the results have been mixed at best.[48] Still, no student of Dulles can afford to discount his background and personality. The evidence presented in the following pages suggests that Dulles was not as inflexible and dogmatic as was once believed. Nevertheless, his confidence in his judgments was unshakable, and he assumed office with a well-defined and articulated set of concepts concerning America's place in the world and how he should protect and promote it. These predispositions and preconceptions may not have determined all of Dulles's perceptions and behavior; their influence, however, was pervasive.

[48] Dulles's personality and demeanor tend to turn many students of his life and career into armchair psychologists. Representative of the most informed and sophisticated efforts are Ole Holsti, "Cognitive Dynamics and Images of the Enemy: Dulles and Russia," in David Finlay, Ole Holsti, and Richard Fagen, *Enemies in Politics* (Chicago, 1967), 25–96; and Holsti, "The 'Operational Code' Approach to the Study of Political Leaders: John Foster Dulles' Philosophical and Instrumental Beliefs," *Canadian Journal of Political Science* 3 (March 1970): 123–57.

Although Dulles's life history is hardly a secret, a few of its most salient features must therefore be kept in mind when contending with his tenure as secretary, particularly those features that are not necessarily congruent with the conventional image. All studies of Dulles contain the obligatory references to the influence of his family and their role in his diplomatic education. His parents named him after his maternal grandfather, John W. Foster, secretary of state under Benjamin Harrison; his uncle, Robert Lansing, held that same post when Woodrow Wilson guided the United States through World War I. Dulles's own diplomatic career began in 1907, when he took leave from his junior year at Princeton University to act as his grandfather's secretary at the Second Peace Conference at The Hague. His years at Princeton in the first decade of the century, combined with his service on the Reparations Commission and Supreme Economic Council during the Versailles negotiations, instilled within him deep-seated Wilsonian instincts.

Dulles maintained and abided by these instincts during the succeeding decades. Although he selected the legal profession over America's foreign service, his many foreign clients and government contacts allowed him to keep a firm finger on the global pulse and produce scores of writings that reflected a sophisticated understanding of international affairs. Dulles's prominent role as advisor to Thomas Dewey and Arthur Vandenberg in the 1940s led to his invitation by the Democrats to join the U.S. delegation to the 1945 San Francisco Conference and then the UN General Assembly; his participation in the series of meetings of the Council of Foreign Ministers that followed World War II; and his ambassadorial appointment in 1950 as Truman's special representative with the responsibility for negotiating the peace treaty with Japan. In sum, one would have to go back at least to John Quincy Adams to find a secretary of state who as a student and practitioner of American statecraft was Dulles's peer.[49]

His résumé is impressive, but what does it mean for appraising

[49] The authoritative study of Dulles before his appointment as secretary of state is Ronald Pruessen, *John Foster Dulles: The Road to Power* (New York, 1982). Mark Toulouse, *The Transformation of John Foster Dulles: From Prophet of Realism to Priest of Nationalism* (Macon, Ga., 1985) presents a religious perspective. Less reliable but nevertheless valuable, especially for this period, is Leonard Mosley, *Dulles: A Biography of Eleanor, Allen, and John Foster Dulles and Their Family Network* (New York, 1978). The standard scholarly biographies of Dulles, which span the interpretive spectrum, include Louis Gerson, *John Foster Dulles* (New York, 1967); Michael Guhin, *John Foster Dulles: A Statesman and His Times* (New York, 1972); and Townsend Hoopes, *The Devil and John Foster Dulles* (Boston, 1973). John Robinson Beal, *John Foster Dulles: A Biography* (New York, 1957), is Dulles's authorized biography.

Dulles's record as secretary of state? Is it possible that the lessons he learned from these formidable experiences actually made it more difficult to adapt to the changed environment in which he operated as secretary? With the exception of the Japanese treaty negotiations and a short stint as his uncle Robert Lansing's envoy to Central America, before 1953 Dulles focused exclusively on European affairs. What influence did this Atlanticist perspective have on his grasp of many of the problems he confronted as secretary of state? To what extent did Dulles's personal experiences with Stalin's representatives in the immediate postwar period shape his subsequent images of the Kremlin leadership? These and related questions have no easy answers. They suggest, however, that the relationship between Dulles's background, cognitions, and years in office is an intricate one that must be examined with care.[50]

Similarly, Dulles's religious views and legal training surely affected his policies and outlook. But the degree to which they did so, and in what ways, is difficult to assess. The son of a Presbyterian minister, Dulles's public record is replete with seemingly evangelical diatribes. In his operational code for Dulles, Ole Holsti accuses Dulles of "spiritual determinism," and Townsend Hoopes called his biography *The Devil and John Foster Dulles* in order to draw attention to Dulles's fire and brimstone Weltanschauung.[51] Yet Dulles's most recent and authoritative biographer underscores that Dulles did not actively engage in church activities until relatively late in life, and even then his motives were decidedly secular. Ronald Pruessen argues that Dulles's successful career as an attorney—a profession that placed a premium on pragmatism and flexibility and instilled in him an ethic closer to the businessman than the clergy—exerted a greater influence on his beliefs.[52] On the other hand, an insightful monograph on Dulles's ideas and philosophy argues that he did view "historical events through a religious lens." However, the refraction of that lens changed dramatically.[53] Again, the fundamental point is that Dulles's personal biography is critically important to his diplomatic biography. But he continues to elude those who wish to capture either dimension of him.

[50] On this level of analysis see Robert Jervis, *Perception and Misperception in International Politics* (Princeton, 1976).

[51] Holsti, "Operational Code," 129; Hoopes, *Devil and Dulles*.

[52] Pruessen, *John Foster Dulles*, chaps. 4–9. For a decidedly unflattering review of Dulles's legal career that nevertheless stresses his pragmatism, see Nancy Lisagor and Frank Lipsius, *A Law unto Itself: The Untold Story of Sullivan and Cromwell* (New York, 1988).

[53] Toulouse, *Transformation of Dulles*, xxi, chaps. 8–10 and conclusion.

Based on the currently available documentation and latest scholarship, the following chapters grapple with this network of factors
that have affected previous appraisals of Dulles and produced such
widely divergent interpretations. The questions they collectively address speak not only to the conduct of U.S. diplomacy during Dulles's
tenure but, more fundamentally, to the very nature of America's foreign and national security policy as it led the noncommunist coalition
during the modern era. The authors seek to identify the influences
on policy, determine definitions of interests and objectives, and evaluate strategies and tactics. In doing so they necessarily focus on both
the domestic and international climate, characteristics of the global
system, perceptions of opportunities as well as threats, and the individual and institutional dynamics of the decision-making, policymaking, and implementation process. They also assess the means by
which the administration sought to accomplish its ends.

The chapters can be divided into four thematic categories. The
first two chapters represent an effort to provide an overarching perspective on Dulles's record. Although finding much to criticize, Ronald Pruessen suggests that analysts must be more sensitive to the constraints Dulles confronted. They must also resist generalizing from
the particular. Dulles's policies toward Europe, which reflected his interest and preparation, differed qualitatively from those toward the
remainder of the globe, about which he was largely ignorant. John
Lewis Gaddis investigates three areas central to understanding
Dulles's international outlook: his attitude toward nuclear weapons,
international communism, and negotiations with the Soviet Union.
These issues have served as a litmus test for judging the secretary of
state; Gaddis has uncovered surprising new evidence that must be
incorporated into the final evaluation.

Rolf Steininger and Hans-Jürgen Grabbe, from Austria and the
Federal Republic of Germany, respectively, bring a welcome European perspective to their analyses. Dulles's European policies were at
the heart of his global strategy; the consensus holds that he experienced his greatest successes there. Grabbe's investigation of the "German Question," centering on Dulles's relationship with Konrad Adenauer, reinforces this consensus. Yet by examining Dulles's efforts to
win ratification of the European Defense Community (EDC), considered vital to Europe's immediate security needs and its future integration, Steininger concludes that this praise of Dulles may be mis-
placed.

Dulles has rarely received plaudits for his diplomacy in the Third
World, the third thematic category, and Stephen Rabe shows that
Dulles's approach to Latin America exhibited virtually all of the lim-

itations that contributed to the traditional critique. Wm. Roger Louis, however, suggests that this orthodoxy must be qualified. From the outset of the Suez crisis Dulles displayed a cluster of conflicting impulses that defy generalization.

Finally, in the Far East where Dulles faced his most intractable problems, his scorecard is similarly checkered. Because it set the stage for his subsequent policies and was the linchpin of his strategy for Asia and the Pacific, Dulles's handling of the Japanese Peace Treaty in the last years of the Truman administration commands attention. As Seigen Miyasato emphasizes, Dulles's first exposure to Far Eastern affairs produced his most impressive performance. Dulles's negotiations with the Japanese were not flawless, but he could take pride in the result. The same cannot be said of his Vietnam policy. George Herring shows that Dulles viewed Indochina and Japan in parallel and approached them on the same tack. His short-term success, however, had detrimental long-term consequences. Also exploring a relationship that trapped the United States into commitments not entirely compatable with its national interests, Nancy Bernkopf Tucker offers a differing viewpoint with regard to China. Her concentration on Taiwan reveals that Dulles's support of a Two Chinas solution to that tangle grew out of his frustration with the Nationalists of Chiang Kai-shek as well as recognition of Communist Chinese power and stability. Although his policy could not be implemented, he was neither blindly pro-Chiang nor anti–People's Republic of China. Indeed, with important qualifications, Dulles deserved credit for his pragmatism and discernment.

Pragmatism and discernment are two qualities normally not ascribed to John Foster Dulles. Indeed, in many respects the Dulles portrayed by these authors will be unfamiliar to readers. This is not to say that the chapters forge a new consensus, nor that they will require a complete revision of the conventional wisdom. The reappraisal does, however, break down the simplistic stereotypes that have handicapped previous examinations. The book is not the last word on Dulles; but it does introduce a new vocabulary by which to appraise him.

CHAPTER 1

John Foster Dulles and the Predicaments of Power

Ronald W. Pruessen

EXILED for twenty years from the White House, Republicans were straining at the bit in 1952. John Foster Dulles was certainly among them: he turned down an offer to become the ambassador to Japan, explaining that he preferred the "power house" in Washington to "the end of the transmission line" in Tokyo. The exhilaration that came with control of the "power house" was quickly tempered, however, by the realities of being "in" rather than "out" of office. Though circumstances produced cynical overstatement, there was a kernel of broadly relevant truth in Harry Truman's late 1952 chuckle over the likely fate of his successor: "He'll sit here, and he'll say, 'Do this! Do that!' *And nothing will happen.* Poor Ike—it won't be a bit like the Army. He'll find it very frustrating."[1]

There would be frustration for John Foster Dulles too—and it would spring from encounters with what might be called the predicaments of power: those things that complicate its exercise, that interfere with the ability of the wielder to do what he may want, and that may ultimately limit success or even bring defeat. Dulles found that power is never pure because it is never exercised in a vacuum. Moving in an environment in which other people and other states also move means that strength is always relative. Just as light or sound waves are affected by the nature of the medium through which they pass, moving faster or slower or not at all under different conditions, so the most influential of policymakers in the most influential of states would be inhibited by the circumstances of the real world in which he operates.

Like all modern secretaries of state Dulles had to struggle with several layers of predicaments, each layer inseparably related to the others while maintaining certain distinct characteristics of its own. Initially, he had to deal with the problems inherent in maintaining a

[1] Memorandum of conversation, October 3, 1951, "Re Japan: Offer by President Truman of Ambassadorship," DPP; Stephen Ambrose, *Eisenhower* (New York, 1984), 18 (emphasis in original).

personal power base in the Eisenhower administration. This meant developing and protecting a relationship with the president: an obvious enough priority for any cabinet officer, but Dulles was acutely sensitive to it because of memories of his uncle Robert Lansing's difficulties with Woodrow Wilson. There was also the need to vie for influence over policymaking with other members of the advisory and administrative structure that supported the president.

Secondly, Dulles had to cope with the complexities of the American political system that surrounded his bureaucratic base. Well before the 1950s, of course, democratic practices had given public opinion, especially as revealed in election results, a place in determining the international posture of the United States. The specific structure of U.S. government also gave Congress power over the shaping of foreign policies. Dealing both with voters and their elected legislators were thus inescapable concerns at any time; the particular atmosphere of the 1950s, however, made these tasks that much more complicated. McCarthyite hysteria, "China Lobby" vigilance, Sputnik, and "missile gap" paranoia, among other influences, generated an extraordinarily charged domestic political atmosphere.

Thirdly, and most important, there was confrontation with the predicaments of power in the international arena—with what Raymond Aron and the subtleties of the French language identify as *puissance* as opposed to *pouvoir*.[2] Dulles attended to a cluster of closely related concerns that might all be placed under the heading "the political economy of power." Though universally recognized as the most powerful single state in the world of the 1950s, the United States, Dulles knew very well, was nevertheless but one nation in a global system. There were external forces and circumstances against which or through which it had to move as it sought to protect and advance its interests. There were, as well, significant limitations on the resources it could devote to dealing with those forces and circumstances. The most basic predicament with which Dulles ever had to deal was the process of balancing—or trying to balance—those interests and those resources.

In this respect Dulles's labors have ongoing relevance. The current controversy sparked by Paul Kennedy's *The Rise and Fall of the Great Powers*, among other writings, would have had a familiar ring to the secretary of state of three decades past.[3] Sensitivity to the perceived

---

[2] Raymond Aron, *Peace and War: A Theory of International Relations* (New York, 1969), 47–48.

[3] Paul M. Kennedy, *The Rise and Fall of the Great Powers: Economic Change and Conflict from 1500 to 2000* (New York, 1987).

interplay of resources and interests in the 1950s might well provide greater historical depth and intellectual heft to today's debates.

Some of the resource problems of that earlier decade are well known. Dulles and most other 1950s policymakers never lost sight of the fact that they had finite military power available to them. For example, military planners had to consider manpower constraints, and they recognized that not all weapons systems were appropriate to all situations. In addition, Dulles and the Republicans were highly sensitive to the severe economic strains that an active foreign policy imposed on the United States. Compounding these abstract military and economic limitations were some of the obvious political factors already mentioned: just how many soldiers would the American public be willing to send overseas, especially if those soldiers actually had to fight? Just how large a defense budget would Congress support, especially if it meant an increase in taxes or deficits?

Some of the resource problems of the 1950s—and today—are less traditionally emphasized. Dulles had a fascinating entanglement with the predicaments of *time*, for example. He saw it as a consistently complicating factor in the exercise of power. On an abstract, indeed philosophical level, he had had an almost lifelong respect for what he saw as the potency of time. As early as his graduate student days in Paris, he had been impressed with Henri Bergson's theories of "flux," of the irresistible force of "change" in human affairs. His own writings in the 1930s, especially *War, Peace, and Change*, had made the unending conflict of "static" and "dynamic" forces a key tool for analyzing international affairs.[4]

The vicissitudes of time were not only an ongoing concern in the 1950s; they seemed to have grown more complex. On the one hand, Dulles saw the pace of change quickening to a dizzying speed, perhaps as a result of technological revolutions and the impact of war: "[I]t was a most uncertain world," he told Syngman Rhee in August 1953, "and impossible to anticipate as much as six months ahead."[5] On the other hand, curiously, problems and struggles had taken on a semipermanent character, with a potential for exhaustion as one result. "One of the most dangerous characteristics of the Soviet Communist movement is that it regards itself as timeless," Dulles wrote Eisenhower. "It emphasizes that to achieve its results will require 'an entire historical era.' "[6] On a more mundane, but equally complicated

[4] Ronald W. Pruessen, *John Foster Dulles: The Road to Power* (New York, 1982), 12, 153–57.

[5] Memorandum of conversation, August 7, 1953, *FR, 1952–1954*, 15:1487.

[6] Dulles to Eisenhower, May 17, 1954, WHMS, "White House Correspondence, 1954 (3)," DPEL.

level, Dulles also found himself consistently *short* of time. Endless issues required attention and crises seemed to hound him at every turn: where was the time, where was the opportunity to learn enough about the issues in order to shape appropriate policies?[7]

A final predicament for Dulles represents something of a category of its own because it grew out of efforts to deal with the other facets of "the political economy of power." Involved here is the issue of "allies" and the process of finding them, working with them, and keeping them. Dulles had not the slightest doubt of America's need for allies, or that this dependency was a function of the limitations on American resources.[8] He was to learn, though, that this need was not easily fulfilled. There were unending problems connected with getting allies to do what Washington wanted them to do—or getting them to at least endorse or maintain some sort of "benevolent neutrality" toward what Washington itself wanted to do. Sometimes it was the stronger partners who caused difficulties: British and French attachment to colonial attitudes, for example, created what Dulles called a "very, very fundamental problem" for the United States.[9] What Churchill once dubbed the "tyrannies of the weak" could complicate Dulles's life too: a Syngman Rhee or a Chiang Kai-shek "are not people, under normal circumstances, that we would want to support," Dulles told the Senate Foreign Relations Committee in 1953, and he could quickly have drawn up a list of frustrating maneuvers emanating from Seoul or Taipei. The national interest, the secretary nevertheless believed, gave the United States no choice but to gather allies both strong and weak. As he said of Rhee and Chiang, they were the "lesser of two evils."[10]

The sources of the predicaments confronting John Foster Dulles were certainly varied. Some of them can almost be said to be inherent in the human condition. Others were more precisely located in place and time. Problems involving Congress or elections were in part a product of specifically American institutions and traditions, for example, though they were also a function of the uniquely charged atmosphere of the 1950s.

Whatever the sources, Dulles accumulated only a mixed record in his encounters with the predicaments of power, with the balance tip-

[7] For a fascinating insight into the pressures of time, which Dulles shared, see C. D. Jackson to Eisenhower, January 17, 1958, "Eisenhower, Pres. Corresp. 1957–1958, 1959 (1)," C. D. Jackson Papers, Eisenhower Library, Abilene, Kansas.

[8] See *Executive Sessions of the Senate Foreign Relations Committee, 1954 (Historical Series).* (12 vols.: Washington, 1976–), 6:630 (hereafter *SFRC*).

[9] *SFRC*, 1954, 6:279.

[10] Ambrose, *Eisenhower*, 387; *SFRC*, 5:387.

ping more toward failure than success. His greatest strengths tended to be *intellectual*: Dulles was frequently sensitive to the problems inhibiting his role as secretary of state and sometimes thoughtful and articulate in discussing them. Awareness did not always translate into *achievement* or *practice*, however. In some situations predicaments were so great as to defy attempts to tame them. In others the policies adopted were not sufficiently aligned with the insights that preceded them. And at still other times—the most ironic or tragic of all—the very efforts that Dulles put forth spawned other, even more troubling problems.

. . .

Dulles may have enjoyed his purest success in the realm of bureaucratic politics. He faced the formidable twin tasks of safeguarding a relationship with a president who was not a longtime associate and navigating the complex shoals of a large executive branch. He worked hard at these tasks, and one might argue that if he had not, he would have had a much shorter tenure as secretary of state than he did.

Problems with Eisenhower might have become important, for example, if Dulles had not acted with considerable shrewdness and sensitivity. There were numerous potential pitfalls. Almost from the beginning of their association, the president had qualms about Dulles's "personality." "Foster's a bit sticky at first," he told Harold Macmillan, "but he has a heart of gold."[11] Disagreement about important issues were present too. In the drawn-out battle over the Bricker Amendment, Dulles regularly pressed Eisenhower to be tougher than he seemed inclined to be.[12] As late as May 1956 the secretary of state was complaining to Sherman Adams about the "awkward" and "embarrassing" situation created by the president's apparent refusal to "take the lead" on this matter.[13] Dulles and Eisenhower never completely resolved differences concerning the use of nuclear weapons either, though a curious seesaw pattern emerged in which each tried to rein in the other on different occasions. In December 1953, for instance,

[11] Entry for May 14, 1953, in Robert Ferrell, ed., *The Eisenhower Diaries* (New York, 1981), 237; Harold Macmillan, *Tides of Fortune, 1945–1955* (New York, 1969), 608.

[12] On the Bricker Amendment, see Duane Tananbaum, *The Bricker Amendment Controversy: A Test of Eisenhower's Political Leadership* (Ithaca, 1988).

[13] Memorandum of conversation with the President, July 11, 1955, WHMS, "Meetings with the President, 1955 (3)," DPEL; Memorandum of conversations with the President, May 1, 7, 9, 1956, all in WHMS, "Meetings with the President January–July, 1956 (3)," ibid.

the secretary of state argued with both the president and Pentagon officials about what he saw as their too-hasty readiness to turn to full-fledged war with China in the event of a violation of the Korean armistice. In September 1958, however, it was Eisenhower who questioned Dulles's proposals regarding a resort to tactical nuclear weapons during the second Quemoy-Matsu crisis.[14]

In spite of the pitfalls, a very strong Eisenhower–Dulles relationship evolved. Dulles kept in constant touch with the president, explicitly saying time and again that he wanted to confirm mutual conceptions of policies and clear major speeches or releases. He could also be openly deferential, as when asking what his "place" would be in the follow-up to Eisenhower's "atoms for peace" proposal.[15] Extensive consultation under such conditions allowed both men to recognize how many ideas and judgments they shared. The president certainly came to see it this way: he resisted a number of suggestions to replace his secretary of state, arguing that he was "as nearly indispensable as a human ever becomes." Ann Whitman commented on how "hard hit" Eisenhower was during the last stages of Dulles's cancer, and the president himself referred to his "unique relationship" with Dulles during one of his last visits to Walter Reed Hospital.[16]

Dulles's solid relationship with Eisenhower, which is all the more impressive because of the fragile elements within it, served as both ballast and compass for navigating the executive branch's bureaucratic rapids. And rapids there were. The secretary was rarely able to forget that some of the most important policies he was involved in shaping were subject to input from potent colleagues; he was forced to participate in ongoing discussions, even struggles, with the Treasury Department and the Bureau of the Budget concerning foreign aid and Mutual Security expenditures.[17] There were likewise constant maneuverings and tussles with the Defense Department and the JCS over issues as crucial as preparations for war with China, the future of NATO, and a nuclear test ban.[18] Within the State Department

[14] Memorandum of NSC meeting, December 3, 1953, *FR, 1952–1954*, 15:1638–39; Ambrose, *Eisenhower*, 483.

[15] Memorandum of conversation with the President, September 23, 1953, WHMS, "Meetings with the President, 1953," DPEL; Memorandum of conversation with the President, October 21, 1955, WHMS "Meetings with the President, 1955 (2)," ibid.; Dulles to Eisenhower, January 7, 1954, DHS, "Dulles, John Foster Jan. 54"; AWF.

[16] Eisenhower to Walter Judd, January 4, 1958, DHS, "Dulles–John Foster Jan. 1958 (2)," AWF; Memorandum of conversation with the President, April 13, 1959, WHMS, "Meetings with the President, 1959 (1)," DPEL; Ambrose, *Eisenhower*, 442, 508–9.

[17] Memorandum of conversation with the President, November 30, 1958, WHMS, "Meetings with the President, July–December, 1958 (2)," DPEL.

[18] Memorandum of conversation with the President, April 11, 1955, WHMS, "Meet-

itself there were disagreements on policy matters. These might have proved to be a two-edged sword for Dulles. On the one hand, conflicting advice on Asian issues from men like Walter Robertson and Philip Bonsal or on European developments from Douglas Dillon as opposed to David Bruce surely increased his sensitivity to options.[19] On the other hand, evaluating those options—and stacking them up against those emerging from other segments of the executive branch—increased the complexity of decision-making.

Dulles worked hard at maintaining his influence in the bureaucracy surrounding Eisenhower. On one level, he seems to have calmly taken as a given the need to thrash out policies: where Eisenhower could get angry at Pentagon pressure for money, for example, Dulles could tell him that "it was not entirely surprising" that the military would make "maximum demands for the deliberate purpose of shifting the decision to the political branch."[20] On another level, it was equally natural for him to be a tough advocate himself. He regularly argued budget issues, using what he once called his "day in court" to impress the president and others.[21] Periodically he took swipes at military spokesmen. In May 1954, while coping with the crisis in Vietnam, Dulles pointedly criticized what he saw as too much JCS emphasis on atomic war with China and the Soviet Union and too little attention to "political" and "defensive" options.[22] This, it might be added, was one of the many situations in which Eisenhower's essential agreement with him gave Dulles a successful handle on a policy deliberation. The secretary of state knew that this was a crucial ingredient in his bureaucratic clout, and he was determined to protect his access to the president so that opportunities for persuasion or opportunities for mutual discovery of shared views could continue unimpeded. About this he was blunt even with Eisenhower on the few occasions when the president toyed with reorganization ideas. In late 1956, for example, when the president was considering making the chairman of the Operations Coordinating Board (OCB) a sort of interdepartmental "inspector general," Dulles expressed worries about the pos-

---

ings with the President, 1955 (5)," DPEL; Draft NSC 5433, September 16, 1954, *FR, 1952–1954*, 5:1205–9; Ambrose, *Eisenhower*, 450–51.

[19] Bruce to Department of State, March 2, 1954, *FR, 1952–1954*, 5:882–83; Dillon to Department of State, March 22, 1954, ibid., 906–8; U.S. Delegation minutes, Second Plenary Tripartite Meeting, December 5, 1953, ibid., 1774–86.

[20] Memorandum of conversation with the President, August 14, 1956, WHMS, "Meetings with the President, August–December, 1956 (8)," DPEL.

[21] Memorandum of conversation with the President, November 20, 1958, WHMS, "Meetings with the President, July–December, 1958 (2)," DPEL.

[22] Memorandum of conversation with the President, May 25, 1954, WHMS, "Meetings with the President, 1954 (3)," DPEL.

sibility of an "undesirable conflict of jurisdiction." He insisted that "the Secretary of State should always have direct access to the President . . . and that if he lost that position, it would seriously impair the constitutional functioning of government."[23] It is not clear whether Eisenhower deferred to Dulles or not; he did not carry through with the plan.

Dulles also worked tirelessly and experienced considerable success when confronting predicaments in the domestic arena outside the executive branch. He knew that his ability to achieve almost any foreign policy goal could be dramatically affected by the winning or losing of elections and the maintenance or loss of broad domestic support. As a result he turned his attention to a cluster of interrelated foci: public opinion, relations with the press, and, especially, relations with Congress.

Dulles's sensitivity to the relevance of public opinion was lifelong. Grandfather John Watson Foster drew him into electoral politics as early as the Taft presidency and involvement, usually with the Republican party, was regular thereafter. More than thirty years before his association with Eisenhower, more than twenty years before his work with Thomas Dewey, Dulles was deliberating campaign strategy on foreign policy issues with men like Herbert Hoover and John W. Davis.[24] By 1952 Dulles's sensitivity to public opinion could only have grown. The surprise results of the 1948 election had demonstrated the fundamental importance of attending to first things first. The intervening travails of Dean Acheson had similarly underlined in unmistakable fashion how a secretary of state could be grievously hurt by failing to tend enough of the fences that surrounded the electorate.

Dulles's interest in voter opinion never dwindled once a Republican finally gained the White House, and he at last assumed command at the State Department. Regarding the never-ending battle over foreign aid appropriations, for example, correspondence and minutes of meetings are liberally sprinkled with estimates of public support. And deliberations on several other specific issues were regularly punctuated by reference to confounding public relations problems. Walking with Anthony Eden on a beach in Bermuda in December 1953, Dulles pleaded for British cooperation on dicey questions concerning China: the new administration wanted to devise more "reasonable" policies, but was all too sensitive to the "political dynamite"

---

[23] Memorandum of conversation with the President, December 15, 1956, WHMS, "Meetings with the President, August–December, 1956 (2)," DPEL.

[24] Pruessen, *John Foster Dulles*, chaps. 5, 10.

still in its hands.[25] In 1956 Dulles bemoaned the way "the White House staff was subject to strong political influences" on the subject of arms aid to Israel.[26]

Thus proded, Dulles devoted a portion of his prodigious energies to domestic political tasks. He was active in both the 1952 and 1956 election campaigns, of course, but also put a great deal of time into general public information efforts before and after the successful re-election drives.[27] Such efforts produced mixed results. In 1949, when Dulles was campaigning for a Senate seat, Arthur Vandenberg had praised him for "the facility with which you have shed the language of a million dollar lawyer and dropped into the lingo of Joe Doakes."[28] Throughout the 1950s, however, the "lingo" of a heavy flow of statements, speeches, interviews, and press conferences regularly sparked problems and criticisms. To this day, in fact, the mention of Dulles's name conjures up redolent phrases like "massive retaliation," "agonizing reappraisal," and "brinkmanship."[29]

Media attention often served as the catalyst for criticism of public statements, and Dulles had problems with the press throughout his years at the State Department. When barely in office he had to tangle with the *New York Times* on a story about an informal dinner discussion with reporters that was supposed to have been "off-the-record"; there were testy telephone exchanges between the new secretary and Arthur Krock, complete with threats on never granting another interview.[30] Rough as the press might be, however, Dulles assumed the costs of *not* working with it would be much higher.

Something of the same stoic determination characterized Dulles's approach to Congress. Congressional controls over budgetary allocations and military affairs would alone have compelled his attention; in addition to an uncomfortably large number of Democrats who required courting, the Republican bloc was a regular source of worry. There were prickly, even eccentric leaders, especially in the Senate, and there were prickly issues (like "China") on which it was impossible to devise a universally acceptable position. Yet the legislators' con-

[25] Record of conversation, December 17, 1953, PRO, PREM 11/418.

[26] Memorandum of conversation with the President, March 2, 1956, WHMS, "Meetings with the President, January–July, 1956 (5)," DPEL.

[27] Robert A. Divine, *Foreign Policy and U.S. Presidential Elections, 1952–1960* (New York, 1974).

[28] Arthur Vandenberg to Dulles, September 16, 1949, "Vandenberg, Arthur H.," DPP.

[29] Examples of the reaction to the "brinkmanship" concept are discussed in Townsend Hoopes, *The Devil and John Foster Dulles* (Boston, 1973), 310–11.

[30] Dulles telephone conversation with Arthur Krock, April 9, 1953, TTS, "January–April 30, 1953 (1)," DPEL.

tinuing efforts to reassert their power following the Roosevelt years made him that much more mindful of their sensitivities and prerogatives. Dulles saw a solid relationship with Capitol Hill as a factor in the international credibility of the Eisenhower administration. During debate on the Formosa Resolution in January 1955, for example, he admitted to the Senate Foreign Relations Committee that "[a]s a practical matter, of course, the authority of the President in this field cannot in fact survive effectively any indication on the part of Congress that it is not behind the President."[31] In the context of the 1950s, keeping Congress "behind" desired policies proved to be a task dense with its own particular predicaments.

Dulles worked strenuously to tame them. Consultation with legislators was a constant necessity, with what he once called "Congressional education" taking place in many hours of committee hearings and White House meetings.[32] Dulles also utilized the tried and true mechanism of roping Capitol Hill representatives into conference delegations and other official responsibilities. (It did sometimes prove difficult to carry off, as when he was unable to persuade a single Democrat or Republican to attend the various London conferences designed to deal with the Suez crisis.)[33] Not surprisingly, Dulles singled out key leaders for special attention: Robert Taft was a major concern early on, and close private contacts with him helped cope with the awkward Bohlen confirmation problem; Democrat Walter George, who became chairman of the Senate Foreign Relations Committee, was probably Dulles's most intensively courted senator, though Mike Mansfield and Lyndon Johnson were important counterparts in the process of maintaining a "bipartisan" foreign policy.[34]

All in all, Dulles's efforts to deal with electoral politics, public opinion, and congressional necessities paid some solid dividends. The major reelection success of 1956 was hardly his, of course, but his four years of work as secretary of state were not irrelevant either. Shortly after the election, Dulles pointed with pride to surveys showing a two-thirds public approval of his performance, in contrast to two-thirds disapproval of Dean Acheson some five years earlier. (It should be

[31] *SFRC, 1955*, 7:102.

[32] Memorandum of conversation with the President, March 19, 1958, WHMS, "Meetings with the President, January–June, 1958 (6)," DPEL.

[33] Memorandum of conversation with the President, August 12, 1956, WHMS, "Meetings with the President, August–December, 1956 (8)," DPEL.

[34] For example, see Dulles's telephone conversations with Alexander Wiley, Robert Taft, and Donald Lourie, March 16, 1953, and his conversations with Wiley and Taft, March 17, 1953, TTS, "January–April 1953 (2)," DPEL; Anna Kasten Nelson, "John Foster Dulles and the Bipartisan Congress," *Political Science Quarterly* 102 (Spring 1987): 43–64.

added that Dulles was honest enough to comment on the full range of the statistics, which also showed that 17 percent of those surveyed had never heard of him!)[35] On the legislative front there were regular successes as well: though one can point to shortfalls involving matters like foreign aid or thorny tangles like the "missile gap" debate, it is likewise essential to cite the long record of congressional cooperation on many budgetary recommendations—the Bricker Amendment, the Formosa Resolution, the "Eisenhower Doctrine," and so on.

In retrospect, however, one must recognize that the costs of such successes were sometimes high—and that such costs are prominent reminders of the way predicaments surrounded Dulles's power. There was, for example, a drain on his time and energy: as early as 1953 he confessed that one set of hearings had been "exhausting" and his grumblings about the number of hours spent on Capitol Hill were heard regularly in later years.[36] When public or congressional pressures resulted in modifying administration policies, other costs resulted. Perhaps the most obvious is the toll taken on allied relationships. What Dulles once referred to as a "delicate Senate problem" on China policy, for instance, greatly compounded already tricky Anglo-American coordination.[37]

European allies in general—and some of Eisenhower's and Dulles's friends at home—also grew frustrated with the bending that took place toward Joseph McCarthy. There were angry indictments of the president's timidity on so dramatic an issue, and the secretary of state's readiness to cave in to the likes of Scott McLeod.[38] What made the administration's posture regarding McCarthyism so distressing, it must be added, was the fact that both Eisenhower and Dulles were quite prepared to use shrewdness, toughness, or both to get around congressional or public recalcitrance when they saw the issue as important enough. Among the virtues of the Formosa and "Eisenhower Doctrine" resolutions overwhelmingly approved by Congress, for example, was the greater latitude allowed the executive to deal with Asian or Middle Eastern problems. In hearings on the former, Dulles

[35] Dulles to Eisenhower, January 30, 1957, WHMS, "White House Correspondence, 1957 (7)," DPEL.

[36] Dulles telephone conversation with Attorney General Herbert Brownell, April 6, 1953, TTS, "January–April 1953 (7)," DPEL; Memorandum of conversation with the President, November 12, 1956, WHMS, "Meetings with the President, August–December 1956 (3)," ibid.

[37] Background paper for the U.S. delegation at the Geneva Conference, April 6, 1954, *FR, 1952–1954*, 14:401.

[38] Ambrose, *Eisenhower*, chap. 7.

admitted that "its purpose" was to allow even so extreme an action as a strike at China without further consultations with Congress.[39]

. . .

Though Dulles had to struggle with the costs of policymaking at home, his most serious predicaments came within the international arena. There, grappling with military, economic, and political limitations on American control capabilities absorbed even more of his time and energy without necessarily producing commensurate achievements.

Dulles tried to deal creatively with the major problems he saw confronting the United States on almost every front. He came closest to success when working on the definition of a new "grand strategy" and closely related policies toward Europe.

The Eisenhower administration is well known for its early pronouncement of a "New Look," and there is no question that Dulles was one of its enthusiastic architects. Even before the 1952 election he had begun to speculate on what would soon be called the "Great Equation": finding a way to maintain adequate defense and an active foreign policy without going bankrupt. Dulles is most identified with the emphasis on nuclear weapons, traditionally seen as the key tool chosen for accomplishing this objective, particularly the concept of "massive retaliation." In the slang of the day, "more bang for the buck" could be secured by relying on atomic bombs rather than conventional ground forces, especially since the Soviet Union was seen as being "glutted with manpower."[40]

The New Look, however, has often been analyzed too simplistically, the tendency being to overstate Dulles's attachment to nuclear weapons and to understate his and other policymakers' interest in "flexible" responses to problems and goals.[41] The Eisenhower administration's European policies, for instance, suggest the fuller range of options that Dulles typically considered. There was, to be sure, a 1953–1954 push to bring NATO into line regarding reliance on atomic weaponry, a policy driven by financial as well as strategic considerations. Other policies were pursued, however, each designed to ease limitations or increase opportunities. Perhaps the best known was the

[39] *SFRC, 1955*, 7:93.

[40] Dulles statement to the North Atlantic Council, April 23, 1954, *FR, 1952–1954*, 5:509–14.

[41] For a more accurate description, see John Lewis Gaddis, *Strategies of Containment: a Critical Appraisal of Postwar American National Security Policy* (New York, 1982), chaps. 5–6.

struggle for the notorious European Defense Community, belatedly and successfully transformed into the Western European Union. Though Dulles inherited plans for EDC and had Anthony Eden to thank for the WEU alternative, he was a willing and important worker on behalf of both programs. Relatedly, Dulles steadily encouraged European economic integration via development of institutions like the European Coal and Steel Community and Common Market.

Dulles helped shape important achievements in the New Look and European policies. Simple accounting suggests one: the actual cutting of billions of dollars from defense budgets. The budgets in excess of $50 billion during the Korean War years were reduced to $40 billion by fiscal 1955; even congressional agitation over Sputnik and the "missile gap" produced increases to only $46.6 billion in fiscal 1959 and $45.9 billion in 1960.[42] Other achievements are not so easily measured but are nonetheless impressive. Take Dulles's patience in dealing with old European allies, at least in the period before the Suez crisis. This may seem an odd claim on behalf of the author of the infamous "agonizing reappraisal" speech of December 1953; yet the long battle over EDC as a whole substantiates it quite well. Countless prods to anger and frustration were part of the EDC campaign, many (though by no means all) of them emanating from the byzantine intricacies of French politics and the interminable delays in securing ratification in Paris. Dulles, like many at the time, had his lapses from equanimity: the harsh "agonizing reappraisal" statement was one; a tendency to testiness in dealings with Pierre Mendès-France, another.[43]

Usually, however, Dulles recognized the seriousness and legitimacy of French concerns, ably communicated to him by men like Georges Bidault and American representatives like David Bruce and Douglas Dillon.[44] In any event Dulles decided that patience was the best way to get maximum results. Facing congressional criticism of his reluctance to use threats to achieve West German rearmament, Dulles shrewdly demurred: "When you have a machine that is running in a certain direction you can try to stop it abruptly, in which case you generally get an accident, or you can swing it through a curve, in which case you can conserve a good bit of what you have got." This

[42] Gaddis, *Strategies of Containment*, 164, 185.

[43] Memorandum of conversation, July 13, 1954, *FR, 1952–1954*, 5:1018–23; Dulles to Embassy in France, August 12, 1954, ibid., 1029–31; Smith to Embassy in France, August 16, 1954, ibid., 1042; Dulles to Embassy in France, August 19, 1954, ibid., 1049–50.

[44] U.S. Delegation minutes, Second Plenary Tripartite Meeting, December 5, 1953, *FR, 1952–1954*, 5:1774–86.

was the typical Dulles approach until the much-delayed French ratification of WEU in December 1954. In his congratulatory telegram to
Mendès-France, he specifically commented that "if we here said little
[during the final ratification debate] it was because we felt that silence
was the best contribution we could make."[45]

Dulles's handling of the EDC-WEU tangle can be seen as the tip of
an iceberg of strength as far as European policies are concerned. EDC
was always explicitly connected with the problems of limitations on
American resources; the WEU variation sensibly allowed allies to help
deal with those problems while simultaneously proceeding with their
own programs. The whole issue is therefore closely related to the
"predicaments" of power.

At least some of Dulles's achievements in this area were the result
of his being able enough—or lucky enough—to prevail over the
shortage of time. Because of the nature of his previous life and work,
Dulles came to European issues with more solid intellectual preparation than he could claim concerning any other foreign policy problems. For more than forty years he had traveled back and forth across
the Atlantic, involved in government work at the Paris Peace Conference of 1918–1919 and meetings of the Council of Foreign Ministers
in the 1940s, and involved in a highly successful law practice special-
izing in international business and finance.[46] He had watched and
thought and written; he had devoted the kind of time and accumulated the kind of experience required for a grasp of complexities.
The evidence of this is abundant and underappreciated, though it
can only be suggested here. One example certainly is Dulles's intense
concern for what he described as the "suicidal strife" between France
and Germany: an "old cycle" of war and revenge; a "firetrap" that
had engulfed too many, he believed, and that had to be replaced by
the weaving of "a European fabric of mutual understanding and
common endeavor."[47] Nor was military unification the only or even
most important mechanism. "The supranational aspect of EDC [is] far,
far more important than twelve German divisions," Dulles told
Mendès-France. His own emphasis on economic integration, going
back to the 1930s and shaped in cooperation with friends like Jean

[45] *SFRC, 1953*, 5:322; Dulles to Adenauer, November 20, 1953, *FR, 1952–1954*,
5:855; Dulles to Mendès-France, December 30, 1954, ibid., 1538.

[46] Pruessen, *John Foster Dulles*, chaps. 3, 4–7, 12, 13.

[47] Dulles to the North Atlantic Council, December 14, 1953, *FR, 1952–1954*, 5:464;
Dulles to Embassy in France, August 19, 1954, ibid., 1049–50; Dulles at the Fourth
Plenary Meeting, September 29, 1954, ibid., 1357–61; Dulles to Adenauer, November
20, 1954, ibid., 854–55.

Monnet, suggested the specific direction in which he was most anxious to move.[48]

Sensitivities like these also allowed Dulles to develop his approach to the thorny problem of dealing with the Soviet Union. Conscious of the indigenous nature of European problems, and congruent with his own concern for them as early as the 1920s, he placed Moscow's behavior into a more balanced, less distorted context than many other contemporary analysts. For example, he refused to oversell the anticommunist case for EDC: "Even if there were a genuine detente with the Soviet Union," he told Britain's Lord Salisbury in July 1953, "it would still be virtually necessary to press on with the integration of Europe"; "Even if the Soviet threat were totally to disappear," he told the North Atlantic Council six months later, "would we be blind to the danger that the West may destroy itself? Surely there is an urgent, positive duty on all of us to seek to end that danger which comes from within?"[49] By 1955 Dulles was explicitly acknowledging the relaxation of the cold war in Europe. With West Germany safely nestled into NATO, with economic integration proceeding, and with the Austrian State Treaty concluded, Dulles described the Soviet Union as moving to a "less menacing" position in Europe. In a report on the Geneva summit to the Senate Foreign Relations Committee, he said further: "I think we are getting closer to a relationship [where] we can deal with [the Soviet Union] on a basis comparable to that where we deal with differences between friendly nations. We have differences, and they are hard differences, but we know they will not lead to war."[50]

It would be reasonable to recall that Dulles's—and Eisenhower's—public rhetoric often failed to communicate this sense of historical complexity and/or incipient détente concerning European issues. Does this suggest a weak link in an often impressive chain of analysis and policymaking? Yes. Nor is it the only weak link. Though it is important to identify basic achievements in New Look and European policies, it is equally necessary to recognize that the achievements were compromised in important ways by problems emanating from those very policies. Attempts to cope with or tame predicaments could generate yet others.

Most striking perhaps are the weaknesses inherent in the "massive retaliation" component of the revised grand strategy. Melodramatic

[48] Memorandum of conversation, September 27, 1954, *FR, 1952–1954,* 5:1286; Pruessen, *John Foster Dulles,* 307–12, 324–29, 334–38, 347–53.

[49] Minutes of Third Tripartite Meeting, July 13, 1953, PRO, PREM 11/425; Dulles to the North Atlantic Council, December 14, 1953, *FR, 1952–1954,* 5:461.

[50] *SFRC, 1955,* 7:505, 726.

appraisals can be put aside, to be sure: neither Dulles nor Eisenhower were itching to charge over the brink to blast adversaries back to the Stone Age. Both of them, on the contrary, generally subscribed to "deterrence" theory in shaping their nuclear policies. And both, to their credit, came to appreciate the almost paralyzing character of nuclear weapons as numbers and destructive capacities increased.[51] Nonetheless, nuclear weapons did remain the ultimate component of the American arsenal, and there were too many ways in which the brink might have been jumped in spite of intentions to the contrary. The president and secretary of state were each too enamored of "tactical" nuclear weapons, for example, and failed to appreciate the full potency of these presumably "bullet"-like tools.[52] This is symptomatic of a certain cockiness about control capabilities as well, a sometimes frighteningly naive assumption that the decision to unsheath weapons of mass destruction would always be one's own and would only be taken after mature deliberation. It is in the very nature of nuclear technology, however, that it can take on a demanding life of its own. (David Lilienthal once remarked that trying to stop development of the hydrogen bomb in 1950 was like trying to say no to a steamroller.)[53] The meshing of ever-developing technology with complex political realities further undercut pretensions to firm control. To illustrate, agitation over the Gaither Report and the "missile gap" forced Eisenhower and Dulles to accept budget increases they had no desire to endorse.[54]

Abroad, something similar was possible. For instance, adversaries would influence the way conflict evolved: who could be sure that some initial use of even "tactical" atomic bombs would not trigger an irresistible escalation to Armageddon? Foreign "friends" could be equally complicating. Dulles worried about Chiang Kai-shek's ability to drag the United States into a war with China that was bound to involve nuclear weapons.[55] And within Dulles and Eisenhower themselves, the capacity for *self*-control was not as absolute as either imagined. Though it can certainly be demonstrated that both men kept

[51] *SFRC, 1954*, 6:653; Ambrose, *Eisenhower*, 314, 455.

[52] Memorandum of conversation, April 12, 1954, *FR, 1952–1954*, 5:499–501; Dulles to Eisenhower, March 16, 1955, WHMS, "White House Correspondence, 1955 (6)," DPEL.

[53] Gregg Herken, *The Winning Weapon: The Atomic Bomb in the Cold War, 1945–1950* (New York, 1980), 58.

[54] Charles C. Alexander, *Holding the Line: The Eisenhower Era, 1952–1961* (Bloomington, 1975), 220.

[55] Memorandum of conversation with the President, September 4, 1958, WHMS, "Meetings with the President, July–December, 1958 (6)," DPEL; Memorandum of conversation with the President, September 23, 1958, ibid.

cool heads about atomic bombs during the May 1954 crisis in Vietnam, for example, the same cannot be said about their handling of
the Quemoy-Matsu tensions of 1954–1955 and 1958. In these cases
the speed and psychological pressures of a crisis situation brought
both men dangerously close to shooting from the nuclear hip over
stakes they knew were nowhere near commensurate.[56]

Nor were flaws lacking in some of the other tools Dulles turned to
in his encounter with the predicaments of power. Psychological warfare and covert operations, for example, may have seemed appropriate for political and financial reasons, but they could bring serious
problems in their train. In Europe, certainly, the reasons to doubt
their value are plentiful and apply to programs involving balloon sur-
veillance and propaganda campaigns in Italy, East Germany, and
Hungary, among others.[57] On an abstract level, "psywar" efforts and
dirty tricks compromised American integrity in many quarters. They
also compromised the intellectual consistency of Dulles's usually
shrewder analysis of the European scene and how to deal with the
Soviet Union there. More concretely, any number of covert operations threatened to explode in the face of the United States—or the
faces of those directly involved, as the bloodshed in Hungary in 1956
amply illustrates.

Dulles's personal role in psychological warfare and covert operations is still unclear. At best, these may have been activities that he did
not adequately control, activities that may offer one more demonstra-
tion of the perils of bureaucratic politics—even when they involve a
brother. At worst, Dulles may have been able to control them but
chose not to. Perhaps he indulged them as a sharper and potentially
useful supplement to calmer, more traditional approaches to European problems? In the end, however, whether the story involves inability to control or indulgence, Dulles's record in this area was as
dubious as that of any of his successors.

One additional example of possible limits on the strength of
Dulles's European policies deserves mention. It does not involve bla-
tant failure but suggests the irony that often plagues the policymaker:
even apparently tamed predicaments have a way of evolving into
other problems. Dulles took pride in the evolution of European in-

---

[56] For varying discussions of the Quemoy-Matsu crises, see: H. W. Brands, Jr., "Testing Massive Retaliation: Credibility and Crisis Management in the Taiwan Strait," *International Security* 12 (Spring 1988): 124–51; Gordon H. Chang, "To the Nuclear
Brink: Eisenhower, Dulles, and the Quemoy-Matsu Crisis," *International Security* 12
(Spring 1988): 96–123; John Lewis Gaddis, *The Long Peace* (New York, 1987), chap. 5.

[57] Stephen Ambrose with Richard Immerman, *Ike's Spies: Eisenhower and the Espionage
Establishment* (Garden City, N.Y., 1981), chaps. 12, 17, 19.

tegration in the 1950s. Politically, militarily, and especially economically, he interpreted his own efforts as contributing to those of many others to solve deep historical problems that had long concerned him. There was a trapdoor in such an achievement, however: it was built on a divided Germany. Dulles feared the destabilizing potential of a two-Germany Europe, feared the ability of the Germans to play off those around them against one another, and the ability of the Soviets to play to German desires for reunification.[58] To repeat, there is irony here, not failure. It is easy to debate but not resolve the question of whether any better German-European arrangements could have been secured in the 1950s, and thirty years of relative stability are not irrelevant to the debate in any event.

. . .

The shaping of basic strategy and European policies were major components of Dulles's work as secretary of state, but they obviously do not comprise the whole story. Because he found it necessary to deal with other issues and other quarters of the globe, so must anyone interested in evaluating his performance. As Dulles turned in other directions, however, his efforts were consistently weaker.

Regarding Europe especially, Dulles invested the time and commitment required to understand highly complex problems, thereby allowing himself to shape policies that related to those problems. As well, these policies were in reasonable proportion to what the United States could do without severely straining its resources. In more instances than not these layers of mature policymaking were lacking when Dulles turned to Asia, the Middle East, and Latin America. Something like an inverse pattern actually became the norm in these areas, in fact, and the poorer results that were common seem all too logical because of the change.

This is not to say that elements of strength were absent from Dulles's approach to non-European issues. Even in the 1950s some impressive achievements were obvious, and the passage of time has allowed appreciation of others. Regarding Asia, for example, he shares in the credit for terminating the draining Korean conflict in 1953 and for avoiding a plunge into war in Indochina during the volatile days of 1954.[59] Dulles could also be shrewd in his analytical

[58] Ronald W. Pruessen, "John Foster Dulles and Germany," in Robert Spencer, ed., *Perceptions of the Federal Republic of Germany* (Toronto, 1986), 70–80.

[59] George Herring and Richard Immerman, "Eisenhower, Dulles, and Dienbienphu: 'The Day We Didn't Go to War' Revisited," *Journal of American History* 71 (September 1984).

grasp of the basic dynamics of Asian affairs. For example, he fully recognized the significance of Japan and the value of a close relationship with that former enemy.[60] Though it produced opposite results, he also understood that China was a crucial factor in any regional equation. More to the point, because it contrasts with still common assumptions of U.S. obtuseness regarding Asia in the 1950s, Dulles was not inclined to treat the People's Republic of China (PRC) as a mere puppet of the Soviet Union. As early as December 1953, at the Bermuda conference, he talked at great length to Eisenhower, Churchill, Eden, and Bidault about the "strain" in the Sino-Soviet relationship and Mao Tse-tung's status as an "outstanding Communist leader in his own right."[61]

The same kind of sensitivity surfaced in his overall view of Middle Eastern developments. He knew full well that Arab nationalism had become the dynamic ingredient in that region and that the United States was being plagued by its allies' tendency to "commit suicide" in dealing with it: even the major crisis of 1956, Dulles said at one point, was "not a question of Suez, but . . . really a question of Algeria for the French and position in the Persian Gulf for the British."[62]

In Europe such analytical sophistication was compromised by Dulles's confrontation with the predicaments of power; in Asia, the Middle East, and Latin America, the strengths were overpowered. This happened because the layers of successful policymaking present in the one area were absent in the others. A shortage of time and experience made the foundation for understanding complex problems too shallow, thus helping to produce responses or programs that were either unrelated to the fundamental nature of those problems or beyond the essential capabilities of the United States.

A shortage of time was one of the truly fundamental predicaments in these cases, as in others. "Today's trouble spot is the Gaza strip," was the first line of a 1955 Dulles memo to the president: it was an opening symptomatic of the "crisis" atmosphere that permeated the Eisenhower presidency.[63] At many points the exigencies did not even wait their turn to hold the stage alone. It was bad enough to have to

[60] Pruessen, *John Foster Dulles*, chaps. 16–17.

[61] U.S. Delegation minutes, Second Restricted Tripartite Meeting, December 7, 1953, *FR, 1952–1954*, 5:1808–18. See also chapter 2 in this book.

[62] Memorandum of conversation with the President, October 24, 1956, whms, "Meetings with the President, August–December, 1956 (4)," dpel; Memorandum of conversation with the President, October 30, 1954, whms, "Meetings with the President, 1954 (1)," ibid.

[63] Dulles to Eisenhower, September 1, 1955, whms, "White House Correspondence, 1955 (1)," dpel.

juggle the problems of the Geneva conference after the fall of Dien Bien Phu and then have to cope with Quemoy and Matsu after Geneva, for example; it was obviously even worse to have to simultaneously deal with the climacteric of the EDC imbroglio.

A crisis orientation, almost by definition, makes it more difficult adequately to collect thoughts, analyze complexities, and evaluate alternatives. Even when some of the raw materials for more capable policymaking are present, they may get shunted aside or inadequately utilized because of the confusing pressures of the moment. In the months before May 1954, for example, Dulles fully shared in the often perceptive Washington assessments of problems in Southeast Asia. He was emphatic that the French must thoroughly pull down colonial sails, for instance, and about the importance of maintaining an American sense of proportion: "[N]ot knowing what the French are going to do . . . I am determined not to make Indochina a symbol for all of Southeast Asia so if Indochina is lost we assume that the whole game is up."[64] Such acumen did not survive in the pressure cooker of mid-1954, however, as Dulles helped shape policies that greatly expanded the U.S. role in the region. And hurried resort to mediums like SEATO and the Diem regime meant that the major new efforts would be unrelated to the fundamental problems involved in Vietnam as well.

Approaches to the Middle East in 1958 offer another example of the debilitating impact of a crisis orientation. In spite of earlier discernment about this region's complex politics and dynamics, Dulles and others responded to emergencies in Jordan and Lebanon with almost knee-jerk reactions. "Even though every alternative is 'wrong,'" Dulles admitted, the United States would have to intervene. Marines would be sent, the flag of resistance to communist aggression would be raised, and references to the lessons of the 1930s would be made before the largely irrelevant operation petered out. Though he was hardly one to talk, Anthony Eden caught something of the nature of the episode at the time: "These sudden gusts of improvization, which with Dulles pass for policy," he wrote, "are disastrous for the West. If this is one more of them there will not be much left in the Middle East."[65]

[64] SFRC, 1954, 6:274.

[65] Ambrose, Eisenhower, 466; Memorandum of conference with the President, June 15, 1958 (June 16, 1958), EDS, "June 1958—Staff Memos (3)," AWF; Memorandum of conference with the President, July 24, 1953, EDS, "June 1958—Staff memos (3)," ibid.; David Carlton, Anthony Eden: A Biography (London, 1981), 425.

To compound the complications of shaping policies under pressured conditions, it is worth remembering that the very perception of a "crisis" was not always germane to fundamental problems. President Camille Chamoun's maneuvers in Lebanon, for example, suggest the way in which a "crisis" could be created or manipulated. American policymakers were not averse to this themselves, as the Guatemalan episode of 1954 demonstrates. And whether fabricated and exaggerated or not, emerging policies could be equally damaged by being forged in such an atmosphere. In Guatemala Carlos Castillo Armas hardly offered genuine solutions to the problems requiring attention.[66]

One more point about the predicaments of pressured policymaking deserves brief mention here. Policies conceived under duress may not only be inappropriate for the situations involved, but may actually make them worse. There are a number of examples of this, but the most dangerous probably came during the Quemoy-Matsu crises of 1954–1955 and 1958. Dulles knew that the overall Asian problem confronting the United States was, as he put it, a "ruptured balance of power" in that region; he also knew that Chiang Kai-shek was a wild-card ally and that the United States had become "over-committed" to "two exposed pieces of real estate."[67] In spite of all this, he helped devise policies that coupled the most dangerous of his options: the United States would brandish and seriously discuss use of its nuclear weapons while simultaneously tending a relationship with Chiang that gave him ongoing opportunities to jeopardize a stable balance. That some of the misguided risks of this combination resulted from the domestic political context in which Dulles and Eisenhower were operating is true enough, but to recognize this is only to recall that this is another kind of pressure that can have deleterious effects on policymaking.

Explicit recognition of U.S. "over-commitment" regarding Que-

[66] See, in particular, Richard Immerman, *The CIA in Guatemala: The Foreign Policy of Intervention* (Austin, 1982).

[67] Nsc 166/1, November 6, 1953, *FR, 1952–1954*, 14:279; U.S. summary of minutes of meeting, November 9, 1954, ibid., 1779–83; Memorandum of conversation with the President, August 12, 1958, whms, "Meetings with the President, July–December 1958 (8)," dpel; Memorandum of conversation with the President, September 4, 1958, whms, "Meetings with the President, July–December 1958 (7)," ibid.; Memorandum of conversation with the President, September 11, 1958, whms, "Meetings with the President, July–December 1958 (6)," ibid.; Memorandum of conversation with the President, September 23, 1958, ibid.; Memorandum of conversation with the President, October 24, 1958, whms, "Meetings with the President, July–December 1958 (4)," ibid.

moy and Matsu is a useful signpost to a last point about Dulles's predicaments in Asia, the Middle East, and Latin America: that in calculations of "the political economy of power" in these regions, he—and Eisenhower—tended to incur obligations that would severely, even tragically, strain the resources of the United States over time. Given articulate sensitivity to the pressures of the "long haul" and the New Look's emphasis on conserving strength, the 1950s witnessed an odd but real drift toward the kind of declining American power recently highlighted by Paul Kennedy and others.

Dulles and Eisenhower did successfully avoid the kind of vast vortexes that plagued other American policymakers. Though there were uncomfortably close calls in the Formosa Strait and the Middle East, for example, it is now often recalled that no Korean War and no grand-scale involvement in Vietnam began between 1953 and 1961. This is important and a distinct achievement, but it does not mean that a sense of proportion was always solidly in place. One sign of fragility in this regard was too great a tendency to put a foot in the door of Asian and Middle Eastern affairs or to inch further through already opened doors. Getting started and/or inching along has a way of seeming safe enough or limited enough while it is being done, but the experiences of the 1950s suggest that apparently minor steps have an insidious way of leading to more and more. What could be the harm in playing something of a friendly mediator's role in Anglo-Egyptian negotiations in 1953–1954? And was it not a finely calibrated move to provide assistance to France for its struggle in Indochina? But first steps in Cairo led to the explosive complications of the Aswan negotiations and to thoughts of replacing the British and French through most of the Middle East. And an arms-length role in Vietnam gave way to the elaborate process of organizing "United Action" to salvage something in Geneva and to the actual replacement of the French in Saigon. There was nothing inevitable about this step-by-step process of moving toward grave problems and disasters; decisions to stop or even turn back, however, require a strong, fully mature sense of proportion, and experience suggests that neither Dulles nor Eisenhower nor their successors had this in good enough measure. There is irony in this matter as far as Dulles is concerned. He could be perceptive about exactly this problem. In one early meeting at the 1954 Geneva conference, for example, he dismissed the likelihood of French withdrawal from Indochina by saying "it is one thing to talk about quitting, but another thing actually to quit." In 1957 too, while debating possible support for Turkish intervention in Syria, he told the president "there would be great difficulty in winding up the affair, as we had anticipated in the case of Britain and France in Suez."[68]

.   .   .

In the real world of the 1950s, John Foster Dulles found complex circumstances that constantly hedged his ability to achieve what he would have seen as ideal results with ideal policies. In the end his struggle with those predicaments produced genuine success and serious failure.

Dulles started out with an impressive intellectual foundation, not the least element of which was his recognition that power was finite and that it required energy and creativity to make it as productive as possible. He also had the ability to mobilize his own energy and creativity over an extended period of time. In most aspects of his dealings with European issues, his intellect and his stamina worked well: he was able to understand many of the complexities of the European situation and to shape manageable policies that related to them. In his work on Asian, Middle Eastern, or Latin American issues, he performed less well. Here the predicaments of circumstances and resources often overpowered his efforts to tame them and tended to produce costly policies that were inappropriate and dangerous.

Why was Dulles less successful at grappling with the predicaments of power in some areas than in others? It is tempting to opt for a curt answer: like other human beings, he simply could not understand everything equally well. This is too bald an explanation, however, primarily because Dulles came intriguingly close to an *intellectual* grasp of many more things than is evident in the *policies* he helped shape. Even in Asia and the Middle East, for example, he often had more sophisticated *perceptions* than his *behavior* would suggest. The real question, then, is what interfered with the progression from sometimes shrewd analysis to less shrewd policymaking? Why did Dulles practice what might be called "intellectual brinkmanship" and fail to follow through his insights to their logical conclusions?

Part of the answer is surely tied up with the predicament of time, which complicated Dulles's work in several ways. His own life had given him extensive experience in European affairs but very limited

---

[68] Memorandum of conversation, April 28, 1954, *FR, 1952–1954*, 16:597; Memorandum of conversation with the President, October 1, 1957, WHMS, "Meetings with the President, 1957 (3)," DPEL.

contact with Asia or the Middle East. In the pressured, crisis-oriented years he served as secretary of state, would this not have made a difference? Is it surprising that deeper familiarity with one area gave views there a solidity that could survive the pressure—or that shallower, even if perceptive familiarity with other areas would prove more fragile?

In a sense the predicament of time can be said to have imposed itself in the path of Dulles's power, making it easier to detour away from directions his intellect might have suggested. The other obstacle that encouraged detour was self-imposed, though probably unconsciously. It involved the identification of goals or interests that were simply beyond the capacities of the United States, no matter how much time was available to tend them. For all his sensitivity to the limitations on American power, Dulles could allow ambitions and appetites to predominate his more abstract calculations of the political economy of power. Though he genuinely understood the scale of problems in Asia, for example, the thought of accepting the inevitability of a less prominent role there was just too unpalatable. On one hand he could tell Chiang Kai-shek's ambassador, Wellington Koo, that "even the Japanese had got themselves completely bogged down" in dealing with China—it "was a big country, with a lot of people."[69] On the other hand, he could struggle for years to force the PRC to accept what the United States had decided were severe but necessary limitations on its regional role in spite of contrary advice from Japanese and Indian leaders, in spite of difficulties with allies, in spite of the blood of Korea and Indochina, and in spite of great numbers of problems elsewhere.[70] John McCloy may have had just such an approach in mind when he once asked Eisenhower whether his administration's foreign policies had "too much of an 'Atlas' complex" about them.[71]

Of course, Dulles was hardly unique in allowing appetite to sometimes triumph over logic. Like many of his Washington associates, like many American policymakers in other years, and like many leaders elsewhere throughout history, he experienced a tug of war often basic to human nature. Ironically, the attempt to make power do more than it is capable of doing seems to come most dramatically at

[69] Memorandum of conversation, May 19, 1954, *FR, 1952–1954*, 14:423–24.

[70] I have discussed this issue with respect to China in particular in "Pondering the 'Evil Fact' in Asia: John Foster Dulles and China, 1953–1954," paper delivered at the annual meeting of the Society for Historians of American Foreign Relations, June 1987.

[71] Memorandum of meeting with the President, June 22, 1959 (June 29, 1959), Presidential Subseries, "Meetings with the President, 1959 (1)," WHOSANSA.

those times when power is already great. In this respect, Dulles and other Americans of the cold war era had something in common with the Persians described by Herodotus or the "exorbitant court" of Louis xiv described by Ranke. Perhaps it has something to do with Henry Kissinger's notion that "power is the great aphrodisiac."

Nor was Dulles unique in *struggling* with his ambitions and the predicaments they brought, though here his company is more exclusive. One thinks of Napoléon, for example, who could advise Metternich that "he who wills a thing must also will the means to bring it about," but could also complain to one of his generals that "you write to me that it's impossible; the word is not French." Or one thinks of Bismarck, deeply troubled by German compulsions after 1890, but so responsible for having set them in motion. Dulles's similar confrontation with contradictory impulses makes him a figure equally worthy of careful study. Such similarity may offer no comfort, of course. The experiences of Napoléon's France and Bismarck's Germany—and Dulles's America—suggest all too clearly how high a price is paid for failing to carry the confrontation to a wise conclusion.

CHAPTER 2

The Unexpected John Foster Dulles: Nuclear Weapons, Communism, and the Russians

John Lewis Gaddis

THE CARTOON IMAGES, thanks to the malicious genius of Herblock, still stick in our minds: John Foster Dulles as a pudgy Superman, pushing an alarmed Uncle Sam over the brink with the reassuring comment, "Don't be afraid—I can always pull you back." Or a complacent secretary of state following Chiang Kai-shek down into a swamp filled with rotting garbage and voracious alligators, pulling a befuddled Eisenhower and—again—a worried Uncle Sam along behind him. Or a sour-faced Dulles standing with bags packed for the summit, swathed in layers of coats, blankets, earmuffs, scarves, and caps, grimly clutching a hot water bottle and an umbrella, while a smiling short-sleeved Eisenhower tells the Russians over the telephone: "Yes, we'll be there, rain and shine." Or Dulles as an aloof grocer, presiding over a freezer stocked with "frozen attitudes," "frozen platitudes," and "frosted fruitless policies," while a frustrated American housewife plaintively asks: "Don't you ever have anything fresh?"[1]

It has often been said of Dulles that he lent himself to caricature: the public appearance of sanctimonious stuffiness; the tendency to let self-confidence become self-congratulation; the penchant for grandiloquent phrase-making; the apparent lawyer-like rigidity in the face of change; and even his obvious fondness for dashing around the world on airplanes. All these traits seemed to confirm Herblock's image of the determined but narrow-minded ideological crusader, relentlessly assaulting the ramparts of monolithic communism, brandishing nuclear weapons at every opportunity, heedless of the risks this involved to the nation, and to the world.

Like most caricatures this one did less than justice to its subject, a fact that has not escaped the attention of Dulles's biographers. Early

---

[1] The cartoons in question are reproduced in Townsend Hoopes, *The Devil and John Foster Dulles* (Boston, 1973), 292, 309, 416, 447.

studies by Louis Gerson and Michael Guhin suggested something of the extent to which the real Dulles only approximately resembled his public image.[2] Townsend Hoopes's 1973 biography, though basically critical of Dulles and certainly quite wrong in its underestimation of Eisenhower, was a still more balanced account than its unfortunate title suggested.[3] And, most recently, Ronald Pruessen has given us an impressive account of Dulles's career up to the time he became secretary of state, one that takes fully into account the multidimensional character and sometimes puzzling complexities of the man.[4]

But there still is no major reassessment of Dulles's role as secretary of state in the light of the vast body of archival materials on the Eisenhower administration that has been opened for research since the mid-1970s. Eisenhower's own reputation has soared as these documents have become available, and it is generally accepted now that he, and not Dulles, really ran foreign policy.[5] But the secretary of state was by no means a cipher: despite his careful deference to the president, Dulles significantly influenced administration policy. The new documents suggest that the positions he took on the issues and the manner in which he dealt with them are, in some ways, as surprising as what we have now learned about the president himself.

What follows is a preliminary reconstruction of Dulles's thinking, based on these new materials, with regard to three important issues: nuclear weapons, international communism, and negotiations with the Soviet Union. Because much of this documentation is new I have thought it best to let Dulles speak for himself as much as possible, although I do venture some analytical conclusions at the end of the chapter. My intent is twofold: to suggest the need for reassessing the nature of Dulles's influence on the Eisenhower administration's foreign and national security policy; but also to make the more general point that even those public figures whose outward behavior persuades us that we know them very well can in fact remain largely unknown to us. If we are to avoid oversimplifying the role of individuals in positions of leadership, we will need to take into account the possibility that these "hidden" or "unexpected" characteristics—as

[2] Louis Gerson, *John Foster Dulles* (New York, 1967); Michael Guhin, *John Foster Dulles: A Statesman and His Times* (New York, 1972).

[3] Hoopes, *Devil and Dulles*.

[4] Ronald W. Pruessen, *John Foster Dulles: The Road to Power* (New York, 1982).

[5] See, for example, Fred Greenstein, *The Hidden-Hand Presidency: Eisenhower as Leader* (New York, 1982), 87–90; also Richard Melanson and David Mayers, eds., *Reevaluating Eisenhower: American Foreign Policy in the Fifties* (Urbana, 1987), especially 1–10.

well as those we know all too well—played a role in determining "what actually happened."[6]

. . .

Dulles's ideas on nuclear weapons had become widely known, even before he became secretary of state, through a controversial article he had published in *Life* magazine in May 1952. Appropriately titled "A Policy of Boldness," it had criticized the Truman administration's approach to containment as too costly: the expenditures necessary to sustain a policy of resisting aggression wherever it occurred, without either escalation or capitulation, were unbalancing the budget, alarming allies, and even eroding civil liberties. If a single limited war in Korea could produce these effects, Dulles seemed to be saying, where would more serious conflicts lead? "Ours are treadmill policies which, at best, might perhaps keep us in the same place until we drop exhausted."

The solution, Dulles argued, was to regain the initiative: to find ways to make containment work more efficiently at less cost. One way was to rely to a greater extent than in the past upon American technological superiority over the Russians—particularly as reflected in the development of nuclear weapons and the means of delivering them—to *deter* the outbreak of war. Those devices had been thought of, up to that point, as instruments with which to *fight* wars. If war occurred, though, "it will be because we have allowed these new and awesome forces to become the ordinary killing tools of the soldier when, in the hands of the statesmen, they could serve as effective political weapons in defense of the peace." The way to ensure peace was to *"develop the will and organize the means to retaliate instantly against open aggression by Red armies, so that, if it occurred anywhere, we could and would strike back where it hurts, by means of our own choosing."*[7]

Curiously though, Dulles did not stress his strategy of "retaliation" during the early months of the Eisenhower administration, despite the fact that the president himself had been quick to raise the possibility of actually using nuclear weapons to end the fighting in Korea.[8] It was true that the Russians had succeeded "in setting atomic weapons apart from all other weapons," the new secretary of state told the

[6] For an excellent example of how "unexpected" or "hidden" characteristics can affect leadership, see Greenstein, *Hidden-Hand Presidency*.

[7] John Foster Dulles, "A Policy of Boldness," *Life* (May 19, 1952): 146–60. Emphasis in original.

[8] See, on this point, John Lewis Gaddis, *The Long Peace* (New York, 1987), 124–29.

National Security Council (NSC) in February 1953. As a consequence, there was a "moral problem" that tended to inhibit their actual military use in limited war situations like Korea. "We should try to break down this false distinction."[9] But when Dulles briefed the NSC the following month on prospects for global war, he did not even mention nuclear deterrence as a way to prevent it, placing his emphasis instead on solidarity with allies, the retention of outposts around the periphery of the Soviet bloc, and the possibility of "inducing the disintegration of Soviet power" by taking advantage of its overextension.[10]

Dulles did lecture the NSC in June 1953 on the virtues of what would later come to be known as "brinkmanship." The United States, he suggested, should "undertake certain efforts to prevent further significant expansion of Soviet power, even at the risk of war." These would not require actually going to war, "but rather that we would take actions which the Soviets, if they chose, could consider a *casus belli*." It was unlikely, Dulles thought, that they would do so: the formation of NATO and the signing of the Japanese Peace Treaty had "greatly irritated" the Russians, but they had not gone to war. Washington should not refrain from acting simply out of fear that it might push the Russians into initiating hostilities.[11]

But Dulles also stressed that unilateral threats of nuclear retaliation, if they risked disrupting relations with allies, could be dangerously counterproductive. News that the Russians had tested their own thermonuclear weapon in August 1953 caused the secretary of state to begin to worry about how long the United States could maintain military bases overseas, especially "if the countries containing these bases increasingly look upon them as lightning rods rather than umbrellas." Alternatively though, if the United States were itself to reduce its conventional forces in Europe—as the administration's "New Look" strategy seemed to imply it might—this would appear to Europeans as "final proof of an isolationist trend and the adoption of a 'Fortress America' concept. . . . The balance of world power, military and economic, would doubtless shift rapidly to our great disadvantage."[12] The presence of American bases therefore invited allied demoralization through the threat of Soviet attack; but the prospect of eliminating those bases was equally certain to demoralize allies by raising fears of American abandonment.

[9] Memorandum of NSC meeting of February 11, 1953, *FR, 1952–1954*, 15:770; see also memorandum of NSC meeting, October 7, 1953, *FR, 1952–1954*, 2:533.
[10] Memorandum of meeting, March 31, 1953, *FR, 1952–1954*, 2:265–66.
[11] Memorandum of NSC meeting, June 5, 1953, *FR, 1952–1954*, 2:374–75.
[12] Dulles to Eisenhower, September 6, 1953, *FR, 1952–1954*, 2:458–59.

The dilemma suggests the importance Dulles accorded to alliances. Just because one had nuclear superiority did not mean that one was free to act as one liked, without considering what allies might think. When an American thermonuclear bomb test in the Pacific accidentally irradiated the crew of a Japanese fishing boat in March 1954, the secretary of state reacted very strongly, warning Atomic Energy Commission Chairman Lewis Strauss of the need to be sensitive to "the tremendous repercussions these things have." A "wave of hysteria" had resulted that "is driving our Allies away from us. They think we are getting ready for a war of this kind. We could survive but some of them would be obliterated in a few minutes. It could lead to a policy of neutrality or appeasement."[13]

Several weeks later Dulles recommended a nuclear test moratorium to the NSC, provided it could be demonstrated that the recent series of tests had placed the United States ahead of the Soviet Union, and if the moratorium could be policed. He observed that the basic reason why the British had not been more helpful in sustaining the American position at the Geneva Conference on Indochina "was their obsession over the H-bomb and its potential effect on the British Isles." Comparisons were even being made between American "militaristic" tendencies and "Hitler's military machine." It simply was not possible to "sit here in Washington and develop bigger bombs without any regard for the impact of these developments on world opinion. In the long run it isn't only bombs that win wars, but having public opinion on your side."[14]

Dulles in the end abandoned the idea of a moratorium for a variety of reasons: it might impede the enterprise of American atomic scientists by discouraging experimentation; it might be difficult to monitor; the Russians might be able to turn to their advantage any moratorium "tailored" to preserve American superiority; and such a moratorium could create a "climate" of opinion in which it might be difficult to resume testing if that became necessary.[15] The decision not to seek a moratorium, Dulles told the NSC on June 23, "illustrated the power of reason against the power of will," because the hope had

[13] Memorandum of Dulles–Strauss telephone conversation, March 29, 1954, *FR, 1952–1954*, 2:1379–80.

[14] Memorandum of NSC meeting, May 16, 1954, *FR, 1952–1954*, 2:1424–28. Eisenhower in this case appeared to agree with Dulles's strongly expressed views: he commented during the course of the meeting that "everybody seems to think that we're skunks, saber-rattlers and warmongers." Ibid., 1428.

[15] Livingston Merchant to Robert R. Bowie, May 25, 1954, *FR, 1952–1954*, 2:1448; Memorandum of NSC meeting, May 27, 1954, ibid., 1453–54; Dulles to James S. Lay, Jr., June 23, 1954, ibid., 1463–67.

been to be able to reach a different conclusion. But as long as the United States remained opposed to the total abolition of nuclear weapons except as part of a general disarmament program, it could not accept "any position which would in effect set these weapons apart from other weapons as morally bad."[16]

The secretary of state returned to the difficulty of dealing with allies when the NSC reconvened the following day. Because of what appeared to be the growing danger of atomic war, he insisted, "our 'tough policy' was becoming increasingly unpopular throughout the free world; whereas the British 'soft policy' was gaining prestige and acceptance both in Europe and Asia." The Joint Chiefs of Staff had recommended that the United States take full advantage of its nuclear superiority to exert pressure on the Soviet Union. "If we do so, however, very few of our allies will follow us." Geneva had provided confirmation that "the tide is running against us in the channel of this tough policy. If we are to continue to pursue it we shall lose many of our allies, and this in itself compels a reappraisal of our basic policy. . . . We must recognize the fact that we can no longer run the free world, and accordingly review our basic security policy."[17]

Dulles further developed his position in an NSC discussion in August 1954. NSC 5422/1, a revision of the administration's basic New Look strategy, had contained language providing that "if general war should occur, the United States should wage it with all available weapons and should continue to make clear its determination to do so." Dulles expressed no objection to this contemplated use of "all available weapons" in all-out war, but he did find unwise the "boast of our nuclear capabilities" that the statement implied. "Talk of atomic attack," he noted, "tended to create 'peace at any price people' and might lead to an increase of appeasement sentiment in various countries. The Russians are smarter on this question because they never talk about using atomic weapons."[18] It would be difficult to overesti-

[16] Memorandum of NSC meeting, June 23, 1954, *FR, 1952–1954*, 2:1468–69. Eisenhower accepted the conclusions upon which Dulles (and the committee he headed on this subject) had agreed but dissented vigorously from the proposition that nuclear abolition required total disarmament: "[I]f he knew any way to abolish atomic weapons which would ensure the certainty that they would be abolished, he would be the very first to endorse it, regardless of general disarmament." Surely the United States with its vast resources could "whip the Soviet Union in any kind of war that had been fought in the past or any other kind of war than an atomic war." The difficulty was not morality, the president insisted: "The real thing was that the advantage of surprise almost seemed the decisive factor in an atomic war, and we should do anything we could to remove this factor." Ibid., 1469.

[17] Memorandum of NSC meeting, June 24, 1954, *FR, 1952–1954*, 2:694–95.

[18] Memorandum of NSC meeting, August 5, 1954, *FR, 1952–1954*, 2:706–7. Eisen-

mate the importance, he added a week later, of appearing before the world "as a peaceful state. Propaganda picturing us as warmongers on account of our atomic capabilities has done incalculable harm."[19]

It is worth pointing out that all of these comments—with their clear implication that the most fundamental aspects of national strategy needed rethinking—came only months after Dulles had called, in his much-quoted January 1954 speech to the Council on Foreign Relations, for reliance on the "deterrent of massive retaliatory power" as a way to show potential aggressors that they could not, henceforth, hope to achieve their aims.[20] The comments also followed the secretary of state's careful reformulation of his public position in the April 1954 issue of *Foreign Affairs*.[21] And they came after Dulles had told a NATO ministerial meeting that same month that "it should be our agreed policy, in case of either general or local war, to use atomic weapons as conventional weapons against the military assets of the enemy whenever and wherever it would be of advantage to do so, taking account of all relevant factors."[22] Such statements suggest, at a minimum, that Dulles's conspicuous statements about the virtues of "massive retaliation" were a less than complete reflection of what he actually believed.

It might well be, Dulles acknowledged in a top-secret assessment of national strategy late in 1954, that "the increased destructiveness of nuclear weapons and the approach of effective atomic parity are creating a situation in which general war would threaten the destruction of Western civilization and of the Soviet regime, and in which national objectives could not be attained through a general war, even if a military victory were won. A situation of mutual deterrence to general war could result." Miscalculations could, of course, always happen. Efforts by the communists to spread their influence by means short of war would still take place. But because "total war would be an incalculable disaster," the primary aim of American policy would have to be "to deter any Communist armed aggression and to avoid the danger that such aggression would develop into general nuclear war."

---

hower qualified Dulles's generalization by pointing out that the Russians had from time to time boasted that the United States no longer had an atomic monopoly.

[19] Memorandum of NSC meeting, August 12, 1954, *FR, 1952–1954*, 2:1485.

[20] Speech to the Council on Foreign Relations, January 12, 1954, *DSB* 30 (January 25, 1954): 108.

[21] John Foster Dulles, "Policy for Security and Peace," *Foreign Affairs* 32 (April 1954): 353–64.

[22] Dulles statement to closed NATO ministerial meeting, Paris, April 23, 1954, *FR, 1952–1954*, 5:512.

What that required was for the United States and its allies to "maintain sufficient flexible military capabilities, and firmness of policy, to convince the Communist rulers that the U.S. and its allies have the means to ensure that aggression will not pay and the will to use military force if the situation requires." The West should, however, "forego actions which would generally be regarded as provocative" and "be prepared, if hostilities occur, to meet them, where feasible, in a manner and on a scale which will not inevitably broaden them into total nuclear war." These cautions were necessary "to assure the support of our allies against aggression and to avoid risks which do not promise commensurate strategic or political gains."[23] The distance separating the architect of "massive retaliation" from what would later come to be known as the doctrine of "flexible response" was, it seems, less than one might think.

The basic policy the United States had followed through the end of 1954, Dulles admitted, had been "pretty good," even if "it hasn't got us into war." Not getting into a war, after all, was no bad thing. The positions the United States had taken with regard to the German question, Indochina, and the Chinese offshore islands could hardly be described as "craven": "it would be difficult to argue that our policies are not strong, firm, and indicative of a willingness to run risks. But our policy was none the less one which fell short of actually provoking war."

That policy had assumed, though, continued American nuclear superiority. The great difficulty Dulles saw on the horizon was "the forthcoming achievement of atomic plenty and a nuclear balance of power between the U.S. and the USSR." It was not at all clear how the United States could prevent the Russians from achieving that "nuclear balance" without going to war with them. More active policies in such areas as Indochina or China, of the kind the Joint Chiefs of Staff had advocated, would not solve that problem.[24]

Dulles expanded on this argument at an NSC meeting later in December 1954. He could not help but have some sympathy for the Joint Chiefs' call for "greater dynamism" in American policies toward the Russians and the Chinese Communists: he himself had campaigned on just this point in 1952. "However, experience indicated that it was not easy to go very much beyond the point that this Administration had reached in translating a dynamic policy into courses of action, and in any case we had been more dynamic than our pred-

[23] "Basic National Security Policy (Suggestions of the Secretary of State)," November 15, 1954, *FR, 1952–1954*, 2:772–75.

[24] Memorandum of NSC meeting, November 24, 1954, *FR, 1952–1954*, 2:789–90, 794–95.

ecessors." Preventive war was "of course" ruled out. Strong and force-ful efforts to change the character of the Soviet system, or to over-throw communist regimes in Eastern Europe and China, or to detach those countries from the Soviet bloc "would involve the United States in general war." Even if the United States could somehow break up Soviet control over Eastern Europe and China, "this in itself would not actually touch the heart of the problem: Soviet atomic plenty." And although these more aggressive policies, if successful, "might re-sult in the disintegration of the Soviet bloc, they would almost cer-tainly cause the disintegration of the free world bloc, . . . for our allies would never go along with such courses of action as these."[25]

In the end, Dulles concluded, the only real solution for the prob-lem of expanding Soviet nuclear capabilities might be nuclear aboli-tion. It was true, he admitted, that if the United States should agree to eliminate nuclear weapons alone, "we would be depriving our-selves of those weapons in which the U.S. was ahead and would not be taking action in the area of Soviet superiority, the conventional armaments field." It was unlikely that the means would ever be de-veloped to monitor conventional force disarmament. But "it could be argued that atomic weapons are the only ones by which the U.S. can be virtually destroyed through a sudden attack, and if this danger of destruction should be removed by eliminating nuclear weapons this would help the U.S. by enabling retention intact of our industrial power which has acted both as a deterrent against total war and as a principal means of winning a war."[26]

A year later, almost on the eve of the famous *Life* magazine inter-

---

[25] Memorandum of NSC meeting, December 21, 1954, *FR, 1952–1954*, 2:833–36. Is-suing ultimatums to the Russians to refrain from further attempts to expand their influence beyond their borders, Dulles argued, would probably also alienate the allies. Moreover, "the remaining areas into which the Soviets could expand their powers were not areas—except perhaps in the case of the Middle East—whose acquisition would notably increase the actual power of the Soviet bloc, although the prestige of the latter might gain." The NATO area was secure, as was Latin America. The situation in the Pacific was "pretty well in hand," except for Indonesia. South and Southeast Asia re-mained areas of concern, but the countries in question "lie so close to the orbit of the USSR and China, and all of the countries in question are so weak themselves, that they cannot but pose very serious problems to us. . . . Yet if one looked at the other side of the picture, these countries are not really of great significance to us, other than from the point of view of prestige, except that they must be regarded as staging grounds for further forward thrusts by the Communist powers." Only the Middle East and Indo-nesia remained as areas both vulnerable to Soviet expansion and vital to the interests of the United States. Ibid.

[26] Dulles conversation with State Department advisers, December 29, 1954, *FR, 1952–1954*, 2:1585–86. It is worth noting that Eisenhower had made a similar argu-ment in a meeting with Dulles and other advisers on January 16, 1954. Ibid., 1342–43.

view with James Shepley in which he had extolled the virtues of going to the brink of war as a means of preserving peace, Dulles discussed the future of nuclear deterrence with a recuperating Eisenhower—the president had suffered his heart attack three months earlier—in the White House. As Dulles himself recorded the conversation: "I said that I had come to the conclusion that our whole international security structure was in jeopardy. The basic thesis was local defensive strength with the backing up of United States atomic striking power. However, that striking power was apt to be immobilized by moral repugnance. If this happened, the whole structure could readily collapse."

Dulles went on to say that he had come to believe "that atomic power was too vast a power to be left for the military use of any one country." Its use, he thought, should be "internationalized for security purposes." The United States might well consider calling together the forty-two nations with which it had security treaties, placing before them a proposal for an international group that would decide "when and how to use atomic weapons for defense—always reserving of course the right of the United States, in the event that it was directly attacked, to use whatever means it had." If and when the Soviet Union was prepared to forgo the right of veto, the group might then transfer this responsibility to the UN Security Council "so as to universalize the capacity of atomic thermonuclear weapons to deter aggression." Eisenhower's response was that the idea was "an interesting one."[27]

Encouraged by the president to develop his ideas, the secretary of state prepared a long memorandum early in 1956 in which he noted that Soviet nuclear capabilities might well grow, within a few years, to the point at which they could "at a single stroke, virtually obliterate our industrial power and . . . simultaneously gravely impair our capacity to retaliate." That retaliatory capacity would then lose its deterrent effect, and "the United States might become endangered as never before." Indeed, the *psychological* loss of superiority might well precede its *actual* loss, because "it would be generally assumed that the use of our nuclear power is so restricted by constitutional and democratic processes and moral restraints that we would never be able to use it *first*; and conditions could be such that only the first use would have great significance." Dulles explained that "repugnance to

---

[27] Dulles memorandum of conversation with Eisenhower, December 26, 1955, WHMS, "Meetings with the President, 1955 (1)," DPEL. Eisenhower added that perhaps the sequence should be reversed: the Russians could be asked to give up the right of veto in the Security Council, and then if they refused, the group of forty-two nations could be formed. Ibid.

the use of nuclear weapons could grow to a point which would depreciate our value as an ally, undermine confidence in our 'collective defense' concepts, and make questionable the reliability of our allies and the availability to sac of our foreign bases."

All of this only reflected the fact that "there is throughout the world a growing, and not unreasonable, fear that nuclear weapons are expanding at such a pace as to endanger human life on this planet. . . . The peoples of the world cry out for statesmanship that will find a way to assure that this new force shall serve humanity, not destroy it." This responsibility very largely fell to the United States, but meeting it would require more than the "Atoms for Peace" or "Open Skies" proposals that had already been put forward. If the nation failed to meet that responsibility, "our moral leadership in the world could be stolen from us by those whose creed denies moral principles."

The solution, Dulles suggested, would be to vest a veto-less UN Security Council with control "of sufficient atomic weapons, and means of delivery, as to overbalance any atomic or other weapons as might be surreptitiously retained by any nation." Prior to this the United States might seek commitments from nations possessing nuclear capabilities to use them only in accordance with recommendations from the General Assembly. Regional groups, too—NATO would be the model—could be set up "to study and plan the means by whereby nuclear weapons could most effectively be used to deter armed attack and to preserve peace in each region." The critical task would be to get the United States away from its "present vulnerable position [of having] virtually the sole responsibility in the free world with respect to the use of nuclear weapons, . . . a responsibility which is not governed by any clearly enunciated principles reflecting 'decent respect for the opinions of mankind'."[28]

Although nothing came of Dulles's sweeping proposals, he continued throughout the rest of his term as secretary of state to reiterate with Eisenhower the concerns he had articulated. For example, in December 1956 in the immediate wake of the Suez and Hungarian crises, Dulles warned that in his view "a 'showdown' with Russia would not have more than one chance in three of working, and two chances out of three of making global war inevitable."[29] But the Russians too would have difficulty translating nuclear strength into political advantage. In November 1957, in connection with a discussion of

[28] Untitled Dulles memorandum, January 28, 1956, ss, "Papers on Nuclear Weapons 1/56 (1)," DPEL.

[29] Memorandum of conversation with Eisenhower, December 3, 1956, WHMS, "Meetings with the President, August–December, 1956 (2)," DPEL.

Strategic Air Command (SAC) vulnerabilities, Dulles dismissed the possibility of a Soviet surprise attack as "remote" on the grounds that "such an attack without provocation involving casualties of perhaps one hundred million would be so abhorrent to all who survived in any part of the world that I did not think that even the Soviet rulers would dare to accept the consequences."[30]

In April 1958 Dulles again raised with Eisenhower "the question of our national strategic concept." The difficulty was that "this too much invoked massive nuclear attack in the event of any clash anywhere of U.S. with Soviet forces." There were, Dulles argued, "increasing possibilities of effective defense through tactical nuclear weapons and other means short of wholesale obliteration of the Soviet Union, and . . . these should be developed more rapidly." It was a vicious circle: "so long as the strategic concept contemplated this, our arsenal of weapons had to be adapted primarily to that purpose and so long as our arsenal of weapons was adequate only for that kind of a response, we were compelled to rely on that kind of a response." It was, of course, the case that "our deterrent power might be somewhat weakened if it were known that we contemplated anything less than 'massive retaliation' and therefore the matter had to be handled with the greatest care."[31]

What this new evidence suggests, then, is that the traditional view of Dulles as an uncritical enthusiast for strategies based solely on nuclear deterrence is wrong; that, indeed, the secretary of state himself anticipated many of the criticisms advocates of "flexible response" would later make of such strategies; and that he even contemplated, as a long-range goal and on both geopolitical and moral grounds, the abolition of nuclear weapons altogether.

.   .   .

A second area in which the documents suggest we need to revise our thinking about John Foster Dulles concerns his understanding of international communism. In his first televised address as secretary of state only a week after the Eisenhower administration took office, Dulles dramatically unveiled a map showing the "vast area" stretching from Central Europe to Kamchatka and including China, "which the Russian Communists completely dominate." In the few years since

[30] Memorandum of conversation with Eisenhower, November 7, 1957, WHMS, "Meetings with the President, 1957 (2)," DPEL.

[31] Memorandum of conversation with Eisenhower, April 1, 1958, WHMS, "Meetings with the President, January–June 1958 (5)," DPEL. I am indebted to Fred Greenstein for this reference.

the end of World War II, the number of people under their rule had expanded from 200 to 800 million, "and they're hard at work to get control of other parts of the world." The strategy was one of "encirclement": "Soviet Communists" would seek to avoid all-out war but would work "to get control of the different areas around them and around us, so they will keep growing in strength and we will be more and more cut off and isolated. And they have been making very great progress."[32]

At first glance, the tone and content of this speech appear to fit the widely held view of Dulles as an ideological literalist, convinced that adherence to the doctrines of Marx and Lenin automatically meant subservience to Moscow. Dulles himself encouraged this view. All one had to do to anticipate communist behavior, he repeatedly said, was to read Stalin's *Problems of Leninism,* "the present-day Communist bible, . . . [that] gives us the same preview Hitler gave in *Mein Kampf.*"[33] Associates recall him pulling the book off the shelf at the slightest provocation and citing it "with surprising accuracy" to prove his point.[34] The world confronted, Dulles liked to stress, "a vast monolithic system which, despite its power, believes that it cannot survive except as it succeeds in progressively destroying human freedom."[35]

But Dulles said something else in that initial January 1953 television address that should have suggested a more complex view of international communism than what could be gleaned from reading Stalin on Lenin. Resorting to what one student of the subject has called "gastronomic" imagery, Dulles reminded his audience that although the "Russian Communists . . . have swallowed a great many people to date, . . . there is such a thing as indigestion. People don't always get stronger by eating more." Signs of indigestion were already apparent within the Soviet bloc: "perhaps in time the indigestion will become so acute that it might be fatal." At the time these references seemed simply to echo Dulles's calls, made during the 1952 campaign, for the "liberation" of the Soviet Union's East European satellites; the secretary of state himself suggested as much in his speech.[36] But the documents show that a deeper and more sophisti-

[32] Dulles radio and television address, January 27, 1953, *DSB* 28 (February 9, 1953): 212–16.

[33] Dulles speech at Colgate University, July 7, 1950, *DSB* 24 (July 17, 1950): 88.

[34] Andrew H. Berding, *Dulles on Diplomacy* (Princeton, 1965), 7–8, 30–31.

[35] Dulles speech at Geneva Conference on Korea, April 28, 1954, *DSB* 30 (May 10, 1954): 706.

[36] Dulles radio and television address, January 27, 1953, *DSB* 28 (February 9, 1953): 215–16. The term "gastronomic" imagery was first suggested to me by Professor John F. Zeugner of Worcester Polytechnic Institute.

cated understanding of international communism lay behind these pronouncements.

The "great weakness in the present brand of communism," Dulles had written in a memorandum to himself in 1949, "is insistence on absolute conformity to a pattern made in Russia. That does not work in areas where the economic and social problems are different from those in Russia and where there are deep-seated national and cultural loyalties."[37] China, he thought, was such an area. "It is not necessary to reconquer China by subsidizing a vast military operation," he wrote Senator Homer Ferguson. "Communism will disintegrate in China, and the Chinese themselves will take care of that, because of its inability to solve the problems of China."[38] The outbreak of the Korean War and China's intervention in it convinced Dulles that the break with the Soviet Union would not come soon. But, as he wrote to Dean Acheson in November 1950, in the long run "[o]ur best defense lies in exploiting potential jealousies, rivalries, and disaffections within the present area of Soviet communist control so as to divert them from external adventures to the problem of attempting to consolidate an already over-extended position."[39]

Where Dulles differed from Acheson was not over whether the Sino-Soviet alliance would break up, but on how one could best accelerate that process. Even after the Chinese had intervened in Korea, Acheson still thought it might be possible to wean Peking from its ties with Moscow, whether by convincing Mao and his advisers that the Russians had imperial aspirations in Asia or through surreptitious contacts with shadowy groups believed capable of overthrowing Mao.[40] Dulles disagreed. "My own feeling," he wrote Chester Bowles early in 1952, "is that the best way to get a separation between the Soviet Union and Communist China is to keep pressure on Communist China and make its way difficult so long as it is in partnership with Soviet Russia." The Yugoslavs had not broken with Moscow "because we were nice to Tito. On the contrary, we were very rough with Tito." If China could win American favors while remaining in the Kremlin camp, "then there is little reason for her to change."[41]

---

[37] Untitled memorandum, June 16, 1949, "Council of Foreign Ministers," DPP.

[38] Dulles to Homer Ferguson, June 28, 1949, "Homer Ferguson," DPP.

[39] Dulles to Acheson, November 30, 1950, "Korea, 1950," DPP.

[40] For details, see Gaddis, *The Long Peace*, 170–73. In order to promote consistency with documents from the 1950s, Wade-Giles spelling will be used throughout this book.

[41] Dulles to Bowles, March 25, 1952, "Chester Bowles," DPP. See also the transcript of a Dulles interview on "Meet the Press," February 10, 1952, as quoted in David Allan Mayers, *Cracking the Monolith: U.S. Policy against the Sino-Soviet Alliance, 1949–1955* (Baton Rouge, 1986), 119.

The ultimate force that would defeat international communism, Dulles believed, was the same force that had defeated all empires: internal contradictions. In his 1950 book, *War or Peace*, he had noted that "[d]ictatorships usually present a formidable exterior. They seem, on the outside, to be hard, glittering, and irresistible." But in fact, "they are full of rottenness."[42] The death of Stalin was likely to reveal the "rottenness" that lay within the Soviet system. Soviet power, he told the NSC soon after Eisenhower took office, was "already overextended and represents tyrannical rule over unwilling peoples. If we keep the pressures on, psychological and otherwise, we may either force a collapse of the Kremlin regime or else transform the Soviet orbit from a union of satellites dedicated to aggression, into a coalition for defense only." There could be "no real replacement for Stalin the demi-god."[43]

Dulles elaborated on this strategy in a remarkable briefing he gave for President Eisenhower, British prime minister Winston Churchill, and French foreign minister Georges Bidault at the Bermuda conference in December 1953. There was evidence of strain in Sino-Soviet relations, Dulles noted. This was only logical, because "Mao Tse-tung was himself an outstanding Communist leader in his own right." With the death of Stalin and the absence among his successors of anyone whose prestige exceeded Mao's, it was becoming necessary for the Russians to treat Mao "as an equal partner on the world scene." That fact was important and "may eventually give us an opportunity for promoting division between the Soviet Union and Communist China in our own common interest."

There were two theories about how to do this. "One was that by being nice to the Communist Chinese we could wean them away from the Soviets, and the other was that pressure and strain would compel them to make more demands on the USSR which the latter would be unable to meet and the strain would consequently increase." The British, Dulles pointed out (and he might have included as well the Truman administration prior to and even during the Korean War), had followed the first approach, but with meager results. This was not surprising, because "competition with the Russians as to who would treat China best . . . put China in the best of worlds." The better approach would be to apply "pressure . . . on Communist China both politically and economically and, to the extent possible without war, military pressure should likewise be maintained." It was within that context, Dulles added, that American assistance to Chiang Kai-

---

[42] John Foster Dulles, *War or Peace* (New York, 1950), 242.
[43] Memorandum of NSC meeting, March 31, 1953, *FR, 1952–1954*, 2:267–68.

shek and the Chinese Nationalists should be viewed: "this was another of the measures we liked to pursue on the theory of exerting maximum strain causing the Chinese Communists to demand more from Russia and thereby placing additional stress on Russian-Chinese relations."[44]

The Eisenhower–Dulles strategy on Quemoy and Matsu has generally been seen as reflecting the assumption that the Chinese Communists were Soviet puppets, together with deference to pressures from the pro-Nationalist China Lobby in the United States.[45] But this new evidence suggests the need to revise that assessment. Domestic politics may indeed have played a role in shaping the American hard line on this issue, but the view that Mao took orders from the Russians clearly did not. Indeed, the strategy was intended to drive Mao *toward* Moscow, not away from it, in the belief that this course of action would most quickly weaken the Sino-Soviet relationship.

One of Dulles's initial recommendations after the first Quemoy-Matsu crisis broke in August 1954 was to take the issue to the UN Security Council, a move that "could put a serious strain on Soviet-ChiCom relations." If the Soviet Union vetoed UN action, it would "gravely impair" their ongoing "peace offensive" and thus cause them to lose support in world opinion. If, alternatively, they did not veto such action, "the ChiComs could react adversely, . . . defy the UN, [and] . . . again become an international outcast."[46] The forth-

[44] U.S. Delegation minutes, Eisenhower–Churchill–Bidault meeting, Bermuda, December 7, 1953, *FR, 1952–1954*, 5:1809–14. See also NSC 166/1, approved by Eisenhower on November 6, 1953, which noted: "As the inevitable differences in interest, viewpoint, or timing of actions develop between the Russians and the Chinese; as the Chinese tend to become importunate in their demands for Russian assistance or support; or as the role of the Chinese as vice-regents for international communism in the Far East becomes too independent and self reliant—there will be strong temptation for the Russians to attempt to move in the direction of greater disciplinary control over the Chinese Communists. If the time ever comes when the Russians feel impelled to contest with the Chinese Communist leaders for primacy in the domestic apparatus of control of the Chinese regime, the alliance will be critically endangered. For . . . the Chinese Communist leaders are Chinese as well as Communists." NSC 166/1, "U.S. Policy Towards Communist China," November 6, 1953, *FR, 1952–1954*, 14:297.

[45] See Hoopes, *Devil and Dulles*, 262–63, 268.

[46] Dulles memorandum, September 12, 1954, *FR, 1952–1954*, 14:612. During the previous summer, Dulles has received from Senator William F. Knowland information purporting to come from Peking indicating that the Russians were less than enthusiastic about supporting the Chinese if they got into a war with the United States, and that the Chinese had expressed "mild resentment" over this. "Information from Peiping Concerning the Geneva Conference," attached to Dulles to Knowland, June 30, 1954, CS, "June 1954 (1)," DPEL. Early in 1955 UN Secretary-General Dag Hammarskjöld, with Washington's approval, invited representatives from the PRC to partici-

coming defensive treaty between the United States and Nationalist China, Dulles told the National Security Council in November, would be a "major challenge" to the Chinese Communists.[47]

As Dulles explained in a conversation with British ambassador Sir Roger Makins in February 1955, the long-term objective of American policy was to bring about "sufficient independence between Peiping and Moscow as to create the beginning of a balance of power relationship." With the two communist giants embroiled with each other, and with the gradual return of Japanese power, "the U.S. would not have to be so fully involved in the Far East as it now is."[48] Both the Soviet and Chinese communist regimes were overextended, he told Chinese Nationalist foreign minister George Yeh a few days later. Moreover, Washington regarded "the disintegrative process as inherent in the nature of a Communist dictatorship, and as inevitable." The communist regimes were "bound to crack," if for no other reason than their inability to satisfy the needs of their own people. What was required was "faith that the dissolution of this evil system is gradually taking place even when there is no surface evidence." After all, as St. Paul had said faith "is the substance of things hoped for, the evidence of things not seen." "We must know in our hearts that Communism contains the seeds of its own destruction. External pressures hasten the destructive process."[49]

How long did Dulles think all this would take? Here his views varied. He told Yeh that the breakup could come within a year, but that no one could tell: "it might be some years away."[50] Several months earlier he had speculated that it might take as long as twenty-five years, and had wondered whether the West could afford to wait that long.[51] By early 1956 Dulles had become even more pessimistic. "[T]hese natural rivalries might take 100 years to assert themselves," he told British foreign secretary Selwyn Lloyd. Precisely for that reason the West could not relax its pressure. "[I]n World War II, it was

---

pate in a Security Council debate on the offshore islands crisis, but the Chinese refused to do so. Editorial notes, *FR, 1955–1957*, 2:178–79, 202–3.

[47] Memorandum of NSC meeting, November 24, 1954, *FR, 1952–1954*, 2:789.

[48] Dulles conversation with Sir Roger Makins, February 7, 1955, *FR, 1955–1957*, 2:236.

[49] Dulles–Yeh conversation, February 10, 1955, *FR, 1955–1957*, 2:253–58. See also Dulles memorandums of conversations with Chiang Kai-shek, March 4, 1955, and with Australian Prime Minister Robert Menzies, March 14, 1955, ibid., 323, 369.

[50] *FR, 1955–1957*, 2:254.

[51] Memorandum of NSC meeting, August 18, 1954, *FR, 1952–1954*, 14:534. Dulles had noted in an earlier NSC meeting on August 5 that "there should be long-range plans for a rollback in the satellites, in Iran, etc., but . . . these plans would have to be very long-range indeed." Ibid., 2:711.

freely predicted that the Axis partners would split, should they win. But the Allies did not stop fighting on that account."[52] Certainly Dulles showed no inclination to explore feelers from Peking, extended in the aftermath of the Quemoy-Matsu crisis, that might have led to a more amicable relationship.[53]

One thing was clear, though: the West should not push so hard in seeking to fragment the international communist monolith as to provoke a violent response. Dulles warned Yeh in February 1955 that "a totalitarian regime when near the point of break-up may lash out recklessly in order to avoid or postpone an internal crisis." World War I, he thought, had resulted more from "such a lashing out by the Austro-Hungarian and the Russian autocracies, which were near the break-up point in 1914, than by Prussian militarism."[54] Seven weeks earlier the secretary of state had told the NSC that any overt attempt to overthrow the Chinese regime or to detach Eastern Europe from Soviet control would lead to general war. The preferable course was to wait for time to bring about changes within international communism, however long it took. Once it developed that the Soviet Union could no longer "decide upon and take sudden action without considering the views of its allies and associates," then the threat posed by that nation would be "greatly diminished." Nationalism was the key: indeed it was possible "to foresee the growth within the Soviet bloc of so wide a distribution of power that no single individual could decide on a course of action which would bind all the rest."[55]

By mid-1956—largely as a result of the Khrushchev "de-Stalinization" speech to the Twentieth Party Congress, which the Central Intelligence Agency had arranged to have distributed throughout the world[56]—Dulles had become convinced that "the process of disintegration" within international communism was well under way. "So-

---

[52] Memorandum, Dulles–Lloyd conversation, January 31, 1956, *FR, 1955–1957*, 3:292. See also Dulles's speech at San Francisco, June 28, 1957, ibid., 564.

[53] See Kenneth T. Young, *Negotiating with the Chinese Communists: The United States Experience, 1953–1967* (New York, 1968), 91–128.

[54] Dulles–Yeh conversation, February 10, 1955, *FR, 1955–1957*, 2:258.

[55] Memorandum of NSC meeting, December 21, 1954, *FR, 1955–1957*, 2:836. Dulles records himself the following day as having told the president that, "in my opinion, the possibilities of change which would be in the interest of the United States would come from either (a) the traditional tendency of the Chinese to be individualistic or (b) the traditional Chinese dislike of foreigners which was bound in the long run to impair relations with Russia." Dulles notes Eisenhower as responding that "under present conditions, no change of our attitude was possible, but that if the Chinese Communists met certain quite obvious requirements, then the situation might be different." Dulles memorandum of conversation with Eisenhower, December 22, 1954, *FR, 1952–1954*, 14:1048.

[56] See John Ranelagh, *The Agency: The Rise and Decline of the CIA* (New York, 1986), 285–88.

viet Communism is in deep trouble," he told the Senate Foreign Relations Committee in June of that year.[57] The Russians faced the dilemma, he explained to Eisenhower, "of either allowing liberal forces to grow and obtain recognition, or else revert to [a] Stalinist type of repression, in which case they would lose the ground they had been trying to gain with the free nations as having become more civilized and more liberal."[58] The administration itself, through the Voice of America and by other means, had done much "to revive the influences which are inherent in freedom, [and] have thereby contributed toward creating strains and stresses within the captive world."[59] Where countries "were physically adjacent to the Soviet Union and where Soviet troops were there to sustain a pro-Soviet government, the people had little recourse. However, that was not the case where a country was not adjacent to the Soviet Union and where Soviet military power was not available to support the government."[60]

The speed and brutality with which the Soviets suppressed the Hungarian revolution of October–November 1956 confirmed that last proposition. It also suggested that Moscow's ability to keep its satellites in line had not eroded to the extent that Dulles thought it had. Still, even that event had its positive side, as the secretary of state pointed out to the President in mid-December: the sixty satellite divisions could "no longer be regarded as an addition to Soviet forces— in fact they may immobilize certain Soviet forces."[61] The difficulty was knowing how much further one could prudently push the Russians. "[T]he successive setbacks of the Soviet rulers in terms of the Communist satellite parties in free countries, in satellite countries in Eastern Europe and internal unrest in Russia itself," Dulles warned, "combined to make it hard for them to accept any further setbacks."[62]

Hope might now have to lie in the gradual evolution of communist systems into something better, a theme the secretary of state began to

[57] "Notes for Foreign Relations Committee Appearance," June 26, 1956, "Soviet Union," DPP.

[58] Memorandum of conversation with Eisenhower, July 13, 1956, WHMS, "Meetings with the President, January–July, 1956 (1)," DPEL.

[59] Dulles to Eisenhower, September 9, 1956, WHMS, "Correspondence—General 1956 (2)," DPEL.

[60] Memorandum of conversation with Eisenhower, September 17, 1956, WHMS, "Meetings with the President, August–December, 1956 (5)," DPEL. Dulles made these points in the context of discussing Soviet-Egyptian relations during the Suez Canal crisis.

[61] Memorandum of conversation with Eisenhower, December 15, 1956, WHMS, "Meetings with the President, August–December, 1956 (2)," DPEL.

[62] Memorandum of conversation with Eisenhower, December 22, 1956, WHMS, "Meetings with the President, August–December, 1956 (1)," DPEL.

emphasize publicly during the last year of his life. "I am not sure that Communism as a social and economic structure will wither away," he told a British television interviewer in October 1958. But "I do see an evolution, away from what I call international communism . . . which tries to spread its creed all over the world . . . to a system which puts more emphasis upon national welfare . . . and will give up this fantastic dream of world conquest."[63] Later that year, in a speech at San Francisco, Dulles returned to his favorite image of "materialistic despotisms [that] with their iron discipline, their mechanistic performance, their hard and shiny exterior, always seem formidable." But these dictatorships suffered from a great internal contradiction: if they were to develop into modern industrial states, they would have to educate their people. They would then find that "minds so educated also penetrate the fallacies of Marxism and increasingly resist conformity." Internal difficulties such as these "are bound to alter the character of the Communist regimes, particularly if these regimes are denied the glamor and prestige of great external successes."

Here Dulles came as close as he ever did in public to laying out the basis of his strategy toward the communist world: "To deny external successes to International Communism is not merely a negative, defensive policy. It accelerates the evolution within the Sino-Soviet bloc of governmental policies which will increasingly seek the welfare of their own peoples, rather than exploit these peoples in the interest of world conquest." If the noncommunist nations could "hold fast to policies which deter armed aggression; if they prevent subversion through economic and revolutionary processes; and, above all, if they demonstrate the good fruits of freedom, then we can know that freedom will prevail."[64]

Dulles's final word on this subject came in an undated fragment of a speech draft that was probably composed around January 1959. "The pattern of the future," he noted, "is, I think, predictable in its broad outlines." The communists had imposed their rule on some 900 million people. There was no way for the West to disrupt that rule from the outside, "for we renounce the destructive power of so-called 'preventive war'. But we can prevent that pattern from prevailing and we can confidently expect that in due course it will be altered from within."[65]

Again, a revision of traditional interpretations seems to be called for, because Dulles clearly did not see international communism as

---

[63] State Department transcript, Dulles interview with William D. Clark of British Independent Television, October 23, 1958, "Deterrent Strategy," DPP.

[64] Dulles speech at San Francisco, December 4, 1958, "Massive Retaliation," DPP.

[65] Undated speech fragment, "Soviet Union," DPP.

monolithic. More than that, he had a sophisticated long-term strategy for encouraging fragmentation within the communist world that almost certainly influenced U.S. policies, and that may also—although at present we have no reliable way of confirming this—even have contributed to the breakup of the Sino-Soviet alliance. It was a strategy pursued with caution: the "pressure" by which Dulles sought to achieve fragmentation was always to be applied by means short of war. In Dulles's last years, he even came to see that internal changes within communist states might alter their external behavior more rapidly than the deliberate application of pressure from without. Whether one agrees with it or not, Dulles's understanding of the communist world—like his thinking on nuclear weapons—turns out to have been based on a good deal more than the rigid and narrow view of the world his critics have so often attributed to him.

· · ·

A third commonly held view of Dulles has been that he was reluctant to acknowledge the possibility of change within the Soviet Union, or to contemplate in any serious way the prospect of negotiations with that country. Townsend Hoopes best summed up this line of argument when he wrote that "Stalin did Dulles a philosophical and practical disservice by dying, but Dulles retaliated by continuing to act as though the death had not occurred."[66] Dulles himself reinforced his image as an uncompromising hard-liner with repeated warnings about the Soviet capacity for deception, "for making concessions merely in order to lure others into a false sense of security, which makes them the easier victims of ultimate aggression."[67] His whole attitude toward the Soviet Union seemed to be summed up in his famous suggestion to Eisenhower, once the Geneva summit had become unavoidable, to avoid social functions at which he might be photographed with Bulganin and Khrushchev, and to maintain "an austere countenance on occasions where photographing together is inevitable."[68]

But was the secretary of state's view of the Russians really that rigid? Enough evidence is available to suggest, once again, a more complex—and more interesting—Dulles than one might expect.

Early in September 1953 the secretary of state raised with Eisen-

[66] Hoopes, *Devil and Dulles*, 171.

[67] Dulles remarks to New York State Republican dinner, New York, May 7, 1953, *DSB* 28 (May 18, 1953): 707.

[68] Dulles undated draft, "Estimate of Prospects of Soviet Union Achieving Its Goals," "Atomic Energy," DPP.

hower the possibility of making "a spectacular effort to relax world tensions and execute such mutual withdrawals of Red Army forces and of U.S. forces abroad" as would permit the stabilization of NATO and of West German forces "at a level compatible with budgetary relief," and creation of a "strategic reserve" in the United States. The result would be a "broad zone of restricted armament in Europe, with Soviets withdrawn from satellites and U.S. from Europe."[69] The basis for this extraordinary suggestion—which resembled, as nothing else, George F. Kennan's much-criticized proposal for "disengagement" put forward in his Reith Lectures five years later[70]—was Dulles's concern that what would later come to be called "extended deterrence" would not, in itself, discourage Soviet aggression in Europe. American military bases there and elsewhere were becoming an "irritant," and the new Soviet "peace offensive" threatened to invite "wishful thinking, on the part of NATO partners and Japan, that the danger is past and that neutralism and military economy are permissible."

If combined with Soviet political liberalization in Eastern Europe—Dulles mentioned the example of Finland in this respect—and with an end to Moscow's efforts to spread "world revolution," an opening-up of East–West trade, and progress toward the international control of nuclear weapons, then the kind of settlement he proposed to Eisenhower could increase American influence in the world while minimizing costs; "it would also end the present state of strain which breeds distrust and intolerance which undermine our traditional American way of life."[71]

The president in response expressed "emphatic agreement that renewed efforts should be made to relax world tensions on a global basis" and acknowledged that "mutual withdrawals of Red Army Forces and of United States Forces could be suggested as a step toward relaxing these tensions." But he also reminded Dulles that although it was true that overseas bases might be unpopular, "any with-

[69] Dulles memorandum, September 6, 1953, *FR, 1952–1954*, 2:459.

[70] See George F. Kennan, *Memoirs: 1950–1963* (Boston, 1972), 229–61. Kennan had, of course, put forward a similar proposal within the government in 1948–1949, known as "Program A." See his *Memoirs: 1925–1950* (Boston, 1967), 421–26; also PPS 37/1, "Position to Be Taken by the U.S. at a CFM Meeting," November 15, 1948, *FR, 1948*, 2:1320–38.

[71] Dulles memorandum, September 6, 1953, *FR, 1952–1954*, 2:459. Dulles brought up the example of Finland as a model for future Soviet–East European relations several months later in a conversation with Churchill and Eden, but Eden pointed out that "considerable autonomy was permissible to Finland from Russia because Finland was 'the road to nowhere,' but the satellite countries were 'the road to somewhere else.'" Dulles memorandum of conversation with Churchill and Eden, April 12, 1954, WHMS, "Meetings with the President, 1954 (4)," DPEL.

drawal that seemed to imply a change in basic intent would cause real turmoil abroad."[72] Dulles subsequently told his Policy Planning Staff director, Robert Bowie, that Eisenhower had been "entirely sympathetic" to the proposal, but that "if we made a fair offer and it was rejected then we had no alternative but to look upon the Soviet Union as a potential aggressor and make our own plans accordingly." The way to proceed would be a public declaration: the president "was not inclined to look with favor upon secret preliminary discussions with the U.S.S.R. or the U.K."[73]

By October 1953 the idea of a mutual withdrawal of forces in Europe had been incorporated into the drafts, already under way, of a presidential speech on the international control of nuclear weapons.[74] But, as Bowie pointed out, there was a difficulty. "The withdrawal of U.S. troops is linked to control of nuclear weapons, because we cannot withdraw our forces at the same time the Russians do without abandoning our bases. Obviously we cannot abandon forward bases until nuclear weapons are controlled."[75] Dulles himself soon came to the view that no serious discussions with the Russians on these matters should take place until progress had been made in establishing the European Defense Community. "I think there may be a fair chance of some settlement with the Russians," he wrote the president, "if we have a firm foundation in Western Europe—but not before."[76] As a result, he later recalled, Eisenhower's speech was limited to the subject of atomic energy: "The broader aspects on analysis were difficult of reduction to concrete acceptable proposals."[77]

Dulles's second thoughts did not mean, though, as one recent biographer of Eisenhower has written, that the secretary of state "had no faith whatsoever in any disarmament proposal [and] believed in dealing with the Russians only from a position of overwhelming strength."[78] It might well "be possible to reach general agreements

---

[72] Eisenhower to Dulles, September 8, 1953, *FR, 1952–1954*, 2:460.

[73] Dulles to Bowie, September 8, 1953, WHMS, "Correspondence 1953 (2)," DPEL.

[74] See C. D. Jackson to Eisenhower, October 2, 1953, *FR, 1952–1954*, 2:1224–26.

[75] "Summary of Discussion of State Draft of Part Two of Presidential Speech," October 19, 1953, *FR, 1952–1954*, 2:1228.

[76] Dulles to Eisenhower, October 23, 1953, *FR, 1952–1954*, 2:1234.

[77] Dulles to Eisenhower, May 12, 1954, WHMS, "Correspondence 1954 (3)," DPEL. This memorandum was written in reply to one from Eisenhower, enclosing—as was often the president's habit—an unsigned proposal for Dulles's comments, in this case one advocating a "really grand effort to achieve whole peace for the whole world." The proposed package included a mutual withdrawal of Soviet and American forces in Europe, an agreement on free elections in Korea and Indochina, and a worldwide reduction in military forces. Eisenhower to Dulles, May 6, 1954, ibid.

[78] Stephen Ambrose, *Eisenhower*. Vol. 2: *The President* (New York, 1984), 132.

with the Soviets . . . on reduction of armaments," Dulles told the NSC in October 1953, but "we were certainly not in a position to impose such settlements on them. Such settlements would have to be mutually acceptable." If the United States was prepared to accept a quid pro quo, then "we are in a position to settle Korea and possibly even East Germany." Negotiations by no means excluded "unilateral efforts by the United States to increase its relative power position vis-à-vis the USSR," or even "to push our power position forward against the USSR." But "we could not reduce tensions with the USSR if in each case we expected to gain all the advantage and the Soviets none."[79]

Nor did Dulles regard the Russians as impossible negotiating partners. They had been "rather cautious in exercising their power," he told the NSC in December 1954. "They were not reckless, as Hitler was." The very fact that they relied primarily upon subversion rather than military force to achieve their objectives was an indication of that caution; it was also "natural," because the Communist party was "in essence revolutionary and conspiratorial." Kremlin leaders calculated that it would not be worth risking what they had achieved through subversion by indulging in aggressive acts that would be hard to reconcile "with their world-wide propaganda line in favor of peace and co-existence." What this meant for the West was that if it could build up regimes "capable of maintaining internal security and . . . which can't be overthrown except by overt, brutal acts of aggression, it will be possible to withstand the present Soviet threat."

Eisenhower drew out the implications of what Dulles had said: to assume that entering into negotiations with the Russians "would cause the free world to let down its military guard" was to assume "that the State Department was incapable of distinguishing fraudulent from honest changes in the Soviet attitude." Besides, "we cannot hope to get the continued support of public opinion in the free world if we always say 'no' to any suggestions that we negotiate with the Soviet Union. . . . [W]e should negotiate wherever and whenever it looks profitable."[80]

[79] Minutes of NSC meeting, October 7, 1953, *FR, 1952–1954*, 2:529–30. It is worth noting that Eisenhower, somewhat surprised by Dulles's tone, observed "with a smile" that "this was not the way that the Secretary of State usually talked to him about this problem." Ibid., 529. No one had the right to assume, Dulles argued in a May 1954 public address, "that he sees the future so clearly that he is justified in concluding either that war is inevitable or that methods of conciliation are futile. Efforts for honorable peace are required out of a decent respect for the opinion of mankind." Dulles speech at Williamsburg, Virginia, May 15, 1954, *DSB*, 30 (May 24, 1954): 780. Negotiations had the additional advantage, the secretary of state noted pragmatically, that "they clarify the issues."

[80] Memorandum of NSC meeting, December 21, 1954, *FR, 1952–1954*, 2:842–43. It

By early 1955, Dulles was distinguishing in public between the "aggressive fanaticism" of the Chinese Communists and the "coldly calculated" but "deliberate" behavior of the Russians: "They have stated that their program will involve an entire historical era, and so far at least they have not taken reckless risks."[81] He was not optimistic about achieving a "significant political settlement" with Moscow, he told a press conference in April, "but I believe it is something that we have always got to keep trying for. . . . Sometimes the unexpected is what happens. It seems to me that in dealing with the Soviet Union it is oftentimes the unexpected which is more apt to happen than the thing that one anticipates."[82]

The secretary of state was modest in his assessment of what the Geneva summit conference actually achieved. It had made relations between Russia and the West "less brittle." It also meant that "for the predictable future, we can subject our differences to the patient processes of diplomacy with less fear that war will come out of them."[83] Divided countries like Germany, Korea, and Vietnam still remained, to be sure, but there were advantages in not carrying out reunifications by means of war: "By war you may then unify . . . only for insects and not for human life."[84] Noting the recent agreement with the Russians on the withdrawal of occupation forces from Austria, Dulles acknowledged the difficulty of knowing "whether what is going on now marks a genuine change of purpose or whether it is merely a maneuver." It was necessary to plan for both contingencies. "We must not rebuff a change which might be that for which the whole world longs. On the other hand, we must not expose ourselves to what could be mortal danger."[85]

Dulles clearly distrusted the Soviet positions on disarmament in the wake of the Geneva summit. Fear of nuclear war and its consequences had induced uncritical attitudes in the West toward the Kremlin's proposals, he told the NSC early in 1956: "[W]e in the

had been true, Dulles added, that the State Department had been reluctant to participate in the Berlin foreign ministers' conference or in the Geneva conference on Korea and Indochina, held earlier in the year. But it had done so in order to secure allied cooperation in the rearmament of West Germany, and because "world opinion demanded that the United States participate in these negotiations with the Communists." Ibid., 844.

[81] Dulles remarks at Advertising Club of New York, March 31, 1955, *DSB* 32 (April 4, 1955): 552.

[82] Dulles press conference, April 5, 1955, *DSB* 32 (April 18, 1955): 642.

[83] Dulles press conference, July 26, 1955, *DSB* 32 (August 8, 1955): 218.

[84] Dulles press conference, August 10, 1955, *DSB* 33 (August 22, 1955): 299.

[85] Dulles speech to the American Legion, Miami, October 10, 1955, *DSB* 33 (October 24, 1955): 639. See also memorandum of a conversation with Eisenhower, October 11, 1955, WHMS, "Meetings with the President 1955 (2)," DPEL.

United States who take real responsibility must always explain the true meaning of proposals, and see that nothing unsound is done." Panaceas such as "ban the bomb" would not work, but there might be room for progress in cutting the amounts of fissionable material that went into weapons, "or even to agree if this can be done safely that after a certain point all future uses of fissionable material would be dedicated to peaceful purposes."[86] By mid-1957 he was publicly listing a wide range of possibilities for agreement with the Russians in the field of disarmament, while continuing to warn against superficial solutions and simple reliance on promises.[87]

Moreover, there were beginning to be encouraging signs, as well, of change within the Soviet Union. "[W]e . . . primarily are looking to the day when Russia will be something that we can be friends with and not have to treat as enemies [sic]," Dulles told a press conference in April 1956. "And if, in fact, the Soviet Union is not as much to be feared as it was, if it has become more tolerant, if it has put aside the use of violence, if it is beginning to move in a liberal way within, then I would call that progress toward victory in the cold war."[88] In his private communications with Eisenhower Dulles was even more encouraging: "within the last three years, Russia has done far more than we would have dared to expect in terms of doing away with the barbarisms of Stalin and seeming, at least, to become a respectable member of the society of nations." There were dangers in this, to be sure: "that kind of a Russia has more acceptability and less ostracism than the other kind. I wonder, however, who would like to go back to the conditions which we had three years ago."[89]

Even the suppression of the Hungarian uprising late in 1956 appears not to have shaken Dulles's conviction that trends toward liberalization were continuing inside the Soviet Union. He told a press conference in July 1957 that Khrushchev's consolidation of power had confirmed the victory of those who were willing to allow more flexibility and improvement in the condition of the Russian people. It was an "irreversible trend," he added, and "I think we have done quite a bit to promote this trend."[90] Moscow's new emphasis on "po-

[86] Memorandum of NSC meeting, February 7, 1956, AWF.

[87] Dulles radio and television address, July 22, 1957, *DSB* 37 (August 12, 1957): 267–72.

[88] Dulles press conference, April 24, 1956, *DSB* 34 (May 7, 1956): 749. See also Dulles's press conference of May 15, 1956, *DSB* 34 (May 28, 1956): 885.

[89] Dulles to Eisenhower, May 18, 1956, WHMS, "Correspondence—General 1956 (4)," DPEL.

[90] Dulles press conference, July 17, 1957, *DSB* 37 (August 5, 1957): 228–29. Dulles did note, during a cabinet meeting several months later, that in a recent hard-line speech Khrushchev had seemed to be "moving in two opposite directions at the same

litical-economic offensives" was, of course, "highly dangerous," Dulles wrote Eisenhower in March 1958, but "there has been a definite evolution within the Soviet Union toward greater personal security, increased intellectual freedom and increased decentralization. This also increases the changes of peace."[91]

It was chiefly the fear of attack that kept the arms race going, Dulles argued in a letter to West German chancellor Konrad Adenauer in June 1958. If that fear could be done away with, "then I think there would almost automatically come about reduction on both sides." The Soviets would not want to carry the heavy expense of armament "if conditions preclude its being put to effective aggressive use." Nor would the United States wish to sustain comparable expenses "if they are not necessary to deter or withstand sudden attack." It ought to be possible "to find ways to minimize this awful risk of massive surprise attack and . . . in the calmer atmosphere that succeeded this, other measures might be taken."[92]

The secretary of state did remain skeptical about summitry. Very little had come out of such conferences in the past, he told the BBC late in 1957, "primarily because the Soviets cannot be relied to live up to their promises."[93] In his June 1958 letter to Adenauer he came out against any summit that would involve "a renunciation of our just and legitimate political positions . . . merely in the hope of some significant disarmament agreement."[94] But by August Dulles was telling Eisenhower that "I thought it would be useful if the President and Khrushchev could have a private talk to emphasize our firmness," so long as it did not degenerate into "a low-level 'slugging match.' "[95]

Early in 1959, just months before his death, Dulles assessed long-term prospects for Soviet-American relations before a bipartisan meeting of congressional leaders at the White House. Because of the regimented nature of their societies, he noted, communist countries had "possibilities for economic growth which we do not possess in a free society." There was no way for the West to stop this growth—or the "feeling of exuberance" that it produced—short of preventive war, "which is unthinkable." But the United States and its allies had

---

time." But Ambassador Llewellyn Thompson speculated that "much of the fanatical was done by Khrushchev because of being under pressure internally." Cabinet minutes, February 7, 1958, EDS, "Staff Notes, February, 1958," AWF.

[91] Dulles to Eisenhower, March 25, 1958, WHMS, "Correspondence—General 1958 (6)," DPEL.

[92] Dulles to Adenauer, June 30, 1958, "Atomic Weapons (1)," DPP.

[93] Dulles BBC interview, December 3, 1957, *DSB* 37 (December 23, 1957): 988.

[94] See note 92.

[95] Memorandum of conversation with Eisenhower, August 3, 1958, WHMS, "Meetings with the President, July–December, 1958 (9)," DPEL.

held firm the previous year through crises in the Middle East and East Asia. There was every sign, as well, that NATO would not allow Khrushchev's recent threats to drive it out of Berlin. "[T]ime is working for us if we use this time correctly," because the economic growth that had produced communist "exuberance" could not be sustained. The economic system that the Russians were attempting to implement required educating their people, but "this education will militate against an attitude of servility." And, as Churchill had pointed out in his *History of the English-Speaking Peoples*, servility was necessary in order for despotisms to survive. "All this adds up to a dangerous period we are in; but . . . eventually the current abnormal situation will change."[96]

In an unusual dictated note to himself early in 1958, Eisenhower acknowledged that Dulles had "a lawyer's mind." "He consistently adheres to a very logical explanation of these difficulties in which we find ourselves with the Soviets," the president went on, "and in doing so—with his lawyer's mind—he shows the steps and actions that are bad on their part; and we seek to show that we are doing the decent and just thing." It was necessary to do this; still, Eisenhower could not help but question "the practice of becoming a sort of international prosecuting attorney."[97] There is no question that Dulles did assume—certainly more frequently than Eisenhower did—a prosecutorial tone in his public pronouncements on the Soviet Union. But the still-incomplete documentary evidence suggests that behind this lay a greater understanding of Soviet realities than one might have thought, together with a more optimistic assessment of prospects for eventually stabilizing the Soviet-American relationship—for making it more "normal"—than most of the secretary of state's critics at the time would have suspected.

. . .

In his thoughtful study of John Foster Dulles's life up to the time he became secretary of state, Ronald W. Pruessen comments on the extent to which his subject seemed simultaneously to elicit and to resist categorization. "Where some have described an unbalanced idealist with his head in the clouds, I have described a frequently devout pragmatist with a fundamental concern for the condition of the American economy. Where some have focused on deep religiosity,

---

[96] Minutes, Bipartisan Congressional Meeting, January 5, 1959, EDS, "Staff Notes, January, 1959 (2)," AWF.

[97] Eisenhower dictated note, EDS, "DDE Diary January, 1958," AWF.

even fanaticism, I have pointed to a selective Presbyterian piety that always involved cognizance of the materialistic side of the Calvinist coin. Where some have condemned the ideologue that Dulles could be, I have cited the Dulles who knew the uses of ideology and melo-dramatic rhetoric." The secretary of state, Pruessen concludes, was "a complex amalgam, many of whose characteristics . . . may seem con-tradictory in their complexity, but . . . they were all expressions of Dulles's ultimately human nature."[98]

The new documents suggest that the same complexity persisted throughout Dulles's career as secretary of state. He was capable of articulating the doctrine of "massive retaliation" while at the same time harboring a deep and growing pessimism about the long-term effectiveness—indeed, even the morality—of nuclear deterrence. He could characterize international communism in public as monolithic while pursuing strategies behind the scenes designed to exploit the fissures he knew existed within it. He could warn repeatedly that changes inside the Soviet Union might be subtle snares to lure the West into complacency, while at the same time quietly welcoming such changes as evidence that the USSR was ending its "abnormal" alienation from the established international order.

One might conclude from all of this simply that Dulles was devious: that he deliberately said things he knew not to be true. This may well have been the case in his strategy for fragmenting the Sino-Soviet bloc. To have explained openly what he was trying to do—to accom-plish fission by encouraging fusion—would very likely have wrecked the entire initiative. A "hidden-hand" in this instance—very much in the Eisenhower style[99]—was probably the only way to proceed.

With regard to nuclear strategy, though, one has the impression that Dulles was undergoing a painful learning experience. It had been easy enough to design the New Look during the 1952 cam-paign, but when one had the actual responsibility for implementing it—and, at the same time, for keeping the alliance together in the face of growing Soviet nuclear capabilities—unforeseen difficulties arose. Left to himself Dulles might well have dealt with these by moving toward some kind of "flexible response" strategy. What kept that from happening, one suspects, was Eisenhower's supreme self-confi-dence in his own crisis-management abilities, together with his deter-mined opposition to increasing military spending.[100]

The gap between the public and private Dulles is least apparent—

---

[98] Pruessen, *John Foster Dulles*, xii.

[99] See Greenstein, *Hidden-Hand Presidency*.

[100] See, on this point, John Lewis Gaddis, *Strategies of Containment: A Critical Appraisal of Postwar American National Security Policy* (New York, 1982), 174–75.

although it is still there—in his assessments of prospects for negotiation with the Russians. A careful reading of what the secretary of state actually said in public would not sustain the view that he was unalterably opposed to substantive diplomatic contacts with Moscow, or that he viewed the Soviet Union itself as unalterably cast in a Stalinist mold for all time to come. His private observations—particularly from 1956 on—are surprisingly optimistic about the prospects for change within the Soviet system.

The question might fairly be asked, though: what good was Dulles's sophistication if conceptualization did not lead to implementation? After all, nuclear strategy was not rethought, and the number of nuclear weapons in the American arsenal was allowed to grow beyond any rational justification.[101] The communist "monolith" would almost certainly have fragmented whether Dulles had sought to apply his "fission through fusion" strategy or not; that strategy made no provision for seeking an accommodation with Peking after a split with Moscow had occurred. Despite his more charitable view of the Soviet Union, relations with that nation at the time of Dulles's death remained locked in a pattern of confrontation that may well have been more dangerous—as crises over the U-2, Berlin, and Cuba would soon show—than the one that existed at the time he took office.

But from a larger perspective, what the archives have revealed about Dulles's influence on postwar American foreign policy and, of course, about Eisenhower's as well, is of considerable importance. Both men, we now know, differed from their predecessors in their assumption that time was on the side of the West. Neither accepted the view, widely held within the Truman administration, that a period of "peak danger" existed in the near future by which the United States and its allies, if they did not sustain crash rearmament efforts, would find themselves vulnerable.[102] Both had a clearer sense than their predecessors of Soviet and Chinese vulnerabilities; both saw clearly that if an approximate status quo could be sustained over time, the West more than the communist world would benefit from it; both accepted almost instinctively the possibility that continued Soviet-American competition, far from being an "abnormal" condition in international relations, could in fact become a "normal" environment within which limited agreements acceptable to both sides might eventually evolve. Both played a major role, in short, in accomplishing the transition from a ragged and unstable postwar *settlement* to a

[101] See David Alan Rosenberg, "The Origins of Overkill: Nuclear Weapons and American Strategy, 1945–1960," *International Security* 7 (Spring 1983): 3–71.
[102] For the "peak danger" concept, see Gaddis, *Strategies of Containment*, 96–97.

postwar international *system* that has, whatever else one might say about it, at least kept the peace.

Oversimplification in the writing of history—as in the drawing of maps—is a necessary exercise: reality is always too complex to replicate precisely. But one particular form of oversimplification, the caricature, is best left to cartoonists. The historian should always be suspicious of the tendency to describe individuals exclusively in terms of images, categories, or even first impressions. As the scholars who have discovered the "hidden" Eisenhower have found out, those who make history are generally a good deal more complicated—and therefore more interesting—than their public images might suggest. It is high time we applied this lesson, as well, to the "unexpected" John Foster Dulles.

CHAPTER 3

John Foster Dulles, the European Defense Community, and the German Question

Rolf Steininger

IN TERMS of foreign and national security policy, the Eisenhower administration, from John Foster Dulles's perspective, faced manifold problems upon taking office in 1953. The ultimate solution to these problems, according to the Republican party platform, was a redesigned global strategy, one that seized the initiative from the communist aggressors and took full advantage of America's nuclear superiority. Yet before the United States could assume a more offensive posture, Dulles recognized, it had to address the immediate defensive needs it inherited from the Democrats. American interests appeared threatened on almost every front: in Korea, Indochina, Iran, and Guatemala, to cite only a few flashpoints. But Dulles's Atlanticism and Wilsonianism drove him to focus on Europe. Europe—Central Europe—was where East met West; more than that, it was the fulcrum of the international balance of power. Notwithstanding the stabilizing influence of the Marshall Plan and NATO, Central Europe was threatened by internal unrest, volatile economies plagued by the dollar gap, and, of course, the Soviet Union. The Soviets—with the world's largest conventional army; poised at the threshold of developing thermonuclear capability; and skilled in subversion—presented a clear and present danger.

No one believed more strongly than Dulles that the situation required a fundamental, and radical, response. His goal was nothing less than the establishment of a fully integrated, united states of Europe. This was an objective that evolved directly from his experience as legal adviser to the Commission on Reparations at Versailles; the services he rendered to his many European clients during the interwar years; his chairmanship of the Commission to Study the Bases of a Just and Durable Peace; and his own writings on war, peace, and change. Dulles did not delude himself into believing that this objective could be accomplished in the near future, if indeed it was realizable at all. But he was convinced that the security of the free world demanded progress in this direction, and time was of the essence.

The coup in Czechoslovakia, the Berlin blockade, and the outbreak of the Korean War had all contributed to Dulles's sense of urgency. So did the incoming administration's fiscal conservatism, which ruled out massive expenditures for either defense or foreign aid.

As someone schooled in the lessons of Versailles, Dulles predictably shared the view of Eisenhower and most of the State Department that a secure and viable European community required the incorporation of Germany. By Germany Dulles meant all of Germany—a truncated version was in his opinion artificial and unnatural. A divided Germany would prove a constant irritant to inter-European relations, deny the free world alliance valuable resources and, perhaps most important, dampen the German people's enthusiasm for affiliating with the West. Dulles assumed that the cost of German allegiance was the allies' commitment to reunification.[1]

Yet as with the case of European integration, this long-term strategic objective required tactical compromises. In his famous note of March 1952, Stalin had made it clear that he would agree to a unified Germany only on the condition that it not become a member of any military alliance.[2] The European allies' forward defense strategy, however, depended on the contribution of West German troops. Thus Dulles's chief priority had to be to secure West German participation in a European military pact even though this ran counter to his promotion of German reunification. Dulles accepted this compromise without great difficulty. He remained confident that West Germany's integration into the West would strengthen the Federal Republic of Germany politically as well as militarily, thus providing additional impetus for Germany's reunification under democratic principles. In addition, this process of incremental unification would militate against Germany's resurgence as an aggressive power or its using its potential for tilting the balance of power to advance nationalist goals. Germany must not be permitted to "play both ends against the middle," Dulles warned. The secretary of state's concerns, as was typical of his entire perspective on Europe, precisely paralleled his president's. Integration must be effected in a manner, Eisenhower advised, that would not present West Germany with the opportunity to "blackmail the other powers and say 'meet my terms or else.' "[3]

Ironically, the major obstacle Dulles confronted was not the West

---

[1] John Foster Dulles, *War or Peace* (New York, 1950).

[2] Rolf Steininger, *Eine Chance zur Wiedervereinigung: Die Stalin-Note vom 10. März 1952* (Bonn, 1985).

[3] Ronald W. Pruessen, *John Foster Dulles: The Road to Power* (New York, 1982), 344; U.S. minutes of Second Plenary Tripartite Meeting, December 5, 1953, *FR, 1952–1954*, 5:1783.

Germans but the French. Chancellor Konrad Adenauer wholeheartedly supported the incorporation of the Federal Republic into the alliance. Due to both his pro-Western orientation and his desire to prove West German loyalty and responsibility in order to end the Occupation Statute by the quickest method possible, he was more than willing to provide the West German troops. Moreover, suspicious of his own countrymen's aggressive nationalism as well as the Soviets' ambitions, Adenauer held grave reservations about reunification, in the immediate or distant future. All these considerations pointed toward a preferred policy that combined a contribution by the Federal Republic to the defense of Europe with the establishment of political sovereignty.[4]

The French, on the other hand, bore too many scars from World War II to accept German—divided or unified—rearmament with equanimity. Further, with the Indochina War exacting a terrible toll on its officer corps, France feared that it would not be able to match West Germany's contribution on the continent. These concerns had prompted Defense Minister René Pleven in 1950 to propose a European army as a substitute for the inclusion of the Federal Republic in NATO. The creation of a European army, with unified command and procurement arrangements, would preclude an independent West German force and, Paris assumed, guarantee that the West Germans would remain under another country's—that is, France's—control. By this mechanism a West German contribution to European defense on the order of twelve divisions could be tolerated. After tortuous negotiations France, the Federal Republic of Germany, Italy, Belgium, the Netherlands, and Luxembourg signed the European Defense Community (EDC) treaty in May 1952, along with a protocol assuring that any attack upon one of its members would be considered an attack upon a member of NATO. Tied to contractual agreements ending the occupation and granting West German sovereignty, the treaty was turned over to each individual government for ratification.[5]

Great Britain had never been enthusiastic about EDC; indeed, arguing that it was not a Continental power, Britain refused to join. Not surprisingly, therefore, Paris demonstrated little inclination to ratify the treaty. With the situation in Indochina deteriorating, France felt more vulnerable in Europe. Without direct British assistance, it ques-

[4] Thomas Schwartz, "The 'Skeleton Key'—American Foreign Policy, European Unity, and German Rearmament, 1949–1954," *Central European History* 19 (December 1986): 376.

[5] Dean Acheson, *Present at the Creation: My Years in the State Department* (New York, 1969), 458–59, 622–50.

tioned its ability to offset West German power on the Continent. Moreover, its collective national pride reeling from the successive blows of World War II and Indochina, France seriously questioned whether it could risk surrendering any of its sovereignty to a European army. From the American viewpoint, the French were holding EDC hostage in order to extract additional support for Indochina.[6]

Therefore by 1953 the EDC ratification process had ground to a standstill. Dulles found this situation intolerable. He viewed EDC not only as *a* way to secure the Federal Republic's military commitment, but *the* way. Dulles perceived EDC as the logical successor to the European Coal and Steel Community (ECSC). In other words, its supranational character and emphasis on "community" would promote European political and economic integration, as well as military integration. And in doing so, it would continue the momentum toward Franco-German reconciliation. To Dulles the institutionalization of this rapprochement, begun by the ECSC, was more than the sine qua non for free world security. It was, as the wise "European statesmen" had been "preaching" for generations, "the indispensable foundation for lasting peace."[7]

In his first national address as secretary of state, Dulles highlighted the administration's focus on EDC. He underlined the importance of West European integration and warned, as he would frequently over the next eighteen months, of the negative consequences of a failure to ratify the treaty: "If . . . France, Germany and England should go their separate ways . . . certainly it would be necessary to give a little rethinking to America's own foreign policy in relation to Western Europe."[8] Underlying this rhetoric was the conviction, also shared by Eisenhower, that there was no alternative to EDC. Given French concerns, Dulles saw the JCS's preference for a West German national army within the NATO framework as politically unworkable. Although he did call for the examination of alternatives to EDC such as "peripheral defense," he considered them not as viable solutions but a means of applying pressure toward ratification: "We are not thinking of how to give up the EDC; the question is how to get the EDC," he explained. "An alternative is necessary if we are going to get it."[9]

On his tour of the West European capitals in late January and early

[6] George C. Herring, *America's Longest War: The United States and Vietnam, 1950–1975* (New York, 1985), 23.

[7] U.S. Delegation at Berlin Conference to Department of State, January 26, 1954, *FR, 1952–1954*, 7:830.

[8] "Survey of Foreign Policy Problems," *DSB* 28 (February 9, 1953): 214.

[9] Memorandum of State–Mutual Security Administration–JCS meeting, January 28, 1953, *FR, 1952–1954*, 5:713.

February 1953, Dulles found the sentiment for EDC ratification encouraging. Only in Paris was there strong opposition to the treaty. In
the ten months since the signing of the EDC treaty and the Bonn contractuals, French fear had grown that an economically, politically,
and militarily resurgent Federal Republic might come to dominate
Western Europe. Prime Minister René Mayer and Foreign Minister
Georges Bidault told Dulles that EDC ratification by the National assembly depended on four issues: agreement on protocols interpret-
ing the treaty; stronger British association with EDC to help offset
West German influence; settlement of the Saar dispute with West
Germany; and active U.S. support of the war in Indochina.[10] Dulles
considered none of these conditions insurmountable problems. Returning to Washington, he informed the administration that the trip
had taken the project "out of the mothballs" and the "odds were now
about 60–40" that the EDC treaties would be ratified.[11]

The "peace offensive" undertaken by the Soviet collective leadership after Stalin's death in March 1953 complicated efforts to press
for ratification. Although Dulles saw Premier Georgii Malenkov's
outspoken support of disarmament and political dialogue as a mere
tactical shift to undermine support for Western unity,[12] in May Churchill declared his support for a high-level summit to test Soviet motives and intentions. In the course of the next few weeks, both Bidault
and Adenauer, though sharing Dulles's skepticism about Soviet motives, argued that in increasing numbers their constituents were favorably disposed to a high-level meeting. Bidault claimed that such a
meeting with the Soviets was a political necessity before movement on
EDC ratification could take place;[13] Adenauer wanted to extend an
invitation to the Soviets before the Bundestag elections in September
to deflect domestic criticism that his policy of integration was destroying all hope of reunification.[14]

Dulles accepted a meeting with the Soviets as a prerequisite for
progress on EDC, thus reversing his opposition to it. During the tripartite conference of foreign ministers in Washington at the beginning of July he agreed that an invitation for talks in September
should be extended to the Soviets. He insisted, however, that the
agenda be limited to Germany and Austria, and that talks take place

[10] Holmes to Department of State, February 4, 1953, *FR, 1952–1954*, 5:1560–61.
Paris and Bonn disagreed over the final disposition of the Saar Valley.

[11] Memorandum of NSC meeting, February 11, 1953, *FR, 1952–1954*, 5:1580.

[12] U.S. minutes of North Atlantic Council meeting, April 24, 1953, *FR, 1952–1954*,
5:373–74.

[13] U.S. Delegation to Department of State, July 10, 1953, *FR, 1952–1954*, 5:1615.

[14] Memorandum of conversation, July 10, 1953, *FR, 1952–1954*, 5:1606–7.

on the foreign minister level. The Soviets responded by rejecting the Western offer of this narrow agenda and called for a broader meeting on both European and Asian problems with Communist Chinese participation.

In the wake of the U.S. decision to pursue four-power talks on Germany and the abortive East Berlin uprising of June 17, 1953, the administration reformulated its German policy. Nsc 160/1, approved on August 17, underlined administration support of the twin goals of German reunification and European integration. The statement defined the ultimate objective of U.S. policy as a "united Germany enjoying full internal freedom; free to determine its external relations and alignments, including the right to participate in European defense and in the free European Community; and oriented to the West." Such a Germany, the report continued, "would represent a major step in rolling back the iron curtain and enlarging the basis for an enduring peace in Europe."[15]

At the same time, the authors of NSC 160/1 doubted the Soviet Union would accept this arrangement. They predicted that it would offer German unity under conditions of neutrality, a dangerous proposal from the Western point of view:

> A "neutralized," unified Germany, with or without armed forces, would entail sacrifices and risks to the West incommensurate with any possible gains. It would deny German strength to the West, wreck present and prospective plans for building augmented European strength through union, and open up the whole of Germany to Soviet intrigue and manipulation which would aim at the absorption of Germany into the Soviet bloc.

To counter such a proposal, the West should develop its own detailed plan for German unity, based on free elections and the right of a unified German state to rearm and join alliances.[16]

Nsc 160/1 also emphasized the importance of EDC, although it acknowledged ratification would have to await the outcome of the proposed four-power meeting. Dulles successfully resisted Defense Department efforts to insert into the text a ratification deadline of January 1, 1954, after which the United States should take concrete steps toward the creation of a West German national army. He clung to his conviction that EDC was the best and only politically feasible way to rearm the West Germans. Dulles, however, did acknowledge the need to examine alternatives, should EDC ultimately fail, and not merely in order to raise the stakes in favor of the treaty. By year's

[15] Nsc 160/1, August 17, 1953, *FR, 1952–1954*, 7:515.
[16] *FR, 1952–1954*, 7:515–17.

end, nevertheless, there was no agreed-upon State–Defense draft on alternatives.[17]

The reelection of Adenauer's coalition in September buoyed Dulles's hopes for ratification. At the London tripartite foreign ministers' conference in mid-October, the secretary of state stressed U.S. "anxiety" about EDC but enthusiastically greeted Bidault's assessment that ratification would be possible before year's end. The major obstacle, Bidault said, was a settlement of the Saar issue.[18] But the lack of French-German cooperation on this issue during the weeks following the conference discouraged Dulles. Moreover, the U.S. high commissioner in Germany, James Conant, informed the secretary that the West Germans themselves were becoming impatient and the possibility existed, however remote, that Adenauer was flirting with the notion of establishing a national West German army within the NATO framework. This prospect further unsettled Dulles, who read Eisenhower this portion of Conant's letter.[19] The secretary of state stepped up American urgings for ratification, expressing concern that EDC opponents could delay ratification until "the 'critical' period next spring, when pressure resulting from Congressional impatience and German insistence on independent status will reach breaking point."[20]

The decision of Mayer's successor as prime minister, Joseph Laniel, to postpone debate on EDC within the Assembly until after the presidential election called for December indicated the gravity of the situation. In a note to the embassy in Paris, Dulles wrote, "Laniel should know that patience of American people and Congress is running out on EDC. . . . Unless we go forward together in our agreed purposes, we inevitably face the disintegration of all our great common efforts and achievements in the past few years to secure the safety and the prosperity of free Europe."[21] Dulles's efforts notwithstanding, prospects for ratification in France did not improve. Laniel only barely survived a vote of no confidence on November 27; it was clear that he did not have the votes needed for EDC approval.

The day before the vote in the French Assembly, the Soviet Union had finally agreed to the Western proposal of a four-power conference on Germany and Austria. When Eisenhower, Churchill, Laniel,

[17] Memorandum of NSC meeting, August 13, 1953, *FR, 1952–1954,* 7:504–7; Memorandum of the Policy Planning Staff, December 10, 1953, *FR, 1952–1954,* 5:863.

[18] U.S. Delegation to Department of State, October 18, 1953, *FR, 1952–1954,* 5:826–28.

[19] Conant to Dulles, October 28, 1953, *FR, 1952–1954,* 5:832; Dulles to Conant, November 9, 1953, ibid., 839.

[20] Dulles to Embassy in France, October 29, 1953, *FR, 1952–1954,* 5:834, n. 3.

[21] Dulles to Embassy in France, November 8, 1953, *FR, 1952–1954,* 5:838–39.

and their foreign ministers met in Bermuda a week later, the four-power conference and the EDC problem were high on the agenda. The Western leaders accepted the Soviet proposal for a foreign ministers' meeting in Berlin and suggested that it convene in January. They could not, however, make substantive progress on EDC. Laniel and Bidault argued that for EDC to be ratified in the National Assembly, the United States and Great Britain would have to guarantee the continued presence of their forces in West Germany at present levels for the length of the treaty—a proposal that was rejected by the Americans and the British.[22] Conversely, Churchill's assertion that the West German national army's integration into the NATO structure was the only viable alternative to EDC, and might in fact be preferable, provoked both French and American protest.[23] At odds with both of their allies, Eisenhower and Dulles resorted to lecturing Laniel and Bidault on the need for quick ratification. They pointed out that Congress had appropriated half of the funds earmarked for European defense to the EDC in 1954, and that French failure to ratify would cause the United States to rethink its commitments.[24] Dulles made the same point in less diplomatic fashion at the NATO foreign ministers' conference in Paris a week later.

> If, however, the European Defense Community should not become effective, if France and Germany remain apart so that they will again become potential enemies then there would indeed be grave doubt as to whether Continental Europe could be made a place of safety. That would compel an agonizing reappraisal of basic United States policy.[25]

Despite Dulles's frustration, he recognized that progress toward French ratification would have to await the outcome of the Berlin conference, which met between January 25 and February 18, 1954. Before leaving for Berlin, Dulles predicted that no agreement on Germany would be reached; this might create momentum in France toward EDC ratification.[26] On the first score, at least, he was right. The plan for reunification presented by Eden called for free elections to be followed by the drafting of a constitution and the formation of a German government that would be free to join the Western alliance. Molotov countered by insisting that the formation of a German gov-

[22] U.S. minutes of Third Plenary Tripartite Meeting, December 6, 1953, *FR, 1952–1954*, 5:1801–3.
[23] U.S. minutes of Second Plenary Tripartite Meeting, December 5, 1953, *FR, 1952–1954*, 5:1780–85.
[24] Eisenhower–Laniel meeting, December 5, 1953, *FR, 1952–1954*, 5:1770–73.
[25] Dulles to the North Atlantic Council, December 14, 1953, *FR, 1952–1954*, 5:463.
[26] Memorandum of NSC meeting, January 21, 1954, *FR, 1952–1954*, 7:781–82.

ernment should precede elections, and that Germany, once unified, should be kept neutral. The only surprise of the conference was Molotov's suggestion of an all-European security treaty as an alternative to EDC, which the Western foreign ministers rejected out of hand.[27]

But deadlock on the German question did not, as Dulles had also predicted, create momentum for EDC ratification in France. In his meeting with Dulles, Bidault continued to stress that the preconditions for ratification were a settlement of the Saar issue and closer association of the United States and Great Britain with EDC.[28] Most critical, however, was the need for U.S. military and diplomatic help in Indochina, where the French position was steadily worsening. At considerable political cost (realizing the growing connection between EDC ratification and the situation in Indochina) Dulles reversed his original opposition to a five-power conference on Indochina with Communist Chinese participation. The foreign ministers agreed to add Indochina to the agenda for the forthcoming conference in Geneva.[29]

In the weeks before the Geneva conference opened on April 26, both the administration and the British government made public assurances of their intended close association with EDC. But as the French position at Dien Bien Phu became critical, it was obvious that any movement on ratification would have to await a clarification of the situation in Indochina. The United States refused to help the beleaguered French with a bombing campaign as long as British refusal made "united action" impossible. When Dien Bien Phu finally fell on May 7, as did the Laniel government on June 13, hopes of EDC progress dimmed. Pierre Mendès-France, Laniel's successor, had never been an outspoken supporter of EDC.

It was in the context of allied discord at Geneva over the Indochina negotiations that Prime Minister Churchill and Foreign Secretary Eden visited Washington from June 25 to 29, 1954. The impasse over EDC, nevertheless, dictated that West German rearmament would command equal attention. Eisenhower and Dulles presented the administration's position without mincing words. Dulles emphasized that the American military authorities were becoming restive and impatient. The JCS felt that if a start were not soon made, the opportunity to rearm West Germany in a controlled and effective fashion might pass. In addition, there were, of course, problems connected with the supply of equipment from American sources. Eisenhower

[27] U.S. Delegation to Department of State, February 16, 1954, *FR, 1952–1954*, 7:1121–22.

[28] Memorandum of conversation, February 17, 1954, *FR, 1952–1954*, 7:1150–51.

[29] Dulles to Bidault, February 23, 1954, *FR, 1952–1954*, 5:879.

interjected that if the Mendès-France government did not proceed with EDC, it ought to be confronted with the choice of admitting West Germany to NATO. The Assembly should be asked to vote on one side or the other. It must be able to choose between NATO and EDC in the near future, Eisenhower remarked. Otherwise, he could only conclude that the French had become "a hopeless, helpless mass of protoplasm."

Churchill and Eden indicated their concurrence. Echoing Eisenhower's opinion, the prime minister asserted that if Paris proved incapable of deciding between EDC and NATO, it would be necessary to proceed without them on the basis of the "real elements of strength in the Western alliance." These lay in the United States, Britain, and the Federal Republic. Eden did not disagree. But he was uncomfortable with the implied dichotomy between NATO and EDC. After all, he pointed out, as Pleven had recognized four years earlier, the French could not enthusiastically accept the Federal Republic's entry into NATO. On the other hand, if anyone in France believed that West Germany would simply enter NATO and accept nearly all the restrictions Bonn had been willing to accept in EDC, he was under a severe illusion. Dulles agreed, arguing that failure to ratify would necessitate separate action on the contractuals. Eden then suggested that Britain and America approach the French jointly, confronting them with the realities of the situation. Given the growing impatience in West Germany, which was weakening Adenauer's position, the foreign secretary emphasized that if something were not done soon to establish West German sovereignty, the Soviets would be able "to pull the Germans across the line." Eisenhower closed the discussion by noting that it was important that this program be put to the French "in the most effective light and in the absence of open threats."[30]

Two weeks later Dulles flew to Paris to discuss America's representation at the Geneva conference with Mendès-France and Eden. Predictably, he used the opportunity, as Eden had suggested, to confront the new prime minister with the realities of the EDC situation. Every signatory nation except for France and Italy had ratified the treaty during the first few months of 1954. Dulles told Mendès-France that by delaying the Assembly's vote he was playing directly into the Kremlin's hand. Their primary objective was to keep France and West Germany divided, to create disunity in Europe, and ultimately obtain control over West Germany. The Soviet Union held important

---

[30] This summary of the Anglo-American talks is based on "Top Secret Record of Conversation at the White House, June 27, 1954," PRO, PREM 11/618, and the U.S. Department of State memorandum of conversation, June 27, 1954, *FR, 1952–1954*, 5:985–86.

cards in this game, and if it played them it might indeed neutralize and reach an agreement of some sort with West Germany. At the same time Dulles emphasized congressional impatience with Paris's delays. French refusal to agree to the Federal Republic's participation in European defense would lead to "the strongest pressures for the U.S. to engage in a peripheral form of defense." In short, Dulles warned that the postponement of a decision on EDC was a direct invitation to the Soviets to drive a wedge between the NATO powers.[31]

Mendès-France's response was that he personally had long been a staunch advocate of European unity. However, he did not believe that there was at present a majority for EDC in the French Parliament. What he did not wish was to put EDC to a vote and have it turned down. This would represent a Soviet victory of the first magnitude and would constitute disaster for France, NATO, and Western unity. In fact, contrary to Dulles's view, Mendès-France was convinced that even a slender majority in favor of EDC would be unsatisfactory. France would be left weak and divided. Far better to continue to postpone the vote, he concluded, until additional support could be generated. His objective was to find a formula to yield a substantial majority in the Assembly.[32]

Mendès-France followed his own instincts. He waited until a settlement to the Indochina War was achieved, and then immediately turned his attention to securing a coalition in favor of EDC. America's ambassador to France, C. Douglas Dillon, reported that the prime minister made it clear to his cabinet ministers and other advisers that the EDC treaty could not be ratified in its present form and that a "compromise" including substantial changes had to be found; Mendès-France himself made no proposals. "In summary," Dillon— together with U.S. observer to the Interim Committee of EDC David Bruce—cabled on August 5, "tension is mounting in Paris on both sides of EDC question as Mendès continues successfully to conceal his views and intentions."[33]

On August 12 Mendès-France made his second move and revealed to Dillon and the British chargé d'affaires in Paris, Patrick Reilly (Ambassador Gladwyn Jebb was on vacation), in "extreme secrecy" his views on how to handle the EDC question. The difficulties facing him on EDC had proven even greater than he had expected and, in particular, he had to take account of the Russian proposals for another meeting on Germany and the effect these had had on French

[31] Memorandum of conversation, July 13, 1954, *FR, 1952–1954*, 5:1018–23.
[32] Memorandum of conversation, July 13, 1954, *FR, 1952–1954*, 5:1018–23.
[33] Bruce and Dillon to the Department of State, August 5, 1954, *FR, 1952–1954*, 5:1023–26.

public opinion and in Parliament.[34] Mendès-France's scheme was to coordinate the ratification process with planning for a four-power meeting. He would seek a preliminary vote on EDC from the National Assembly, but he would postpone final approval until Soviet intentions could be put to the test. If the Kremlin's initiatives turned out to be disingenuous, he was certain he would be able to secure a firm majority for EDC. Moreover, by proceeding in this manner, opponents of EDC would not be able to argue that he was sabotaging efforts to reach a détente with the Soviets. Finally, because Italy's ratification timetable called for a vote in December, this approach would not delay putting EDC into force.[35]

Reilly remained skeptical. It looked to him that Mendès-France "may now regard threat of ratification primarily as a means to get agreement on a unified but disarmed Germany." The British chargé admitted that the prime minister was justified in seeking means to increase support for the treaty. He warned the Foreign Office, nevertheless, that those tactics "which he is now contemplating are dangerous and it is important to find out what precisely he is aiming at. He may not realize how strong are objections of Her Majesty's Government and United States Government to any proposal for neutralization of Germany. In replying to his present approach it may therefore be desirable to leave him no possibility of doubt on this point."[36]

For his part Dulles wrote Dillon in Paris that he was "deeply shocked and disheartened." The secretary of state considered the French prime minister's proposals further proof of French unreliability. He was convinced that Mendès-France was prepared to abandon EDC if the Soviets would agree to unify Germany by free elections. This could only mean that France would agree to neutralize Germany as a basis for unification. To Dulles this posture would "completely destroy NATO defense plans." As he put it, "an attempt to neutralize [a] unified Germany will be illusory and seriously menace European stability and security." The Mendès-France proposal would "split basic Western position and solidarity, thereby providing Soviets with opportunity they have sought for years," and it would "probably destroy Adenauer" by substantiating his opposition's thesis that German unity should take priority over EDC.[37]

[34] On July 24, 1954, only three days after the Geneva conference had ended, the Soviets had sent a note on European security to the Western powers, and on August 4 they had made an oral presentation proposing a preliminary four-power meeting on a general European security conference.

[35] Reilly to Foreign Office, August 12, 1954, PRO, PREM 11/618; Dillon to Department of State, August 12, 1954, FR, 1952–1954, 5:1026–29.

[36] Reilly to Foreign Office, August 12, 1954, PRO, PREM, 11/618.

[37] Dulles to the Embassy in France, August 12, 1954, FR, 1952–1954, 5:1029–31.

On Dulles's instructions Ambassador Dillon saw Mendès-France the next morning and went over the secretary's message carefully with him. The prime minister argued that Dulles had not only misread his intentions, but he also demonstrated a poor understanding of France's political dynamic. Mendès-France maintained that his position did not constitute a new delaying tactic. He was moving as rapidly as he could to obtain ratification, he said, reminding Dillon that rejection would put an unbearable strain on the Western alliance. Further, the prime minister would stake the continuance of his government on approving EDC. Therefore he wanted to increase chances for a successful result. Only by placing ratification in a context where it would force the Russians to show their cards and put them "*au pied du mur*" could ratification be assured. This, Mendès-France concluded, would represent the "most telling," in fact the "vital argument" for ratification and demonstrate that he was not in favor of a neutralized Germany.[38]

As far as it went, Mendès-France presented a solid defense. Dulles, nevertheless, was far from reassured. And London felt that the French prime minister left out some critical dimensions. More than Dulles, the British understood Mendès-France's parliamentary difficulties. However, they criticized his preoccupation with them, a circumstance that clouded his perception of the dangers facing the Western powers in Germany. Mendès-France, the Foreign Office held, did not realize that a decision on Germany had to be taken "this autumn, if the situation there is not to slip very dangerously." It also believed he was making a grave mistake in connecting EDC and the Russian note publicly. Mendès-France's new proposals would mean indefinite delays that would be used by the Russians and neutralists everywhere to prevent not only EDC ratification but also the adoption of any practical arrangement to ensure West German association with the West, that is, to bring the Bonn contractuals into force.

Eden accordingly instructed Reilly to speak to Mendès-France in support of the U.S. representations already made by Dillon and to leave the prime minister in no doubt that the British government was "certainly not prepared to agree to any such dangerous course." Reilly should also take the opportunity to remind Mendès-France of the essential background to the West German situation: "Dr. Adenauer's whole policy of associating a democratic Germany with the West is now at stake." In addition, the chargé should point out that Mendès-France's view seemed to be that Germany could be reunited at the price of abandoning the EDC and the whole policy of West Ger-

[38] Dillon to Department of State, August 13, 1954, *FR, 1952–1954*, 5:1031–33; Reilly to Foreign Office, August 13, 1954, PRO, PREM 11/618.

man integration with the West. He should be warned that "there is no assurance that Germany would accept neutralization under Four Power Control. If we attempted to impose such a solution strong forces would probably depose Dr. Adenauer and seek by direct negotiation with the Russians to improve Germany's position."[39]

The negative reactions by both Washington and London to Mendès-France's proposed procedure had, in the words of Permanent Under Secretary Sir Ivone Kirkpatrick, "some slight effect." The prime minister now disclaimed all intention of putting EDC to a provisional vote or telling the deputies that they would have an opportunity to reverse themselves. Nevertheless, the thrust of Mendès-France's plan remained intact. If during the debate opponents of the treaty declared that ratification would provoke Russia or indicate France's unwillingness to negotiate with the Soviets, he would deny that France refused to negotiate and declare France's intention to attend a four-power conference if the Russians provided grounds for believing that such a conference would be useful. Indeed, he would frame the debate so as to portray a vote for EDC as a vote in favor of a conference. Mendès-France felt it imperative that the National Assembly perceive the treaty as purely defensive and a means to strengthen the West's negotiations, not military power.[40]

The British felt Mendès-France's thinking represented an "improvement" over his previous position, but ratification would depend on the "tone" of his presentation to the National Assembly.[41] They were not optimistic. Indeed, even as the Eisenhower administration clung determinedly to EDC, London, if not convinced the treaty would be defeated, decided prudence dictated the development of contingency plans. Eisenhower and Dulles feared that any discussion of an alternative might be interpreted as a weakening of American support for EDC, a premise supported wholeheartedly by Adenauer.

[39] Dulles to Embassy in Paris, August 13, 1954, *FR, 1952–1954*, 5:1033, n. 5; Secret minute PM/IK/54/127 and top secret minute PM/IK/54/126 "M. Mendès-France and E.D.C." by Sir Ivone Kirkpatrick for Churchill, August 13, 1954, PRO, PREM 11/618.

[40] Secret minute PM/IK/54/133, "France and E.D.C." by Kirkpatrick for Churchill, August 16, 1954, PRO, PREM 11/618. The same day G. Jebb had sent two long telegrams to the Foreign Office. In a minute for Churchill, Kirkpatrick commented:

I do not at all agree with everything Sir G. Jebb says. In particular, his proposal to induce M. Mendès-France to say that if the Russians were to accept our *desiderata* a new situation would arise seems to me very dangerous. It would undo everything we have done in the last few days. Accordingly I am asking Sir G. Jebb to come over and discuss all this here. We have a little time because the Debate in the French Parliament has been postponed and will not take place for another 12 days. (minute PM/IK/54/132, August 16, 1954, PRO, PREM 11/618)

[41] Secret minute PM/IK/54/133, August 16, 1954, PRO, PREM 11/618.

Eden and Churchill, however, considered this approach dangerously shortsighted. If EDC failed they had to have an alternative ready, and the only viable one seemed to be West Germany's controlled rearmament within the NATO framework. To remain wedded to EDC was to refuse to confront reality.

History demonstrates the wisdom of the British—in contrast to the American—approach. On August 30, 1954, the French National Assembly refused to ratify EDC. This "black day for Europe," in Adenauer's words,[42] would have been even worse had London not prepared for it. The Churchill government had long considered West Germany's membership in NATO not only a possible alternative to EDC but, in certain respects, preferable. The more suspicious it became of Mendès-France's ability—or willingness—to win ratification, the more it concentrated on what Churchill described as the "NATO solution," which he was sure could be arranged. Hence concurrent with voicing Britain's objections to Mendès-France's plan to tie EDC to a four-power meeting with the Soviets, the seventy-four-year-old prime minister wrote Washington on August 14 to urge the administration to show some flexibility.[43]

Left in charge of the State Department while Dulles was away from Washington, Walter Bedell Smith received Churchill's entreaty from the counselor of the British Embassy, Adam Watson. Smith sat Watson down and explained his estimate of the situation. More so than his superior, the under secretary of state was willing to concede that the prospects for EDC were extremely poor. But he shared the view of both Dulles and Eisenhower that admitting the Federal Republic of Germany to NATO was not an alternative. The keynote of U.S. policy on the Continent was to anchor West Germany firmly to the West; Smith wondered "whether NATO was a strong enough anchor." The West Germans were so efficient and so inclined to abdicate their own judgment and sense of responsibility "in the name of *Dienst*," he maintained, that once they possessed the means to reunify their country by force, "how were we to control them?" The wisest word about the Germans was Churchill's phrase: they are always either at your throat or at your feet.

Smith's analysis reflected the paradox that permeated the administration's attitude toward West Germany. Bluntly put, it did not completely trust the country on which so much of its security depended. World War II was too recent a memory for Dulles, Eisenhower, Smith, and most of the other key actors in Washington for them to

---

[42] Konrad Adenauer, *Erinnerungen 1953–1955* (Stuttgart, 1966), 289.
[43] Churchill to Dulles, August 14, 1954, *FR, 1952–1954*, 5:1037.

look to the future without considering the past. They had enthusiastically embraced EDC as a means of squaring the circle, but now the availability of that option was highly problematic. That would leave the West with four courses: NATO; a bilateral agreement between West Germany and the United States that Britain would support; German neutralization; or a peripheral defense strategy.

All of these options were, to quote Smith, "set with grave dangers." The under secretary and longtime Eisenhower aide's gloom was, as Watson described the conversation in a letter to Sir Frank Roberts, "clearly due in part to his own illness and weariness. But there is no doubt that the developments of the last few days have discouraged people here a good deal. They were therefore especially comforted by the forthrightness and vigour of H.M. Government's reaction."[44]

Churchill characteristically refused to succumb to his allies' pervasive despondency—and paralysis. Even before the final vote in Paris, the experienced prime minister had all but given up hope of getting EDC through. In view of the "impotence of the French Chamber" and the gloomy outlook in Washington, Churchill determined that the only course open was for the British to assume the initiative. On August 19 he telegraphed Dulles "[W]e surely ought to create some variant of NATO." He then informed the American secretary of state that he would take the lead. "I am having the problem studied here and may have some ideas to put before you and the President," he wrote. "I am distressed at Adenauer's position. I feel we owe him almost a debt of honour after all the risks he has run and patience he has shown. It ought to be possible to devise some safeguards for a NATO arrangement."[45]

The same day Churchill prepared a top-secret note and sent copies only to Kirkpatrick and the minister of defense, Field Marshal Earl Alexander of Tunis. His position was simple and to the point: "[W]e must work out a good plan for bringing Germany into the N.A.T.O. front. It must be ready soon; the study is urgent. . . . We should propose that Germany should join N.A.T.O. If France uses a veto we should make a new N.A.T.O. . . . , if necessary without the French." Churchill's impatience and frustration with Washington were evident. The new NATO should be in a form "which we can put before the Americans. They ought to have seen that EDC was hopeless a year

[44] Sir R. Scott to Foreign Office, August 14, 1954, and J.H.A. Watson to Sir F. Roberts, August 16, 1954, both in PRO, PREM 11/618. See also Smith to Embassy in Belgium, August 14, 1954, *FR, 1952–1954*, 5:1036–37.

[45] Churchill to Dulles, August 19, 1954, *FR, 1952–1954*, 5:1050–51. Draft in PRO, PREM 11/618.

ago."[46] For his part Dulles remained "not optimistic about a NATO substitute."[47]

Churchill's sense of urgency, as well as his irritation, grew commensurately with EDC's declining fortunes. On August 14, 1954, Mendès-France communicated to the other EDC governments a "Draft Protocol of Application of the EDC Treaty." It contained proposals for a modification of the treaty that the six EDC foreign ministers who met at Brussels on August 19 were to consider. When the Bonn Foreign Office analyzed the draft it noted that there were, in all, some sixty-five suggestions, of which forty-seven would involve alterations to the EDC Treaty. Nearly half of these would need to be passed by the Bundestag, the West German Federal Assembly, by a two-thirds majority. Three suggestions were particularly noteworthy. The French now proposed that for eight years following the entry into force of the treaty, any member state should have the right to veto decisions. In order words, there would be no supranational institutions during this period. Mendès-France also wanted to limit the integration of basic units to land and air forces stationed in the *"zone de couverture."* Thus only in the FRG itself were the West German and allied forces to be integrated. Finally, and most revealingly, the draft protocol stipulated that in case of the unification of Germany, member states should be free to leave the community if they wished.[48]

When Adenauer saw Mendès-France's proposal he immediately arranged for one of his closest advisers, Robert Pferdmenges, to hand-deliver a letter to Churchill. The chancellor drew the British prime minister's attention to the "extremely critical situation which is now developing." The French proposals, he wrote, were "much worse than anything" he had expected; he did not think that he would be able to get a simple majority, let alone the two-thirds necessary, in favor of them in the Bundestag.[49]

Indeed, it appeared to Adenauer that Mendès-France, or to be charitable, his advisers, intended to "sabotage" EDC and sacrifice it in return for an agreement with the Soviets to neutralize Germany. The real question to address, he told Denis Allen of the British Foreign Office, was "whether or not the French Parliament wanted EDC." The essential feature of EDC was that it should last for fifty years. This

[46] Note for Foreign Office (Kirkpatrick) and Minister of Defense (Earl Alexander of Tunis), August 20, 1954, and draft with numerous handwritten corrections by Churchill, August 19, 1954, both in PRO, PREM 11/618.

[47] Dulles to Churchill, August 20, 1954, *FR, 1952–1954*, 5:1051.

[48] German translation in *Keesing's Archiv der Gegenwart* (1954), 4691ff; R. Allen to Foreign Office, PRO, PREM 11/618.

[49] Foreign Office to Bonn, August 17, 1954, PRO, PREM 11/618.

principle had come from the French, and now they were the ones who were abandoning it.[50]

Washington initially was of a similar mind. Ambassador Dillon, who as a rule sympathized with the French government's travails, described the proposals as "unacceptable beyond our worst expectations."[51] David Bruce added that in view of their "confused, chauvinistic and destructive" nature, which he attributed to Mendès-France having "ignorantly outsmarted himself," the agreement on external aid should not be signed pending the outcome of the Brussels conference.[52] Dulles listed four major objections to the French proposal: they would cause further delay in the ratification; they would virtually eliminate EDC's supranational features; they discriminated against the West Germans; and they raised new questions about America's and Britain's roles in West European defense.[53] The Americans' reaction was understandable; yet they had no positive alternative to propose. The Americans feared the defeat of EDC but could not bring themselves to plan for that contingency.

Although no less disappointed than the West Germans or Americans, the British continued to focus on finding an escape from the quagmire. This was definitely not the time to table the NATO alternative. As summed up in Washington, London's position was "not to 'rock the boat.' "[54] Accordingly, while Churchill wrote Adenauer in an effort to cheer him up, the Foreign Office scrutinized Mendès-France's draft protocol. Conceding that the proposals presented the danger that EDC would be "paralysed from the start," it nevertheless tried to salvage as much as possible from the situation. After all, the allies' distress with France must not overshadow the "vital need for obtaining an early solution to the problem of German association with the West." They must recognize that Mendès-France could not return from Brussels empty-handed if the treaty were to have any chance of ratification. Even if the French were "opening their mouths rather wide," as Sir Gladwyn Jebb put it colorfully, Mendès-France still "remains our best bet, and if he fails to get EDC ratified, it certainly will never be." Therefore all the concerned nations should go as far as possible to meet the French proposals. Above all, they should not reject them "out of hand."[55]

---

[50] D. Allen to Foreign Office, August 18, 1954, PRO, PREM 11/618.

[51] Dillon to Department of State, August 15, 1954, *FR, 1952–1954*, 5:1039.

[52] *FR, 1952–1954*, 5:1042, n. 2.

[53] Dulles to Embassy in Belgium, August 17, 1954, *FR, 1952–1954*, 5:1046–47.

[54] Memorandum of conversation, August 17, 1954, *FR, 1952–1954*, 5:1046.

[55] German translation of Churchill's letter in *Keesing's Archiv der Gegenwart* (1954),

The other conferees at Brussels refused to heed London's advice. They attacked Mendès-France so fiercely that the chairman, Belgian foreign affairs minister Paul-Henri Spaak, finally felt compelled to intervene. On August 20 he declared the situation so "very bad" that the conference could not proceed.[56] Mendès-France complained that his record did not justify the hostility he was encountering. He observed that the other EDC partners' distrust of France and his government ran "far deeper than anything he had realized before." Like Spaak, Mendès-France concluded that nothing constructive could be accomplished within this atmosphere.[57]

Dulles reacted differently. Refusing to accept defeat, somehow, some way, he hoped to save EDC. Disbanding the conference would run counter to this objective. But he was no more amenable to the British approach. Dulles believes that rather than compromise with the French, the allies should induce Mendès-France to withdraw the odious proposals. His strategy was to escalate pressure on Mendès-France. Toward this end he wrote the prime minister on August 21 that there would be a "great crisis" should the conference break up with no agreement. In that event, the United Kingdom and those EDC countries that had ratified the treaty would immediately proceed without France to discuss steps toward West German sovereignty and rearmament. Spaak was informed accordingly.[58]

The groundwork thereby laid, Dulles next wrote Churchill, emphasizing that it would be an incalculable disaster if Adenauer's policy to ally West Germany with the West and to prevent the revival of West German militarism failed. He remained pessimistic about a NATO substitute for EDC; the treaty simply had to be ratified. The following day Dulles sent Churchill another, even more urgent message, stressing the importance of a West German defense contribution and reiterating that EDC was the only means of achieving it. Protracted delays would erode Adenauer's domestic strength and do nothing to resolve the problem of a French veto. In this situation there were in his opinion two essentials: "We must while there is still a chance for the EDC keep our eyes exclusively on the EDC. . . . Secondly we must not permit Mendès-France to think that in event of failure we can forget all that has happened and start afresh with France in a position

4691ff; Jebb to Foreign Office, August 15, 1954, PRO, PREM 11/618; Foreign Office to Washington, August 17, 1954, ibid.

[56] C. Warner to Foreign Office, August 20, 1954, PRO, PREM 11/618.

[57] Bruce to Department of State, August 21, 1954, FR, *1952–1954*, 5:1062.

[58] Dulles to Mendès-France and Spaak, August 21, 1954, delivered August 22, 1954, FR, *1952–1954*, 5:1058–60.

to block what we know to be vital to our interests. . . . We need to stand together on this."[59]

Dulles's mixture of threats and alarmist predictions only exacerbated the tension at Brussels, not that his positions were without foundation. As far as the United States was concerned, neither the neutralization of Germany nor the revival of West German militarism was acceptable. The possibility that the United States might negotiate bilaterally with the West Germans, or convene a conference without French participation, was undoubtedly a powerful lever to prevent either of these developments. Still, given the climate of suspicion and incrimination in Brussels, Dulles's tactics may have been self-defeating. The day after he warned Mendès-France that a "great crisis" would ensue should the conference break up without agreement, it did in fact break up without agreement. To Dulles this was the worst possible scenario; yet if anything he had contributed to it.

Neither the British nor the French perceived the situation as disastrously as did Dulles. Two days before the conference's adjournment, in an effort to control the damage, Mendès-France made plans to stop off in London before returning to Paris. Kirkpatrick retained the hope, expressed to the U.S. chargé d'affaires in London, that the French might "at eleventh hour" finally ratify.[60] Churchill was thinking more of a NATO alternative to EDC than of EDC itself, but either method of remilitarizing West Germany would require a serious modification of the French position. Therefore he prepared to use all his persuasive powers to bring Mendès-France around to his view. The prime minister wrote Dulles immediately after receiving the secretary of state's second telegram, "Mendès-France arrives here noon tomorrow [Monday, August 23] and I shall urge him to stake his political fame on getting EDC through. I shall make plain the awful consequences which might follow from a flop. It is a choice between peace through strength and subjugation through weakness. . . . We might all of us be in on a winner. We must keep in the closest touch. This is a time for vehement moral action. I suppose you could come over if need be. . . . Code name BITE, quite like old times. Winston."[61]

Dulles, greatly cheered by this message, cabled back that he was prepared to "bite" hard to get something "not only digestible but in-

[59] Dulles to Churchill, August 21, 1954, *FR, 1952–1954*, 5:1060–61; Dulles to Churchill, August 22, 1954, PRO, PREM 11/618; attached were the messages to Spaak and Mendès-France.

[60] Alger to Department of State, August 20, 1954, *FR, 1952–1954*, 5:1056; Penfield to Department of State, August 22, 1954, ibid., 1069.

[61] Churchill to Dulles, August 22, 1954, *FR, 1952–1954*, 5:1070–71. Draft and original telegram in PRO, PREM 11/618.

vigorating." He would eagerly await the results of Churchill's talks with Mendès-France.[62] Still, he was not quite sure what Churchill was up to. Age was catching up with the prime minister, and he appeared at times to lose touch with reality. A few months earlier the U.S. ambassador in London, Winthrop Aldrich, had written that Churchill was "imaginative, unpredictable, firm in belief in his own genius, and apparently determined to attempt one last crowning act on world stage."[63] Also, Churchill's obsessive fear of a nuclear war, and his concomitant obsession with convening a summit, had become a serious irritant to Anglo-American relations. As a result, on August 21, 1954, Dulles cabled Aldrich that "in view uncertainty line Churchill may take with Mendès-France at Chequers [*sic*] meeting," American presence should be avoided if an invitation was offered.[64]

Dulles need not have worried. No invitation was offered. Although the annoyance expressed by Dulles in his message of August 21 to Mendès-France was "understandable," as Kirkpatrick put it, Eden was "against any move now which excludes or isolates France." Churchill, despite having written Dulles that he "supposed" the secretary could attend, endorsed this opinion. The prime minister wanted to be able to digest and possibly discuss with Mendès-France the latest findings of his own military without American interference.[65]

Only hours before Mendès-France arrived in England, Churchill had Lord Alexander's answer to his memorandum of August 20. The Chiefs of Staff had concluded that the only satisfactory alternative to EDC that would provide reasonable safeguards over West German rearmament would be to bring West Germany into NATO. But should France veto this option and the West proceed with a new NATO without the French, they saw serious consequences. They assumed that, in those circumstances, France would be neutral and deny the new NATO powers the use of her territory. The results would be extremely serious. To begin with, the chiefs maintained, the West would cease to have the use of supply ports on the Channel and Atlantic coasts and of transportation facilities in France. This would completely disrupt the lines of communication and the plans for supporting the British forces on the Continent in war. Similarly, the allies would also have to replace the headquarters and signal communications system,

[62] Dulles to Churchill, August 23, 1954, *FR, 1952–1954*, 5:1071.

[63] Aldrich to Dulles, November 27, 1953, *FR, 1952–1954*, 5:1721. See also entry for June 26, 1954, Robert Ferrell, ed., *The Diary of James C. Hagerty: Eisenhower in Mid-Course, 1953–1955* (Bloomington, Ind., 1983), 77–78.

[64] *FR, 1952–1954*, 5:1051, n. 3.

[65] Minute by Kirkpatrick for Churchill with handwritten note by Churchill, PRO, PREM 11/618.

which had been built in France. Lord Alexander was likewise concerned with the potential loss of the use of French airfields vital to the defense of the central sector, and the use of naval ports and bases on the Mediterranean coast and in North Africa.

The Chiefs of Staff concluded, in addition, that the French contribution to the armed forces of the Supreme Allied Commander, Europe (SACEUR)—14⅓ division, about 500 aircraft, 4 major and about 40 minor naval units—would be withdrawn. There would be, in time, a West German contribution of about equivalent size and "almost certainly of greater operational value." But NATO planning required the West German contribution in addition to the forces already at SACEUR's disposal. With their worldwide commitments the British could not possibly offer additional forces to replace the French forces, and Lord Alexander was sure that the Americans would not be prepared to augment their forces in Europe. For all these reasons the British Chiefs of Staff regarded it of the "utmost importance to get France to agree either to West Germany joining NATO or to an arrangement which would permit the rearming of Germany with safeguards, while France herself remains in NATO."[66]

Churchill had this report in mind when he met Mendès-France at Chartwell for a four-hour talk. He began by describing the general world situation and warning his French counterpart that there were four alternative policies for the West in Europe. They were not original. The West could either ratify EDC, which was much the best option, or it could bring West Germany into NATO, which was the next best. If France accepted neither of these alternatives, the allies could adopt the "empty chair policy." The other countries would be forced to go ahead without France with a reasonable West German policy, leaving a chair for France to take when she was ready to do so. This would be "regrettable but might become inevitable." The fourth possibility was the peripheral defense, which Churchill was very much afraid that the United States might turn to with "all its grave dangers."

For his part, Mendès-France stated flatly that France would reject EDC. Assuming his prediction proved correct, however, it would "never dare to reject an alternative, even that of German entry into NATO." But, Mendès-France insisted, he must receive help in order to get the necessary results within the next few weeks. Specifically he alluded to the United Kingdom's agreeing to associate with the Continental powers in some modified NATO structure. At the same time

---

[66] Alternatives to EDC, Memorandum by Field Marshal Alexander for Prime Minister, August 23, 1954, PRO, PREM 11/618.

Mendès-France spoke strongly against Dulles's proposal for a meeting without France. "This would do no good and might do much harm," he warned.[67]

The Americans were unconcerned with Mendès-France's warning about a meeting without France's participation. Indeed, in their view it was the French prime minister's meeting with Churchill that had done no good and might have done much harm. Dillon reported from Paris that at a briefing that morning Mendès-France had given the "clear impression" that his talk with Churchill had prepared the way for an alternative solution should EDC be defeated; that treaty opponents considered their hand had been greatly strengthened; and that there was considerable press speculation that if and when EDC was defeated it would be possible to agree in relatively short time on a seven-nation formula involving a military pact within the NATO framework. Dillon suggested that if such innuendos were to be effectively countered, high-level protestations by the United Kingdom of their endorsement of EDC would not be enough: "What would be required is clarification that if EDC fails, Great Britain will move in concert with U.S. for creation of German National Army." Otherwise, the ambassador stated, "erroneous impression will persist here that there is easy way out" of the EDC crisis.[68] In a cable to Churchill, President Eisenhower added that there must be "some way to bring Mendès-France to see his historic opportunity or to put a little backbone into the French Assembly." If this could be done, "there would be an immediate spiritual transformation throughout the whole region."[69]

Bruce, with Dillon's support, came up with a solution for Eisenhower. Essentially he recommended that the United States continue Dulles's tactic of applying pressure on Mendès-France. Washington should strike at the "weakest point in Mendès-France's armor," dramatizing what he had been trying to conceal: namely, "his great fear that the French Public and French Parliamentarians will become aware of his Country's isolated position vis-à-vis its partners." This could be done by Eisenhower and Churchill jointly calling a meeting for August 30 to be attended by the six EDC foreign ministers and special representatives of the president and the prime minister. The invitations should be in the hands of the recipients by noon London

[67] Conversation at Chartwell with M. Mendès-France on August 23, 1954, PRO, PREM 11/618. See also telegram to Mr. Dulles from the Prime Minister, draft (with alterations by Churchill) and original, and Eden's personal message to Dulles, both August 24, 1954, ibid., and *FR, 1952–1954*, 5:1077–79.

[68] *FR, 1952–1954*, 5:1079, n. 2.

[69] Eisenhower to Churchill, August 25, 1954, PRO, PREM 11/618.

time, August 27, because the proposal would involve postponing the debate in the Assembly scheduled for August 28. This procedure would expose France's isolation for everyone to see. Bruce prefaced his recommendation by underscoring that it required quick and decisive action. Moreover, it represented "our only chance, and we might just win on it."[70]

Not all of Bruce's colleagues shared his opinion. However, with Dulles once more away from the capital, Smith was again in charge. On balance he liked the idea. Britain's minister in Washington, Sir Robert Scott, reported that the under secretary recognized that this gambit "might cause Mendès-France to fall"; but "that would not be too serious if we got EDC." According to Scott, Smith telephoned to Eisenhower, who was in Colorado. The president expressed his willingness to adopt the proposal provided Churchill and Eden were in complete accord with it.[71]

The British, it turned out, were not in accord. Churchill's and Eden's reaction was "strongly negative."[72] They did not think that this proposal would achieve Bruce's objective of strengthening France's advocates of EDC, especially as they did not believe, as Bruce reported, that Mendès-France was "doing and will do his utmost to defeat the EDC Treaty."[73] The British still believed the allies had to work with, not against, the French prime minister. Accordingly, a meeting would be useful only if there was a new proposal to put before it. Conversely, London saw the danger that the isolation argument "may boomerang" because many Frenchmen were already arguing that if EDC meant that France was to be bullied and placed in a minority of one before the treaty had even been signed, she had better not become a member of the community at all.[74]

With Churchill's refusal to join Eisenhower in summoning the allies to this extraordinary meeting aborting Bruce's idea, America's well of proposals ran dry. Washington could suggest nothing to do other than to await Paris's final verdict. The British would also wait, but they would keep very busy while doing so. Just hours before informing the State Department of its decision not to support Bruce's

[70] Bruce to Department of State, August 26, 1954. *FR, 1952–1954*, 5:1079–81, 1081, n. 1.

[71] Sir R. Scott to Foreign Office, August 26, 1954 (six different telegrams), PRO, PREM 11/618.

[72] Cf. *FR, 1952–1954*, 5:1081f.

[73] Bruce to Department of State, August 26, 1954, *FR, 1952–1954*, 5:1079–81.

[74] Bedell Smith to Bruce and Dillon, August 26, 1954, *FR, 1952–1954*, 5:1081–82. The original to Washington, August 26, 1954, with slightly different wording, in PRO, PREM 11/618.

initiative, the Foreign Office completed for Eden a memorandum entitled "Alternatives to the European Defense Community." Predicated on the assumption that the French would not ratify the treaty, it reviewed the alternatives suggested by Churchill's discussions with Mendès-France. The adoption of a peripheral defense was not considered. Rather, potential options included admitting the Federal Republic to NATO; a European organization in which Great Britain would join a modified EDC while retaining the NATO framework; and a triangular alliance among the United Kingdom, United States, and West Germany that would be superimposed upon NATO. The "best bet," in Eden's eyes, was "Germany's entry into NATO" on the condition that its rearmament be restricted. However, this safeguard would not guarantee that, as a "territorially dissatisfied Power," the FRG would not be constantly tempted "to modify its Eastern frontiers by force and to drag the whole of the NATO Alliance into war for that purpose." This was a risk Eden was willing to accept. To prolong the negotiations much longer might lose West Germany to the West altogether.[75]

The cabinet authorized Eden to use the memorandum as the basis for new consultations with the Americans, French, and West Germans. Further, he was instructed to arrange a meeting among the six EDC nations and the British and Americans as well as one with the North Atlantic Council. The cabinet acted none too soon. Three days later, on August 30, the French National Assembly behaved as predicted; it rejected EDC. Although expected, the vote had "a stunning effect upon our partners in the Western Alliance," Eden reported to his colleagues.[76]

Eden did not exaggerate, particularly with regard to the United States. In the first draft of a public statement, Dulles called the French rejection of EDC a "grave event."[77] In fact, after reading the draft, America's deputy chief of mission in London, W. Walton Butterworth, described it as the secretary's "lament on the death of EDC" and suggested some revisions. Butterworth hoped that they would do "some good in helping to remove the tone of bitterness and preserve our position of leadership," but he still feared that Dulles's statement would hinder "the cause of European integration—which we must

[75] Cabinet memorandum by the Secretary of State for Foreign Affairs, August 26, 1954, PRO, PREM 11/618.
[76] Cabinet Conclusions (54), 57th Conclusion, August 27, 1954, PRO, CAB 128/27; Cabinet Conclusions (54), 58th Conclusion, September 1, 1954, ibid.
[77] Dulles to Embassy in France, August 30, 1954, FR, 1952–1954, 5:1114. He later changed the adjective to "saddening." Ibid., 1120.

not think of as dead because EDC has been defeated."[78] Back in Washington Eisenhower agreed. "[W]e cannot sit down in black despair and admit defeat," he wrote Bedell Smith.[79]

Yet by this time the United States had forfeited its position of leadership, and even if the administration refused to admit defeat, it did not have any constructive proposals to advance. It had bet everything on the implementation of EDC; it had refused to accept that when they finally brought the treaty to a vote the French would actually fail to ratify it. Consequently it was up to the British to save the day, and they willingly grasped the challenge. Eden already had his agenda; his plan was to move quickly in order to forestall proposals from other quarters, including the Americans, that "might not seem to us wise." Thus his first step was to convene a meeting of the EDC powers along with Britain and the United States, which he hoped would take place in London. Eden recognized that he would confront serious obstacles. Surely France would resist admitting West Germany to NATO for the same reasons it had voted down EDC, and Bonn would insist on the same treatment it was to receive through EDC, especially with regard to sovereign rights. Hence difficult negotiations lay ahead. Moreover, there remained supplementary—albeit highly emotionally charged—issues such as the disposition of the Saar Valley. The British strategy was to induce Adenauer to declare immediately, before the nations gathered together, that he recognized that the Federal Republic's contribution to Western defense was subject to certain restrictions and that he renounced any intention of taking advantage of the allies' current predicament. At the same time the powers must make clear that left with a choice between proceeding without France or leaving West Germany free to pursue an independent policy, possibly involving some arrangement with the Soviet Union, "we should," Eden flatly asserted, "be bound to choose the former."[80]

With Churchill's cabinet in full accord, Eden pushed forward as rapidly as possible. On September 7 he wrote Dulles to suggest the nine-power meeting. The secretary of state at first hesitated. He was anxious to avoid a repetition of the Brussels meeting, and suspected that the British might be "deliberately attempting to rush us in order to put across some plan of their own which we may or may not approve."[81] Because Dulles was at the time in Manila negotiating the

[78] Butterworth to the Assistant Secretary of State for European Affairs (Merchant), September 1, 1954, *FR, 1952–1954*, 5:1127.

[79] Eisenhower to Smith, September 3, 1954, *FR, 1952–1954*, 5:1145.

[80] Cabinet Conclusions (54), 57th Conclusion, August 27, 1954, PRO, CAB 128/27; Cabinet Conclusions (54), 58th Conclusion, September 1, 1954, ibid.

[81] Dulles to Eden, September 8, 1954, *FR, 1952–1954*, 5:1155; Dulles to Smith, September 7, 1954, ibid., 1150.

SEATO treaty, and would not return to Washington until September 12, he suggested that the administration use his need to consult with Eisenhower, his colleagues, and the congressional leadership as an excuse for delaying the meeting. Further, Adenauer himself was reluctant to commit to anything final, including the type of declaration Eden wanted, until he was sure that both British and American opinion would support West German membership in NATO if France remained adamantly opposed. Eden decided not to force the issue. "It now looks as though the meeting of Foreign Ministers," he cabled Dulles, "will need a little more time for preparation."[82]

In the event the powers met in London from September 28 through October 3. By the time they did, however, the results were all but anticlimatic, and again due primarily to the British initiative. Eden flew to Brussels and Bonn where he conferred with the Benelux ministers and, of course, Adenauer. He was "much encouraged" by the meetings. Not only were the ministers sympathetic to admitting the Federal Republic to NATO, but Adenauer appeared ready to provide effective political and military safeguards that would both place restrictions on West German rearmament and establish West German sovereignty without leaving a legal vacuum in regard to the Bonn contractuals. Much work lay ahead, especially with the French, but "all has so far gone better than I could have hoped," Eden wrote Dulles on September 13. "I think we now have the foundation for a practical plan which our experts in NATO could work out quickly with German participation."[83]

Meanwhile the Americans continued to develop their own plans; they came up with little to add to the British program.[84] Dulles responded to Eden's report of his discussions by complimenting him on his progress and conceding that the United States was not yet ready to submit a proposal of its own. All Dulles could do at this time was offer some bromides on the need to grant West German sovereignty promptly and maintain the supranational characteristics of EDC.[85] When Dulles flew to Bonn and London to meet with Eden and Ade-

[82] Conant to Department of State, September 1 and 7, 1954, *FR, 1952–1954*, 5:1122–25, 1152–54; Eden to Dulles, September 8, 1954, ibid., 1156.

[83] Eden to Dulles, September 13, 1954, *FR, 1952–1954*, 5:1184–85.

[84] See, for example, memorandum by the Assistant Secretary of State for European Affairs (Merchant) to Dulles, and attachments, September 10, 1954, *FR, 1952–1954*, 5:1163–70; Paper prepared by Leon W. Fuller of the Policy Planning Staff, September 10, 1954, ibid., 1170–77; Draft statement of policy proposed by the NSC (NSC 5433), September 16, 1954, ibid., 1205–9; Memorandum by the Executive Secretary of the NSC (Lay) to the NSC, and attachments, September 23, 1954, ibid., 1246–53; and NSC 5433/1, September 25, 1954, ibid., 1268–71.

[85] Dulles to Eden, September 14, 1954, *FR, 1952–1954*, 5:1192–93.

nauer on September 16 and 17, he again had little constructive to contribute. He confined his comments primarily to repeating the inherent problems with incorporating West Germany into NATO. However, Dulles was quick to add that he did not mean to "suggest that there was a better way. At any rate he had not thought of it." Indeed, Dulles ended up concluding that "the general scheme or conception that Mr. Eden had developed seemed the best that could be devised to meet the situation which confronts us. The whole conception had been brilliant and statesmanlike."[86]

The evidence suggests that by the time he returned to Washington, Dulles had become convinced that it was in the interests of the United States, and European integration, for the United States essentially to defer to the British. When questioned by Vice President Richard Nixon at the September 24 NSC meeting about whether U.S. leadership was so seriously resented in Europe that any plan it sponsored was likely to meet defeat, Dulles answered that a European plan would have a better chance to succeed. France and Great Britain, he explained, "have now reached a point of no longer wishing to seem tied to the U.S. coattails. They want to throw their weight around a little." Significantly, Dulles omitted the fact that the British had proposed the plan to begin with, and the United States had not thought of an alternative approach. Be that as it may, the secretary did make clear his intention to follow Britain's lead. "What we would face at the London meeting was not a U.S. plan but an indigenous plan." Accordingly, "we should not try to impose a U.S. plan by dangling promises, nor will it be necessary to offer firm commitments as a *quid pro quo*."[87] His attitude, he told Eden upon arriving in London, "would be that the U.S. was there as a friend and counselor and was deeply interested in the results but looked to the Europeans to put forward proposals."[88] He then told Mendès-France that he came "with no plan of our own but only the desire to be helpful."[89]

It was thus with Dulles's compliance as much as cooperation that Eden's nine-power conference proved so successful. With the Americans basically remaining on the sidelines, proceedings evolved much as the British had hoped. The foreign ministers agreed to revive the dormant Brussels Treaty, changing the name of its executive body from the Western Union to the Western European Union (WEU) and inviting both West Germany and Italy to join. The WEU's force struc-

---

[86] Report of Dulles's conversations with Adenauer and Eden, September 16–17, 1954 (September 20, 1954), *FR, 1952–1954*, 5:1209–23.

[87] Memorandum of NSC meeting, September 24, 1954, *FR, 1952–1954*, 5:1263–66.

[88] Memorandum of conversation, September 27, 1954, *FR, 1952–1954*, 5:1277.

[89] Memorandum of conversation, September 27, 1954, *FR, 1952–1954*, 5:1286.

ture and strategy would be wholly dedicated to NATO. By this mechanism the European allies would be able to restrict the size of West Germany's naval and air buildup as well as its manufacture of nuclear and chemical weapons; in return they would grant Bonn sovereignty and membership in the Atlantic alliance. Confirmed in Paris at another conference from October 20 to 22, along with the Saar Statute that provided for a referendum in 1955, the new accords accomplished in months what had eluded the powers for years. In December Mendès-France secured ratification of the package. The timely intervention of the British had proven decisive.[90]

Yet in the final analysis, the British should not receive all the credit. London had always preferred the NATO solution, and the idea of resurrecting the Western European Union was hardly a stroke of genius. Churchill and Eden had been vital catalytic agents; but responsibility for the success lay with all the European nations and their collective recognition that they lived in a less than perfect world and would have to compromise. Hence even as Adenauer agreed to accept a wide range of restrictions on rearmament, his allies understood that should they disappoint the West Germans again they would throw the Bonn government to the opposition and, at a minimum, weaken the Federal Republic's ties with the West. And even as the French were gratified that the United States and Britain would be full-fledged members of the defense pact, they acquiesced to the reality that West Germany was going to rearm whether France was a party to it or not. And overshadowing all else, of course, was the uniform conviction, appropriately captured by Eden, that to fail now "would be a disaster for Europe and triumph for the Kremlin."[91] If any single nation was responsible for the European nations putting aside their differences, therefore, it was ironically the Soviet Union.

On May 5, 1955, the occupation ended and the Western powers formally recognized the Federal Republic of Germany. Four days later they accepted it as a member of NATO. At that time Adenauer announced "West Germany is now a member of the strongest alliance in history. It will bring us reunification."[92] The evidence suggests that the chancellor was being less than sincere. According to a recently declassified British document, Adenauer "was terrified that when he

---

[90] Lawrence S. Kaplan, *NATO and the United States: The Enduring Alliance* (Boston, 1988). For a detailed examination of the British role, see Saki Dockrill, "Britain and a West German Contribution to NATO, 1950–1955," Ph.D. dissertation, King's College, London (1988), 233–378.

[91] Verbatim record, Nine-Power Conference, September 28, 1954, PRO, FO 371/109774/cw/10714/2.

[92] Steininger, *Eine Chance zur Wiedervereinigung*, 87.

disappeared from the scene a future German Government might do a deal with Russia at German expense. Consequently, he felt that the integration of Western Germany with the West was more important than the unification of Germany."[93] Dulles, although there is no record that he ever said it, appears to have arrived at the same conclusion. Faced with what came down to a choice between unification, and a chance to settle the primary cold war irritant, and West German rearmament, which would irrevocably divide Europe but strengthen the Atlantic Alliance's defenses and potentially provide the basis for the eventual retraction of Soviet power, Dulles saw no alternative. In light of the climate of fear and uncertainty that infected all nations, he was probably correct.

[93] Memorandum of conversation, December 16, 1955, PRO, FO 371/118254/WG/1071/1374.

CHAPTER 4

Konrad Adenauer, John Foster Dulles, and West German-American Relations

Hans-Jürgen Grabbe

BETWEEN 1953 and 1958 Konrad Adenauer, who headed the West German government from 1949 to 1963, stood at the apex of his power. Not only did his Christian Democrats (CDU/CSU)[1] command a majority in the Bundestag, but during the crucial years of 1955 and 1956, when the Federal Republic joined NATO and established armed forces, the four-party government coalition controlled two thirds of the vote—a margin sufficient to bring about the constitutional changes necessary for rearmament. In the field of foreign policy Adenauer reigned supreme: after having doubled as foreign minister until 1955, Adenauer made it clear that his successor's responsibilities in the field of foreign policy would not extend much beyond routine operations of the office.[2] This heyday, conventionally described as *Kanzlerdemokratie*,[3] virtually paralleled John Foster Dulles's term as U.S. secretary of state.

In an influential study of West German foreign policy, Wolfram F. Hanrieder borrowed a term coined by James N. Rosenau to label the Federal Republic a "penetrated political system," "one in which non-members of a national society participate directly and authoritatively, through actions taken jointly with the society's members, in either the allocation of its values or the mobilization of support on behalf of its goals." Penetration may also take place without such *direct* participation if the decision-making process of a society is strongly affected by external events and trends.[4] Under the Occupation Statute, which remained in force until May 1955, the United States could always find avenues into Bonn's decision-making process. But, as the elections of 1953 and 1957 showed, West Germany's close association with the United States and the Western alliance was based on a firm societal

---

[1] The Bavarian Christian Social Union (CSU) has an independent party organization but forms a common parliamentary group with the Christian Democratic Union (CDU).

[2] See Konrad Adenauer, *Erinnerungen* (4 vols.: Stuttgart, 1965–1968), 3:121.

[3] Arnulf Baring, *Aussenpolitik in Adenauers Kanzlerdemokratie* (München, 1969).

[4] Wolfram F. Hanrieder, *West German Foreign Policy, 1949–1963: International Pressure and Domestic Response* (Stanford, Calif., 1967), 229–30.

consensus and did not depend exclusively on contractual agreements.[5] A broad majority of the population saw no alternative to political, economic, and cultural alignment with the West. The repressive systems of East Central and Eastern Europe were precariously close; the realization of dependence on American military protection was keen; and pride in the market economy and *Wirtschaftswunder* (economic miracle), which had received an initial boost from Marshall aid, was widespread. Alternative foreign or domestic policies found limited support: "keine Experimente!" (no experiments) read the fitting CDU election slogan for 1957.

The alliance with America has been called the "second *Grundgesetz*" (Basic Law, that is, constitution) of the Federal Republic.[6] This foundation, which goes beyond even what one would expect under the conditions of penetration defined by Hanrieder, is to no small degree the result of the relationship between Dulles and Adenauer.[7] Major crises and serious challenges to the postwar status quo were frequent in the 1950s. The general course of events was determined by the systemic clash between East and West; by bilateral and multilateral interdependence; and by the dictates of respective national interests. Yet the "personal factor" must be considered exceptional in the German-American relationship. Accordingly, my reflections focus on the Adenauer–Dulles connection.

In June 1962 the eighty-six-year-old Adenauer met with a small group of American newspaper writers for one of his famous background interviews or *Teegespräche* (tea conversations), as they were known. This was little more than a year before he was scheduled to leave office, and the chancellor was in a reminiscent mood. One of the participants recalled an incident following the Berlin foreign ministers' conference of 1954. On the way back to Washington, Dulles's plane stopped at Wahn airfield, near Cologne, where the secretary was met by Adenauer. For about thirty minutes the statesmen walked to and fro on the tarmac, discussing and coordinating impending actions while accompanying journalists peeked through the cabin windows.[8]

[5] The element of consensus is crucial in defining a penetrated system. Hanrieder, *West German Foreign Policy*, 229–30.

[6] Walther Leisler Kiep, *Good-bye Amerika—was dann? Der deutsche Standpunkt im Wandel der Weltpolitik* (Stuttgart, 1972), 106.

[7] See volumes 2 and 3 of the authoritative *Geschichte der Bundesrepublik Deutschland*: Hans-Peter Schwarz, *Die Ära Adenauer 1949–1957*, and *Die Ära Adenauer 1957–1963* (Stuttgart and Wiesbaden, 1981–1983); Schwarz, "Das aussenpolitische Konzept Konrad Adenauers," in Rudolf Morsey and Konrad Repgen, eds., *Adenauer-Studien* (Mainz, 1971), 1:71–108, 86.

[8] Informationsgespräch, June 28, 1962, Archives of the Federal Government's Press

At this point in the interview the chancellor was moved to say that his relationship with Dulles had been a "true friendship" based on a great consonance in their thinking. "At Dulles's and particularly at my age,"[9] Adenauer continued, "one doesn't easily find a real friend anymore; but in Dulles I indeed gained a real friend."[10] This statement reflected genuine feeling. Yet to Adenauer "friendship" stemmed from the mind more than the heart. Here was a man whose formative years lay in the nineteenth century, who was intimate with no one outside his closely knit family, and who in the political sphere confided in no one; he was a cynical, at times devious person. To the end he addressed his two lifelong friends, the Belgian-American industrialist Dannie Heinemann and the Cologne banker Robert Pferdmenges, as "Dear Friend" and "Dear Mr. Pferdmenges."[11] "Friendship" meant being akin in substance; it did not mean that common personal traits, similarities of life-style, and the like, existed to any great extent. Adenauer never invited Dulles to his home, and the secretary behaved the same way. Their fifteen bilateral meetings between 1953 and 1959 were ruled by tight agendas, the language barrier had to be bridged by an interpreter, and the statesmen never conferred in strict confidence. But they understood one another.

"I got to know Dulles as a very sober, coolly deliberating person, a logical thinker, willing to listen to the arguments of others," Adenauer wrote in his memoirs. "His reflections were clear, and what he deemed necessary was done in a businesslike, dispassionate manner." He knew "that successful policy needs firm ethical foundations. Like myself he considered communism a serious threat to the culture of the Christian occident. . . . I came to esteem him as a thoroughly fair and square person. . . . Our friendship was based not least on the fact that we talked with total frankness."[12]

Adenauer and Dulles believed in the same basic values, which both often stated publicly in woodcut-like simplicity. When the chancellor, for instance, spoke of the "cataclysmic powers of ungodly totalitarianism," the rhetoric had a distinct Dullesian ring.[13] More substan-

---

and Information Office, Bonn. A memorandum of the conversation between Dulles and Adenauer is printed in *FR, 1952–1954*, 7:1208–15.

[9] Adenauer (1876–1967) was seventy-eight years old, twelve years older than Dulles at the time of the 1954 meeting.

[10] Informationsgespräch, June 28, 1962, archives of the Federal Government's Press and Information Office.

[11] See the letters to Heinemann and Pferdmenges printed in Konrad Adenauer, *Briefe, 1945–1953*, Hans-Peter Mensing, ed. (4 vols.: Berlin, 1983–1987).

[12] Adenauer, *Erinnerungen*, 3:162–63. (All quotes are the author's translations.)

[13] Quote from a speech at Georgetown University in April 1953. Adenauer, *Erinnerungen*, 1:581.

tively, by as early as October 1945 Adenauer had concluded that the partition of Europe was a reality, and he saw little or no short-term possibility for a reconciliation of Western and Soviet interests. The political, military, and ideological challenge that the West faced had to be countered by creating a viable European community, by building a powerful defense network, and by fighting ideology with ideology. This belief, nevertheless, did not preclude sitting down at the conference table with Soviet leaders to explore opportunities for a breakthrough toward détente. Two years later Dulles arrived at the same conclusions.[14]

This is not to say that Adenauer knew much about Dulles prior to the American's becoming secretary of state. Evidently he began to pay attention to Dulles after the latter delivered a speech at a World Council of Churches meeting in Amsterdam in August 1948. Adenauer told the delegates of a subsequent CDU party congress that Dulles, who was likely to play an important role in American foreign policy, believed in the reconstruction of the world according to Christian principles, and sympathized with his concept of Western European political cooperation.[15]

Dulles's rhetoric of "liberation" and "roll back," on the other hand, did not meet with equal approval.[16] Adenauer shared Dulles's hostility toward the Soviet Union, and he was acutely sensitive to the communist threat to Europe. Yet he feared that if the allies responded to the Soviets on the basis of fear and emotion, the consequences could be disastrous. Driving his concerns was the West's behavior during the debate over the European Defense Community. Not only did Adenauer suspect that France still opposed rearming the Federal Republic and granting it sovereignty, but he believed the British, out of panic, were willing to accommodate Moscow. The Kremlin leadership, he was certain, would play the "German card," offering reunification in a neutralized state, with the short-term intention of torpedoing EDC and the long-term goal of drawing all of Germany into its

---

[14] Adenauer to Heinrich Weitz, October 31, 1945, Adenauer, *Briefe*, 1:130, Ronald W. Pruessen, *John Foster Dulles: The Road to Power* (New York, 1982), 302–3.

[15] See Hans-Jürgen Grabbe, *Unionsparteien, Sozialdemokratie und Vereinigte Staaten von Amerika 1945–1966* (Düsseldorf, 1983), 33. Adenauer had also attended the Amsterdam meeting. Adenauer, *Erinnerungen*, 3:161. Excerpts of Dulles's speech are printed in Henry P. Van Dusen, ed., *The Spiritual Legacy of John Foster Dulles: Selections from His Articles and Addresses* (Philadelphia, 1960), 159–93.

[16] Background conversation with German newspaper writers, July 11, 1952, in Konrad Adenauer, *Teegespräche: 1950–1963*, Hanns Jürgen Küsters, ed. (4 vols.: Berlin, 1984–1988), 1:328–29. It is not clear whether Adenauer fully understood the rationale behind these concepts. See John Lewis Gaddis, *The Long Peace* (New York, 1988), 174–76.

orbit. Adenauer worried that Germany either would be ground to pieces between the millstones of East and West—the fragments then to be swallowed up by the Soviet Union—or the East–West negotiations would lead to a "second Potsdam."

While Bismarck had suffered from a *cauchemar des coalitions*, Adenauer lay sleepless because of his "Potsdam nightmare," the ever-present fear that the wartime allies might once again settle the affairs of Germany without the participation of Germans. In his scenario France and Great Britain would opt for détente with the Soviet Union, and the United States, practicing a brand of "new isolationism" frequently associated with Dulles's policy of massive retaliation,[17] would resort to a strategy of "peripheral defense" of Europe, based on an arc from Norway through Britain to the Iberian and Apennine peninsulas, to Greece and Turkey. This vision, he told the executive committee of the CDU in January 1953, made him tremble.[18]

It was in this climate that the Adenauer–Dulles relationship germinated. On February 5, 1953, the secretary of state arrived in Bonn for his first official visit. Dulles's foreign policy goal, evident already in 1919 and dominant after 1945, was "the alteration of the structure and environment of continental Europe." As Ronald Pruessen has demonstrated, "grave doubts about the trustworthiness of Germany" were one of the "key stimuli" for Dulles's thoughts and recommendations in the postwar period. Germany would have to be made incapable of ever conducting war on its own and should be anchored to an economically and financially integrated (Western) Europe. Otherwise the malaise of both the Germans and their neighbors would lead to defeatism or the open espousal of communism. Collapse seemed imminent unless the West German potential—that of the Ruhr in particular—was used to breathe oxygen into the sick body of Western Europe.[19]

[17] Norman Graebner, *The New Isolationism: A Study in Politics and Foreign Policy since 1950* (New York, 1956).

[18] Hans-Peter Schwarz, *Adenauer: Der Aufstieg 1876–1952* (Stuttgart, 1986), 830–33; Günter Buchstab, ed., *Adenauer: "Es musste alles neu gemacht werden": Die Protokolle des CDU-Bundesvorstandes, 1950–1953* (Stuttgart, 1986), 306. As late as October 1953, the U.S. High Commissioner for Germany, James B. Conant, pleaded, in the event of EDC failure, for "the withdrawal of all but token [U.S.] forces from Europe and a so-called peripheral defense rather than a German national army." Conant to Dulles, October 28, 1953, *FR, 1952–1954*, 5:832. It seems, though, that neither the Joint Chiefs nor the State Department considered "peripheral defense" a viable alternative. See memorandum of discussion of State–Mutual Security Agency–Joint Chiefs of Staff Meeting, January 28, 1953, ibid., 712–13, and editorial note, ibid., 694.

[19] Pruessen, *John Foster Dulles*, 307, 311–12, 331–32, 342.

Adenauer shared this assessment and agreed to the proposed remedy. Indeed, it promised a solution to his "Potsdam nightmare." The danger, as Dulles phrased it, that West German politicians might again turn to the methods of yesteryear, "play[ing] both ends against the middle," was equivalent to Adenauer's firm resolve to prevent a revival of the Weimar tradition of *Schaukelpolitik* (seesaw politics) between East and West.[20] Together the statesmen helped to achieve and make permanent what West German scholars call *Westbindung*. The expression is difficult to translate into English; "alignment with the West" comes reasonably close, although the German term encompasses the noncompulsory *and* the mandatory aspects of the Federal Republic's ties. Adenauer intended to lead West Germany and, if possible, all of Germany into the fold of the "Western democracies." He was supported by the Social Democrats, whose leader Kurt Schumacher had declared in April 1946 that Germany should join the countries that had experienced successful bourgeois revolutions.[21] *Westbindung* as an ideological alignment, then, was not in dispute. Adenauer was convinced, however, that a formal and for the foreseeable future irrevocable alliance was necessary to create a permanent marriage between West Germany and the West and thus assure completion of the German democratic revolution.

Adenauer's analysis meshed with the Eisenhower administration's European strategy. In preparation for Secretary Dulles's first trip to Europe, the U.S. permanent representative on the North Atlantic Council, William H. Draper, Jr., underscored America's "controlling interest" in securing "an effective German military contribution to the defense of free Europe on terms which bind [West] Germany to us and our allies, bury age-old Franco-German hostility and reassure our smaller allies." Draper believed that EDC was the only means at hand to achieve these objectives.[22] Dulles agreed: EDC would "combine" West Germany and France "in a manner more trustworthy than a treaty relationship," since treaties may be "torn up."[23]

Nsc 160/1, "United States Position with Respect to Germany," approved by the president on August 13, 1953, reflected these views. The administration considered the "reliable cooperation [of the Federal Republic] with other free European nations . . . indispensable for a strong and stable Europe." U.S. security interests required "that the continent of Europe be made as impregnable as possible against So-

---

[20] Pruessen, *John Foster Dulles*, 337, 344; Adenauer, *Erinnerungen*, 1:96; Schwarz, "Das aussenpolitische Konzept," 85.

[21] Grabbe, *Unionsparteien*, 53.

[22] Draper to State Department, January 26, 1953, *FR, 1952–1954*, 5:709.

[23] Memorandum of discussion, January 28, 1953, *FR, 1952–1954*, 5:712.

viet attack or subversion." Effective protection meant that "the historic enmity between Germany and her neighbors, especially France, must be transcended to permit the kind and degree of collaboration necessary to satisfy [Western] Europe's economic, political, and defense needs." The Federal Republic's contribution to the defense of the West was considered indispensable, and the participation "of a united, democratic Germany from which Soviet occupation forces have been withdrawn" was deemed desirable.

But "[a] united Germany, disarmed or neutralized by four-power agreement," the next sentence read, "would jeopardize these interests by tending to separate Germany from the West and placing excessive military burdens on the U.S. and free Europe." Furthermore, neutralization would "open up the whole of Germany to Soviet intrigue and manipulation which would aim at the absorption of Germany into the Soviet bloc." However, since the German desire for unity was considered strong and likely to get even stronger, reunification based upon free elections as a first step, eventually leading to a Germany with "full sovereign rights, including the right to affiliate itself with the West," could safely be proposed, even if "it might choose to remain neutral or to retain freedom of action. Under present conditions, such a risk must be accepted," particularly as the Soviet Union seemed "unlikely to accept unity on these terms at this time."[24]

Little of this was new. The rationale and the basic objectives of NSC 160/1 went back to deliberations in the Acheson State Department during the spring of 1949 and reflected a broad consensus among policymakers during the final years of the Truman administration. At that time Dulles held the rank of ambassador and acted as the chief foreign policy spokesman of the Republican party.[25] The striking aspect about the Eisenhower NSC document is that the analysis and the objectives might well have come from a state paper of the Adenauer government. The position vis-à-vis the "German Question" as set forth in NSC 160/1 and Adenauer's policy of *Westbindung* were almost identical.

Although the integration of the Federal Republic into the Western alliance took precedence over reunification—echoing Adenauer's priority of "freedom" over unity—NSC 160/1 maintained that Germany would remain a zone of friction and possible conflict with the Soviet

[24] Nsc 160/1, August 17, 1953, *FR, 1952–1954*, 7:510–20. The administration's estimate that Germany's desire for unification was likely to grow was influenced by the June 17, 1953, uprising in East Berlin and other cities in the German Democratic Republic.

[25] Dean Acheson, *Present at the Creation: My Years in the State Department* (New York, 1969), 291; Grabbe, *Unionsparteien*, 179–81.

Union *especially while divided.*[26] This corresponded to the Adenauer government's argument that the East–West conflict in Europe resulted from Germany's continuing division; reunification therefore, would lead to détente.[27] Thus, even the contradictions of NSC 160/1 reflected parallel inconsistencies in Adenauer's position.

Nsc 160/1 made it clear that the West German chancellor was the linchpin of the Eisenhower administration's German policy. This was implicit in the congruity of goals, but it was also spelled out: the political stability of the Federal Republic could not be taken for granted. Its export-oriented economy remained vulnerable; millions of refugees had not been fully integrated; political apathy among the young was widespread; and many war veterans and former Nazis had not fully embraced democracy. Adverse conditions might precipitate extremist nationalism—but not at present. Under the Adenauer government strong anticommunism, firm alignment with the West, and ardent support of European integration rendered conditions in the Federal Republic favorable for America's objectives.[28]

Adenauer had succeeded in portraying himself and his government as the sole guarantors of the closest possible alignment with the West and, significantly if problematically, as the only alternative to instability. The Truman administration had assumed all along that it was in America's interest to back Adenauer;[29] Dulles and Eisenhower went further. A message from Eisenhower, in which the president defended Adenauer's claim that EDC would eventually lead to reunification, was made public at a time when the Federal Constitutional Court was reviewing the treaty. The letter met with widespread criticism in the Federal Republic, which in turn alarmed American diplomats in Bonn. Responding to a request by the American high commissioner in Germany, Dulles promised to examine carefully further action in support of Adenauer lest it boomerang by lending substance to the Social Democratic party's (SPD) portrayal of the chancellor as an "American puppet."[30]

But then came Dulles's statement of September 3, 1953, just two days before the federal elections, that failure to return the Adenauer government would be "disastrous" for West Germany.[31] This could

[26] Nsc 160/1, *FR, 1952–1954,* 7:511 (my emphasis).

[27] This reasoning united supporters and opponents of *Westbindung.*

[28] Nsc 160/1, *FR, 1952–1954,* 7:511.

[29] For examples see Grabbe, *Unionsparteien,* 183, 205–8, 215–16.

[30] Eisenhower to Adenauer, July 23, 1953, U.S. Department of State, *Documents on Germany, 1944–1985* (Washington, 1985), 402; *FR, 1952–1954,* 7:499, n. 3; Grabbe, *Unionsparteien,* 196; Dulles to Conant, July 30, 1953, *FR, 1952–1954,* 7:499.

[31] Dulles press conference statement, *DSB* 29 (September 14, 1953): 353.

only be interpreted as flagrant interference in the internal affairs of the Federal Republic. Why Dulles ignored his promise of caution is not hard to understand. In 1953 West Germany appeared as an "oasis of stability," compared, for instance, to France, with its short-lived governments, and even to Great Britain, where the Conservatives commanded only a narrow majority in the House of Commons. Among the larger West European countries, only the Federal Republic under Adenauer possessed the strong leadership needed to bring about a viable community. As Dulles put it in a letter to Churchill: "It would be an incalculable disaster if there was a failure of his [Adenauer's] pro-Western policy to ally Germany with the West and to prevent the revival of German militarism."[32]

To provide security *for and against* West Germany had been the rationale for EDC. However, the treaty was doomed. In the spring of 1954, the West German Foreign Office submitted alternatives to Adenauer that largely anticipated the outcome of the London Nine-Power Conference and the Treaty of Paris.[33] Dulles, however, continued to support the idea of a Western European army to the very last, as did Adenauer, who contemplated resignation from office when the French Assembly tabled EDC.[34] The "harrowing days" of August 1954 left a permanent mark. As late as December 1965, less than two years before his death, Adenauer called the failure of EDC "the bitterest disappointment and the greatest setback" during his tenure as chancellor.[35] Dulles was equally disappointed; yet the administration had already decided to push ahead in case of EDC's failure. In an undated paper that Dulles received on May 27, 1954, the Office of German Affairs asserted that the United States "and the British must, in order to prevent a complete deterioration in Dr. Adenauer's position, take positive steps (even without the French) to implement the contractual agreements with Germany."[36]

[32] Background conversation with German newspaper writers, October 20, 1953, Adenauer, *Teegespräche*, 1:491; Dulles to Churchill, August 20, 1954, *FR, 1952–1954*, 7:1051.

[33] These alternatives were prepared by Wilhelm Grewe, who had been the West German chief negotiator for the 1952 Bonn and EDC treaties. See Wilhelm G. Grewe, *Rückblenden 1976–1951* (Frankfurt/Main, Berlin and Wien, 1979), 194.

[34] See Heinrich Krone, "Aufzeichnungen zur Deutschland- und Ostpolitik," in Rudolf Morsey and Konrad Repgen, eds., *Adenauer-Studien* (Mainz, 1974), 3:134–201, 3:135. Krone, one of Adenauer's closest political associates, was CDU/CSU faction whip at the time.

[35] Adenauer, *Erinnerungen*, 2:298; Adenauer television interview, broadcast on December 29, 1965, printed in Günter Gaus, *Zur Person: Porträts in Frage und Antwort* (München, 1966), 2:52–59.

[36] Paper prepared in the Office of German Affairs, undated (attached to a memorandum dated May 27, 1954), *FR, 1952–1954*, 7:570–71.

During the debate of 1952 over the signing of the EDC treaty, the SPD opposition had argued that only a fully sovereign Federal Republic could contemplate rearmament. Adenauer, who had pledged a West German military force for reasons of mutual security and as a lever for ending the restrictions imposed by the Occupation Statute, agreed to tie rearmament to the termination of the occupation. But because so much time had elapsed, he felt pressure from his supporters in the Bundestag and from public opinion to make headway with the implementation of political equality.[37] His problems were further aggravated during the summer of 1954 by upcoming state elections, by a metalworkers' strike, and by tensions between the Christian Democrats and the Free Democratic Party (FDP), a small but important coalition partner.[38] Adenauer's domestic difficulties apparently helped to persuade Dulles that it had become essential to provide for an alternative to EDC. On June 23 he told the West German ambassador that he agreed with the chancellor: the Federal Republic should not be kept waiting indefinitely for its freedom and sovereignty.[39]

Rolf Steininger has argued that the solution prepared at the London Nine-Power Conference—the Federal Republic would become a full member of NATO and had to accept armament restrictions regulated through the Western European Union (WEU)—resulted mainly from British endeavors. A caveat must be entered. As Dulles pointed out at an NSC meeting assessing the London agreements, he had "tried throughout 'to play it cagey' " and "had early taken the position that what was to be done at London was up to the European powers." Therefore he avoided "so far as possible any idea that the new settlement had been 'made in the USA.' "[40]

In fact, Dulles's activities in the weeks before and during the London conference had been greater than he claimed. He counseled British foreign secretary Eden against an early nine-power meeting

[37] Telegram from the U.S. High Commission in Bonn, May 15, 1954, *FR, 1952–1954*, 7:570, n. 3. Conant had already reported in December 1953 that the chancellor's position in the Bundestag and in his party appeared to be somewhat weakened. Conant to State Department, December 12, 1953, ibid., 563.

[38] Schwarz, *Ära Adenauer 1949–1957*, 229–39. In the Schleswig-Holstein state elections of September 1954, the CDU lost 15 percent of its vote compared to the federal elections of a year earlier.

[39] Memorandum of a conversation with Ambassador Krekeler, June 23, 1954, *FR, 1952–1954*, 7:574. The ambassador was also told that the matter would be on the agenda of the forthcoming meeting between President Eisenhower and Prime Minister Churchill. Ibid., 576.

[40] See the end of chapter 3 in this book; Memorandum of discussion at the 216th Meeting of the NSC, October 6, 1954, *FR, 1952–1954*, 5:1382–83.

and suggested advance bilateral consultations.[41] These took place not only in London but in Bonn also, allowing the chancellor to coordinate his approach with that of Dulles. Furthermore, the secretary persuaded the other Western powers to comply with Adenauer's wishes and relinquish most of their prerogatives under the Occupation Statute prior to the Federal Republic's entrance into NATO.[42]

During the ninth plenary meeting of the London Nine-Power Conference, the delegates witnessed the remarkable interplay between Dulles and Adenauer. Faced with the prospect of a French veto against West German membership in NATO, the chancellor solemnly declared his readiness to renounce the production of atomic, biological, and chemical (ABC) weapons. Dulles had known since early September that Adenauer, rather than accept limitations on rearmament imposed by the nine powers, might make a unilateral declaration of intent. After Adenauer had finished speaking, Dulles rose, walked to the opposite side of the fairly long conference table where the German delegation was seated and said: "Mr. Chancellor, you have just declared that the Federal Republic promises not to manufacture nuclear, biological or chemical weapons on its territory. I assume that you made this declaration *rebus sic stantibus*—like all binding declarations and commitments under international law." Adenauer replied: "You have interpreted my declaration correctly." The summary of the meeting prepared by the U.S. delegation simply acknowledges Adenauer's initial renunciation of the ABC weapons; it contains nothing about the melodramatic scene which followed.[43]

Two years later, when the Eisenhower administration contemplated offering tactical nuclear delivery systems to its European allies, Dulles took up the question of WEU restrictions on West German armaments. It was unlawful for Bonn to manufacture nuclear weapons, he contended, but not illegal to buy them from Washington. Of course he had only been thinking of carrier systems, not of warheads, Dulles hastened to add.[44] Still, as the 1960 proposals for a NATO nu-

[41] Dulles to Eden, September 8, 1954, *FR, 1952–1954*, 5:1155. Dulles added, significantly, that Adenauer was also opposed to an early meeting.

[42] See the report on Dulles's conversations with Adenauer and Eden (September 16–17), September 20, 1954, *FR, 1952–1954*, 5:1212–13; Memorandum of a conversation between the Assistant Secretary of State for European Affairs, Livingston T. Merchant, and Herbert Blankenhorn, German Foreign Office, September 25, 1954, ibid., 1272; Memorandum of NSC meeting, October 6, 1954, ibid., 1379.

[43] Conant to State Department, September 7, 1954, *FR, 1952–1954*, 5:1153; Adenauer, *Erinnerungen*, 2:347; Telegraphic summary of the 9th Plenary Meeting, October 3, 1954, *FR, 1952–1954*, 5:1324–25.

[44] Memorandum of a U.S.–U.K. conversation in Paris, December 11, 1956, *FR*,

clear force were to indicate, the administration was willing to concede a certain degree of nuclear sharing to the Federal Republic and other "have-nots."[45]

Nuclear sharing through NATO never materialized, though, and the Non-Proliferation Treaty of 1968 closed the loopholes in the declaration of the West German chancellor. Dulles's action at the Nine-Power Conference and the later proposals for a NATO nuclear force were significant because they illustrate that Adenauer's major long-term goal—to secure sovereignty on terms of near equality with Great Britain and France—was well understood and supported by the Eisenhower administration.[46] By interceding in Adenauer's behalf at the London conference, Dulles wanted to make clear that the restrictions the chancellor had advanced could not be interpreted as acquiescence in a permanent *status quo minus* for the Federal Republic.

Dulles's intervention during the negotiations over the final wording of the 1952 Bonn agreements, which took place in Paris during late October 1954, is another example of his sensitivity to West German concerns. His legal ingenuity helped discover the formula for Article 1: "The Federal Republic shall have . . . the full authority of a sovereign state over its internal and external affairs."[47] To experts in international law the difference between this and the earlier phrasing, which had not contained the word "sovereign," might appear negligible. But it did not to Adenauer, who still faced a battle in the Bundestag over ratification of the Bonn and Paris treaties.

At a meeting of the NSC, Dulles had called Adenauer's London declaration a "self-denying ordinance"—"the greatest single contribution in terms of statesmanship" apart from the historic British commitment to WEU. Adenauer had acted as "a true European who made real sacrifices to European principles." After the Federal Republic had been safely incorporated into the Western framework, the chancellor remained important to the American secretary of state because he alone seemed able to rekindle the flame of European integration. British participation in WEU, historic because it tied the United Kingdom more closely to the Continent, brought disadvantages, too: "By virtue of this closer tie, you bring in a country . . . which is not as

---

1955–1957, 4:125. The Atomic Energy Act of 1954 did not permit the United States to supply other nations with nuclear warheads in peacetime.

[45] On the Norstad and Bowie schemes for assigning a nuclear deterrent to NATO, see Catherine McArdle Kelleher, *Germany and the Politics of Nuclear Weapons* (New York and London, 1975), 137–43.

[46] The chancellor had disclosed his intention in an "off the record" conversation as early as June 1951. See Adenauer, *Teegespräche*, 1:93; Schwarz, *Adenauer*, 863–64.

[47] *DG*, 425; "Tea Conversation," October 25, 1954, Adenauer, *Teegespräche*, 1:560.

ready to develop the supra-national agencies," Dulles reminded the NSC. Adenauer saw things the same way.[48]

In 1956 supranational integration had gained momentum. The European Economic Community offered the "promise of opening the way to a genuine United States of Europe," Dulles wrote in a memorandum to the president. The proposed nuclear authority, EURATOM, had the additional advantage of simplifying "control over military uses of atomic energy by the six countries." Further success would tie the Federal Republic more firmly to the Western European community.[49] Dulles apparently believed that *Westbindung* remained in doubt. When formulating the U.S. position on European integration for discussions with British prime minister Eden, scheduled for the end of January, he listed as one of the three most serious obstacles the "problem of tying Germany *organically* into [the] Western Community so as to diminish [the] danger that over time a resurgent German nationalism might trade neutrality for reunification with [the] view [of] seizing [the] controlling position between East and West."[50]

Dulles's anxiety regarding the revival of "seesaw politics" continued, notwithstanding West German membership in NATO. Alliances come and go; only supranational, "organic" cooperation was irreversible. As long as the road toward an integrated community was blocked, his "grand design" fell short of success. There is no indication that Dulles flatly ruled out reunification. It depended on a global rapprochement with the Soviet Union on the control of nuclear weapons, which in itself was the prerequisite for some sort of disengagement in Europe. He also counted on a Sino-Soviet split and expressed his conviction that the communist regimes were "bound to crack," but admittedly not in the foreseeable future. Nearer to the present, he saw "a fair chance of some settlement with the Russians if we [the United States] have a firm foundation in Western Europe— but not before."[51]

Here, too, the affinity with Adenauer's thinking could hardly be greater. The chancellor often declared that a "policy of strength" (which was tantamount to a "policy of Western unity and firmness") would at some time persuade the Soviet Union to seek relief from its

---

[48] Memorandum of NSC meeting, October 6, 1954, *FR, 1952–1954*, 5:1380, 1382; Report on Dulles's conversations with Adenauer and Eden, ibid., 1212.

[49] Dulles to Eisenhower, January 9, 1956, *FR, 1955–1957*, 4:388.

[50] The other two problems were "the weakness of France" and "the solidifying of [the] new relationship between France and Germany." Dulles to the U.S. Embassy in Belgium, January 26, 1956, *FR, 1955–1957*, 4:399 (my emphasis).

[51] See chapter 2 in this book.

many burdens by cooperating with the West in making progress on the road to true disarmament and reconciliation.[52] In a background interview in 1952 he mentioned such problems facing the Kremlin as the short life expectancy, high birth rate, and the food shortage that required the diversion of rivers to irrigate steppes and deserts. After Nikita Khrushchev had told him in 1955 that economic support of China was overtaxing Soviet capabilities, Adenauer became convinced that one day Moscow would have to seek a reduction of military spending. Then reunification might be attained, or Moscow might at least permit East Germany to develop along more "liberal-democratic" lines. In a conversation with the Soviet ambassador in 1958, the chancellor proposed an "Austrian solution" for the German Democratic Republic, but cautioned the diplomat not to make the initiative public because he, Adenauer, risked being "stoned" by his own followers.[53]

Here the Achilles' heel of Adenauer's reunification policy surfaced. In his assessment of the chances for unity the chancellor was a realist, like Dulles. Unlike the secretary of state, however, he displayed an entirely unwarranted optimism combined with rhetorical revisionism in his public pronouncements on the subject. This reflected the dilemma that the only chance of finding a popular and parliamentary majority for rearmament and NATO (or EDC) membership lay in the claim that integration, rather than precluding reunification, would promote it. Certainly, given Adenauer's "policy of strength" axiom, this point might be argued. But for most West Germans—who opened their eyes to postwar realities only after the erection of the Berlin Wall—it was deceptive.

Adenauer believed he had no choice in the matter. The smaller coalition parties were openly nationalistic and the pressure groups of the refugees from the Soviet Zone and from the territories east of the Oder and Neisse Rivers could not be ignored by a CDU-led government. A majority of the electorate supported the famous "triad of values": Freedom—Peace—Unity (unity ranking last!).[54] But Ade-

[52] See Grabbe, *Unionsparteien*, 186–89, for a detailed discussion of Adenauer's "policy of strength."

[53] Conversation with the editor of *The Times* (London), June 3, 1952; Adenauer, *Teegespräche*, 1:301; Adenauer, *Erinnerungen*, 2:527–28 and 3:378. Adenauer's belief in the inevitability of a Sino-Soviet split derived from reading Wilhelm Starlinger, *Grenzen der Sowjetmacht* (Würzburg, 1955). Starlinger was a physician who had served as director of a hospital in Königsberg (now Kaliningrad), East Prussia, until 1947. He subsequently spent several years in a Soviet prison camp. Ambassador Grewe thinks that Starlinger's theses and the fact that Adenauer was impressed by them may have come to Khrushchev's notice. Grewe, *Rückblenden*, 634–35.

[54] See Grabbe, *Unionsparteien*, 320.

nauer suspected that the voters would desert him and withdraw their endorsement of his pro-Western policy if they realized how dim were the prospects of their achieving their national aspirations. This assessment may not have been correct; however, the CDU/CSU assumed it was and preserved the essence of the Adenauer policy until the 1970s.

In Article 7 of the Convention on Relations (the revised Bonn treaty of 1952), signed in Paris on October 23, 1954, the United States, the United Kingdom, and the French Republic declared that a freely negotiated peace settlement for Germany was "an essential aim of their common policy"; that the final determination of the boundaries must await such a settlement; and that they would "cooperate to achieve, by peaceful means, their common aim of a reunified Germany enjoying a liberal-democratic constitution, like that of the Federal Republic, and integrated within the European community." At the London Nine-Power Conference the allies had declared that they considered the government in Bonn "the only German Government freely and legitimately constituted and therefore entitled to speak for Germany as the representative of the German people in international affairs."[55]

In a strictly legal sense these obligations were carried out until Chancellor Willy Brandt, in the early 1970s, redefined the national goals of the Federal Republic. However, as U.S. ambassador to the Soviet Union, Charles Bohlen, wrote, the Geneva summit of July 1955, and the foreign ministers' meeting that followed, "represented the final effort on the part of the West to reunify Germany under conditions that would safeguard the rest of Europe from any renewal of German militarism."[56] Thereafter, the primary value of the Western commitment to reunification was that it provided Bonn with the means to prevent an open consolidation of the European status quo at Germany's expense and to influence talks and negotiations with the Soviet Union that could have a bearing on the "German question."[57]

When arms control was placed on the international agenda in the summer of 1955, the West German foreign office tried to thrust the *Junktim*, or nexus, between arms control and the "German question" upon the reluctant allies: no progress regarding the former without corresponding headway concerning the latter. What the Western powers accepted until the Geneva conference of 1959, where reuni-

---

[55] *DG*, 427–28, 423.

[56] Charles E. Bohlen, *Witness to History, 1929–1969* (London, 1973), 386–87.

[57] Grewe, *Rückblenden*, 213.

fication appeared for the last time as an issue of East–West negotiations, was spelled out in the Berlin Declaration of July 29, 1957:

> The reunification of Germany accompanied by the conclusion of European security arrangements would facilitate the achievement of a comprehensive disarmament agreement. Conversely, if a beginning could be made toward effective measures of partial disarmament, this would contribute to the settlement of outstanding major political problems such as the reunification of Germany. Initial steps in the field of disarmament should lead to a comprehensive disarmament agreement which presupposes a prior solution of the problem of German reunification. The Western Powers do not intend to enter into any agreement on disarmament which would prejudice the reunification of Germany.[58]

A "beginning" could be made toward disarmament without prior or parallel negotiations on German unity. "Initial steps" in the field were possible; comprehensive agreements, however, must at a minimum be preceded by an accord on the procedure for reunification. As the wording indicates, Adenauer had accepted that he could not stand in the way of arms control talks, but he remained adamantly opposed to broader concepts that implied that West Germany's ties to the West would be loosened and its freedom of action impeded. The success of this strategy resulted in part from a well-rehearsed game plan with Dulles.

Scholars have argued that American support for Adenauer's reunification policy in the 1950s prevented an early breakthrough toward détente. The Eisenhower administration, Robert Divine claims, may have missed "a genuine opportunity" immediately following Stalin's death. "[I]n the issue of German rearmament," he continues, "the Western powers had a valuable consideration to exploit in any bargain with the Russians." Divine blames Dulles's "unshakable suspicion" of the Soviet leaders together with "domestic constraints" in the United states for preventing a "more creative diplomacy."[59]

Divine thus slights the possibility that bargaining away rearmament would have led to the fall of the Adenauer government and thereby demolish the "new house of Europe" that the Truman and Eisenhower administrations had struggled to build. Still, to policymakers in Washington, prudence dictated considering alternatives. These were already implicit in NSC 160/1 of August 1953: American military disengagement from West Germany involved "the risk of major dislocations in present U.S. and NATO plans"; it must take into account

---

[58] Declaration on German Reunification, July 29, 1957, *DG*, 511.
[59] Robert Divine, *Eisenhower and the Cold War* (New York, 1981), 109–10.

"the difficulty of finding places in Europe for stationing troops" and "the possible impact of U.S. troop withdrawal from Germany upon European opinion." This type of contingency planning was typical of the administration's national security policymaking. However, it was also pointed out that proper allowance had to be made for "current U.S. atomic superiority." In this light it was significant that an earlier draft of the paper had only contained a reference to "some dislocations" in the event of troop withdrawal.[60]

About two weeks after Eisenhower approved the policy statement, Dulles proposed a "broad zone of restricted armament in Europe." The Red Army would withdraw behind Soviet borders and U.S. forces across the Atlantic. NATO and German forces, presumably reduced in numbers compared with pre–"New Look" planning, would remain.[61] Almost simultaneously a similar idea came from Adenauer. A group of experts had drawn up a plan for a demilitarized zone on both sides of the Oder and Neisse Rivers, encompassing Poland to the Vistula and all of East Germany. West Germany would be garrisoned by EDC troops, Western Europe by NATO troops, and Eastern Europe to the east of the Vistula line by "Satellite" forces. Again the Red Army was to be sent home, but the fate of U.S. forces in Europe was not clearly spelled out.[62]

This concept, the nucleus of the Heusinger Plan of 1955,[63] attempted to square the circle by reconciling reunification, the continuance of NATO, and the security interests of the Soviet Union. For Adenauer it was a tactical device, primarily designed to forestall American and British ideas concerning the neutralization of Germany. In his opinion the various disengagement schemes offered nothing but disadvantages. They would lead to the erosion of NATO because the American troops in Germany would have to be removed. The West Germans would certainly draw nearer to the Soviet Union and equidistance would replace the mutually fruitful alignment with the West. Disengagement could bring no security, as a military vacuum in the neighborhood of the Soviet Union was inherently perilous. The status gains of the Federal Republic vis-à-vis France and Great Britain would be irreclaimably lost, because all proposals limited the demilitarized or denuclearized area in the West to the territory of the Federal Republic. Finally, the still-nascent Western Euro-

[60] Nsc 160/1, *FR, 1952–1954*, 7:518.

[61] Dulles memorandum, September 6, 1953, *FR, 1952–1954*, 2:459.

[62] Conant to State Department, September 16, 1953, *FR, 1952–1954*, 5:806. It was specified later that U.S. strategic air bases in Great Britain and Spain might remain.

[63] See Helga Haftendorn, *Sicherheit und Entspannung: Zur Aussenpolitik der Bundesrepublik Deutschland 1955–1982* (Baden-Baden, 1986), 81–83.

pean community would be doomed, and the price Adenauer had paid for his pro-Western stance would have been paid in vain.[64]

Dulles, however, appears to have been more serious then the chancellor. The planning for a mutual troop withdrawal in Europe was pursued both in the State Department and the White House. Not made public immediately because it seemed dangerous to give up forward bases without progress regarding the control of nuclear weapons, the idea surfaced again in the spring of 1955. President Eisenhower, delighted with the completion of the Austrian State Treaty, promoted the idea of a "neutral belt" in Central Europe and stated his belief, almost inviting misunderstanding, that neutrality of the Austrian or Swiss type had nothing to do with a military vacuum.[65]

Adenauer was horrified, prompting Dulles to explain that "the view of the United States that a policy of neutrality has no application to a country of the character of Germany."[66] During a meeting with the U.S. chiefs of mission in Western Europe in May 1957, the secretary of state interpreted the American position regarding disengagement: The U.S. government did not favor "any plan which takes as its premise the present division of Germany, nor do we favor a plan which particularly would manifest itself by displacing American forces from Germany. The Soviets can go back gradually and we can't. It is all or nothing with us. For both of those reasons we are not sympathetic toward it."[67]

Although reassured by Dulles, Adenauer worried that the administration continued to harbor schemes for neutralization or regional arms control. And in fact, Washington's planning for aerial inspection zones in sensitive areas of the Northern Hemisphere and for mutual, balanced force reductions had resulted in detailed proposals.[68] At a news conference on May 14, 1957, Dulles admitted that a plan for regional arms control in Europe existed, but expressed reservations: it would have to be worked out in cooperation with NATO

---

[64] Adenauer, *Erinnerungen*, 2:446; Grabbe, *Unionsparteien*, 231–32.

[65] Adenauer, *Erinnerungen*, 2:443–44.

[66] Dulles press conference remarks, May 24, 1955, *DG*, 448. The secretary of state added: "It is all well to talk about neutrality for a country such as Austria, a small country with 7 million people. But I do not believe that anybody realistically believes that the German people, 70-odd million of them, are destined to play the role of a neutral country." See also Adenauer, *Erinnerungen*, 2:444.

[67] Minutes of the Western European chiefs of mission conference, Paris, May 6, 1957, *FR, 1955–1957*, 4:586.

[68] See John Foster Dulles, "Challenge and Response in U.S. Foreign Policy," *Foreign Affairs* 36 (October 1957): 25–43. The so-called Radford Plan of 1956 called for an 800,000-man reduction in U.S. troop levels over the next four years. See Kelleher, *Germany and the Politics of Nuclear Weapons*, 44–59.

and the Federal Republic; there were bound to be complications; and it might be that Europe was "not the best place to start because of the complications." Adenauer's views would carry "a great deal of weight" in this context.[69]

The chancellor concluded that Dulles's press conference reflected differences between Eisenhower and his secretary of state; the president had wholeheartedly endorsed regional arms control a few days earlier.[70] Adenauer thought he understood their "division of labor." He had witnessed it during his 1953 visit to Washington, when Eisenhower and Dulles explained American views regarding Soviet behavior: the "former expressing [the] hope that as [a] result [of] new developments, [the United States] may succeed in lessening some of the world's tensions and burdens," and the latter emphasizing the necessity to continue with strong, constructive policies. Settlements with the Soviets could "best be obtained through strength."[71] Adenauer realized that Dulles's political effectiveness depended on his unswerving loyalty to the president. He believed that the secretary of state occasionally had to make statements against his better judgment. Nevertheless, to Adenauer's way of thinking Dulles had often drawn Eisenhower back to the path of virtue. The chancellor flattered himself by assuming that he had a hand in this.[72]

Adenauer put little faith in the president's ability to get the true measure of the Soviet leaders. Early in 1958 he told columnist Joseph Alsop: "You see, President Eisenhower was a soldier; he is an honest, simple, straightforward character. Khrushchev is a liar, a robber, a man who has no moral commitments. And Eisenhower, whom I know quite well, believes . . . that Khrushchev is a decent guy."[73] In fact, Adenauer did not know Eisenhower well and his "character study" was mere conjecture, based on the president's public championing of détente and his faith in summit meetings, which neither Adenauer nor Dulles shared.

Adenauer's belief, mistaken as it was, that Dulles was responsible for ensuring that Washington's policy remained realistic evidently af-

---

[69] U.S. Senate Committee on Foreign Relations (SCFR), *Documents on Germany, 1944–1961*, 87th Cong., 1st sess. (Washington, 1961), 237.

[70] Adenauer, *Erinnerungen*, 3:306.

[71] Dulles to Conant, April 8, 1953, *FR, 1952–1954*, 5:786.

[72] Dieter Oberndörfer, "John Foster Dulles und Konrad Adenauer," in Dieter Blumenwitz, Klaus Gotto, Hans Maier, Konrad Repgen, and Hans-Peter Schwarz, eds., *Konrad Adenauer und seine Zeit.* Vol. 2: *Beiträge der Wissenschaft* (Stuttgart, 1976), 232–33.

[73] Adenauer, *Teegespräche*, 2:255. This assessment of Eisenhower was rather commonplace in Bonn. See Hans-Jürgen Grabbe, "Das Amerikabild Konrad Adenauers," *Amerikastudien/American Studies* 31 (1986): 315–23.

fected the chancellor's personal career decisions. Christian A. Herter, who succeeded Dulles as secretary of state, was, as Adenauer patronizingly declared, "a good man, certainly." But Dulles had been "the most intimate friend of President Eisenhower, with whom he [Dulles] was in complete accord." The prospect of having Eisenhower and Herter determine American foreign policy even contributed to a spectacular about-face: In April 1959 Adenauer had announced his intention to step down and become a candidate for the ceremonial office of federal president. He came to regret it, mainly because the CDU/CSU would not support his candidate for the succession. The chancellor claimed that he decided to continue at the helm of the Federal Republic at Dulles's funeral in May. Now that Dulles was no longer alive, Adenauer explained, his own influence on the Western powers had become even more important.[74]

This statement might seem surprising. Had not Dulles, after the outbreak of the 1958 Berlin crisis, indicated American readiness to recognize East German officials as "agents of the Soviet Union"? Had he not also acknowledged that "reunification by free elections," the agreed-upon formula, might not be the only method available?[75] Both pronouncements—though logical and not very remarkable—created a stir and were seen as evidence of a rift between Dulles and Adenauer.

Such a rift did not exist. The secretary meant to issue a warning that a more flexible approach to East–West negotiations was imperative. Khrushchev had, after all, issued a "Berlin ultimatum" on November 27, 1958, demanding that West Berlin be transformed into an "independent political unit" and threatening unilaterally to revoke four-power rights if no agreement was reached within six months.[76] Dulles saw this as one of the "probing operations" that he expected since the Soviet Union had gained strategic parity—"now that we are all under the guns so to speak." These challenges must be dealt with firmly, but under the awesome responsibilities dictated by the "balance of terror," one had to concentrate on essentials.[77]

For Adenauer the essentials were a continued American presence,

---

[74] Memorandum of a confidential discussion with selected newspaper writers, June 12, 1959, printed in Jürgen Küsters, "Kanzler in der Krise: Journalistenberichte über Adenauers Hintergrundgespräche zwischen Berlin-Ultimatum und Bundespräsidentenwahl 1959," *Vierteljahrshefte für Zeitgeschichte* 36 (1988): 767.

[75] See news conferences of November 26, 1958, and January 13, 1959, SCFR, *Documents on Germany, 1944–1961*, 344, 406.

[76] Extracts of the Soviet note are printed in *DG*, 552–59. See also Jack M. Schick, *The Berlin Crisis: 1958 to 1962* (Philadelphia, 1971).

[77] Memorandum of a conversation at the British Embassy in Paris, December 14, 1957, *FR, 1955–1957*, 4:228.

preferably within the NATO framework, and European supranational cooperation. Issues such as the demilitarization of Berlin under UN auspices, or de facto recognition of the German Democratic Republic and de jure recognition of the other Warsaw Pact countries, were either incorporated as concessions in the secret papers that the *Bundeskanzleramt* (chancellor's office) drew up or regarded as possible developments compelling acquiescence if war were to be averted. Adenauer intended to be prepared for all eventualities but hoped to avoid making these concessions because he was, on the one hand, counting on the intransigence of the Soviet Union and, on the other, on the vigilance and alliance-consciousness of the secretary of state. A similar confidence in Eisenhower and Herter did not develop.[78]

Only once, in 1956, had genuine irritation plagued the Adenauer–Dulles relationship. Proposals calling for a substantial reduction in U.S. Army manpower (the Radford plan) had rekindled Adenauer's old fear of an American withdrawal from Europe. The redefinition of strategy inherent in the New Look seemed to depreciate the value of the nascent *Bundeswehr*, reducing it to the kind of "trip-wire" function envisaged by the JCS during the first stage of the Eisenhower administration's defense planning.[79] Adenauer was furious because he believed that Dulles had deliberately left him in the dark regarding the impending force reductions. But Adenauer was wrong. It was Dulles who showed the greatest concern for and understanding of the situation in the Federal Republic: "It was one thing," he told Eisenhower, "for [the United States] to rely on the new look, not being subject to insurrectionary or conventional attack as the Europeans are, and it is something else to propose it for the Europeans."[80]

The "Carte Blanche" war games of June 1955, which simulated the explosion of 335 nuclear devices on West German soil, had led to an estimate of 1.7 million killed and 3.5 million incapacitated.[81] There-

[78] See Schwarz, *Ära Adenauer 1957–1963*, 85–87; Krone, "Aufzeichnungen," 149–52; see also Adenauer, *Erinnerungen*, 3:538, 4:24–25.

[79] General Omar Bradley had argued in January 1953 that twelve West German divisions would force the Eastern troops to "concentrate," to have a "considerable build-up before they could attack." *Bundeswehr* participation would make it certain that the United States was given warning, because it lacked sufficient nuclear weapons "to plaster all of Europe." See Memorandum of discussion, January 28, 1953, *FR, 1952–1954*, 5:714. For the deliberations of 1956 see *FR, 1955–1957*, 4:89–102; Kelleher, *Germany and Nuclear Weapons*, 44–59.

[80] Grabbe, *Unionsparteien*, 199–200; Memorandum of a conference with the President, October 2, 1956, *FR, 1955–1957*, 4:101.

[81] For "Carte Blanche" and the West German debate on strategy, see James L. Richardson, *Germany and the Atlantic Alliance* (Cambridge, Mass., 1966), 39–48; Kelleher,

after, political support for the strategy of "massive retaliation" and confidence in the continuing value of large ground forces dwindled. Franz-Josef Strauss, the new defense minister, reduced the conscription period from eighteen to twelve months and cut down the ceiling for West German army strength from five hundred thousand to three hundred fifty thousand men. Dulles, however, underscored the continued importance of NATO's conventional strength in the nuclear age: "We must have a measure of flexibility although our main reliance must be on atomic weapons in the event of a major attack."[82] The Eisenhower administration was already modifying its emphasis on "massive retaliation," and Adenauer quickly reconciled himself to the new concept of "graduated deterrence," in particular since the *Bundeswehr* was going to be equipped with nuclear carrier devices.[83]

The crises in Egypt, Iraq, and Lebanon, which paralleled the strategy debate, did not directly affect the Federal Republic. The repercussions were nevertheless felt. NATO, as Adenauer saw it, had malfunctioned; the United States had brought the alliance to the brink of war without having consulted with its allies. Furthermore, American troops had been sent to the Middle East from bases in West Germany without Bonn's prior notice or consent.[84] When the chancellor dispatched special envoys to protest the administration's behavior, Dulles responded with a stern lecture on American leadership: "We are not asking for a blank check from our NATO partners but . . . if we wait in all cases to consult them before reacting to Soviet maneuvers the opportunity to make a riposte might vanish." Adenauer gave in gracefully: "I should like to assure you now," he wrote to Dulles, "that I share fully your concern about the necessity of mutual confidence," signing the letter: "With best wishes, as ever, your faithful Adenauer."[85]

To the last, "mutual confidence" in the Adenauer–Dulles relationship was qualified by the awareness that complete convergence of political interests was unlikely and conflicting assessments of the respective national interests could never be ruled out. Adenauer was to

---

Germany and Nuclear Weapons, 34–43; and Mark Cioc, *Pax Atomica: The Nuclear Defense Debate in West Germany during the Adenauer Era* (New York, 1988), 29–31.

[82] Memorandum of a U.S.–U.K. conversation, December 11, 1956, *FR, 1955–1957*, 4:125. See also Dulles's memorandum for Eisenhower, October 1, 1956, ibid., 97.

[83] Grabbe, *Unionsparteien*, 204, 266–68. NATO's emphasis on nuclear weapons was formalized with the approval of MC-14/2 in December 1956.

[84] Bruce to State Department, November 19, 1957, *FR, 1955–1957*, 4:186–87; Adenauer to Dulles, November 18, 1957, ibid., 187–88.

[85] Memorandum of a conversation between Dulles, Foreign Minister von Brentano and Ambassadors Blankenhorn and Krekeler, November 23, 1957, *FR, 1955–1957*, 4:192; Adenauer to Dulles, December 5, 1957, ibid., 213–14.

repeat time and again in governmental and party circles that Dulles had explained during his 1953 visit to Bonn that the U.S. government was pursuing neither a French nor a German, but an American policy.[86] Still, the chancellor believed that the secretary of state could be trusted to avert rash sacrifices of the Federal Republic's interests.[87]

In volumes two and three of his memoirs, written during 1965 and 1966, Adenauer sang Dulles's praises. This was a time when U.S. troop withdrawals from West Germany, prompted by the war in Vietnam, had rekindled the fear of an American military disengagement, and when the continuing détente process had prompted apprehension of a U.S.-Soviet condominium over Europe. On August 17, 1965, the American draft for a nonproliferation treaty was made public, and Adenauer, now in his ninetieth year, delivered an anti-American harangue against what he termed a "Morgenthau plan squared." The speech included the cryptic remark that there were "good Americans and other Americans"; Dulles had belonged to the former group. The tale of his friendship with the secretary of state, on which he was then working almost daily, was no doubt both influenced by these developments of the mid-1960s and designed to influence German-American relations.[88]

Only during the final months of Dulles's life is there evidence that a genuinely private relationship apart from the political association appears to have developed between the two men. While on his deathbed, Dulles asked his brother Allen to inform the chancellor about the nature of his illness and to tell him that he had not been aware that his cancer had recurred when he denied suffering from the disease when his health was discussed during the last visit to Bonn in early February 1959. Dulles wanted to make certain that Adenauer did not feel deceived.[89]

[86] See for instance Adenauer's remarks at a CDU executive committee meeting, March 11, 1953, Buchstab, *Adenauer*, 431, and at the Industrieklub Düsseldorf, June 23, 1964, printed in Konrad Adenauer, *Reden 1917–1967: Eine Auswahl*, ed. by Hans-Peter Schwarz (Stuttgart, 1975): 459–70.

[87] In this Adenauer was probably not mistaken, as one can infer from Dulles's behavior during the 1956 Anglo-American talks on defense expenditures and allied forces in West Germany, and his reminder during the 1957 consultations with the British government on Soviet disarmament proposals "not to treat Germany different [*sic*] from the rest of the allies." Memorandum of U.S.–U.K. conversation, Paris, December 11, 1956, *FR, 1955–1957*, 4:123–133; Memorandum of conversation, Paris, December 14, 1957, ibid., 228.

[88] Adenauer's account of Dulles's *"rebus sic stantibus* intervention" at the Nine Power Conference of 1954, for which apparently no other evidence exists, is a case in point. See Grabbe, *Unionsparteien*, 454, 499, 505–6, 510.

[89] Adenauer, *Erinnerungen*, 3:477.

As has been pointed out, the Adenauer–Dulles cooperation was based on similarities in outlook, and most of the normal ingredients of friendship were lacking. Both statesmen believed that the high offices that they held precluded the requisite closeness and trust of a personal friendship. What was known about each other's personality could even serve as an operational tool in their diplomacy: the Adenauer–Dulles correspondence shows that both, if they found it expedient, catered to and thus exploited the ideas, inclinations, prejudices, and phobias of the other. And yet, as Lucius D. Clay wrote in a contribution commemorating Adenauer's one-hundredth birthday, when Dulles died the era of "personal diplomacy" in German-American relations also passed away.[90] Dulles, who represented the stronger partner in the German-American relationship, showed a remarkable—in a sense "personal"—sensitivity to the concerns of the politically vulnerable, insecure Federal Republic. The skillful management of this still fragile, difficult relationship is one of his lasting achievements.

. . .

The author would like to thank Roger Daniels (University of Cincinnati) and Richard Immerman for their frank comments that much improved the manuscript.

[90] Lucius D. Clay, "Adenauers Verhältnis zu den Amerikanern und die deutsch-amerikanischen Beziehungen nach 1945," in Dieter Blumenwitz, et al., eds., *Konrad Adenauer und seine Zeit.* Vol. 1: *Beiträge von Weg- und Zeitgenossen* (Stuttgart, 1976), 473–74.

CHAPTER 5

Dulles, Suez, and the British

Wm. Roger Louis

"WE MUST NEVER FORGET," Anthony Eden, the British prime minister, wrote in October 1956, "that [John Foster] Dulles' purpose is different from ours."[1] To Eden the difference could be summed up in two words: "Suez Canal," the artery of the British Empire that was critical to Britain's survival but "in no sense vital to the United States." Dulles's "game," as it appeared to Eden, was "to string us along" for reasons of American politics and now allow the Suez crisis to become an issue in the presidential election of 1956.[2] Thus there was a question of motive as well as perception of national interest. Eden and other prominent British leaders believed that Dulles deliberately misled them. The phrases "up the garden path," "dishonest," and "double cross" characterized British thought of the time, and the interpretation of Dulles as a devious politician has persisted. Dulles not only managed to poison Anglo-American relations but also, according to the extreme judgment of the time, bears the responsibility for the catastrophe of Suez.[3]

Yet there was another British view, less dominant but equally significant, which held that Dulles was an honorable man who differed from the British only in tactics. Sir Roger Makins, the British ambassador in Washington, wrote during the early part of the Suez crisis: "We agree about the substance of the policy, but differ on method and timing."[4] This interpretation held that the "special relationship" between the British and Americans had more than a symbolic meaning, and that Anglo-American friendship would ultimately survive the Suez crisis. These two views had one element in common. The issue of "anticolonialism" exacerbated the situation. "I have noticed

[1] Eden to Selwyn Lloyd, "Top Secret," October 6, 1956, PRO, PREM, 11/1102.

[2] Eden to Selwyn Lloyd, "Top Secret," October 6, 1956, PRO, PREM, 11/1102.

[3] "Dulles has sometimes been saddled with the whole blame for Suez, and it is certainly hard to believe . . . that he was merely unconsciously rude." Hugh Thomas, *The Suez Affair* (London, 1986 edition), 174.

[4] "We press for immediate action," Makins wrote, "while the Americans are inclined to move with greater phlegm and deliberation. This is the opposite of what our natural temperaments are supposed to be." Makins to Lloyd, "Emergency Top Secret," September 9, 1956, PRO, FO 800/740.

before," Makins commented, "this deep seated feeling about colonialism, which is common to so many Americans, occasionally welling up inside Foster [Dulles] like lava in a dormant volcano."[5]

During the Suez crisis the British were caught off guard by Dulles's volcanic sentiments about European colonialism. Anthony Eden himself went so far as to describe Dulles's attitude as "dishonest."[6] Several questions arise from this harsh judgment. Did it only reflect the heat of the moment, a time when Eden's anger interfered with his discernment? For at least two years previously there had been friction between the two men. "[T]here is no doubt that Dulles and A.E. have got thoroughly on each other's nerves," wrote Sir Evelyn Shuckburgh (Eden's private secretary) during the Indochina crisis of 1954, "and are both behaving rather like prima donnas."[7] Did their clash in temperament, and their differences in background and training, merely intensify the disagreement over issues of substance, or was there an unbridgeable gap in intent? How accurate was Eden's perception of the relationship between Dulles and Eisenhower? For that matter, how well did Dulles understand the British? Was there a misperception of motive or a conflict of purpose? What do recently released records reveal about one of Dulles's most acute dilemmas, in which he was caught between the expectations of the European allies and the nationalist aspirations of the non-European world? Perhaps most important of all, how should the historian assess Dulles as a statesman attempting to resolve these issues? The opening of the British archives at the Public Record Office in London affords the opportunity for a reconsideration of those questions.

This reinterpretation also derives from access to the Eisenhower papers at the Presidential Library in Abilene, Kansas, and the Dulles papers at the Seeley G. Mudd Manuscript Library at Princeton University.[8] These collections reveal an Eisenhower at variance with his public image in America, and even more with the predominant view of him in Britain, that portrayed the wartime hero as a benign, slightly incoherent soldier-president somewhat out of his element. Eisenhower cultivated that image. In fact he was highly intelligent,

[5] Makins to Eden, "Secret and Personal," October 4, 1956, PRO, PREM, 11/1174.

[6] Eden's minute on Makins to Eden, October 4, 1956, PRO, PREM, 11/1174.

[7] Evelyn Shuckburgh, *Descent to Suez: Diaries 1951–1956* (London, 1986), 186.

[8] In an essay entitled "Eisenhower, Dulles, and the Suez Crisis," Robert R. Bowie has examined unpublished American sources (in *Suez 1956: The Crisis and Its Consequences*, edited by W. R. Louis and Roger Owen (New York, 1989). I am in general agreement with this fundamental reappraisal. For the present chapter I have reviewed material in the Dulles and Eisenhower papers. Nevertheless, in order not to overlap too much with Bowie's analysis, I have concentrated on British sources.

hardworking, and decisive. He had a keen sense of his own historical reputation, and he guarded it on all flanks. He had a genius for avoiding confrontation. His secretary of state was his stalking-horse. Dulles's dramatic language went down well with the right wing of the Republican party. The American public could understand his Manichaean vision of the Soviet Union as an evil government of communist tyranny and the United States as the land of freedom and constructive capitalism. As a corrective to ideological interpretation, was there an underlying consistency of actual policy applied to specific events? If so, who controlled it—Eisenhower or Dulles?

In the case of Suez the emphatic answer to the latter question is Eisenhower. It was Eisenhower who blocked the British and French and who, coincidentally, forced the Israelis to draw back, thus momentarily reversing the pro-Zionist thrust of American policy. Eisenhower was unalterably opposed to the invasion of Egypt. No doubt one of his motives was to keep the world's attention on the Soviet suppression of the Hungarian revolution. But above all he did not wish to antagonize nationalist sentiment in the Middle East, Asia, and Africa. He did not want to be associated in any way with the antiquated system of British and French colonialism that the United States, in his view, had historic reason to oppose. He also believed that Britain and France no longer possessed the economic or military resources to dominate the Middle East. Inevitably the United States would have to play an increasing part in Middle Eastern affairs, and Eisenhower was determined not to be tarred by association with the British and French at Suez.

What then of Dulles? He agreed in principle and in detail with Eisenhower. Their views were virtually identical. The two of them consulted closely on every issue, and there was indeed an underlying consistency of principle. But Dulles in every sense was the executor of the policy set by Eisenhower, even though he emerges from his secret correspondence and conversations as more passionately anticolonial than Eisenhower. This of course was the popular perception at the time. But one aspect was not apparent: it served Eisenhower's purpose to use Dulles as his lightning rod. Eisenhower wished to keep on good terms with the British government, though privately he was contemptuous of the British claim to be a "world power." He expected Dulles not only to oppose colonialism but also to support Britain and France as the oldest and most valued allies of the United States. Here was a challenge that tested even Dulles's intellectual agility and tore him emotionally.

We can now view the events of the 1950s from the perspective of three decades. Certain problems that faced Dulles are now much clearer than they were to contemporary observers. Two of these are the "Palestine question," as it was called at the time, and the Baghdad Pact, which was conceived as an instrument of Western security in the Middle East. Dulles found himself mainly in agreement with the British over Palestine, but not in accord with them over the defense issue. It is useful briefly to study these two problems as part of the general background to the Suez crisis because they reveal Dulles's method as well as his aims, and because they establish his attitude toward the Arabs and the Israelis as well as toward the British and the French. His pessimistic view of Russian intent was consistent, but his general outlook was nuanced and by no means as unsubtle as some of his own rhetoric suggests.

Dulles was much less in sympathy with Zionist aims than he wished to state in public. His attitude toward Israel probably explains part of the reason for the vitriolic treatment in Herman Finer's indispensable but unbalanced work, *Dulles over Suez*. Writing in 1964, and having thus accumulated his evidence when emotions about the Suez crisis had by no means subsided, Finer had read voluminously and had conducted extensive interviews but had only scant access to archival data. He believed that Dulles's "Wilsonian missionary passion," together with his characteristic determination to be evenhanded, caused him to attach too much significance to the Arab cause. Dulles's inflated assessment of Arab nationalism led him to betray the Israelis and his European allies, the British, and the French. In turn, according to Finer, Dulles jeopardized the Western position in the Middle East by giving advantage to the Soviet Union.[9] What Finer had no way of knowing was that Dulles had played a leading part in the effort for a comprehensive settlement between the Israelis and the Arabs. From Dulles's own point of view in 1956, the British had betrayed their own principles and the Israelis themselves had shattered the prospects of a lasting peace beyond repair. This explains in part what he meant when he stated emphatically during the Suez crisis that "what the British and French had done was nothing but the straight old-fashioned variety of colonialism of the most obvious sort."[10] As will be seen, Dulles expected as much from the French. From the British, however, this was a breach of good faith.

The plan for a comprehensive settlement between the Israelis and the Arabs was known as "Project Alpha." The full records of this ven-

[9] Herman Finer, *Dulles over Suez: The Theory and Practice of His Diplomacy* (Chicago, 1964).

[10] Memorandum of NSC meeting, November 1, 1956, NSCS, AWF.

ture are now accessible in London but not in Washington.[11] They reveal a determined effort by the State Department and Foreign Office from late 1954 to solve the refugee problem by resettlement, mainly in Arab countries. The United States would bear most of the cost of indemnity and repatriation. There would also be a territorial adjustment, which would include a revision of the frontiers to allow direct land communication between Egypt and Jordan. The purpose was to redress one of the principal Arab grievances of the 1948–1949 war. The new boundaries would be guaranteed by both the United States and Britain. The Israelis would have to make concessions in the southern part of Israel, the Negev. In the view of the principal British architect of the scheme, Evelyn Shuckburgh, Israel's blocking of this solution led to the failure of the project. Egypt gave it one of the final blows in March 1956, but Israeli resistance to altering the frontiers was, in Shuckburgh's judgment, the fundamental reason why the scheme came to nothing.

During the latter stage of Eden's tenure as foreign secretary, Shuckburgh served as his private secretary. In late 1954 Shuckburgh took charge of the Middle Eastern policy of the Foreign Office as assistant under secretary, a position of key responsibility. He never believed that the Alpha plan had much chance of success, but his minutes reveal that whatever hope it had depended on Israeli willingness to arrive at a compromise between the boundaries proposed by the UN in 1947 and those established after the Israeli victories in the 1948–1949 war. In retrospect the assumption was extravagant. But Dulles himself believed that some form of Israeli retreat from the 1949 armistice boundaries would be an essential ingredient of the settlement. On that point there was concurrence between the British and Americans. "On the subject of Palestine," Shuckburgh summed up later, "Eden and Dulles at this time saw eye to eye."[12]

Shuckburgh has recently published his diaries under the title *Descent to Suez*. They are an invaluable source for the study of Dulles in the mid-1950s not merely because of the detail about British and American policies in the Middle East and other conflict-ridden regions but also because of the fair-minded portrayal of Dulles. Here is an example of a British official upholding the views that Dulles did not, until Suez, view British and American policies as fundamentally incompatible. Misunderstanding and mutual irritation, much more

[11] And in Jerusalem but not in Cairo. I have benefited from reading an essay that fully utilizes Israeli as well as British sources: Shimon Shamir, "The Collapse of Project Alpha and the End of the Secret-Diplomacy Phase of the Search for an Egyptian-Israeli Settlement," in Louis and Owen, eds., *Suez 1956*.

[12] Shuckburgh, *Descent to Suez*, 242.

than suspicion, characterized the relations between Dulles and Eden. Shuckburgh himself regarded Dulles as a methodical man of sound judgment. "I had a sort of allegiance to Dulles . . . ," he wrote, "and I had considerable respect for him. The trouble, so far as his [Dulles's] relations with Eden were concerned, was that the temper of his mind was entirely out of harmony with Eden's."[13]

Shuckburgh and other British officials knew that on the Middle East Dulles's views were virtually identical with Eisenhower's, above all on the Palestine question. Eisenhower once said privately at a Jewish convention in 1954: "I don't know what I would have done had I been President when the question of Israel's independence came up . . . but Israel is now a sovereign nation to which we have obligations. We shall keep them."[14] Like Eisenhower, Dulles dwelt not on historical controversies about the creation of the State of Israel but rather on the problems to be resolved between Israel and the Arab states. Each nation would have to make sacrifices and commitments, including the United States. Dulles was willing for the American government to guarantee Israel's security as part of the general settlement— but after, and not before, agreement was reached with the Arab states as well. He was explicit on this point: "[T]here should be no question of giving the Israelis the guarantee . . . ahead of and apart from a general settlement."[15] In July 1955 Dulles explained to the British the reasons why the plan should be publicly announced, the sooner the better. According to Shuckburgh's diary, which reveals relief about Dulles's determined attitude in the face of Jewish pressure in America:

> It is not, as I feared, that D. is weakening on the "Alpha" demand for sacrifices from Israel, or is contemplating any abandonment of the position that Israel can only have a US guarantee after the settlement.
>
> His point is that only by getting the US Government publicly committed to this policy now can he insure himself against being compelled later on, in the atmosphere of US elections, to make a much more pro-Israeli stand. . . . There is a lot of force in this.[16]

Harold Macmillan, Eden's foreign secretary in 1955, wrote of Dulles's motives for wishing to make a public statement on the Palestine problem:

[13] Shuckburgh, *Descent to Suez*, 23.
[14] Quoted in Finer, *Dulles over Suez*, 13–14.
[15] "Record of Conversation . . . Alpha," May 12, 1955, PRO, FO, 800/678.
[16] Shuckburgh, *Descent to Suez*, 266.

I am convinced that Dulles has impelling internal political reasons. . . . The thing has risks, particularly from our point of view. But the situation in which we would find ourselves if, at a later date, the U.S. Administration were compelled by Jewish pressure and electoral considerations to move over towards a more obviously pro-Israeli policy, would be even more dangerous.[17]

The British thus understood Dulles's purpose. He was clearly a moving force behind the comprehensive settlement, despite the domestic opposition he was certain to encounter. If the plan succeeded he would attempt to move the United States into the Baghdad Pact.[18]

Here then was Dulles's grand strategy: a settlement between Israel and the Arab states on the refugee question, and a territorial adjustment backed by the United States and Britain. The ground would thus be prepared for an effective alliance system in the Middle East in which the United States would adhere to the Baghdad Pact consisting of Britain, Iraq, Turkey, Iran, and Pakistan—and, it was hoped, eventually other Middle Eastern states if Project Alpha succeeded.

Dulles initially supported the plans for the Baghdad Pact as "precisely [the] kind of basis from which full fledged regional defense organization could grow."[19] But when it became clear that Project Alpha might fail, he became increasingly skeptical. Failing a settlement of the Palestine question, the Baghdad Pact, in his view, would divide the Arab states. The underlying political tensions had to be ameliorated before military security could become a reality. Otherwise anti-Western Arab nationalists would denounce the military measures as designed to keep the Middle East under Western control. At the same time the Soviet Union would become alarmed at a military alliance that paradoxically would not have the military unity or strength to serve its anti-Soviet purpose. "[B]etter to keep it a paper pact," Dulles advised the British.[20]

This apparent vacillation exasperated Eden. "I am sorry that Dulles is so hesitant," he wrote, "I am afraid that we shall miss the tide

[17] Minute by Macmillan to Eden, July 12, 1955, PRO, FO 800/680.

[18] "Dulles has now assured me," Macmillan wrote, "that he is willing to tell the Iraqis that if a Palestine settlement could be achieved the United States would be prepared to join the Pact." Minute by Macmillan to Eden, "Top Secret," July 16, 1955, PRO, FO 800/687.

[19] Secretary of State to Embassy in Turkey, December 31, 1954, *FR, 1952–1954*, 9:2403.

[20] Shuckburgh, *Descent to Suez*, 299.

once again."[21] What seemed to Eden to be faintheartedness, and a wide gap between rhetoric and action, appeared to Dulles to be a matter of pragmatism and common sense. The Baghdad Pact was not developing into an effective military alliance. The divergence of views reflected different aims. Dulles wished to reconcile the nationalists' aspirations and the military requirements of the Western powers in the Middle East, thereby frustrating the expansionist ambitions of the Soviet Union. Eden of course was also wary of Russian aims, but he took a long-range historical view and believed American assessments to be overdrawn. Eden's priority was to preserve British power in the Middle East and, in time, to secure a British line of defense along "a frontier stretching from the Mediterranean to the Himalayas."[22]

"Distinctly disappointing," were the words used by Anthony Nutting of the Foreign Office to sum up Dulles's attitude toward the Baghdad Pact in March 1956.[23] Dulles now seemed to be interested in a UN solution. He appeared to be changing course. But the British were not entirely certain. Dulles spoke ambiguously. His rhetoric had a bearing on substance. Here there were two British views. Perhaps American legal training caused his meaning to be opaque. Perhaps he made vague statements because of the danger of being misinterpreted by Arab or Jew. Perhaps he merely preferred, like Eisenhower, to keep options open. In any case the British could not always be certain of Dulles's intent. For example, what of the danger of Israeli aggression? How would Dulles respond? Their reflections on a UN resolution about the possibility of hostilities breaking out between Israel and the Arab states presents an example of how the British attempted to deduce Dulles's purpose:

> His [Dulles's] unspoken thoughts may conceivably have been something like this: - Israel is more likely to attack the Arab States than they are to attack her; it would be even more difficult for the United States to use force against Israel than against the Arab States; if this has to be done, there must be a clear finding on the part of the United Nations that Israel is responsible, and the United States must be able to vote for such a finding.[24]

That line of reasoning appealed to the Foreign Office. In March 1956 Project Alpha and all hopes for a comprehensive settlement collapsed. The immediate cause was Nasser's rejection of the basis for

[21] Eden to Macmillan, "Secret," November 15, 1955, PRO, FO 800/680.
[22] Quoted in Robert Rhodes James, *Anthony Eden* (London, 1986), 398.
[23] Minute by Nutting, March 6, 1956, PRO, FO 800/734. Nutting was minister of state.
[24] P. M. Crosthwaite to E. M. Rose, "Secret," February 11, 1956, PRO, FO 371/121772.

settlement, which the Americans as well as the British interpreted as his smoldering ambitions against Israel. In Dulles's words, general agreement "is impossible at the present time unless and until Arab hopes *vis-à-vis* Israel are somewhat deflated."[25] For preserving peace in the Middle East, all that remained was the American, British, and French "Tripartite Declaration" of May 1950, which was designed to regulate arms shipments and prevent violations of the armistice frontiers of the previous year.

To the British the Tripartite Declaration had become a most unsatisfactory arrangement, and thus they responded positively to Dulles's hint that the UN might play a greater part in keeping the peace. A UN resolution, in other words, might supersede the 1950 declaration. Shuckburgh now took into account the Czech arms deal to supply Egypt with Soviet weapons, which the British and Americans had learned about in the previous autumn, as well as the 1950 tripartite pledge:

> We are left without a Middle East policy of any kind. The Tripartite Declaration is a mere stop-gap; its sole justification was that it held the ring while a settlement was sought. Now that no settlement is in sight, it operates only to sharpen the Israelis' dilemma. They now have no prospect of peace . . . ; they also have no prospect of arms, while their enemies grow strong.

The dilemma was acute for the Americans as well as for the British. The Israelis might launch a preemptive attack. Then the three Western powers would be compelled, theoretically at least, to intervene in order to fulfill the obligations of the 1950 declaration. Shuckburgh continued, and as he wrote his thoughts became more alarming:

> If the Jews attack, then perhaps we can find means of saving ourselves by falling upon them. But if they do not, the tension and despair of their position will grow rapidly and public opinion in the U.K. and U.S. will find it impossible not to support them and arm them, despite the appalling consequences of doing so. This will destroy the Baghdad Pact and put in jeopardy our oil supplies.
>
> It will lead us direct towards a conflict, with the West supporting Israel and Russia the Arabs. In fact, unless the Israelis commit an aggression, we are becoming daily more deeply committed to go to war against a Soviet-armed Arab world as soon as they feel strong enough or fanatical enough to attack Israel. Every time we refer to the Tripartite Declaration as an

[25] Dulles to Henry Cabot Lodge, March 31, 1956, ss, "Israeli Relations (3)," DPEL.

"obligation" to defend Israel, we get ourselves more deeply in this position.[26]

Shuckburgh therefore favored an initiative through the UN, if only to circumvent the "embarrassing" obligations of the Tripartite Declaration to uphold the 1949 frontiers.[27] The British records reveal, however, that Anthony Eden did not see eye to eye with his Foreign Office advisers on the virtue of the UN. Before, during, and after the Suez crisis, he despaired of effective UN action. He wrote in June 1956: "The United Nations becomes an increasing source of trouble. I wish I could glimpse any good it does."[28] On this point of transcendent importance there was a world of difference in the outlook of Eden and Dulles. In actual crises, for example in Guatemala in 1954, Dulles's tactics may have been manipulative, and his attitude toward UN politics as cynical as Eden's.[29] Nevertheless, for Dulles the UN, despite its flaws, remained the cornerstone of the society of nations.

There was another fundamental difference. Eden believed much more than Dulles that the ruler of Egypt, Gamal Abdel Nasser, was at the heart of all Western troubles in the Middle East. In March 1956, King Hussein of Jordan kicked out Sir John Glubb, the commander of the Arab Legion. Glubb represented the tradition of British proconsuls in the Middle East. His dismissal was an affront. Eden held Nasser responsible. This was an error of judgment on Eden's part, for Hussein himself ousted Glubb without Egyptian help. But to Eden it was an anti-British act of such calculated intent that there had to be a villain comparable to Mussolini or Hitler—a comparison made frequently by Eden but rarely by Dulles.[30] Eden and many officials of the Foreign Office believed that the Americans had not learned the historical lesson of appeasement. "It does not seem," wrote Anthony Nutting, "that the Americans have yet hoisted in that appeasement of Nasser simply does not pay and that whatever 'bargain' you make with him he will break."[31]

A few weeks earlier, in January 1956, Eisenhower and Dulles had met with Eden and Selwyn Lloyd, the new foreign secretary. The president and secretary of state had mixed practical and, to the British, almost naive questions together with a sense of humor. Eisen-

[26] Minute by Shuckburgh, "Top Secret," March 10, 1956, PRO, FO 371/121235.

[27] Minute by Shuckburgh, "Top Secret," April 20, 1956, PRO, FO 371/121738.

[28] Minute by Eden, June 6, 1956, PRO, FO 800/737.

[29] Richard Immerman, *The CIA in Guatemala: The Foreign Policy of Intervention* (Austin, 1982), 168–72.

[30] Dulles did refer to Nasser's "Hitlerite personality." Stephen Ambrose, *Eisenhower.* Vol. 2: *The President* (New York, 1984), 334.

[31] Minute by Nutting, "Secret," March 6, 1956, PRO, FO 800/734.

hower asked, "What kind of fellow is Nasser? Lloyd answered, "[h]e is ambitious, dreams of an Arab empire from the Atlantic to Persian Gulf under his leadership."[32] Eisenhower expressed curiosity. Would other Arab leaders follow him? He suspected that the British view was alarmist, but he saw a critical point. Was Nasser falling irretrievably under Soviet influence? If so the Americans would face the decision whether or not to support the British, French, Israelis, and anti-Nasser Arabs. Whatever might happen to Nasser, this course would further divide the Middle East. Lloyd replied by emphasizing an inflammatory anti-Western speech made by Nasser only the day before. Eisenhower appeared to be skeptical. This exchange was taking place two weeks after publication of the celebrated article in which Dulles boasted about bringing the United States three times to the brink of war.[33] Eisenhower said that it was possible that Nasser "doesn't have [a] good staff to go over his speeches." There was a pause. Then Dulles said, "I wonder what you mean by that."[34] The banter did not convince the British that Eisenhower and Dulles took Nasser seriously enough.

The Americans were in fact alarmed at Nasser, but they responded to some of the major issues differently. For example, the turning points in the background of the Suez crisis were the Czech arms deal and Glubb's dismissal. When Dulles learned of the arms deal in September 1955, his response was almost as indignant, and his sense of frustration just as intense, as Eden's. Dulles remarked to Herbert Hoover, Jr., the under secretary of state:

> We have a lot of cards to play with Nasser—although they are mostly negative. The waters of the Upper Nile: we can strangle him if we want to. We can develop the Baghdad group and [we can] ruin the cotton market. We can switch this year's economic aid from Egypt to Iraq.[35]

Dulles nevertheless curbed his anger. He tried to woo Nasser away from the Russians by emissaries to Cairo and other measures including coordinated efforts with the CIA. The British already doubted whether it was still possible to do business with Nasser, but the critical shift in their policy occurred in March 1956 when Glubb was cashiered. From that time onward, Eden became, in Shuckburgh's

---

[32] This was one of Lloyd's insistent themes: Nasser "aspired to have a pan-Arab union from the Atlantic to the Persian Gulf, dominated by Egypt and with all Western influences eliminated." Lloyd to Jebb, "Secret," March 20, 1956, PRO, FO 800/734.

[33] James Shepley, "How Dulles Averted War," *Life* (January 16, 1956): 70ff.

[34] Shuckburgh, *Descent to Suez*, 329. Shuckburgh continued in the vein of brinkmanship: "The current joke about Dulles is—'three brinks and he's brunk'." Ibid.

[35] Donald Neff, *Warriors at Suez* (New York, 1981), 92–93.

phrase, "violently anti-Nasser."[36] At one point Eden went so far as to exclaim that he wished to have Nasser "murdered."[37]

Both Dulles and Eden agreed on the danger that Nasser represented. But they disagreed on the extent of the danger and the means to combat it. Eden regarded UN action as futile and resolved not to appease Nasser. His approach was basically different from the more cautious tactics of Dulles, who made it clear throughout that he believed in the sanctity of the UN. He held that force should be employed only after all peaceful avenues had been explored and found to be dead ends. These were issues of profound substance, not style or timing, and they endured throughout the Suez crisis.

. . .

"Foster very gradually and very slowly came to realize what we were up against," recalled George Humphrey, the secretary of treasury in the Eisenhower administration. He was describing Dulles's reaction to the possibility that the Egyptians might turn to the Soviet Union for economic as well as military assistance. In the months following the Czech arms deal, the question of the High Dam at Aswan, a project that had been years in planning, acquired urgency—but to the British more than the Americans. Humphrey explained Dulles's reaction in October 1955:

> He [Dulles] had a cablegram from Eden which was . . . very sharp . . . demanding, practically—it was kind of half demand and half threat—that if we did not join them in building this Aswan Dam, that . . . the fat would be in the fire.[38]

So high were the stakes that Eden turned directly to Eisenhower. "I hate to trouble you with this," Eden telegraphed to the president in November, "but I am convinced that on our joint success in excluding the Russians from this [Aswan] contract may depend the future of Africa."[39] Within a month the American and British governments together with the International Bank for Reconstruction and Develop-

---

[36] Shuckburgh, *Descent to Suez*, 341.

[37] Anthony Nutting's original version of this comment in his book *No End of a Lesson* (London, 1967) was that Eden wanted Nasser "destroyed" (34). In a recent interview for the Granada television series "End of Empire" he stated that he had toned down Eden's comment and that the actual word was "murdered." Brian Lapping, *End of Empire* (London, 1985), 262.

[38] George Humphrey interview, JFDOHC.

[39] Quoted in Keith Kyle, "Britain and the Crisis 1955–1956," in Louis and Owen, eds., *Suez 1956.*

ment (IBRD) offered a loan of $400 million toward the initial cost of the High Dam at Aswan.

During the Aswan discussions the question of colonialism emerged as an irritant in Anglo-American relations a well as in the negotiations with the Egyptians. Nasser inquired about the terms of the loan. Would it be a means of regulating or interfering with the Egyptian economy? With the benefit of hindsight it is clear that this was a real and not a fabricated concern, but at the time officials within both the British and American governments believed that he was guilty not merely of ingratitude but of attempting to play the Western powers off against the Soviet Union. Dulles saw Nasser as an opportunist in the cold war as well as an Egyptian nationalist rebelling against European dominance. The dilemma was acute. Sherman Adams, Eisenhower's chief of staff, summed it up after a visit by Eden to Washington in January 1956:

> Eden's visit to Washington did not resolve one serious difference between the American and British positions on the Middle East question; our firm opposition to colonialism made us sympathetic to the struggles which Egypt and the other Arab states were making to free themselves of the political and economic control that the British felt they had to maintain in the Middle East in their own self-interest.[40]

Eisenhower shared Dulles's aversion to British colonialism. On the other hand, members of the Eden government to a man believed that the Americans were misguided in this obsession. As Lord Blake has pointed out, it would be a mistake to lay too much emphasis on the conflict as a running battle between Dulles and Eden. The Suez crisis reflected differences of political judgment and national attitudes.[41]

Nevertheless the British, especially in retrospect, held Dulles responsible for the abrupt cancellation of the Aswan loan and for linking economic assistance to political alignment in the cold war. It is true that he dealt the death blow to the loan in July 1956, but the British in the preceding months were fully abreast of the reasons. From the ambassador in Washington, Sir Roger Makins, the Foreign Office received accurate reports on the mounting domestic protests against the loan by the Israeli lobby, the cotton lobby, and the China Lobby. In May Nasser recognized Communist China, an action that antagonized both the Congress and the public. According to Makins there was real doubt in Congress together with a staggering new debt service that would be incurred by the Aswan project. To give but one

---

[40] Sherman Adams, *Firsthand Report* (New York, 1961), 245.
[41] Lord Blake, *The Decline of Power 1915–1964* (London, 1985), 349.

example of the congressional pressure felt by Dulles, Otto Passman, a Democrat from Louisiana who chaired the foreign aid subcommittee in the House of Representatives, once said to a State Department official, "Son, I don't smoke and I don't drink. My only pleasure in life is kicking the shit out of the foreign aid program of the United States of America."[42] The dam in Egypt became a natural target for such sentiment, particularly after Nasser appeared to align himself with America's enemies in the cold war. Dulles's cancellation of the offer of the loan on July 19, 1956, came as no surprise to the British. They were merely startled that he acted so quickly and decisively. According to William Clark, the press secretary who took the news to Eden:

> [t]his came through, as messages tended to, on the Reuters tape before it came through on the Foreign Office tape. I took it up, always glad to get credit for the press, to the Prime Minister in his bedroom. His comment was, "Oh good, oh good for Foster. I didn't think he had it in him." Then there was a pause and, "I wish he hadn't done it quite so abruptly."[43]

The Foreign Office response indicates the alignment of the two countries at this stage: "Mr. Dulles has taken the decision for us. We were not absolutely in step at the last moment but the difference between us was no more than a nuance."[44]

Dulles was in Peru when he learned of Nasser's nationalization of the Suez Canal Company on July 26, 1956. It is important to bear in mind the word "company" because Dulles correctly saw Nasser's action as the takeover of a concession rather than, in the widespread view of the general public, as territorial aggression. On his return to Washington a few days later he quickly made his views known to the British. "Mr. Dulles sent for me this afternoon," Sir Roger Makins telegraphed to London on July 30. The secretary of state made clear two points on which he remained consistent during the crisis:

> The United States Government thought it necessary to distinguish between the Suez Canal Convention of 1888, which was concluded in perpetuity, and the Canal Company concession, which had been granted for a fixed

[42] Quoted in William J. Burns, *Economic Aid and American Policy toward Egypt 1955–1981* (Albany, N.Y., 1985), 48.

[43] Lapping, *End of Empire*, 262. Eisenhower was also skeptical about Dulles's abrupt tactics. See especially Townsend Hoopes, *The Devil and John Foster Dulles* (Boston, 1973), 343; and Ambrose, *Eisenhower*, 330.

[44] Minute by A.D.M. Ross (head of the Eastern Department of the Foreign Office), July 20, 1956, PRO, FO 371/119056.

term. It was, therefore, *infractions* of the Convention, *rather than the termination of the concession*, on which action could most appropriately be based.

While he agreed that our attitude should be a firm one . . . his view was that so long as there was no interference with the navigation of the canal, and no threats to foreign nationals in Egypt, *there was no basis for military action*.[45]

All the emphasis was Eden's. "Why?" he had written in the margin in response to Dulles's emphasis on the Suez Canal Convention of 1888, which secured the right of passage of vessels of the signatory states. Dulles was pointing out, implicitly at least, that each nation has the sovereign right to nationalization, which in his view could not be effectively challenged in international law unless questions arose about fair compensation or efficient management. Thus there was no basis for intervention, at least for the time being. On that point, at least, Eden was obviously clear about Dulles's meaning, even though it was open to the charge of hypocrisy in view of various acts of American intervention. Eden himself doubted that effective action could be taken on the basis of a nineteenth-century convention. "Theft" was the straightforward word he used to describe Nasser's action.

The problem was that Dulles seemed to be speaking at two levels. One was the academic and legal, as if he were arguing his case before a court. The other was the popular and robust vernacular, which Eden and everyone else could easily comprehend. In meeting with Eden and others in London on the first of August, Dulles said: "A way had to be found to make Nasser disgorge what he was attempting to swallow." Here, as in the case of taking his country to the brink of war, Dulles's spontaneous remarks got him into trouble. Eden wrote in his memoirs about Dulles wishing to make Nasser disgorge: "These were forthright words. They rang in my ears for months."[46] Allowing for an element of exaggeration, what Eden wrote was no doubt true. Dulles gave the impression that he sympathized with the British and would support them, in the last resort with force, if they first pursued legal and peaceful methods, in Eden's phrase, to bring Nasser to his senses.

It will not be my purpose to discuss Dulles's tactics that led to the creation of the Suez Canal Users' Association (SCUA), by which the waterway would be placed under international supervision.[47] I shall instead briefly examine the two incidents that revealed to the British

---

[45] Makins to Lloyd, "Top Secret," July 30, 1956, PRO, PREM 11/1098.
[46] *The Memoirs of Anthony Eden: Full Circle* (Boston, 1960), 487.
[47] For the SCUA see Robert R. Bowie, *Suez 1956* (New York, 1974), 35–51.

what appeared to be his true sentiments. These episodes have had an adverse influence in Anglo-American relations to the present day. There is, however, a preliminary point that needs to be made about SCUA because it indicated Dulles's underlying objective. It is one of the more important revelations from the opening of the British archives. Those officials in the British government who studied Dulles's methodical statements in writing and in committee, as well as his casual comments in conversation and his provocative remarks in press conferences, were certain of his intention. Adam Watson, the head of the African Department of the Foreign Office, wrote on the eve of the invasion by the expeditionary force in late October 1956: "The fact is that he [Dulles] always really intended SCUA as a means for negotiating a settlement, not for pressure on Nasser."[48]

Dulles and Eden both made basic miscalculations. Dulles believed that "the danger of bellicose action would disappear if negotiations were prolonged."[49] Eden assumed that if the British supported the proposal for a "Users' Club" (what became known as SCUA), then Dulles would back them in the application of economic sanctions and, if necessary, force. Eden said at one stage that SCUA was "a cock-eyed idea, but if it brings the Americans in, I can go along."[50] He wished to bring the crisis to a head as quickly as possible, thereby not losing momentum in protracted negotiations. Dulles by contrast hoped to gain time. But contrary to what might seem to be the natural course, he did not wish to turn to the UN, where the Soviet Union would be certain to block any chance of peaceful resolution of the issue. According to a memorandum written by Dulles on August 30, 1956, after a conversation with Eisenhower, which summed up the basic points that they both endorsed,

> I [Dulles] said I had come to the conclusion that, regrettable as it might be to see Nasser's prestige enhanced even temporarily, I did not believe the situation was one which should be resolved by force.
>
> I could not see any end to the situation that might be created if the British and the French occupied the Canal and parts of Egypt. They would make bitter enemies of the entire population of the Middle East and much of Africa. Everywhere they would be compelled to maintain themselves by force and in the end their own economy would be weakened virtually beyond repair and the influence of the West in the Middle East and most of Africa lost for a generation, if not a century. The Soviet Union would reap

---

[48] Watson to G. E. Millard, "Secret," October 31, 1956, PRO, FO 11/1175.
[49] Robert Murphy, *Diplomat among Warriors* (London, 1964), 468.
[50] Thomas, *The Suez Affair*, 83.

the benefit of a greatly weakened Western Europe and would move into a position of predominant influence in the Middle East and Africa. No doubt it was for this reason that the Soviets were seeking to prevent a peaceful adjustment of the Suez problem.[51]

The secretary of state noted for the record that "The President said he entirely agreed with me in this basic analysis."

Dulles's thoughts that he voiced intimately to Eisenhower were consistent with his public statement affirming the premise of American policy on September 13, 1956. This extemporaneous comment was the first of the two incidents in which Dulles, in the British interpretation, revealed his true colors. It was the occasion of his famous remark that the United States would not force its way through the canal. In response to a question about the possibility of Egypt blocking passage of American ships under the auspices of scua, Dulles had replied, in the phraseology of the headlines throughout the world, *"We do not intend to shoot our way through!"*[52] To Eden the statement was an act of betrayal. He held to the end of his days that Dulles had misled him into believing that, if all else failed, the United States would support intervention.

The records released in London reveal that Sir Ivone Kirkpatrick, the permanent under secretary at the Foreign Office, was well aware of Dulles's attitude and was determined to take advantage of it. Eden trusted Kirkpatrick. He was one of the few officials within the Foreign Office who favored intervention. He had written the week before Dulles's pronouncement against shooting one's way through the canal that the time had come to apply "economic and psychological measures of pressure" against Nasser:

> We seem to me to be in a good position to do this because the Americans are so frightened that we may use force that we might bulldoze them into suitable economic and psychological measures simply by threatening that if they do not agree we shall have no alternative but to have recourse to force.[53]

Kirkpatrick thus gave careful thought to the ways in which the Americans might be manipulated. Though such evidence does not diminish Eden's genuine surprise at what he believed to be Dulles's treachery, it does indicate a deadly set of interlocking miscalculations.

[51] Memorandum of conversation with the President, August 30, 1956, whms, "Meetings with the President, August–December 1956 (6)," dpel.

[52] See Finer, *Dulles over Suez*, 229 (emphasis in original).

[53] Minute by Kirkpatrick, September 4, 1956, pro, fo 371/119154.

Kirkpatrick hoped that Dulles could be nudged from economic and psychological measures into political and military action, or at least into acquiescence in the British use of force. Kirkpatrick furthermore believed that the Americans would prefer not to know about the military plans against Nasser. According to another Foreign Office official, "nothing had been said to the Americans because we assume that they did not wish to be told."[54] In trying to understand Dulles and Eisenhower's reaction to the crisis, this was a fatal misjudgment.

The second incident was a press conference Dulles held on October 2, 1956. He elaborated on the SCUA. If his previous public remarks had left any uncertainty, his comments how were explicit that SCUA would remain a voluntary association. Dulles's basic idea had always been that an international authority would schedule pilots to provide passage, collect tolls, and compensate the Egyptian government. The users of the canal would thus be in a position of collective bargaining against Egypt. But the international authority would have no power to enforce Nasser's compliance. "There is talk," Dulles said, "about teeth being pulled out of the plan, but I know of no teeth; there were no teeth in it."[55] As if this further renunciation of the use of force were not enough, Dulles at this juncture connected the canal controversy with the volatile issue of colonialism. The United States, he stated, "cannot be expected to identify itself 100 per cent either with the colonial Powers or the Powers uniquely concerned with the problem of getting independence as rapidly, and as fully, as possible." All but suggesting that the British, together with the French, still possessed a nineteenth-century mentality, Dulles maintained that the colonial regimes should be dismantled. It should be the goal of the United States, in his view, to facilitate the shift from colonialism and "to see that this process moves forward in a constructive, evolutionary way, and does not come to a halt or go forward through violent, revolutionary processes."[56] Dulles was apprehensive about the instability that might be caused by decolonialization. Yet he also gave the impression that the European colonial powers were not moving fast enough toward a transfer of power.

Those comments caused great bitterness. The Suez crisis to the British public did not represent a colonial issue but, in the words of *The Times* (London), "one of elementary international law and order

---

[54] Minute by Donald Logan (private secretary to the foreign secretary), August 23, 1956, PRO, FO 371/119123.

[55] *The Times* (London), October 3, 1956. According to Eden's recent biographer, Robert Rhodes James, "In the unhappily long saga of Anglo-American duplicity, this ranks very high." *Anthony Eden*, 515.

[56] *The Times* (London), October 3, 1956.

affecting a waterway which is many times as important for western Europe as the Panama Canal is for North America." Beyond the merits of the canal dispute Dulles had cast a slur on the British colonial record. From the distance of some three decades it is difficult to recall the intensity of the debate about the end of the British Empire. The British, sometimes under American pressure and despite their better judgment, had quickened the pace of decolonization. For Dulles to call into question the British colonial record was entirely unjustified from both Tory and Labour points of view. His animosity now seemed almost to rival the ill will demonstrated by Nasser. *The Times* well expressed the sense of wounded pride and national indignation at Dulles's innuendo that Britain was not a progressive colonial power:

> Britain's record as a colonial Power stands in voluntarily bestowing independence on four great Asian countries after the war, in withdrawing from the Palestine mandate—at little benefit to peace in the Middle East—in 1947; in delaying settlement with Egypt because the latter refused to grant like independence to the Sudan, and in granting independence to Malaya and the Gold Coast next year at a time when even some nationalist politicians are forcibly expressing their doubts as to its immediate desirability.
>
> Britain has nothing to learn from anybody about the task of bringing progress, freedom, and self-government to the emergent peoples.[57]

With his remarks about colonialism, Dulles earned a permanent reputation as a hostile critic of Britain's imperial mission. Eden was further exasperated, and he drew a practical lesson: "We have been misled so often by Dulles' ideas that we cannot afford to risk another misunderstanding. . . . Time is not on our side in this matter."[58]

During the crisis Eden received conflicting advice. Sir Ivone Kirkpatrick represented one powerful view, cogently presented whenever the occasion arose, that whatever the Americans might do, the British would soon face a choice between "the use of force or surrender to Nasser."[59] On the other hand Eden certainly did not lack counsel that intervention would be a mistake unless the Americans acquiesced. Certain officials read the minds of Eisenhower and Dulles much better than others, and one of them stands vindicated in view of the events of late October through early November 1956. Sir Roger Makins wrote from Washington that he did not know the "inner thoughts" of those in London making decisions about possible "mili-

---

[57] *The Times* (London), October 3, 1956.
[58] Eden to Selwyn Lloyd, "Top Secret," October 8, 1956, PRO, FO 800/741.
[59] Kirkpatrick's draft telegram to Makins, September 10, 1956, PRO, FO 800/740.

tary action"—but "to attempt it without full American moral and material support could easily lead to disaster."[60]

.   .   .

Dulles's papers indicate that he had no knowledge of the British, French, and Israeli plans for the invasion. When he learned of the Israeli attack on October 29, he explained his reaction to the British chargé d'affaires, John Coulson (Makins had completed his tour of duty as ambassador and his successor, Sir Harold Caccia, had not yet arrived). Dulles said he was appalled not only at the Israelis but also the French, whose brand of imperialism he warmly detested. According to Coulson, "the French had in a sense involved us [the British] in their own Middle Eastern and African troubles and would try to use us further." Both Eisenhower and Dulles, Coulson continued, harbored "the profoundest suspicions" about the French.[61] At this initial stage of the invasion Dulles still hoped that the Israelis and the French might be checked. He did not yet know the extent of British involvement. A record of a conversation among Eisenhower and others, shortly before Coulson's arrival, reveals what Dulles had in mind when he made his pointed remarks about the French: "[t]here has been a struggle between the French and ourselves to see who will have the British allied with them in the tense situations in the Middle East and North Africa. . . . [T]here was still a bare chance to 'unhook' the British from the French."[62]

The British estimate of Dulles in the second day of the fighting reveals a man left with no doubt about the collusion. London and Paris had issued an ultimatum for the Israelis and Egyptians each to withdraw from within ten miles of the canal, and to allow French and British troops to occupy the area of the canal itself. "A pretty brutal affair," Dulles said to Coulson. How could the Egyptians, who had been attacked, be expected to give up their own territory and submit again to occupation?[63] To Dulles the veil of camouflaged intent had been lifted. He now had no doubt that the British were acting in concert with the French and the Israelis. Dulles's intuition and judgment were accurate on this point. He saw the true nature of the situation quicker than many of the British themselves. One can sympathize with Coulson, who in good faith believed that his government had

[60] Makins to Lloyd, "Top Secret," September 9, 1956, PRO, FO 800/740.

[61] Coulson to Lloyd, "Top Secret," October 29, 1956, PRO, FO 800/741.

[62] Memorandum of conference with the President, October 29, 1956, WHMS, "Meetings with the President, August–December 1956 (3)," DPEL.

[63] Coulson to Lloyd, "Top Secret," October 30, 1956, PRO, FO 800/741.

issued the ultimatum in order to stop the fighting. "Mr. Dulles was obviously profoundly disturbed and depressed," Coulson reported on October 31. Nothing could alter the view of Dulles or Eisenhower that they had been deceived. "What rankles the most," Coulson concluded—and here he touched the heart of the matter—"is what they believe to be deliberate concealment on our part, if not an actual plot with the French and Israelis."[64] Some practitioners of international politics might have assumed that deception was part of the game. But Dulles and Eisenhower were genuinely offended.

On November 1, Dulles explained to the members of the National Security Council the significance of the "concerted moves" of the British, French, and Israelis. He again lashed out at the French who had "for some time been supplying the Israelis with far more military equipment than we knew anything about." He then warmed to his subject. He spoke against the background of British bombers over Cairo and Molotov cocktails in Budapest. What the world witnessed at Suez was a revival of European colonialism at a time when the Hungarians were in revolt against their colonial masters. The United States now had to stand on its own historic principles. Summaries of NSC minutes do not ordinarily make for dramatic reading. But the following excerpt represents Dulles's creed as an American anti-imperialist. He spoke passionately—"with great warmth," in the euphemistic words of the minutes.

For many years now the United States has been walking a tightrope between the effort to maintain our old and valued relations with our British and French allies on the one hand, and on the other trying to assure ourselves of the friendship and understanding of the newly independent countries who have escaped from colonialism. . . . Unless we now assert and maintain this leadership, all of these newly independent countries will turn from us to the USSR. We will be looked upon as forever tied to British and French colonialist policies. In short, the United States would survive or go down on the basis of the fate of colonialism if the United States supports the French and the British on the colonial issue. Win or lose, we will share the fate of Britain and France. . . .

It is no less than tragic that at this very time, when we are on the point of winning an immense and long-hoped-for victory over Soviet colonialism in Eastern Europe, we should be forced to choose between following in the footsteps of Anglo-French colonialism in Asia and Africa, or splitting our course away from their course.[65]

[64] Coulson to Lloyd, "Top Secret," October 31, 1956, PRO, FO 800/741.
[65] Memorandum of NSC meeting, November 1, 1956, NSCS, AWF.

Later the same day Dulles delivered a speech at the UN in which he reiterated in somewhat more lofty tone the same themes. It was one of the historic events of the Suez crisis. He subsequently stated that he would stand by every word, and indeed that he would choose the UN oration as his epitaph.[66] But for the vintage, unvarnished, anticolonialist Dulles, his true epitaph was his comment earlier in the day to the NSC.

Within days after the UN speech, Dulles fell ill and was taken to Walter Reed Hospital. The new British ambassador, Sir Harold Caccia, reported later in November that, though Herbert Hoover, Jr., the acting secretary of state, wished to work back "towards the old relationship," the State Department without Dulles seemed to be adrift: "[i]t does not look as if the Administration without Dulles has much idea of any coherent programme of action."[67] What also seemed to emerge as an undeniable truth to the British at this juncture was the control over the crisis exerted by Eisenhower himself. Eisenhower was a strong president served by a strong secretary of state. According to a ranking British military officer who had served extended tours of duty in Washington, Air Chief Marshal Sir William Elliot, "the President is the only man who matters, and there is no one near him, except Foster Dulles, who is the slightest good."[68]

The impression of Caccia and Elliot were not contradictory. In the British view, Dulles provided Eisenhower with the systematic policy that reinforced Eisenhower's own principles. In the emotionally charged debate about the Suez crisis in the NSC, the combination of Eisenhower and Dulles easily carried the anticolonial sense of the meeting against those, notably Harold Stassen (the president's special assistant on disarmament), who wished to have a less condemnatory judgment on the British and French. So strongly did Eisenhower and Dulles feel about colonialism that they were prepared to nail the American colors to the mast, even though there might be adverse reactions during the election campaign. During the discussion on October 29 at the White House, the president had said (in the indirect words of the minutes of the meeting):

[H]e does not care in the slightest whether he is re-elected or not. He feels we must make good on our word. He added that he did not really think

[66] Hoopes, *Devil and Dulles*, 379. For the speech see especially Finer, *Dulles over Suez*, 393–96. Finer attacks Dulles, here as elsewhere, for "anger and excessive moralism," and lack of nerve and imagination. "[H]e was afraid of a world war, a figment of his own trepidation, and especially of the hostility of the Arab-Asian peoples" (395).

[67] Caccia to Lloyd, "Secret," November 30, 1956, PRO, FO 800/742.

[68] "Record of Conversation," November 18, 1956, "Top Secret Guard," PRO, PREM 11/1176.

the American people would throw him out in the midst of a situation like this, but if they did, so be it.[69]

Eisenhower may have been unduly modest about his political ambitions. Nevertheless, he was certainly right about the sentiment of the American public. Dulles interjected that one development would probably be "a wave of anti-Semitism through the country." Others at the meeting agreed. Eisenhower continued:

> The President next asked whether we should call Congress back into session, and specifically whether we could call them for the day following the election. He said that referral to the United Nations was not enough. We must take more definite action, since we are the only people the British and the French will listen to.[70]

So much for the view that Eisenhower and Dulles would hold back because of domestic political reasons. They were on solid political ground.

Even those who sympathized with the British purpose did little to end the rift. The Middle Eastern crisis had become a crisis in Anglo-American relations. Members of the Eisenhower administration believed that the Eden government had flouted the office of the U.S. presidency by concealing the plans at Suez. According to Selwyn Lloyd, the traditional pro-British sentiment that usually characterized any administration in Washington had been transformed:

> [T]he hard core of policy-makers, some of whom have been strongly pro-British in the past, are now against us. . . . Their feeling is that we have to purge our contempt of the President in some way.
>
> [T]he Americans have no intention of lifting a finger to help to preserve us from financial disaster until they are certain that we are removing ourselves from Port Said quickly. . . . Much of this American attitude is quite irrational and as they frankly admit contrary to their own long-term interests, but they . . . are temporarily beyond the bounds of reason and even threats to withdraw ourselves from the United Nations, N.A.T.O., etc. would not bring round those who have to make the decisions to a sense of reality.[71]

In Washington the new ambassador agreed with that assessment. "We have now passed the point where we are talking to friends," Caccia reported. "[W]e are on a hard bargaining basis and we are dealing

---

[69] Memorandum of conference with the President, October 29, 1956, WHMS, "Meetings with the President, August–December 1956 (3)," DPEL.

[70] Memorandum of conference with the President, October 29, 1956, WHMS, "Meetings with the President, August–December 1956 (3)," DPEL.

[71] Lloyd to R. A. Butler, "Top Secret," November 28, 1956, PRO, FO 800/742.

with an Administration of business executives who rightly or wrongly consider that they are animated by the highest principles."[72] Those included, of course, Dulles. Once the British announced their plans to withdraw, he worked quickly and pragmatically to restore the alliance. In Caccia's judgment, Dulles's "new found fervour for the Afro-Asians" would probably not interfere with a realistic approach to other problems, but Caccia was determined to review the relationship "Without mincing matters at any point."[73]

On November 16 Lloyd, together with Caccia, visited Dulles in the hospital. "Dulles was up and looked remarkably well," Lloyd wrote to Eden. What struck them on this occasion was Dulles's willingness to end the estrangement, repair the damage, and look toward the future. He emphasized that British and American policies differed not in aim but in method; not on the danger but on how to combat it. Here was the view that the British and Americans differed in timing and style, not the goal, which was, one way or another, to get rid of Nasser. There followed a startling remark. Dulles lamented that the British had not finished the job. This is a comment that has been discussed many times, but here is the excerpt from the original telegram:

> He [Dulles] agreed that there was no point in arguing about the past. The thing was to concentrate on the future. He said that he had no complaint about our objectives in our recent operations. In fact they were the same as those of the United States but he still did not think that our methods of achieving them were the right ones. Even so he deplored that we had not managed to bring down Nasser.[74]

What is one to make of the last sentence? Was Dulles merely saying, as did Churchill, that once begun the task should have been finished? Did he intend it as an interrogative comment, to discover why the British had pulled back? Did he mean to imply that the British had botched the operation, but said no more because of the obvious rejoinder that the Americans had caused them to do so? If he had been

[72] Caccia to Foreign Office, "Top Secret," November 28, 1956, PRO, FO 800/742.

[73] Caccia to Foreign Office, "Top Secret," November 28, 1956, PRO, FO 800/742.

[74] Lloyd to Eden, "Secret," November 18, 1956, PRO, FO 371/118873. One of the more embroidered versions appears in Finer, *Dulles over Suez*, 446–44: "He [Dulles] said, seriously, 'Well, once you started, why didn't you go through with it and get Nasser down?'" Selwyn Lloyd answered, "Foster, why didn't you give us a wink?" Dulles answered, "Oh, I couldn't do anything like that!" According to Lloyd's own posthumously published memoir in 1978, Dulles asked, "Selwyn, why did you stop? Why didn't you go through with it and get Nasser down?" Lloyd replied, "Well, Foster, if you had so much as winked at us we might have gone on." Selwyn Lloyd, *Suez 1956: A Personal Account* (London, 1978), 219.

pressed by Caccia and Lloyd, how would he have reconciled the top-pling of Nasser with the principle of anticolonialism? Would he have replied that Nasser would have been best taken care of in the way that the CIA and MI6 dislodged Musaddig as the head of the Iranian government in 1953—in other words, by covert action? If so there was an echo of a previous conversation between Lloyd and Dulles: "The Americans' main contention is that we can bring Nasser down by degrees rather on the Mossadeq lines."[75] Unfortunately Dulles did not elaborate, either earlier or later. But the British took his comment about failure to bring down Nasser as further evidence of double-dealing.

There was no love lost between Caccia and Dulles. Caccia believed that the Suez expedition would have been a success had the United States not forced the British prematurely to withdraw. He held Dulles responsible. The root of the trouble, in Caccia's view, went back to Dulles's duplicity on the SCUA. Early in 1957 he and Sir Anthony Head, the minister of defense, decided to confront Dulles with the basic grievance:

> What we complained of most was the way in which we were misled by his scheme for a Users' Association. He had held this out to us as a method of bringing joint pressure to bear on Egypt; but, as soon as we accepted it, he had watered it down to nothing at all. I said that, frankly, we felt we had been "led up the garden path" and that from that moment onwards the British Government had lost all confidence in the friendly intentions of the American Government.
>
> Dulles seemed momentarily embarrassed by this.[76]

The occasion for the renewal of this acrimonious discussion was another of Dulles's spontaneous public comments. Appearing before the Senate Foreign Relations Committee in January 1957, he stated that "if I were an American soldier who had to fight in the Middle East, I would rather not have a British and a French soldier, one on my right and one on my left." To Caccia this was an intolerable re-mark. He recalled Dulles's previous outburst on colonialism and other extemporaneous comments. He now reviewed the record. "All [his words] have been said under pressure and the words have not been deliberately chosen. But after all allowances they do show a cast of thought which we should ignore at risk."[77] Thus Dulles was a men-ace, and he had done harm, in Caccia's judgment irreparable dam-

[75] As alluded to in Eden to Macmillan, "Top Secret," September 23, 1956, PRO, FO 800/740.

[76] Head to Macmillan, "Secret," January 28, 1957, PRO, PREM 11/1178.

[77] Caccia to Lloyd, "Secret," January 26, 1957, PRO, PREM 11/1178.

age, to Anglo-American relations. That certainly was Eden's view as well.

Eden long outlived Dulles and continued to blame him for the fiasco at Suez. In his retirement he venomously referred to Dulles as "as tortuous as a wounded snake, with much less excuse."[78] The language was poisonous, but it was consistent with the underlying attitude in his memoirs, which have had a lasting influence on historical interpretation. Dulles served as a convenient scapegoat. Eisenhower was still alive, and Eden had to be wary of him while writing *Full Circle*.[79] But Dulles could be painted, subtly but firmly, as the villain. This view persists. Whatever the more balanced judgment might be, one thing is certain. Dulles left an enduring impression on the public consciousness in Britain. The words of a contemporary critic sum it up: Dulles had a "hypocritical obsession with the evils of British colonialism."[80] He himself was responsible for this lasting reputation because of his extravagant rhetoric. But for those who studied Dulles's more careful language and consistent attitudes, they found a steadfast determination not to use force, as well as views on colonialism shared widely by his countrymen. The Suez crisis caused his bedrock sentiments to erupt with the force of a volcano.

[78] Rhodes James, *Anthony Eden*, 617.
[79] See Blake, *The Decline of Power*, 349. Blake assisted Eden in the writing of the memoirs.
[80] Quoted in Thomas, *The Suez Affair*, 174.

CHAPTER 6

Dulles, Latin America, and Cold War Anticommunism

Stephen G. Rabe

SCHOLARS have given scant attention to John Foster Dulles's foreign policy toward Latin America because they believe the secretary of state concentrated his attention and energies on Europe, Asia, and the Middle East and neglected inter-American affairs.[1] This chapter challenges these traditional interpretations of Dulles and Latin America. It agrees with new studies that portray President Dwight D. Eisenhower as a strong and effective leader capably in charge of his own foreign policy.[2] President Eisenhower, not Dulles, directed the Latin American policy of the United States. And Eisenhower and Dulles did not ignore Latin America. They developed a coherent, consistent strategy for the region: they wanted Latin Americans to support the United States in the cold war, adopt free trade and investment principles, and oppose communism. But this chapter disagrees with those "Eisenhower revisionists" who argue that Eisenhower and Dulles's foreign policy was characterized by moderation, prudence, and restraint. In the name of anticommunism the administration expanded the measures deemed permissible to protect U.S. security, thereby violating the national sovereignty of Latin Americans.

. . .

During the presidential campaign of 1952 the Republicans promised to change the hemispheric policy of the United States. In a speech in

---

[1] Louis Gerson, *John Foster Dulles* (New York, 1967), 310. For other traditional interpretations of U.S. policy in Latin America in the 1950s, see Samuel Baily, *The United States and the Development of South America, 1945–1975* (New York, 1976), 68–79; Gordon Connell-Smith, *The United States and Latin America* (New York, 1974), 187–225; Federico G. Gil, *Latin American–United States Relations* (New York, 1971), 189–221; and F. Parkinson, *Latin America, the Cold War, and the World Powers, 1945–1973* (Beverly Hills, 1974), 52.

[2] For the new Eisenhower scholarship, see Stephen Ambrose, *Eisenhower*. Vol. 2: *The President* (New York, 1984); Robert Divine, *Eisenhower and the Cold War* (New York, 1981); and Fred Greenstein, *The Hidden-Hand Presidency* (New York, 1982).

New Orleans on October 13, 1952, Dwight Eisenhower charged that the neighbors to the south had lost confidence in the United States. Although Latin Americans had stoutly supported the United States during World War II, the Democrats had betrayed their trust by reneging on promises of postwar economic cooperation. The result, Eisenhower alleged, was economic distress "followed by popular unrest, skillfully exploited by Communist agents there." "Through drift and neglect" the Truman administration had turned a good neighbor policy into a "poor neighbor policy."[3]

In lambasting the Truman administration's Latin American policy, Eisenhower accurately depicted the disillusionment that Latin Americans felt over inter-American relations. The Truman government had decided to subordinate regional concerns to the more significant task of rebuilding Western Europe and Japan and containing the Soviet Union. Neither economic aid or a "Marshall Plan for Latin America" was feasible because the United States needed to rush money to Asia and Europe, the first lines of defense against international communism.[4]

Although it identified economic development as the key issue in inter-American relations, the new administration focused on political problems. Secretary of State Dulles set the tone for the administration's approach. During his confirmation hearings Dulles told the Senate Foreign Relations Committee that Soviet communism was "not only the gravest threat that ever faced the United States, but the gravest threat that has ever faced what we call western civilization, or, indeed, any civilization which was dominated by a spiritual faith." As for Latin America, Dulles saw a well-organized communist movement in most countries and a fascist apparatus in Argentina. These totalitarians were allied in their "hatred of the Yankee" and their determination "to destroy the influence of the so-called Colossus of the North in Central and South America." Dulles warned that "conditions in Latin America are somewhat comparable to conditions as they were in China in the mid-thirties when the Communist movement was getting started." He concluded: "The time to deal with this rising menace in South America is now."[5]

Historians have argued that such alarmist statements should not be taken seriously. Eisenhower and his aides used militantly anticom-

[3] Eisenhower's speech in sps, "Sept. 26–Oct. 13, 1952," awf.

[4] Stephen G. Rabe, "The Elusive Conference: United States Economic Relations with Latin America, 1945–1952," *Diplomatic History* 2 (Summer 1978): 279–94.

[5] U.S. Senate Committee on Foreign Relations, *Nomination of John Foster Dulles, Secretary of State-Designate*, 83rd Cong., 1st sess., 1953, 10, 30–31. See also John Foster Dulles, *War or Peace* (New York, 1950), 150–51.

munist rhetoric to hold the support of extremists and zealots in the Republican party. Unlike its rhetoric, the administration's policies were moderate and considered. It wisely declined, for example, to "liberate" Eastern Europe.[6] Yet in regard to Latin America the private discussions and classified policy statements of administration officials differed little from their public positions. Secretary Dulles's private views, in particular, coincided with his public pronouncements. In a telephone conversation he told his brother Allen, the director of the Central Intelligence Agency (CIA), that "the Communists are trying to extend their form of despotism in this hemisphere." He informed the cabinet that he would have to convince Latin Americans that communism was "an internationalist conspiracy, not an indigenous movement." Indeed, in 1956 for example, Dulles instructed an aide to tell Juscelino Kubitschek, the president of Brazil, that the communists had established within Brazil and the United States "nerve centers" that directed "the operations of this international conspiracy." The objectives of the communists were contained in a "master plan" about which "we know a good deal." These conspirators intended to retard economic progress in countries like Brazil and "to separate each American state from every other American state in order that politically and in a military sense we would not be as strong or as coordinated an enemy in the event of another war."[7]

Convinced that Kremlin-directed communist aggression imperiled the world, the Eisenhower administration set out to construct its Latin American policy. The administration's first substantive discussion of inter-American relations took place on February 18, 1953, at a National Security Council meeting. The NSC received an unsettling briefing from CIA Director Dulles, who reported that Latin America was "deteriorating not only in terms of cordiality of relationships with the United States but in the economic and political spheres of most of the Latin American states. The Kremlin was exploiting this situation." Dulles compared developments in Latin America with revolutionary movements in the Middle East, with "trends in the direction of economic nationalism, regionalism, neutralism, and increasing Communist influence." In particular, "Communist infection" in Guatemala was "such as to mark an approaching crisis." These develop-

[6] Michael Guhin, *John Foster Dulles: A Statesman and His Times* (New York, 1972), 2–10, 304–6; William B. Pickett, "The Eisenhower Solarium Notes," *Newsletter of the Society of Historians of American Foreign Relations* 16 (June 1985): 1–10.

[7] Dulles to Allen Dulles, February 25, 1954, TTS, "January–February 1954 (2)," DPEL; Cabinet meeting, February 26, 1954, Cabinet Series (Minnich Notes) "C-12," WHOSS; Memorandum of conversation between Dulles and Kubitschek, January 6, 1956, *FR, 1955–1957*, 7:685–89.

ments endangered U.S. access to Latin America's strategic materials and retarded inter-American military cooperation. "Deeply disturbed" by Dulles's report, Eisenhower ordered the NSC staff to prepare expeditiously a paper on Latin America.[8]

A month later, on March 18, 1953, Eisenhower had a new policy for Latin America, NSC 144/1. Although described by Under Secretary of State Walter Bedell Smith as a paper "prepared in some haste" that represented a "shotgun approach," NSC 144/1 served as the basis for all subsequent statements on "United States Objectives and Courses of Actions with Respect to Latin America."[9] The document interpreted inter-American affairs solely within the context of the Soviet-American confrontation. It had little to say about political and social democracy or human rights in Latin America, except to note that the United States favored "orderly political and economic development" in the region. What the United States wanted was for Latin America to support the U.S. position at the UN, eliminate the "menace of internal Communist or other anti-U.S. subversion," produce strategic raw materials, and cooperate in defending the hemisphere. After cursory debate Eisenhower approved the paper.[10]

Beyond enumerating U.S. objectives, NSC 144/1 reflected the frustration government officials felt about Latin Americans' failure to understand the dangers of international communism. In the annex to NSC 144, the staff study that served as the basis for NSC 144/1, the administration lamented that Latin American leaders, preoccupied with domestic demands for rapid social and economic change, ignored their international responsibilities. Therefore, Washington had to reconsider the U.S. commitment to nonintervention and the Charter of the Organization of American States (OAS), which prohibited any state from intervening "directly or indirectly, for any reason whatever, in the internal or external affairs of any other state." The study noted that "it is probable that the majority of Latin American governments do not yet favor even limited multilateral intervention," and it speculated that collective action "would probably be supported" only if a "clearly identifiable communist regime should establish itself in the hemisphere." Still, the study concluded that "overriding security interests" required the United States to consider acting unilaterally, albeit recognizing that "this would be a violation of our

[8] Memorandum of NSC meeting, February 18, 1953 (February 19, 1953), NSCS, "132nd Meeting of the NSC, February 18, 1953," AWF.

[9] FR, 1952–1954, 4:2. Other key NSC statements on Latin America were: NSC 5432/1 of 1954; NSC 5613/1 of 1956; NSC 5902/1 of 1959; and the draft revision of NSC 5902/1 of late 1960.

[10] FR, 1952–1954, 4:1–10.

treaty commitments, would endanger the Organization of American States . . . and would probably intensify anti-U.S. attitudes in many Latin American countries."[11]

With NSC 144/1 as guidance the Eisenhower administration worked to hold Latin American support for the cold war and to eradicate communists in the hemisphere. Its initiatives were evident in its public relations, propaganda, labor, military aid, and recognition policies. Secretary of State Dulles often played a vital role in implementing these policies. To demonstrate that the administration did not "neglect" Latin America, officials attempted to "dramatize" U.S. interest. In 1953 Eisenhower dispatched his brother, Milton, to South America. The president also attended a dinner for Latin American ambassadors, and spoke on Pan American Day at the OAS center in Washington. Similarly, the State Department tried to show that the United States was paying more attention to Latin America by inviting Latin Americans for visits, issuing commemorative stamps, and distributing movies that "would be particularly effective in getting our message to the illiterate masses."[12] Such efforts, Dulles told Eisenhower, were "a very good way of doing things," for "you have to pat them a little bit and make them think that you are fond of them."[13]

The administration coupled its "fondness" campaign with tough anticommunist measures. It aimed its information and cultural programs at alerting Latin Americans to "the dangers of Soviet imperialism and communist and other anti-U.S. subversion." The U.S. Information Agency spent about $5.2 million a year producing and distributing such items as ninety thousand anticommunist cartoon books for Central America; anticommunist comic strips for over three hundred Latin American newspapers; and scripts for twenty-six anticommunist radio shows in Cuba. The administration also opened a fifty-thousand-watt radio broadcast station in El Salvador, which in the State Department's view would be useful both for "overt propaganda and news" and "in the covert propaganda field as well."[14] In addition, the department tried to disrupt what it considered communist-front conferences, including youth festivals and student con-

[11] Annex to NSC 144, March 6, 1953, "NSC 144," WHOSANSA.

[12] First progress report on NSC 144/1, July 23, 1953, *FR, 1952–1954*, 4:12–14; Assistant Secretary of State for Latin America John Moors Cabot to Dulles, March 28, 1953, DSRG 59, 611.20/3-2853.

[13] Dulles telephone conversation with Eisenhower, February 26, 1953, TTS, "January–April 1953," DPEL.

[14] Progress report on NSC 5432/1, January 19, 1955, *FR, 1952–1954*, 4:106–7; State Department officer R. Richard Rubottom to Cabot, March 19, 1953, DSRG 59, 611.20/3-1953.

gresses. It asked all Latin American countries to deny visas and passports for travel to communist-sponsored conferences. Most countries acceded to the U.S. request, although the large countries—Argentina, Brazil, and Mexico—declined to issue new regulations, citing constitutional restrictions.[15]

The administration's anticommunist offensive was also launched on the labor front. One of the objectives of NSC 144/1 was to encourage the development of the regional Inter-American Organization of Workers, an anticommunist trade-union movement in Latin America sponsored by the American Federation of Labor (AFL). The administration's policies included gathering information on the Latin American labor movement, inviting labor leaders to visit the United States, and investigating the backgrounds of union officials in plants that were to receive technical cooperation under the Point Four program. In implementing these policies the State Department consulted with U.S. union officials. George Meany, the president of the AFL, assured department officers that his union's goal in Latin America was "to create friendship and support for the U.S. in opposition to the attempt of the Communists to seek the same support and friendship of Russia." Meany and others added, however, that their task of creating a democratic labor movement would be easier if the United States did not recognize dictatorships and if U.S. firms in Latin America established fair labor practices.[16] Nonetheless, State Department officials were impressed by the anticommunist fervor of U.S. trade unions, and Assistant Secretary of State John Moors Cabot recommended to Dulles that "we be prepared to supplement the financial contributions of U.S. labor on a highly secret basis."[17]

[15] Dulles to U.S. Embassies in Latin America, August 18, 1953, DSRG 59, 720.001/8-1853; Dulles to U.S. Embassies in Latin America, April 19, 1954, ibid., 720.001/4-1954; U.S. Ambassador Francis White, Mexico City, to Dulles, April 21, 1954, ibid., 720.001/4-2154.

[16] Meany quoted in Cabot's memorandum of conversation with Meany, March 12, 1953, DSRG 59, 820.06/3-1253. See also Cabot's memorandum of conversation with Paul Reed of the United Mine Workers, March 16, 1953, ibid., 820.06/3-1653; Under Secretary Smith to U.S. Embassy, Santiago, Chile, April 23, 1953, ibid., 820.00TA/4-2353; Dulles to U.S. Embassies in Latin America, June 29, 1953, ibid., 820.062/6-2953.

[17] Cabot's recommendation to Dulles cited in memorandum of J. T. Fishburn, State Department labor adviser, to Cabot, March 23, 1953, DSRG 59, 820.06/3-2353. The March 16 memorandum of Cabot to Dulles, which Fishburn cited, was not found in the appropriate decimal file. It cannot de determined whether Secretary Dulles accepted the recommendation to fund the U.S. trade movement, but in the late 1960s allegations arose that, beginning in 1959, the CIA had transferred funds to noncommunist labor movements in Latin America. See New York Times, February 19, 1967, February 22, 1967. See also George Morris, CIA and American Labor: The Subversion of the AFL-CIO's Foreign Policy (New York, 1967), 78–79, 150–56.

In addition to sponsoring anticommunist measures in Latin America, the Eisenhower administration tried to arm the region. During the 1950s military assistance, which amounted to approximately $400 million, was the only significant U.S. aid program for Latin America. The program was a legacy of the Truman administration, and Eisenhower, who had testified in favor of military aid in the 1940s, heartily backed its continuation. Recalling his efforts during the Truman years, the president told the NSC that he had "never wholly sympathized with the State Department view that munitions sent to Latin America would be used by the republics for hostilities against each other." Military aid was crucial because the United States needed Latin America's strategic materials and because "we can't defend South America if this Communist war starts."[18]

Eisenhower's strong views notwithstanding, the United States could not immediately deliver weapons to Latin America. By mid-1954, $105 million in military aid had been appropriated, but only $20 million in matériel had been shipped. Other regions, such as French Indochina, had a greater claim on U.S. military aid than did Latin America. When informed of the delay, Eisenhower instructed the Department of Defense to "investigate the feasibility of accelerating deliveries of military equipment to Latin American republics." But, although promising to expedite deliveries, the Joint Chiefs of Staff and defense officials resisted giving Latin America priority for U.S. military equipment. Their decision left Latin America, in the words of Under Secretary Smith, "at the bottom of the heap as far as military priorities were concerned."[19]

This decision suggested that fears of Soviet aggression against Latin America were exaggerated. Indeed, the activities of defense planners continually belied the need for inter-American military cooperation. Over one hundred thousand U.S. troops served in the Western Hemisphere during World War II—but virtually all of them were located in the Caribbean, guarding the Panama Canal. According to NSC 144/1, the United States would insist that Latin Americans continue to accept "U.S. military control of defense of these areas." Moreover, although ostensibly part of a multilateral plan, military assistance agreements were bilateral pacts. The Inter-American Defense Board, which was composed of U.S. and Latin American military officers, had functioned since 1942; but the United States largely ignored the defense board, and the board did not coordinate or su-

[18] Memorandum of NSC meeting, April 28, 1953, *FR, 1952–1954*, 4:146–47; Eisenhower conversation with Senator Malone, July 20, 1954, AWD, "July 1954 (2)," AWF.

[19] Eisenhower quoted in editorial note, *FR, 1952–1954*, 4:44; Memorandum of NSC meeting, September 2, 1954, ibid., 79.

pervise the bilateral agreements. In any case by arming Western Europe, Japan, the Philippine Islands, and South Korea, the United States was moving its lines of defense far from the American continents.[20]

Whereas the strategic benefits of inter-American military cooperation may have been slight, the political advantages of military aid were significant. Training and assistance programs gave the Eisenhower administration access to the Latin American military caste, a bulwark of anticommunism. U.S. Army Chief of Staff J. Lawton Collins, in supporting military aid for Anastasio Somoza's Nicaragua, noted that "the Latin American officers who work with us and some of whom come to this country and see what we have and what we can do are frequently our most useful friends in those countries." Because military officers either ruled or dominated many Latin American nations, this friendship was essential. Ambassador to Paraguay George Shaw reported that the U.S. military mission lent prestige to the Paraguayan military establishment and demonstrated that "the United States is backing the government of Paraguay and the party in power, which remains in power largely because of the military." Ambassador to Venezuela Fletcher Warren advised Washington that the United States should sell sophisticated military equipment to dictator Marcos Pérez Jiménez because he had "broken diplomatic relations with Soviet Russia and Czechoslovakia, and embarked upon the closest supervision of the activities of Communist front groups." Officials in Washington agreed that the primary purpose of military aid was to maintain "good U.S. military relations with the Latin American military," although they declined to say so publicly when defending aid programs.[21]

Secretary Dulles recognized that military assistance had little strategic value and was used by Latin American military rulers to enhance their prestige and power. On September 6, 1956, at an NSC meeting, he voiced those concerns to the president. Dulles questioned whether, "the United States really wanted to build up large military

[20] NSC 144/1, March 18, 1953, FR, 1952–1954, 4:9; John Child, Unequal Alliance: The Inter-American Military System, 1938–1978 (Boulder, 1980), 120; Stephen G. Rabe, "Inter-American Military Cooperation, 1944–1951," World Affairs 137 (Fall 1974): 132–49; Robert D. Tomasek, "Defense of the Western Hemisphere: A Need for Reexamination of United States Policy," Midwest Journal of Political Science 3 (November 1959): 355–59.

[21] Memorandum of meeting between State Department and Joint Chiefs of Staff, May 22, 1954, FR, 1952–1954, 4:150–53; Shaw to State Department, September 4, 1953, ibid., 1473–80; Warren to State Department, May 11, 1953, ibid., 1643–47; George O. Spencer, special assistant for inter-American military assistance, to Assistant Secretary Henry Holland, November 4, 1954, DSRG 59, 720.MSP/11-454.

establishments in these Latin American Republics." He observed that, given the unstable nature of some governments, the United States could not "estimate reasonably what use they will make of larger military establishments." Perhaps one republic would use arms to threaten another. In fact, the State Department was receiving reports from officers in the field that "much of the military equipment maintained by Latin American countries is obtained in an effort to counter equipment which they fear might be used against them by some rival country." Dulles suggested that the United States "would be better off if by itself it undertook to protect the sea lanes of communication and the Panama Canal."[22]

Admiral Arthur Radford of the Joint Chiefs of Staff replied "with emphasis" to Dulles. If the United States drastically changed its military aid policy, it would be difficult to "keep the Latin American republics in line." They would purchase arms elsewhere and perhaps establish foreign military missions. Moreover, because Congress authorized military aid for hemispheric defense, the Joint Chiefs had to define a military role for Latin America. In the face of the admiral's assault, Dulles rapidly retreated from his position. He admitted that Radford was correct about the terms of the Mutual Security Act, and he conceded that it was "better that such additional armament come from U.S. stocks than from some foreign sources."[23]

President Eisenhower saw merit in both views. He recalled that most of the Latin American leaders he had met in Panama at a conference in 1956 wore military medals, which were "struck for their own purposes," and that "only two or three of the leaders of the Latin American Republics wanted to be called by other than some military title." He did not wish to encourage further dependence on the military. He also doubted the ability of the armed forces of Latin America to contribute to hemispheric defense. Yet, he "agreed with Admiral Radford that what we want to preserve above all is the good will of the Latin American Republics" and "to assure their internal security, without which their good will would be useless to us." Eisenhower ruled that military aid would continue.[24]

Perhaps chastened by the president's decision and in view of his own staunch anticommunist views, Dulles never again challenged

---

[22] Memorandum of NSC meeting, September 6, 1956, *FR, 1955–1957*, 6:106–7; Report of J. Lawton Collins and Ambassador John C. Hughes, February 23, 1957, "Latin American Trip," U.S. President's Citizen Advisers on the Mutual Security Program (Fairless Committee) Records, Eisenhower Library.

[23] Memorandum of NSC meeting, September 6, 1956, *FR, 1955–1957*, 6:107–13.

[24] *FR, 1955–1957*, 6:108–13; Memorandum of NSC meeting, September 20, 1956, ibid., 116–18.

military assistance. In 1958, Democrats on the Senate Foreign Relations Committee, led by J. William Fulbright, bluntly criticized inter-American military programs. Military assistance had bolstered unrepresentative regimes, created a militaristic image of the United States, and built and perpetuated hierarchies that "endanger the very values of individual freedom which we seek to safeguard."[25] Dulles advised President Eisenhower to deflect the Democrats' charges by appointing a committee, the Draper Committee, to issue a public report to put military assistance "on a sound long-term basis." Although Dulles shared Fulbright's concern about excessive military aid, he told the senator in early 1959 that "if we carried out the theory too rigidly the practical result would be that many friendly governments would collapse and Communism would take over."[26] In conducting its investigations the Draper Committee would learn from U.S. military officers that the Soviet Union posed no military threat to Latin America. But Acting Secretary of State Christian Herter, writing in 1959 for the ailing Dulles, found that irrelevant. The key question was: "Is the country on our side?" Communism threatened the United States; therefore, "a more urgent value—security and survival—must take precedence over an absolute commitment to the promotion of democracy."[27]

A commitment to democracy and human rights did not always characterize the Eisenhower administration and Dulles's diplomacy toward Latin America. When they took office, the Republicans pledged to restore the traditional de facto recognition policy of the United States and conduct normal diplomatic relations with noncommunist Latin American republics. The new administration was reacting to the Truman administration's Argentine policy. First as ambassador to Argentina and then as assistant secretary of state, Spruille Braden had between 1945 and 1947 interfered in Argentine politics, denouncing the military rulers of Argentina as erstwhile sympathizers of Nazi Germany. Colonel Juan Perón cleverly seized upon Braden's impolitic behavior and turned the Argentine election of February 1946 into a campaign against Yankee imperialism; he won a

[25] The senators' letter is in U.S. President's Committee to Study the U.S. Military Assistance Program (Draper Committee) Records, *Composite Report*, 185–87, Eisenhower Library.

[26] Dulles to Eisenhower, September 13, 1958, Subject Series, Alphabetical Subseries, "ICA(3)," WHOSS; Memorandum of conversation with Fulbright, February 2, 1959, GCMS, "Memos of conversations–General–E through I (1)," DPEL.

[27] Admiral Robert B. Carney to William Draper, February 13, 1959, "Sixth Committee Meeting folder," and Dulles (Herter) to Draper, February 17, 1959, "Letter to John Foster Dulles folder," both in Draper Committee Records, Eisenhower Library.

landslide victory.[28] Thereafter, relations between the United States and Perón's Argentina remained strained.

In both private discussions and public pronouncements, Secretary of State Dulles explained the administration's policy. In 1953 he turned aside a suggestion by the president that the United States urge freedom of the press by speaking on behalf of the embattled Argentine newspaper, *La Prensa*. Such a step would upset Perón and violate "our policy and commitments against intervention in the internal affairs of the other American nations."[29] At a news conference in 1956 Dulles observed that he realized that "the American Republics are much divided among themselves on the question of democratic governments as against so-called dictator governments." But he added that, whatever the U.S. views, he did not think it "wise or profitable to carry those views into the current conditions of our relations with those countries."[30] Assistant Secretary of State for Latin America Henry Holland assured his boss that he was implementing the correct policy. In Holland's view, "the genius of the Eisenhower administration was to get along with all countries." To denounce dictators would be "going back to Bradenism."[31]

With dictators firmly ensconced in power in thirteen of the twenty Latin American countries by 1954, the Eisenhower administration and Dulles had little choice but to work with tyrants. The administration went beyond dealing, however, with "so-called dictator governments" to supporting them. Secretary Dulles worked assiduously, for example, for a rapprochement with Perón. In his confirmation hearings Dulles had charged that there were fascists in Argentina. But Perón was an anticommunist and by the early 1950s his economic policies had so disrupted the Argentine economy that he needed U.S. assistance. As Dulles explained to Eisenhower, it was "of the greatest importance" to take advantage of Perón's new orientation in order to "develop a sound basis of solidarity with the Argentine government to prevent it becoming a possible threat to inter-American security and solidarity." Accordingly, by the end of 1954 the United States had sold Argentina a government-owned rolling mill for the production of steel; had agreed to loan $60 million through the Export-Import Bank to help build a new steel mill; and had begun to consider

[28] Roger R. Trask, "Spruille Braden versus George Messersmith: World War II, the Cold War, and Argentine Policy, 1945–1947," *Journal of Inter-American Studies and World Affairs* 26 (February 1984): 69–95.

[29] Dulles to Eisenhower, November 19, 1953, *FR, 1952–1954*, 4:450–52.

[30] Dulles quoted in Richard P. Stebbins, *The United States in World Affairs, 1956* (New York, 1957), 238.

[31] Holland to Dulles, September 28, 1956, TTS, "July–September 1956 (1)," DPEL.

including Argentina in its military assistance program.[32] These effects to curry favor with Perón gained little, nevertheless, for U.S. diplomacy. The Argentine economy continued to flounder and the Perón regime began to disintegrate in early 1955. Argentine military officers overthrew Perón in September of that year.

The administration not only aided Latin American strongmen but also fawned over some of the region's most unsavory tyrants. The president awarded a Legion of Merit, the nation's highest honor for foreign personages, to both Manuel Odría, the military dictator of Peru, and Marcos Pérez Jiménez of Venezuela. Both men had earned Washington's gratitude by dutifully following the anticommunist line. The Venezuelan, for example, received his medal in October 1954 in a grand ceremony conducted by U.S. Ambassador Fletcher Warren. The award's announcement cited the dictator's "indefatigable energy and firmness of purpose" for having "greatly increased the capacity of the Armed Forces of Venezuela to participate in the collective defense of the Western Hemisphere," as well as noting that "his constant concern toward the problem of Communist infiltration has kept his government alert to repel the threat against his country and the rest of the Americas."[33] Other ambassadors were as "intimately cordial" with anticommunist dictators as was Warren. Ambassador to Cuba Arthur Gardner and his wife frequently socialized with Fulgencio Batista and his wife. Ambassador to the Dominican Republic William Pheiffer characterized Rafael Trujillo Molina, in a speech, as "an authentic genius who thinks and labors, primarily, in terms of the best interests of his people."[34]

During the Eisenhower years anticommunism, in addition to earning dictators lavish praise, protected them from criticism. Labeling it

[32] Dulles to Eisenhower, June 18, 1953, *FR, 1952–1954*, 4:440–41; Harold F. Peterson, *Argentina and the United States, 1810–1960* (New York, 1964), 489; Dulles to Secretary of Defense Charles Wilson, June 3, 1955, *FR, 1955–1957*, 7:360–61. The administration's economic relations with Perón are documented in *FR, 1952–1954*, 4:469–84.

[33] Stephen G. Rabe, *The Road to OPEC: United States Relations with Venezuela, 1919–1976* (Austin, 1982), 127; Assistant Secretary Holland to Dulles, December 20, 1954, *FR, 1952–1954*, 4:1674–75.

[34] Warren to Director Rollin Atwood, Office of South American Affairs, December 8, 1954, *FR, 1952–1954*, 4:1674–75; for accounts of Gardner's activities, see Philip Bonsal, *Cuba, Castro, and the United States* (Pittsburgh, 1971), 13; Earl E. T. Smith, *The Fourth Floor: An Account of the Castro Communist Revolution* (New York, 1962), 20; David Atlee Phillips, *The Night Watch* (New York, 1977), 63–64; Pheiffer quoted in G. Pope Atkins and Larman C. Wilson, *The United States and the Trujillo Regime* (New Brunswick, N.J., 1972), 71.

"an internal Venezuelan matter," Assistant Secretary Cabot in 1953 turned away appeals from U.S. citizens who wanted the State Department to intercede on behalf of the political prisoners rotting in the dungeons of Pérez Jiménez. A year later, after Holland succeeded Cabot, the State Department further pandered to Pérez Jiménez by harassing and threatening to revoke the political asylum of the exiled democrat Rómulo Betancourt.[35] On the other hand Ambassador to Columbia Philip Bonsal's liaisons with democrats such as Alberto Lleras Camargo, a past and future president of Columbia, earned him the wrath of dictator Gustavo Rojas Pinilla and reassignment orders from the Department of State.[36]

John Foster Dulles received blame for these policies. As U.S. Ambassador to the OAS John Dreier recalled, Dulles would have been happy to see "flourishing little democracies" in Latin America, but "I think that he was somewhat inclined to feel that governments which contributed to a stability in the area were preferable to those which introduced instability and social upheaval, which would lead to Communist penetration." Dulles, therefore, was "very tolerant" of dictatorships, "as long as they took a firm stand against communism."[37] José Figueres, the popularly elected president of Costa Rica, was less charitable. In reviewing inter-American relations in the 1950s, he charged that "our main enemy was Mr. John Foster Dulles in his defending corrupt dictatorships."[38] Ambassador to Costa Rica Robert Woodward agreed with Figueres. The veteran foreign service officer alleged that at a staff meeting Dulles had "laid down with vigor" the policy to "do nothing to offend the dictators; they are the only people we can depend on."[39]

Dulles may have believed that dictators were dependable allies of the United States. But the secretary of state was implementing his superior's policy. Like Dulles, President Eisenhower preferred to work with leaders who protected civil and human rights. At an NSC meeting he sharply disagreed with Secretary of Treasury George

[35] Cabot memorandum of conversation with members of the Inter-American Association for Freedom and Democracy, December 30, 1953, DSRG 59, 611.20/12-3053; Bainbridge C. Davis, Office of South American Affairs, to Holland on exile of Betancourt, July 14, 1954, ibid., 731.00/7-1454; Robert J. Alexander, *Rómulo Betancourt and the Transformation of Venezuela* (New Brunswick, N.J., 1982), 361–62; *FR, 1952–1954*, 4:1669–74.

[36] Bonsal, *Cuba, Castro, and the United States*, 27.

[37] John Dreier interview, JFDOHC.

[38] José Figueres interview, Harry S. Truman Library, Independence, Mo.

[39] Woodward related this charge to Adolf Berle. See diary entry, February 8, 1955, Adolf A. Berle, Jr., Papers, Franklin D. Roosevelt Library, Hyde Park, New York.

Humphrey who argued that the United States "should back strong men in Latin American governments" because "whenever a dictator was replaced, Communists gained." The president pointed out to his advisers that "he firmly believed that if power lies with the people, then there will be no aggressive war." "In the long run," therefore, "the United States must back democracies."[40]

But Eisenhower could also be ambivalent about dictators. In July 1956 Eisenhower attended a ceremonial inter-American conclave in Panama with the leaders of other American republics; he also met individually with each leader. The president did not raise questions of human or civil rights with any dictator. Instead he confided to his diary that Anastasio Somoza of Nicaragua and General Alfredo Stroessner, the military dictator of Paraguay, "stood out" among those he had met. Stroessner had perhaps earned Eisenhower's admiration by assuring him that "Paraguay was one-hundred percent anticommunist and would continue to be so." The obsequious Somoza told Eisenhower that "if the United States desired a canal in Nicaragua, it was all right with him."[41]

The same stance on dictatorships was evident during Vice President Richard Nixon's tour of Central America and the Caribbean in early 1955. State Department officers briefed Nixon not to raise questions of civil liberties with tyrants; he should, however, urge them to guard against communism. In regard to Batista, for example, the department noted its disappointment that the Cuban leader did not hound Cuban Communists but added that "his continuance in office is probably a good thing from standpoint of U.S."[42] The vice president obeyed his instructions. Before cameras he gleefully embraced Trujillo and Batista. And in a toast to Batista he compared the Cuban to Abraham Lincoln. When Nixon returned to Washington he proudly reported to the cabinet; he called Batista "a very remarkable man" and found that Trujillo had given his people clean, drinkable water, an obsession with progress, and pride in being on time. The price may have been dictatorship, but as Nixon saw it, "Spaniards had many talents, but government was not among them."[43]

[40] Memorandum of NSC meeting, February 17, 1955, FR, 1955–1957, 6:2–5.

[41] Entry for July 25, 1956, in Robert Ferrell, ed., The Eisenhower Diaries (New York, 1981), 328; Memorandum of Eisenhower conversations with Stroessner and Somoza, both July 23, 1956, IS, "Panama Chronology July 23–24, 1956," AWF.

[42] Briefing on Cuba, January 31, 1955, box 1, series 361, Richard M. Nixon Papers, Federal Archives Center, Laguna Niguel, Calif.; Briefing on Dominican Republic, February 3, 1955, ibid.

[43] Nixon's toast to Batista (n.d., but February 1955), Nixon Papers, series 362; Cabi-

However controversial the policies that flowed from NSC 144/1 on issues such as public relations, labor, inter-American military cooperation, and democracy and human rights, they were pursued by President Eisenhower and Secretary of State Dulles in the name of national security. But their fears about Soviet imperialism in the Western Hemisphere derived more from inference and analogies from other areas of the world than from dispassionate analyses. Through the 1950s, communism did not seem to threaten Latin America any more than it had in 1948, when the Truman administration, in NSC 16—the first NSC document devoted exclusively to Latin America—decided that "communism in the Americas is a potential danger, but that, with few possible exceptions, it is not seriously dangerous at the present time."[44] For example, in September 1953 Assistant Secretary Cabot responded to an NSC inquiry about communism in the hemisphere. He conceded that the major source of friction in inter-American relations was not the machinations of the Soviet Union but rather the intense resentment Latin Americans felt about the absence of a Marshall Plan for them. Latin Americans, including political radicals, were absorbed with domestic, not international problems. As Cabot told the NSC, "we must remember that many of them are essentially native Communists."[45]

Soviet diplomacy and economic influence was similarly minimal. Until 1960 the Soviets had embassies in only Argentina, Mexico, and Uruguay. Soviet trade with Latin America usually amounted to less than 2 percent of the value of Latin America's annual international trade. Russia's only significant trading partners in the hemisphere were Argentina and Uruguay. Russia badly needed their beef, wheat, and wool but had few valuable goods, except petroleum, to sell in return. The bilateral balance of trade favored the Latin Americans. Argentina and Uruguay traded with the Soviets because the hemisphere's wealthiest nations, Canada and the United States, did not need their products, for they also produced abundant quantities of beef, wheat, and wool.[46] The Eisenhower administration, in fearing a

net meeting, March 11, 1955, Cabinet Series (Minnich Notes), "C-22," WHOSS. See also Nixon's report to NSC, memorandum of NSC meeting, March 10, 1955, *FR, 1955–1957*, 6:614–18.

[44] *FR, 1948*, 9:193–206.

[45] Cabot to NSC, September 9, 1953, DSRG 59, 611.20/9-953.

[46] Aldo César Vacs, *Discreet Partners: Argentina and the USSR since 1917* (Pittsburgh, 1984), 13–17; Cole Blaiser, *The Giant's Rival: The USSR and Latin America* (Pittsburgh, 1983), 27; National Intelligence Estimate on Argentina, March 9, 1954, *FR, 1952–1954*, 4:463–64; Robert Loring Allen, *Soviet Influence in Latin America: The Role of Economic Relations* (Washington, 1959), 6.

communist conspiracy in Latin America, had interjected global concerns into what were regional affairs.

A confusion of regional and global issues also marked the administration's most extreme anticommunist measure, the overthrow in June 1954 of President Jacobo Arbenz Guzmán of Guatemala. The story of how the Eisenhower administration overthrew the Arbenz government has been well told elsewhere, and only the role Secretary Dulles played in the *golpe de estado*—or coup—will be emphasized here.[47] The administration destroyed the Arbenz government because it believed that Guatemala was or soon would be under the domination of communists loyal to Moscow. President Arbenz was suspect because of his friendship with Guatemalan Communists, his expropriation of the holdings of the United Fruit Company, and his purchase of arms from the Soviet bloc in May 1954. As Ambassador to Guatemala John Peurifoy put it after his first conversation with Arbenz, "if the President is not a Communist he will certainly do until one comes along."[48] The administration ultimately rejected arguments of Guatemalan government officials that Guatemala was a democratic country; that communists could be controlled best in the open; and that their reforms, like the redistribution of land, would undermine the appeal of communism. The U.S. position was that communism was international in scope, that it was directed by Moscow, and that it constituted intervention in the internal affairs of Latin American states. A Guatemalan Communist was by definition a subversive, not a nationalist reformer.[49]

During the latter part of 1953 President Eisenhower ordered the CIA to organize a program, code named PBSUCCESS, to undermine the Arbenz government. Eisenhower confined knowledge of the conspiracy to his closest advisers. Probably only the president, the Dulles brothers, Under Secretary Smith, and Special Assistant for National Security Affairs Robert Cutler were intimately aware of all details. In all likelihood Eisenhower controlled the operation through oral communications with Secretary Dulles.[50]

[47] Good accounts can be found in Richard Immerman, *The CIA in Guatemala: The Foreign Policy of Intervention* (Austin, 1982); Stephen Schlesinger and Stephen Kinzer, *Bitter Fruit: The Untold Story of the American Coup in Guatemala* (Garden City, N.Y., 1982); David Wise and Thomas B. Ross, *The Invisible Government* (New York, 1964), 165–83; Bryce Wood, *The Dismantling of the Good Neighbor Policy* (Austin, 1985), 152–90.

[48] Peurifoy to State Department, December 17, 1953, *FR, 1952–1954*, 4:1091–93.

[49] Memorandum of conversation between Eisenhower and Ambassador Guillermo Toriello of Guatemala, January 16, 1954, *FR, 1952–1954*, 4:1095–97; Cabot to Acting Secretary of State, February 10, 1954, ibid., 279–92.

[50] Immerman, *CIA in Guatemala*, 133–68; Schlesinger and Kinzer, *Bitter Fruit*, 99–117.

Secretary Dulles's public role in the anti-Arbenz campaign was to head the U.S. delegation to the Tenth Inter-American Conference at Caracas in March 1954 and secure an anticommunist resolution or, in his words, to extend "the Monroe Doctrine to include the concept of outlawing foreign ideologies in the American Republics."[51] On the surface the Caracas conference went well for the administration. Dulles fervently pressed the anticommunist case, and after two weeks of debate the resolution, which called the "domination or control of the political institutions of any American state" a "threat" to the entire hemisphere, carried by a vote of 17-1-2. Only Guatemala opposed the resolution; Argentina and Mexico abstained. Guatemala's lone opposition underscored the administration's contention of communist penetration. Secretary Dulles proclaimed that the Monroe Doctrine had become a multilateral pact.[52]

Although Dulles obtained his resolution it lacked, in his word, "vitality." Dulles labored to secure his anticommunist manifesto. Latin Americans, led by representatives from Argentina, Mexico, and Uruguay, offered fifty-one amendments designed to weaken the resolution. Dulles was able to fend off fifty, defeating many of the amendments by votes of 11-9. His allies were the Caribbean and South American dictators, something Dulles confessed in executive congressional testimony "was sometimes a bit embarrassing."[53] The one amendment that carried seriously weakened the resolution. Instead of calling for immediate action against "Communist control or domination," it merely recommended that the American states meet to consider the adoption of measures in accordance with existing treaties. In short, the Latin Americans rejected the administration's contention that communism in Latin America constituted external aggression. Louis Halle, of the State Department's Policy Planning Staff, opined that the message of Caracas was "that there was more fear of U.S. interventionism than of Guatemalan communism."[54]

Nonetheless, although Dulles preferred "support from others than

[51] Dulles quoted in memorandum of NSC meeting, March 18, 1954, *FR, 1952–1954*, 4:304–6.

[52] Dulles's statement in U.S. Department of State, *DSB* 30 (March 29, 1954): 466; Dwight D. Eisenhower, *Mandate for Change, 1953–1956* (Garden City, N.Y., 1963), 507–11.

[53] Dulles's testimony in U.S. House of Representatives, Committee on Foreign Affairs, *Selected Executive Session Hearings of the Committee, 1951–1956*. Vol. 16: *Middle East, Africa, and Inter-American Affairs* (Washington, 1980), 502–15; Memorandum of NSC meeting, March 18, 1954, *FR, 1952–1954*, 4:304–6.

[54] Jerome Slater, *The OAS and United States Foreign Policy* (Columbia, 1967), 118–20; Halle to Director of Policy Planning Staff, May 28, 1954, *FR, 1952–1954*, 4:1148. See also analysis of Caracas resolution by John Moors Cabot in his interview, JFDOHC.

the Somozas in the hemisphere," the Caracas resolution proved useful to the administration. It served as diplomatic cover and a propaganda tool, helping, as Secretary Dulles circumspectly told his brother Allen, to "make other things more natural."[55] The CIA-backed and -sponsored "invasion" of Guatemala from Honduras by the forces of Colonel Carlos Castillo Armas began on June 18, 1954, and within ten days the Arbenz government had collapsed. Thereafter, Guatemalan military officers wrangled over who should lead their nation. After receiving authorization from Secretary Dulles to "crack some heads together," Ambassador Peurifoy arranged a settlement on July 2 that left Colonel Castillo Armas, the CIA's man, the president of the junta.[56]

The Eisenhower administration was immensely pleased that its bold policy had succeeded. President Eisenhower congratulated Allen Dulles for having "averted a Soviet beachhead in our hemisphere." Secretary Dulles boasted to colleagues that Guatemala was "the biggest success in the last five years against communism," and Eisenhower pointed to Guatemala with pride during the 1956 presidential campaign.[57] But although pleased by the fall of Arbenz, Secretary Dulles and others were slightly troubled that they had prepared and executed a golpe when they knew the case against Arbenz was based on "circumstantial" evidence. On May 11, 1954, Dulles admitted to the Brazilian ambassador that it would be "impossible to produce evidence clearly tying the Guatemalan Government to Moscow; that the decision must be a political one and based on our deep conviction that such a tie must exist." In early June the secretary of state pleaded with the U.S. Embassy in Honduras to produce evidence linking strikes against United Fruit in that country to agitation by Guatemalan Communists; the embassy gloomily reported, "facts few, convicting and convincing evidence scarce." After the golpe, intelligence agents combed through Guatemalan archives; but a year later, Assistant Secretary of State for Intelligence W. Park Armstrong informed Dulles that "nothing conclusive" had been found linking Guatemalan Communists with Moscow.[58] Whatever the merits of the

[55] Dulles quoted in discussion with Eisenhower in memorandum of NSC meeting, May 27, 1954, *FR, 1952–1954*, 4:1134; Dulles to Allen Dulles, April 7, 1954, TTS, "March–April 1954 (1)," DPEL.

[56] Peurifoy to State Department, July 7, 1954, *FR, 1952–1954*, 4:1202–8; Immerman, *CIA in Guatemala*, 161–77; Schlesinger and Kinzer, *Bitter Fruit*, 191–225.

[57] Eisenhower quoted in Phillips, *Night Watch*, 50–51; Dulles telephone conversation with Carl McCardle, June 29, 1954, TTS, "May–June 1954 (1)," DPEL.

[58] Memorandum of conversation between Ambassador João Carlos Muniz of Brazil and Dulles, May 11, 1954, *FR, 1952–1954*, 4:1106; Ambassador to Honduras Whiting

administration's case against Arbenz, it had violated the OAS Charter. Latin Americans, the State Department's Bureau of Inter-American Affairs predicted in a staff study, would judge the covert intervention as "a Czechoslovakia in reverse in Guatemala."[59]

In addition to celebrating its Guatemalan victory the Eisenhower administration vowed to be more precise in its attitude toward communism in Latin America. In NSC 144/1 it had questioned whether the United States could be bound by the OAS Charter in the midst of cold war. The Guatemalan imbroglio demonstrated that the influential, more democratic Latin American nations cherished the nonintervention principle and that they did not subscribe to the U.S. version of a monolithic, international communist conspiracy. Covert intervention had resolved both problems: it had eliminated the Arbenz government and preserved the appearance of nonintervention. Nevertheless, the administration decided to stiffen its resolve to combat communism. In September 1956 in NSC 5613/1—the administration's first comprehensive review of the political features of its Latin American policy since the overthrow of Arbenz—the administration declared that "closer relations between the Soviet Union and Latin America are against the security interests of the United States." It accordingly inserted in NSC 5613/1 the warning that "if a Latin American state should establish with the Soviet bloc close ties of such a nature as seriously to prejudice our vital interests," the United States would "be prepared to diminish governmental economic and financial cooperation with that country and take any other political, economic, or military actions deemed appropriate."[60]

It was the Joint Chiefs of Staff who suggested this tough language. The statement, which codified and extended to Latin America the interventionist policies pursued against Guatemala, evoked little debate among NSC members. Secretary Dulles initially objected, believing the language to be "so broad as not to give very clear guidance to those who were obliged to carry out the policy." But after some minor changes and Eisenhower's observation that "this issue struck him largely as a matter of semantics," the president ruled that he favored the Joint Chiefs' recommendation.[61]

Willauer to State Department, June 9, 1954, ibid., 1164, n. 4; Armstrong quoted to Immerman, *CIA in Guatemala*, 185.

[59] Staff Study of Bureau of Inter-American Affairs, August 19, 1953, *FR, 1952–1954*, 4:1083. For Latin American reaction to the overthrow of Arbenz, see Schlesinger and Kinzer, *Bitter Fruit*, 188–89; Slater, *OAS and United States Foreign Policy*, 128.

[60] Paragraph 16-e of NSC 5613/1, September 25, 1956, *FR, 1955–1957*, 6:119–27.

[61] Memorandum of NSC meeting, September 6, 1956, *FR, 1955–1957*, 6:102. For a

The administration did not immediately need to fulfill its pledge to take any "political, economic, or military actions deemed appropriate" to sever Soviet ties in Latin America. By the end of 1957 and early 1958, administration officials were satisfied that, through the policies of NSC 144/1 and NSC 5613/1, they had secured the hemisphere from communism. In November 1957 Secretary Dulles assured journalists that although communists could be counted on to make trouble, "we see no likelihood at the present time of communism getting into control of the political institutions of any of the American Republics." The administration's confidential analyses confirmed the secretary of state's public optimism. Reviewing the progress of NSC 5613/1, the Operations Coordinating Board (OCB) concluded that "there are at present no critical or strategic problems or difficulties which are major threats to United States security or which seem likely to cause changes in the generally satisfactory status of United States relations with the area." In February 1958, in executive congressional testimony, CIA Director Dulles agreed with his brother and the OCB that although there were "soft points," communism in Latin America was not "a situation to be frightened of as an overall problem."[62]

Latin Americans, however, vehemently disputed the description of inter-American relations as "satisfactory." For them the inter-American system had to be more than an anticommunist alliance; the true test of hemispheric friendship would be inter-American economic cooperation. The region was desperately poor, with a per capita annual income of approximately $250. For economic growth and development, Latin Americans believed that they needed U.S. grant assistance and commodity agreements to stabilize the prices of their chief exports, such as coffee. But, like the Truman government, the Eisenhower administration continued to deny economic assistance to Latin America. During the 1950s the United States allocated about one percent of its development assistance to Latin America, with only perennially indigent Bolivia, Haiti, and post-Arbenz Guatemala receiving aid.[63] According to the Eisenhower administration, the region's

---

history of this statement on intervention, see Stephen G. Rabe, "The Johnson (Eisenhower?) Doctrine for Latin America," *Diplomatic History* 9 (Winter 1985): 95–100.

[62] John Foster Dulles quoted in Richard P. Stebbins, *The United States in World Affairs, 1957* (New York, 1958), 259–60; Progress report of OCB on NSC 5613/1, September 11, 1957, *FR, 1955–1957*, 6:194–212; Allen Dulles testimony, February 7, 1958, *SFRC, 1958, 10:111.*

[63] Celso Furtado, *Economic Development of Latin America* (London, 1970), 35–48; U.S. Department of State, Agency for International Development, *U.S. Overseas Loans and Grants, 1945–1975* (Washington, 1976), 33–61.

economic salvation would be found not in economic aid but in international capitalism. As NSC 144/1 pointed out, the primary economic objective of the United States was to encourage "Latin American governments to recognize that the bulk of the capital required for their economic development can best be supplied by private enterprise and that their own self-interest requires the creation of a climate which will attract private investment."[64]

As it was in the politico-military field, U.S. foreign economic policy for Latin America was the policy of President Eisenhower. At the outset of his administration Eisenhower expressed a strong distaste for foreign aid for Latin America, observing to cabinet officers that "we put a coin in the tin cup and yet tomorrow we know the tin cup is going to be there." If Latin Americans "want our money, they ought to be required to go after our capital."[65] In any case, in Eisenhower's calculation Latin America was not eligible for economic aid, for it was not on the front line of the cold war. "Countries like Burma, Thailand, and the remaining parts of Indochina are directly open to assault. This does not apply in South America." Eisenhower wanted an enduring "good partner" relationship with Latin America which could be encouraged by loans instead of grants; this would "apply whether or not the Communist menace seems to increase or decrease in intensity."[66]

Secretary of State Dulles agreed with the president's views on foreign economic policy. He recommended free trade and investment and "the private enterprise philosophy" to Latin Americans and stoutly opposed nationalistic economic policies. In testimony to the Senate Finance Committee in 1955, for example, Dulles commended Venezuela, with its over $2 billion in U.S. investment, as "a country which had adopted the kind of policies which we think that the other countries of South America should adopt." Dulles added that if other nations emulated Venezuela in creating "a climate which is attractive to foreign capital . . . the danger of communism in South America, of social disorder will gradually disappear." Dulles reiterated these points in discussions with aides, lamenting that Brazil, with its government oil company, PETROBRÁS, had an "aversion to private capital." The United States, Dulles observed, "had been developed by British and French capital in the main." Unfortunately "nationalistic sentiments in Brazil stood in the way of a similar process." Dulles backed his views on economic development by refusing to consider

[64] Memorandum of NSC meeting, March 18, 1953, *FR, 1952–1954*, 4:2–8.

[65] Cabinet meeting, July 3, 1953, Cabinet Series (Minnich Notes), "C-6," WHOSS.

[66] President Eisenhower to Dr. Milton Eisenhower, December 1, 1954, EDS, "December 1954 (2)" AWF.

U.S. loans for PEMEX, the national oil company of Mexico, and by pressuring impoverished Bolivia to settle with former owners of the nationalized tin mines.[67]

To be sure Dulles was not oblivious to poverty in Latin America. He feared that the raw-material-producing economies of the region were dangerously sensitive to world market conditions. He wrote to the president that "at times we need their raw materials badly, and then they have feverish prosperity. Then the need falls off, and they go into economic decline with unemployment, which, nowadays, the Communists organize against us." In addition, he pointed out to the NSC and the cabinet that "in the absence of adequate assistance from us the Latin American countries might well go Communist."[68] Despite these beliefs, Dulles did not press the case for economic aid for Latin America with the president. In waging his anticommunist campaign the secretary did not assign the same priority to economic issues that he did to political matters. He declined, for example, to attend the two inter-American economic conferences, the Rio conference of 1954 and the Buenos Aires conference of 1957, both of which Latin Americans perceived as dismal failures. By comparison, Dulles devoted two weeks to gaining his anticommunist resolution at the Caracas conference.[69]

Dulles and his colleagues would have to reconsider their positions on economic aid, democracy, and human rights in 1958. In May the administration's smug confidence in its Latin American policy was abruptly shaken when Vice President Nixon, who was touring South America, was greeted by angry protesters throughout the continent and nearly killed by a howling mob in Caracas, Venezuela. The demonstrators blamed the United States for Latin America's social ills: the Eisenhower administration supported repressive regimes, had denied Latin America economic assistance, and was now imposing tariff barriers against Latin American exports. Venezuelans, for example,

---

[67] Dulles on Venezuela in Rabe, *Road to OPEC*, 130; Dulles on PETROBRÁS in memorandum of conversation, Department of State, August 28, 1957, *FR, 1955–1957*, 7:761–63; Dulles on PEMEX in Dulles to Eisenhower, March 19, 1957, ibid., 6:745–46; Dulles on Bolivia in memorandum of conversation with Bolivian Foreign Minister, October 3, 1957, ibid., 7:615–16. See also Holland to Dulles on U.S. foreign economic policy, December 13, 1955, ibid., 6:354–56.

[68] Dulles to Eisenhower, September 3, 1953, WHMS, "White House Correspondence, 1953 (2)," DPEL; Memorandum of conversation between Dulles, Cabot, and others, October 2, 1953, *FR, 1952–1954*, 4:197–201.

[69] Dulles to Eisenhower on Rio conference, November 1954, DHS, "November 1954 (1)," AWF; Dulles to Eisenhower on Buenos Aires conference, August 5, 1957, DHS, "August 1957 (2)," ibid.; Assistant Secretary Rubottom to Dulles on Buenos Aires conference, *FR, 1955–1957*, 6:510.

denounced the administration for its past connivance with the deposed Marcos Pérez Jiménez and its present harboring of the fugitive dictator and his chief of secret police, the notorious Pedro Estrada. They also feared, correctly, that in order to protect domestic producers the United States was about to limit imports of Venezuelan fuel oil.[70]

The tumult in Venezuela was evident in the rest of Latin America. Between 1956 and 1960, ten military dictators fell from power. The dictators had been unable to produce the stability and economic growth they had promised, and Latin Americans tired of the rampart repression and corruption that characterized military rule. The dictators were also undermined by the collapse of their economies. The U.S. recession of the late 1950s reverberated throughout the hemisphere. Economic growth came to a standstill. Metal prices collapsed, as the United States established quotas on imports of lead and zinc. The price of coffee beans, the region's principal export, fell sharply. The price of Colombian coffee, for example, steadily declined from eighty cents a pound in 1954 to fifty-two cents a pound in 1958.[71]

The unhappy Nixon trip sparked a debate about the Latin American policy of the United States. The administration initially focused on identifying the demonstrators. In his report to the cabinet Nixon stressed that the extremists "without any doubt were Communists." The fact that the protesters chanted all the same slogans "was absolute proof that they were directed and controlled by a central Communist conspiracy." The vice president conceded in a speech, however, that although "Communists spearheaded the attack, they had a lot of willing spear carriers with them." Secretary Dulles took up Nixon's communist conspiracy theme, telling the cabinet that the Soviets had cleverly infiltrated mass political movements in Latin America.[72] But CIA Director Allen Dulles thought it too facile to blame the international communist movement. He rebuked his brother, informing the secretary of state that "there would be trouble in Latin America if there were no Communists." Moreover, his agency could find no evidence that Moscow had inspired or directed the attacks on Nixon. Indeed, in a mid-1958 study the CIA concluded that Moscow consid-

[70] Richard M. Nixon, *Six Crises* (Garden City, N.Y., 1962), 183–230; R. Richard Rubottom interview, JFDOHC; Rabe, *Road to OPEC*, 134–35.

[71] Tad Szulc, *Twilight of the Tyrants* (New York, 1959), 3–8; Jonathan Hartlyn, "Military Governments and the Transition to Civilian Rule: The Colombian Experience of 1957–1958," *Journal of Inter-American Studies and World Affairs* 16 (May 1984): 245–81.

[72] Cabinet meeting, May 16, 1958, Cabinet Series (Minnich Notes), "C-45," WHOSS; Nixon, *Six Crises*, 223; Richard P. Stebbins, *The United States in World Affairs, 1958* (New York, 1959), 354–55.

ered Latin America an appendage of the United States and therefore "the bloc leadership has been reluctant to allocate to Latin America any substantial proportion of the bloc's total political, economic, and propaganda resources devoted to foreign penetration activities."[73]

While publicly blaming the communists for the attack on Nixon, the administration knew it needed a new approach to restore public confidence and to assuage Latin Americans. Vice President Nixon called for a revised recognition policy, arguing that the United States should adhere to the nonintervention principles of the OAS but should make it clear that it preferred to work with democracies. As he cleverly put it, "a formal handshake for dictators; an embrace for leaders of freedom."[74] Nixon's suggestion was both artful and brazen—during his 1955 tour of Central America, he had, of course, hugged Batista and Trujillo. But Secretary Dulles opposed Nixon's formula. In a meeting with the president he mocked Nixon's idea, asserting that "it was not possible in a brief trip to many countries to come back with a formula for a solution." Dulles also held that when uneducated masses took over they were "not going to practice democracy as we know it"; instead, he foresaw "dictatorships of the proletariat" or populist dictators "of the Nasser type."[75]

Dulles lost the argument. After mid-1958 it was politically unacceptable to claim that socioeconomic elites could best protect the interests of the United States in Latin America. As one congressional committee investigating the Nixon trip reported, the United States had to stop creating the impression in Latin America that it was "indifferent to the sufferings of oppressed people."[76] In February 1959

[73] Memorandum for Secretary of State from CIA Director Dulles, May 28, 1958, GCMS, "A.W.D. Conv. with Dulles (Intelligence Material) (3)," DPEL; Allen Dulles telephone conversation with John Foster Dulles, June 19, 1958, TTS, "June–July 1958," ibid.; Annex B, "CIA Intelligence Annex: Sino-Soviet Bloc Activity in Latin America," April 15, 1958, in OCB progress report on NSC 5613/1, June 3, 1958, Policy Papers Subseries, "NSC 5613 (1)," WHOSANSA; Annex C, "CIA Intelligence Annex: Sino-Soviet Bloc Activity in Latin America," November 12, 1958, in OCB progress report on NSC 5613/1, December 2, 1958, ibid.

[74] Cabinet meeting, May 16, 1958, Cabinet Series (Minnich Notes), "C-45," WHOSS; S. Everett Gleason to Robert Cutler, "Report on Nixon Oral Briefing to NSC," May 26, 1958, "U.S. Policy toward Latin America (3)," Briefings Subseries, WHOSANSA; Nixon, Six Crises, 191–92.

[75] Memorandum of conversation between Dulles and President, May 18, 1958, WHMS, "Meetings with President, January–June 1958 (2)," DPEL; Dulles to Nixon, May 19, 1958, TTS, "April–May 1958," ibid.; Cabinet meeting, May 16, 1958, Cabinet Series (Minnich Notes), "C-45," WHOSS.

[76] U.S. House Committee on Foreign Affairs, Subcommittee on Inter-American Affairs, Report on United States Relations with Latin America, House Report No. 354, 86th Cong., 1st sess., 1959, 3.

President Eisenhower approved NSC 5902/1, which called upon the United States to give "special encouragement" to representative governments.[77]

Instead of awarding medals to dictators Eisenhower began to express publicly his preference for political democracy and respect for human rights. In August 1958, in a ceremony that received wide notice throughout the hemisphere, the president heartily welcomed the new Venezuelan ambassador and declared that "authoritarianism and autocracy of whatever form are incompatible with the ideals of our great leaders of the past." Eisenhower's statement marked the first time that a high administration official had openly and unequivocally recommended representative government for Latin America. Over the next two years, the president repeatedly reaffirmed that position and wrote open letters of support to embattled democratic leaders.[78]

Beyond altering its stance on dictatorships the Eisenhower administration also had to modify its foreign economic policy for Latin America. Although the attacks on the vice president captured international attention, Nixon's private meetings with South American leaders centered on what most troubled Latin Americans: raising the living standards of the poor. As President-elect Alberto Lleras Camargo warned, "if a better way of life could not be available to the people, an 'explosion' was inevitable."[79] The warnings and pleas Nixon heard were reiterated for the administration by the redoubtable president of Brazil, Juscelino Kubitschek. Two weeks after the attack on Nixon, Kubitschek wrote an open letter to Eisenhower that called for a "thorough revision" of hemispheric programs. The harried Eisenhower responded first by sending Assistant Secretary of State R. Richard Rubottom, and then Dulles, to Rio de Janiero to meet with Kubitschek. The Brazilian president emphasized to U.S. officials that "the problem of underdevelopment will have to be

[77] Paragraph 22-b of NSC 5902/1, February 16, 1959, "NSC 5902/1 (1)," Policy Papers Subseries, WHOSANSA.

[78] Eisenhower's statement of August 14, 1958, in "OF-227-Venezuela," WHOF; Atkins and Wilson, *United States and Trujillo Regime*, 14–15; Eisenhower to Rómulo Betancourt, December 20, 1958, "OF-227-Venezuela," WHOF; Dulles to Eisenhower on President-elect Jorge Alessandri of Chile, October 29, 1958, IS, "Chile (5)," AWF; Briefing memorandum for Eisenhower on visit of Colombian President Alberto Lleras Camargo, March 31, 1960, IS, "Colombia (2)," ibid.

[79] Memorandums of Nixon conversations with Arturo Frondizi of Argentina, May 6, 1958; Lleras Camargo, May 11, 1958; Camilo Ponce Enríquez of Ecuador, May 9, 1958; and Luis Batlle Berres of Uruguay, April 29, 1958, all in box 1, series 397, Nixon Papers; Memorandum of conversation with Hernán Siles Zuazo of Bolivia, May 5, 1958, Bolivia-Maps folder, box 2, series 401, ibid.

solved if Latin American nations are to be able more effectively to resist subversion and serve the Western cause." Specifically, Kubitschek thought the United States should pledge $40 billion in foreign aid to Latin America over the next twenty years. His program, dubbed "Operation Pan America," was, of course, the enduring hemispheric quest: the Marshall Plan for Latin America.[80]

Few U.S. officials supported President Kubitschek's grandiose plans. Dulles, for example, thought the Brazilian "unreasonable" for wanting the economic development of Latin America to be "our primary obligation."[81] Nonetheless, Kubitschek's views strengthened the position of those who believed that the administration had to alter its foreign economic policies. These officials included Rubottom, Dr. Milton Eisenhower, John Moors Cabot, State Department economic officer Thomas Mann, and Under Secretary of State for Economic Affairs C. Douglas Dillon. These men warned that the United States was unwittingly jeopardizing its security by ignoring Latin America's economic needs. Dillon, Mann, and Rubottom had attended the 1957 inter-American economic conference and were appalled by the administration's arrogant rejection of Latin American proposals.[82] Led by Dillon, the group succeeded in convincing President Eisenhower to allow the United States to participate in international discussions to stabilize the prices of coffee, lead, and zinc. In addition, in August 1958 Dillon announced that the United States would establish an Inter-American Development Bank with the United States supplying 45 percent of the bank's initial capitalization of $1 billion.[83] Dulles supported these announcements. The secretary of state had brought Dillon to Washington in 1957, perhaps recognizing that the administration's anticommunist policies needed an economic component. In any case, as Dulles informed the president,

[80] Kubitschek to Eisenhower, May 28, 1958, IS, "Brazil (8)," AWF; DSB 38 (June 30, 1958): 1090–91; Eisenhower to Kubitschek, June 5, 1958, IS, "Brazil (8)," AWF; Dulles to Eisenhower on Rubottom meeting with Kubitschek, June 20, 1958, IS, "Brazil (7)," ibid.

[81] Dulles to Eisenhower on meeting with Kubitschek, August 5, 1958, DHS, "August 1958," AWF.

[82] C. Douglas Dillon interview, Columbia University Oral History Collection, New York, N.Y.; Rubottom interview, JFDOHC; Thomas Mann interview, Eisenhower Library; Cabot to Milton Eisenhower, October 23, 1957 and December 12, 1957, both in part 1: Latin America, microfilm reel #1, John Moors Cabot Papers, University Publications of America, Frederick, Maryland; Milton Eisenhower, The Wine Is Bitter (Garden City, N.Y., 1963), 161–63, 205–9. For the U.S. position at Buenos Aires, see FR, 1955–1957, 6:511–20.

[83] Thomas Zoumaras, "Eisenhower's Foreign Economic Policy: The Case of Latin America," in Richard Melanson and David Mayers, eds., Reevaluating Eisenhower: American Foreign Policy in the Fifties (Urbana, 1987), 176–78.

Kubitschek's schemes had to be addressed, for "life constantly requires getting along with unreasonable people, or at least those who seem to us to be unreasonable."[84]

Although the Eisenhower administration had proposed new initiatives, it had not yet radically restructured its policies. It continued to oppose spending vast sums in the region. Its proposal for an Inter-American Development Bank was modest, especially compared to President Kubitschek's suggestion of an initial capitalization of $5 billion for the bank. Moreover, in 1959 the administration asked Congress for only $25 million in development assistance, with the bulk of that assistance again going to Bolivia and Guatemala. By comparison the administration expanded military aid programs, asking for over $160 million for Latin America in 1959–1960.[85]

Despite the shock of the Nixon trip the Eisenhower administration declined to reshape its policies in 1958–1959 because its two senior officials resisted fundamental change. President Eisenhower was stunned and angered by the ferocious criticism his foreign policy was subjected to—even his beloved brother, Milton, chided him for granting "special" recognition to dictators. But he was stubborn, continuing to hold that Latin Americans needed to attract private investment and to root out radicalism. At a cabinet meeting in February 1959, for example, Eisenhower received a briefing from Thomas Mann on Operation Pan America; he responded by remarking that he approved of Latin American leaders who "battled" their people and then noted that he had given Adolfo López Mateos, the new president of Mexico, a book on the dangers of communism.[86] As usual Secretary of State Dulles agreed with his president. Although he backed Dillon's initiatives, Dulles still preferred a political approach to foreign affairs. When in the summer of 1958 he went to confer with Kubitschek, Dulles tried to turn the subject of conversation away from underdevelopment to communism. Upon returning to Wash-

[84] Dulles to Eisenhower on meeting with Kubitschek, August 5, 1958, DHS, "August 1958," AWF.

[85] Burton I. Kaufman, *Trade and Aid: Eisenhower's Foreign Economic Policy, 1953–1961* (Baltimore, 1982), 166; Stebbins, *United States in World Affairs, 1958*, 367–69; Richard P. Stebbins, *The United States in World Affairs, 1959* (New York, 1960), 366–67; U.S. Senate, Committee on Foreign Relations, *Hearings on the Mutual Security Act, 1959*, 86th Cong., 1st sess., 1959, 217, 543–60; U.S. Senate, Committee on Foreign Relations, *Hearings on the Mutual Security Act, 1960*, 86th Cong., 2nd sess., 1960, 345–75.

[86] President to Dr. Eisenhower, November 26, 1958, "Report to President," Milton S. Eisenhower Papers, Eisenhower Library; Dr. Eisenhower's statement to NSC contained in memorandum from Gordon Gray to Philip J. Halla, February 9, 1959, Briefing Notes Subseries, "U.S. Policy toward Latin America (2)," WHOSANSA; President quoted in cabinet meeting, February 27, 1959, Cabinet Series (Minnich Notes), "C-49," WHOSS.

ington, Dulles reported to the president that he was mystified by the Brazilian's "reluctance to have used the word 'Communism' in our communique." For his part Kubitschek called Dulles "a tenacious, intransigent debater, almost incapable of compromise."[87]

Eisenhower and Dulles rejected Kubitschek's program because they discounted the region's vulnerability to direct communist penetration. To be sure the administration's reflex response to Nixon's troubles was to blame it on the international communist movement. And it perceived its military aid program as an anticommunist insurance policy. But Eisenhower and Dulles, backed by intelligence analysts, did not believe that the Soviet Union had immediate plans for Latin America. After the overthrow of the Arbenz government, Secretary Dulles concluded that Moscow had altered its strategy, believing that communists had "learned from their Guatemalan experience that, even if opportune, an isolated Communist seizure of control tends to undercut over-all Communist objectives for the area by alarming and rallying the hemisphere against international communism." Citing pronouncements by Nikita Khrushchev and Mao Tsetung, Dulles predicted that the communists would go "the indirect aggression" route with a "national front" strategy. They could be expected to unite with political groups advocating socially progressive causes. By exaggerating nationalist objectives and setting unrealistic timetables for fulfilling legitimate aspirations, the communists would then arouse anti-American feelings in the region.[88] The "fundamental objective" of the United States, therefore, must be "to retain its ascendancy as the leader of the Western Hemisphere and to undercut efforts of International Communism to disengage Latin America from its traditional alignment with this country."[89]

In view of these analyses, administration officials remained sanguine about inter-American relations. They actually concluded that the vice president's unhappy experience had had salutary effects, for it has alerted them to potential dangers. But until 1960 the Eisenhower administration continued to hold to the tenets of NSC 144/1;

[87] Dulles to Eisenhower, August 7, 1958, WHMS, "Meetings with the President, July–December 1958 (9)," DPEL; Kubitschek quoted in Stanley Hilton, "The United States, Brazil, and the Cold War, 1945–1960: End of the Special Relationship," *Journal of American History* 68 (December 1981): 622.

[88] Dulles testimony, July 2, 1954, in *SFRC, 1954*, 6:466; Dulles testimony, May 19, 1958, in *SFRC, 1958*, 10:232–37; Dulles to Eisenhower, August 3, 1958, WHMS, "Meetings with the President, July–December 1958 (9)," DPEL.

[89] Annex C, "Sino-Soviet Bloc Activities in Latin America," November 12, 1958, in OCB report on NSC 5613/1, December 2, 1958, Policy Papers Subseries, "NSC 5613/1 (1)," WHOSANSA; "Communist Strategy in Latin America," in Annex B, "General Considerations," NSC 5902/1, February 16, 1959, ibid., "NSC 5902/1 (1)," WHOSANSA.

that is, a secure and stable hemisphere could be achieved basically with free trade and investment policies, military aid, and admonitions to Latin Americans not to form ties with Moscow or local communist parties.

. . .

The year 1960 witnessed a dramatic shift in the Latin American policy of the Eisenhower administration. In early 1960 the administration suddenly feared that the United States could lose the cold war in Latin America. Cuba, under the fiery leadership of Fidel Castro, had been abruptly transformed from a client state of the United States into a radical, anti-American nation. The charismatic Cuban had also stirred the Latin American people, who now demanded economic development and social justice. Moreover, U.S. officials speculated that Castro might allow the Soviet Union to use Cuba as a beachhead for communist expansion throughout the Western Hemisphere. Confronted by this "Castro-Communist" challenge, the Eisenhower administration rapidly revised its Latin American policies. It prepared to overthrow Castro and dismantle the Cuban revolution. It further worked to remove dictators like Trujillo from power, reasoning now that Latin American tyrants created "Batista-like" conditions, forcing desperate people into the hands of communists. The administration also decided that to prevent radicalism from spreading it had to underwrite a thoroughgoing reform of Latin America's archaic political, social, and economic institutions. This included devising an extensive economic aid package for Latin America. In effect, the Eisenhower administration started the Alliance for Progress, the decade-long effort to reform and modernize Latin American societies, in order to make them resistant to communist subversion.[90]

These far-reaching changes in the U.S. approach to Latin America occurred after the death of Secretary of State Dulles. Whether Dulles would have favored these new policies cannot be definitely determined. But anticommunism had been the keystone of his diplomacy in Latin America; he had consistently interpreted hemispheric developments within the context of the East–West confrontation. As such, it seems certain that Dulles would have labored diligently to implement President Eisenhower's new cold war policies for the region.

[90] Stephen G. Rabe, *Eisenhower and Latin America: The Foreign Policy of Anticommunism* (Chapel Hill, 1988), 135–73. Material in this chapter that is drawn from my previously published book and cited here is reproduced by permission of the University of North Carolina Press.

CHAPTER 7

John Foster Dulles and the Peace Settlement with Japan

Seigen Miyasato

ALTHOUGH the shooting war between Japan and the United States ended in 1945, no peace treaty had been signed as of May 18, 1950, when Harry S. Truman (and Secretary of State Dean Acheson) assigned John Foster Dulles the primary responsibility for negotiating a treaty with Japan. That the settlement ending the occupation marked a turning point in the evolution of U.S. policy not only toward Japan but toward the entire Far East is indisputable. Yet, as a recent historiographic essay on the cold war in Asia commented, it "has escaped close scholarly scrutiny."[1] This chapter seeks to rectify this oversight.

[1] Robert J. McMahon, "The Cold War in Asia: Toward a New Synthesis," *Diplomatic History* 12 (Summer 1988): 323. This is not to say that there is not an extensive literature on Dulles's participation in the negotiations. There is, and it encompasses several specific considerations not discussed here. On bipartisanship and congressional relations, for example, see Louis Gerson, *John Foster Dulles* (New York, 1967), 62; and Tetsuo Umemoto, "Congress and the Japanese Peace Settlement," *American Review* [Tokyo] 17 (March 1983): 129–52. For the relationship of the negotiations to the question of recognizing the PRC, see Masataka Kosaka, *Saisho Yoshida Shigeru* [Prime Minister Shigeru Yoshida] (Tokyo, 1968), 60–61; and Chihiro Hosoya, *San Furansisuko Eno Michi* [The Road to San Francisco] (Tokyo, 1984). On the economic aspects of Dulles's policy toward Japan, the following are helpful: Michael Schaller, *The American Occupation of Japan: The Origins of the Cold War in Asia* (New York, 1985); William S. Borden, *The Pacific Alliance: United States Foreign Economic Policy and Japanese Trade Recovery, 1947–1955* (Madison, 1984); and Nancy Bernkopf Tucker, "American Policy Toward Sino-Japanese Trade in the Postwar Years: Politics and Prosperity," *Diplomatic History* 8 (Summer 1984): 183–95. On the peace settlement itself, Frederick S. Dunn, *Peace-Making and the Settlement with Japan* (Princeton, 1963) is the classic and remains useful. A more recent work on the subject is Michael M. Yoshitsu, *Japan and the San Francisco Peace Settlement* (New York, 1983). Marie D. Strazar's essay, "Japanese Efforts to Influence a Peace Settlement, 1945–1951," in Thomas W. Burkman, ed., *The Occupation of Japan: The International Context* (proceedings of a symposium at Old Dominion University, October 21–22, 1982, The MacArthur Foundation), 194–211, advances a stimulating thesis that highlights Tokyo's skill: "Through long-range planning and research, through the maintenance of appropriately deferential behavior, through the employment of deftly assertive and timely initiatives, and through a sound knowledge of the behavioral patterns and culture of the opposition, that is, the United States, the Japa-

My specific purpose is threefold: first, to analyze Dulles's role in resolving the impasse that existed within the U.S. government between the Departments of State and of Defense on the question of whether to negotiate a settlement; second, to analyze his role in negotiating with Prime Minister Shigeru Yoshida, focusing on the Japanese rearmament issue; and third, to draw some conclusions about the significance of Dulles's contribution to the success of the negotiations and, ultimately, to his subsequent conduct of the Eisenhower administration's affairs of state.

. . .

After two years of study and debate, the National Security Council (NSC) decided in October 1948 not to press for a treaty of peace with Japan. The reasons, as explained in NSC 13/2, emphasized "the differences which have developed among the interested countries regarding the procedure and substance" of a treaty and, moreover, the dangerous situation "created by the Soviet Union's policy of aggressive communist expansion."[2] In mid-1949 the State Department, however, began to reexamine the decision because reports from Tokyo indicated mounting Japanese discontent with the prolonged American occupation. The department feared that the occupation had reached a stage of "diminishing returns" and that continued delay of a treaty might create a situation that the Soviets could exploit by offering peace terms more favorable to Japan than those offered by the United States. In May, therefore, State requested that the NSC obtain the Joint Chiefs of Staff's (JCS) evaluation of security requirements for the posttreaty defense of Japan.[3] This request gave rise to a series of discussions, which eventually precipitated an impasse.

Replying to the State Department's request on June 9, 1949, the JCS emphasized both the necessity of denying Japan's manpower to the Soviet Union and the strategic importance of Japan as a staging area for possible U.S. actions on the Asian mainland or on Soviet territory. Japan was considered the key to America's offshore island chain of defense in the Pacific. Because a peace with Japan would

---

nese government was able 'to generate intended negotiating outcomes,' ultimately influencing the final form of the peace settlement" (208). She asserts that "the Japanese won on the issue of rearmament" but she does not fully develop the thesis on rearmament. Because of a lack of systematic analysis, a consensus on this and many other issues has remained elusive.

[2] Nsc 13/2, October 7, 1948, *FR, 1948*, 6:858–62.

[3] Memorandum by the Director of the Office of Far Eastern Affairs to the Under Secretary of State, May 19, 1949, *FR, 1949*, 7:752; the Acting Secretary of State to Acheson, May 27, 1949, ibid., 758–60.

weaken the posture enjoyed by the United States during the occupation, the JCS concluded that "a peace treaty would, at the present time, be premature." If for political reasons a treaty were nevertheless necessary, the JCS proposed the following preconditions: a prior assurance of domestic stability and pro-Western orientation in Japan; existence of indigenous security forces capable of maintaining international order; and a limited Japanese rearmament plan that could immediately be implemented before the departure of American occupation forces.[4]

In a memorandum distributed on October 4, 1949, the State Department extensively criticized the JCS's position by underscoring the saliency of nonstrategic considerations. Because the communist threat to Japan might take the form of concealed aggression rather than direct and overt attack, State argued, Japan's defense would greatly depend on its situation. "The orientation of any people toward a foreign country," it commented, "is a subjective political-psychological condition. It is the product of domestic political, economic and social factors, together with the nature and quality of a nation's relations with foreign nations. This being the case, the United States can neither impose nor enforce pro-Western orientation on any foreign people, including Japan." Pro-Western orientation could be accomplished by fostering friendly feelings among the Japanese, so an early peace was essential.[5]

Under Secretary of the Army Tracy Voorhees and his aides countered with a further argument against an early peace. A peace treaty that would meet American military requirements in Japan (American military bases in Japan, limited Japanese rearmament, etc.) would be unacceptable to the Soviet Union and the People's Republic of China (PRC); but a treaty concluded without Soviet and Chinese participation would give them a legal pretext to argue that such a treaty violated the Potsdam Declaration and the surrender terms. Under such a pretext the Soviets and the PRC might undertake harassing actions against Japan. Voorhees thus reiterated that at this time a settlement was premature and instead proposed the so-called "stand-by" SCAP (the Supreme Commander of Allied Powers). Under this arrangement SCAP would be retained, but its personnel would be reduced to a "skeletonized and virtually a stand-by form," delegating powers to

---

[4] Enclosure to NSC 49, Report by the Joint Chiefs of Staff, June 9, 1949, *FR, 1949*, 7:771–77.

[5] Enclosure to note by the Executive Secretary (Souers) to the National Security Council, October 4, 1949, *FR, 1949*, 7:870–73.

the Japanese government while the United States maintained base rights in Japan.[6]

In order to break the deadlock the State Department began in early 1950 to study a posttreaty security arrangement for Japan. It first considered concluding an "Agreement on the Restoration of Normal, Political and Economic Relations with Japan," which was similar to Voorhees's "stand-by" SCAP, and second, "a Peace Treaty which authorizes the maintenance of U.S. or Western Allied bases in Japan."[7] But the department considered the first approach to possess too many legal complications; the second had "serious political drawbacks." As a third plan, it proposed a Pacific pact. On February 20, 1950, Secretary of State Dean Acheson obtained President Truman's approval to prepare a paper on the pact to be presented to the NSC as a "matter of urgency."[8] By March 9 State's position paper was completed. Representatives presented it to the Joint Chiefs of Staff on April 24.

The Pacific pact proposed a multilateral security arrangement including the Far Eastern Commission countries and Japan to defend one another against aggression by Japan and to protect Japan against aggression from any source. For purposes of this second objective Japan would grant the United States whatever bases and rights deemed necessary by military planners. State hoped that this multilateral arrangement "would facilitate the signature by other members of a non-punitive peace treaty with Japan and help to assure them against resurgence of Japanese aggression." At the same time it would strengthen Japan's resistance to communist pressures.[9]

State's position thus came closer to that of the JCS by accepting the possibility of Japan's eventual rearmament. Still, a basic difference between the State Department and the JCS military chiefs remained as to Japan's strategic importance and, as a consequence, on the timing of a peace treaty. State recognized Japan's vital role in America's defense posture but felt that such security considerations had to be

[6] Memorandum for the Chairman of the JCS, April 22, 1950, JCSRG 273, CJCS 092.2 Japanese Peace Treaty; and Report by the JSSC to the JCS on Impact of an Early Peace Treaty with Japan on U.S. Strategic Requirements, November 30, 1949, ibid., JCS 1380/75, JCS 388.1 Japan, Section 1.

[7] Tab. A, Outline for meeting with the Secretary on Japanese Peace Settlement, attachment to Memorandum by the Assistant Secretary of State for Far Eastern Affairs (Butterworth) to Acheson, January 18, 1950, *FR, 1950*, 6:1117–19.

[8] Memorandum by the Special Assistant to the Secretary (Howard) to the Assistant Secretary for Far Eastern Affairs (Butterworth), March 9, 1950, and attachment, Position of the Department of State on United States Policy toward a Japanese Peace and Security Settlement, *FR, 1950*, 6:1138–49.

[9] *FR, 1950*, 6:1144–48.

tied to political and diplomatic ones. In the April 24 meeting, Secretary of Defense Louis Johnson, after a heated debate, agreed to reevaluate the military situation. After another meeting in early May it was agreed that a final decision would be made after Johnson's scheduled visit to Tokyo in June.[10]

· · ·

Facing strong partisan criticism from the Republicans, particularly on its China policy, the Truman administration needed someone who could deflect the criticisms. Dulles was considered the most useful and qualified for the job because of his experience in international affairs—especially as a member of the Reparations Commission at the Versailles Peace Conferences and as an adviser at the San Francisco Conference that established the UN—and for his close relationship with Governor Thomas Dewey and the Republican leadership. He was also an acknowledged proponent of bipartisan foreign policy. Dulles had served under the Truman Democratic administration as a staff member of the U.S. delegation at the Council of Foreign Ministers in London in 1945, and, together with Senator Arthur Vandenberg, had elicited the support of a number of Republican senators for the North Atlantic Treaty Organization.[11]

At the time of Dulles's appointment as adviser to Acheson on April 6, 1950, Acheson probably had not intended to assign Dulles the primary responsibility for negotiating a treaty with Japan. However, in light of the escalating tensions at home and abroad that followed the fall of China in October 1949, some focused initiative toward the Far East was almost inevitable. Dulles himself is reported to have suggested that someone with responsibility and accountability to the secretary of state be appointed to effect a peace settlement with Japan. Although the evidence is inconclusive, Acheson apparently agreed and decided Dulles possessed the appropriate credentials.[12]

Any new official brings to his office what may be called "intellectual baggage." Historical experiences—especially those in which the official was a participant—influence perceptions and judgments.[13] Dulles

[10] Walter S. Poole, *The History of the Joint Chiefs of Staff, 1950–1952* (Washington, 1979), 439; Memorandum of conversation by the Special Assistant to the Secretary, April 24, 1950, *FR, 1950*, 6:1175–81.

[11] Ronald W. Pruessen, *John Foster Dulles: The Road to Power* (New York, 1982), 280–84, 395–97.

[12] Pruessen, *John Foster Dulles*, 436–37; Dunn, *Peace-Making*, 97.

[13] Richard Neustadt and Ernest May, *Thinking in Time: The Uses of History for Decision-Makers* (New York, 1986).

was no exception, and in this instance two sets of preconceptions are relevant to the peace settlement with Japan: the "lessons of Versailles" and his views on the Soviet Union.

The first lesson of Versailles for Dulles was that the imposition of severe economic restrictions on a defeated enemy is destructive because such a treaty invites vengeance. Therefore, justice, fairness, and humanity are in reality the essential elements for a lasting and successful peace. Dulles believed in the economic origins of conflict, or "political economic determinism," which implied that alliance cooperation could not be sustained on purely military bases. No less important was the second lesson he learned from President Woodrow Wilson's handling of the Versailles treaty: "an inability or refusal to make certain compromises to political realities usually spells a prescription for failure."[14] This second lesson relates not only to Dulles's keen sensitivity to congressional opinion but also to his focus on pragmatic solutions.

As for his views of the Soviet Union, following his encounters with the Soviets at the San Francisco Conference in 1945 and London meeting of the Council of Foreign Ministers in 1946, Dulles concluded that Soviet communism was the greatest threat to world peace. He also feared that the communist offensive was shifting from Europe to the Far East and emphasizing indirect subversion rather than overt attack.[15] Dulles's approach to the negotiations reflected these preconceptions. In addition, as a prospective secretary of state and a proponent of bipartisan foreign policy, he had a personal stake in making the peace settlement a success: he had to prove his effectiveness as a broker in the government and as a negotiator in the international arena.

Two days after his appointment as adviser to the secretary of state, Dulles requested a briefing from the State Department on the peace settlement. Assistant Secretary of State for Far Eastern Affairs W. W. Butterworth and Special Assistant to the Secretary John B. Howard went to New York to brief Dulles, bringing him up to date on the differing arguments of the respective departments. Drawing on his personal experience and strategic preferences, Dulles immediately rejected any idea of Japanese neutrality and voiced support for an early "liberal" treaty with Japan. He was "skeptical about the future utilities of small bases scattered around the world," and considered that "bases in a hostile country would be useless." American military

[14] Dunn, *Peace-Making*, 67–68, 98–99; Michael Guhin, *John Foster Dulles: A Statesman and His Times* (New York, 1972), 31.

[15] Pruessen, *John Foster Dulles*, 276–330, 439–42.

bases in Japan should be retained only at the specific request of the Japanese. On a Pacific pact, he held "grave doubts" about a NATO-type commitment, but was favorably disposed toward the pact proposed by the State Department. He was particularly critical of Voorhees's "stand-by" SCAP arrangement for its exaggerated estimate of the legal difficulties involved in a peace treaty without Soviet and Communist Chinese participation.[16]

Within two months of acquiring prime responsibility for the peace settlement, Dulles, with a small State Department staff, prepared a memorandum covering a wide range of problems involved in the peace settlement. In this June memorandum Dulles and his colleagues first established a comprehensive long-range objective: the Japanese should be peaceful; should respect fundamental human rights; should be part of the free world; and should be friendly to the United States. Japan should also develop self-respect by avoiding dependence on outside charity, and it should demonstrate to the rest of Asia the advantages of the free world, thereby helping in the effort to resist communism. Moving from the general to the particular, the memorandum then surveyed various geographic, economic, political, ethical, social, and military problems. Dulles and his colleagues assumed that Japan's proximity to the Soviet Union and PRC made it vulnerable to communist intrigue and subversion as well as attack. Some counteroffensive of a propaganda and covert character "designed to prevent easy communist penetration" was important, although the memorandum recommended no specific measures to be taken. It did mention the importance of developing "some sense of governmental responsibility to resist indirect agression in Japan," pointing to the need to develop a police force, constabulary, and coast guard. Referring to economics, the memorandum recognized that "[t]here is natural and historical economic interdependence between Japan and the now communized parts of Asia." Because these areas were "the natural sources of raw materials," a question arose concerning Japan's ability to find, outside of the communist areas, adequate sources of raw materials and markets for its industry. Otherwise, the United States might find it expedient to actually encourage trade with communist areas, albeit with restrictions. Dulles exhibited acute interest in these economic problems.[17]

The memorandum also addressed racial problems. It noted both the "Western sense of white superiority" and the Japanese desire "to

[16] Memorandum of conversation, April 7, 1950, *FR, 1950*, 6:1162–63.
[17] Memorandum by Dulles to Acheson, June 7, 1950, *FR, 1950*, 6:1207–12; Memorandum by the Director of the Office of Northeast Asian Affairs, June 14, 1950, ibid., 1213.

be treated as social equals by the West." Lasting harmony between the two nations required the amelioration of this tension. One enlightened measure the memorandum recommended was to permit at least limited Japanese immigration into the United States. But although necessary, this liberal immigration policy was not sufficient. The memorandum concluded: "[A] Treaty alone will not be adequate unless there are important parallel efforts along other fronts. It may be that the principal attention to hold Japan in the Free World will be a capitalizing on their desire to be an equal member of the family of free nations."[18]

This June memorandum was unquestionably a carefully crafted document and provided an essential framework for subsequent proposals. Nevertheless, because it was in line with previous planning within the State Department, Frederick Dunn, the author of the standard study of the negotiations, concludes that it is inaccurate to refer to Dulles as "the architect of the Japanese peace treaty." Dunn's contention is not without validity, but only in the most technical sense. The memorandum articulated State's position more clearly than previously, and moreover, represented a workable synthesis of many inchoate ideas. In addition, as Dunn himself admits, security provisions had been left undecided within the State Department. In terms of adjusting differences between State and the JCS, a real and urgent problem was a posttreaty security arrangement. Though the memorandum suggested a special arrangement consistent with the UN Charter, it admitted that there was "no hard and fast opinion in the Department" on the problem. It would be Dulles's responsibility to forge a consensus.[19]

Learning that Secretary of Defense Johnson and the JCS were scheduled to travel to Tokyo in June to confer with Douglas MacArthur and that discussion of security was postponed until their return, Dulles likewise decided to visit Japan's capital. Not only did he feel it necessary to explore security arrangements with the other actors in this focused manner, but he wanted to know precisely what the JCS wanted before he tried to reconcile its views with those of State. As was his habit, on his way to Japan Dulles wrote down his thoughts on the problem: "Much depends on whether the JCS want to use Japan generally as a major advanced *offensive* air base. That decision, if adopted as U.S. policy, would have many consequences in terms of relations with, and responsibilities for, the Japanese." "An alterna-

[18] Memorandum by Dulles to Acheson, June 7, 1950, *FR, 1950*, 6:1208–9.

[19] Memorandum by the Director of the Office of Northeast Asian Affairs to the Acting United States Political Advisor for Japan, June 14, 1950, *FR, 1950*, 6:1212; Dunn, *Peace-Making*, 85–86.

tive" was, the note continues, "some form of *defensive* guarantee, stiffened by a continuing presence of some skeleton U.S. forces." Dulles favored the "alternative," but the note shows that he was concerned that it might not be accepted by the Joint Chiefs. Dulles realized that a meeting of minds between them and State officials would be extremely difficult to achieve.[20]

Secretary Johnson and his party remained in Tokyo from June 17 to 23; Dulles's party stayed there from June 21 to 27. Available records do not show that, during the three days that both parties were in Tokyo, all of them conferred with MacArthur to discuss posttreaty security arrangements for Japan. William J. Sebald, political adviser to SCAP, speculates that because of "the differences over Japanese security" Dulles may not have met with Johnson and the JCS at all. Dulles's report on the trip to Secretary Acheson, however, states that the security problem was "thoroughly discussed" by Johnson, Omar Bradley (chairman of the JCS) and Dulles. In light of what we know about Dulles's methods and objectives, his report seems more credible although, as will be discussed below, Johnson's subsequent reluctance to negotiate any treaty with the Japanese suggests that the discussions were probably less thorough than Dulles claimed.[21]

In Tokyo Dulles found MacArthur equally concerned over the policy impasse in Washington and eager to bring the State and Defense Departments together. On June 14 the general drafted a memorandum proposing an alternative security arrangement: to maintain American troops at some points in Japan "so long as 'irresponsible militarism' exists in the world as a threat to 'peace, security and justice' in Japan." MacArthur claimed that this arrangement was "in complete consonance with the status of neutrality" of Japan because it was based on his interpretation of the Proclamation to Japan issued at the Potsdam Conference (Potsdam Declaration). But this interpretation was so broad as to constitute a distortion of the meaning of "irresponsible militarism." "Irresponsible militarism" in the proclamation referred specifically to the threat of Japanese militarism; MacArthur interpreted the phrase to embrace the Sino-Soviet threat to Japan. Whether Dulles as a seasoned lawyer objected to this distortion is not clear. He did not indicate that he did. What is clear is that Dulles feared MacArthur's proposal to maintain American troops

[20] Memorandum by Dulles to Acheson, June 15, 1950, *FR, 1950*, 6:1222–23 (emphasis in original).

[21] William J. Sebald with Russell Brines, *With MacArthur in Japan: A Personal History of the Occupation* (New York, 1965), 252; Annex to a letter from Dulles to the Secretary, December 28, 1951, "Japanese Treaties, Chronological [Series]—John Foster Dulles, November–December 1951 (1)," DPP.

temporarily at some points in Japan would not meet the JCS's demand to use Japan as a primary base in case of a global war with the Soviet Union.[22]

Dulles suggested that MacArthur prepare another memorandum. It took the general but one day to complete it. Two days before the outbreak of war in Korea he presented it to Dulles and Johnson separately. The memorandum stated that "[t]he entire area of Japan must be regarded as a potential base for defensive maneuver with unrestricted freedom reserved to the United States." It further stated that "despite Japan's constitutional renunciation of war its right of self-defense in case of predatory attack is implicit and inalienable." Dulles's concerns had evidently impressed MacArthur. This second memorandum appears to have met the requirements of the Joint Chiefs.[23]

Of course, Tokyo also had to accept the principles. Consequently, when requesting the second memorandum, Dulles encouraged MacArthur to cast the security provisions "in the mold of overall international peace and security rather than in terms of any special advantage to the United States at the expense of Japan." Dulles's suggestion was to provide that "pending Japan's admission to the United Nations and the coming into force of Article 43 agreements, . . . Japan would make comparable agreements for military facilities with the United States acting under the Potsdam Declaration as representatives of the signatories." If this broad right was acknowledged by the Japanese, details containing the JCS's requirement would be possible. MacArthur concurred and incorporated Dulles's recommendation into his memorandum, which Dulles subsequently used to establish the framework for negotiating the security agreement with Japan.[24]

Soon thereafter the Korean War broke out. Dulles was now more convinced than ever that the United States should quickly move toward an early peace with Japan. He immediately defined the North Korean incursion as a threat to Japan as well and cabled Acheson that if Seoul proved unable to repel the attack the United States must engage its forces. To fail to respond immediately would probably precipitate a chain reaction leading to a third world war.[25] The silver

[22] Memorandum by the Supreme Commander for Allied Powers (MacArthur), June 14, 1950, *FR, 1950*, 6:1220–21; Proclamation to Japan, July 26, 1945, *FR, 1945*, 2:1475–76.

[23] Memorandum on Concept Governing Security in Post-war Japan, June 23, 1950, *FR, 1950*, 6:1227–28.

[24] Attachment to memorandum by Dulles to Acheson, June 30, 1950, *FR, 1950*, 6:1230.

[25] Pruessen, *John Foster Dulles*, 454.

lining in Dulles's alarmist cloud was his belief that, with Japan having been in "somewhat of a postwar stupor," the Korean War was "awakening" its population to the threat of communism.[26] The United States should take advantage of this mood to sustain Japan's Western orientation and achieve a favorable settlement. On July 27 Dulles completed a draft of provisions on "International Peace and Security" that might be used in a treaty with Japan. It consisted of only four short chapters. Chapter 1 stated that Japan as a prospective member of the UN would act in accordance with the principles of Article 2 of the UN Charter. Chapter 2 provided that at Japan's request the United States would provide armed forces, and "the Japanese Government on its part shall provide such assistance and facilities, including rights of passage, as may be determined by the United States in consultation with the Japanese Government." In chapter 3 Japan promised not to allow another power to establish military facilities in Japan. And chapter 4 stipulated that the provisions would remain in effect until Japan had been admitted to the UN and the special agreements referred to in Article 43 of the UN Charter, which provided that facilities be made available to the Security Council "for the purpose of maintaining international peace and security," came into force. In a footnote Dulles's draft indicated that details would be provided in a separate agreement.[27]

When Dulles telephoned Secretary Johnson to discuss submitting his draft, the latter expressed hesitancy over negotiating any peace treaty with Japan during the Korean War. Under the terms of the occupation the United States could use bases in Japan at will, but a peace treaty, in spite of the agreement in Tokyo, would impinge upon this flexibility. Johnson's reluctance to accept Dulles's draft of provisions was also due to his impression at "first reading" that it was phrased too broadly to guarantee America's rights to adequate bases. Johnson thought that Dulles was unfamiliar with MacArthur's June 23 memo. Dulles assured Johnson that he had based his draft on that second memorandum, and that it was "designed to give, in a form as inoffensive as possible to the Japanese, the broad power in the United States to place military forces wherever in Japan the United States may determine to be desirable from the standpoint of maintenance of international peace in the Japan area."[28]

Thus Dulles accomplished much in the short time since his assign-

---

[26] Memorandum by Dulles to Acheson, July 19, 1950, *FR, 1950*, 6:1243.

[27] Memorandum by Dulles to Acheson, July 27, 1950, *FR, 1950*, 6:1259–61. For the text of Article 43 see *DSB* 12 (June 24, 1945): 1125.

[28] Memorandum of telephone conversation, by Dulles to Acheson, August 3, 1950, *FR, 1950*, 6:1264–65.

ment to the peace settlement. In less than one month he drew up a comprehensive framework, took advantage of Johnson's trip to Tokyo, successfully persuaded MacArthur to accede to the JCS, and drafted a memorandum covering the compromise. The JCS, however, remained unsatisfied.

Replying to the Dulles draft on August 22, the Joint Chiefs withdrew objections to a treaty concluded without the participation of the Soviet Union and China but criticized Dulles's guidelines for not meeting military requirements. They listed several conditions for concluding a peace treaty, one of which was a new condition that a peace treaty "must not be effective until after favorable resolution" of the Korean War. The State Department objected. In its view the Korean War should serve as a catalyst for hastening agreement. To await a favorable resolution would cost valuable momentum. Eventually a compromise was reached that gave priority to an early *start* at peace negotiations. A joint State–Defense memorandum for the president that included these requirements was drafted, and Truman approved it as NCS 60/1 on September 8, 1950. Nsc 60/1 included all of the JCS's military demands. In return Dulles obtained authorization to proceed with peace negotiations.[29]

In order to begin talks with allied representatives in New York, Dulles drew up on the basis of NSC 60/1 a seven-point statement of general principles of a peace treaty with Japan. Point four represented a major initiative, for it addressed the lingering problem of a security arrangement. This newest Dulles draft provided that "[t]he Treaty would contemplate that, pending *satisfactory alternative security arrangements* such as UN assumption of effective responsibility, there would be continuing cooperative responsibility between Japanese facilities and U.S. and perhaps *other forces* for the maintenance of international peace and security in the Japan area" (my emphasis). According to Robert A. Fearey, Dulles's deputy during the treaty talks, one of the "satisfactory alternative security arrangements" could include "the existence of adequate Japanese defense forces," and "other forces" could be Japanese. This reflected one of the security agreements listed in NSC 60/1, which envisioned no prohibition of Japanese rearmament. By drawing on the skill acquired during his many years as an international lawyer, Dulles was able to arrive at a

---

[29] Attachment to memorandum for Johnson, August 22, 1950, *FR, 1950,* 6:1278–82; Memorandum by the Director of the Office of Northeast Asian Affairs (Allison) to Acheson, August 24, 1950, ibid., 1282–88; memorandum by Allison to Acheson, August 29, 1950, ibid., 1288–93; Memorandum for the President (approved as NSC 60/1), September 7, 1950, ibid., 1293–96.

wording that could satisfy the Japanese while protecting what the JCS argued were America's security interests.[30]

· · ·

On November 24, 1950, MacArthur launched a large-scale offensive in Korea "to end the war." Barely two days later Chinese "volunteers" intervened. By mid-December the Eighth Army had crossed back over the 38th parallel and continued to retreat south. Washington feared that its troops might be expelled entirely from Korea and, in fact, the JCS gave permission to MacArthur to redeploy to Japan, rationalizing that Japan's defense was his primary reponsibility. On December 15 President Truman proclaimed the existence of a national emergency. In mid-January 1951, however, American troops slowly began advancing northward again, and by the end of march had retaken Seoul and reached the 38th parallel.[31]

During the acute crisis in late 1950 and early 1951 the State Department again seriously discussed the timing of a peace treaty with Japan. Dulles, along with his deputy and future ambassador to Japan John Allison, was concerned with Tokyo's subsequent reliability as a member of the free world. Dulles continued to view the Korean conflict as a possible first step on the communists' road to Japan. "Developments in Asia," wrote Dulles to Acheson in November 1950, "confirm that there is a comprehensive program, in which the Soviet and Chinese communists are cooperating, designed as a present phase to eliminate all Western influence on the Asiatic mainland, and probably also in relation to the islands of Japan." He later complained to Arthur Vandenburg that militarily Japan was "encircled by the Soviet Union" while it was economically deprived of the China market.[32]

There was no time to lose. With the Korean War dramatizing the need to expand America's defense perimeter so that it encompassed the entire noncommunist area of Asia and the Pacific, Washington had to secure bases in Japan without delay. Moreover, its strategic posture would require the authority to station both American troops and planes on Japanese soil. Dulles hoped that a treaty would provide

[30] Unsigned memorandum prepared in the Department of State, September 11, 1950, *FR, 1950*, 6:1297; undated memorandum by Robert A. Fearey of the Office of Northeast Asian Affairs, ibid., 1329, n. 4.

[31] DA [Department of the Army] to CINCFE [Commander in Chief, Far East], January 23, 1951; and MacArthur to DEPTAR [Department of the Army], January 10, 1951, both in MacArthur Library; Poole, *History of the JCS*, 79–80.

[32] Dulles to Acheson, November 30, 1950, "Acheson, Dean, 1950," DPP; Dulles to Arthur H. Vandenberg, January 17, 1951, "Vandenberg, Arthur H., 1951," DPP.

the foundation for Japan's own rearmament and contribution to regional defense, but that was negotiable. America's rights were not. From a less specific perspective, Dulles recognized that for Japan to exercise its designated role in the containment scheme, it had to reestablish its international credibility and standing while projecting an image sufficiently benign so as to allay the residual fears of its neighbors. A treaty would serve both purposes. By restoring Japan's sovereignty the United States would formally welcome Japan back into the community of nations, thus sending a signal to its neighbors that the time had come to resume political, commercial, and even military relations. At the same time, however, the treaty would assure those nations, especially those who had suffered at Japan's hand during World War II, that the United States would be an active participant in regional affairs. An added benefit, as far as Dulles was concerned, was the likelihood that ending the occupation would deprive leftists in Japan of an inviting target and promote Japanese-American harmony.

Dulles thus strongly recommended that the United States press for an early treaty and irrevocably commit Japan to the cause of the free world before the Japanese became so alarmed over the military and political implications of the situation in Korea that Tokyo started to entertain thoughts of accommodation. Because he considered time so precious, Dulles asked Acheson to send a special presidential representative to Tokyo to determine what price the United States had to pay for keeping Japan in the free world. The price Dulles had in mind included a nonpunitive peace treaty, America's commitment of substantial armed forces for the defense of the offshore island chain, and economic assurances.[33]

What economic assurances meant, Dulles told Charles Wilson, director of the Office of Defense Mobilization in a meeting on January 18, 1951, was guaranteeing Japan that "its industry can keep running and that it will receive sufficient quantities of the necessary raw materials." The assurances would also include procurements for U.S. military forces, particularly in the Pacific area, and other purchases that supported the military assistance programs in Southeast Asia. In his initial June 1950 memorandum outlining the settlement's problems, Dulles had expressed uncertainty as to whether Japan should be prohibited from the Chinese market. He recognized that Sino-Japanese trade was potentially of mutual benefit. But the communist intervention in the Korean War had led to stringent controls of the

---

[33] Dulles to Acheson, November 30, 1950, "Acheson, Dean, 1950," DPP; Dulles to Arthur H. Vandenberg, January 17, 1951, "Vandenberg, Arthur H., 1951," DPP.

China trade. Therefore Japan's only alternatives appeared to be U.S. military procurement and increased access to Southeast Asian markets. In his meeting with Wilson and other Truman officials Dulles emphasized that these economic assurances were essential "if Japan is to be on the side of the Free World." Wilson promised full support.[34]

Undoubtedly mindful of the European Defense Community proposal, Dulles believed that a Pacific pact was necessary in order to generate support from Asian allies on a peace treaty that contained no restriction on Japanese rearmament. The pact would also make it possible for Japan to circumvent Article 9 of the Japanese Constitution. As Dulles wrote to MacArthur, it "would provide a framework within which a Japanese force, if developed, could have an international status rather than a purely national status and thus might ease reconciliation with the present Japanese Constitution." Article 9 provided that "the Japanese people renounce war as a sovereign right of the nation and the threat or use of force as means of settling international disputes." The maintenance of an armed force or other instruments that could be used for such purposes was expressly forbidden. Drawing once again upon his legal expertise, Dulles reasoned that although the article "prohibits Japanese national forces for war," it "may not exclude Japanese participation in collective security arrangements such as contemplated by the United Nations Charter."[35]

Acheson found the thrust of Dulles's arguments persuasive. As a first step toward implementing them he proposed to the Defense Department to amend the stipulation in NSC 60/1 that a peace treaty could not be concluded until after a successful resolution of the Korean War. But the JCS, while agreeing to explore the possibility of a Pacific pact (to be limited to the island chain), strongly opposed an early peace. The JCS had reluctantly gone along with Dulles's desire to commence the negotiations; acquiescing to a final settlement, however, was a very different matter. Fortunately for Dulles and the State Department, Truman had recently replaced Louis Johnson with George C. Marshall as secretary of defense. The World War II hero was highly regarded by the president and could work well with Ache-

[34] Memorandum of conversation, January 18, 1951, *FR, 1951*, 6:804–5; the Assistant to the Secretary of Defense for International Security Affairs (Burns) to the Deputy Under Secretary of State (Matthews), February 20, 1951, ibid., 887–88.

[35] Dulles to MacArthur, December 20, 1950, MacArthur Library. Press conference with Mr. Sakai, representing the Japanese press, September 15, 1950, "Japan and the Japanese Peace Treaty [1951]," DPP; and "Japan's Future: Interview with John Foster Dulles," *Newsweek*, September 10, 1951, "Japanese Peace Treaty and Security Related Material," ibid.

son. With Marshall's support the administration finally agreed on January 8, 1951, to go ahead with a peace treaty. Dulles received authorization to conclude the negotiations, if possible, without awaiting a favorable outcome of the Korean War. A few weeks later, having obtained the support of Wilson and others on economic matters, Dulles headed the mission back to Japan.[36]

When Dulles had visited Japan in June 1950, he had met a number of prominent Japanese leaders, including leaders of opposition parties. Nearly all of them suspected that the United States favored Japanese rearmament only for its own security interest. Aware that these suspicions were not without foundation, Dulles sought to put a different American foot forward. He therefore requested John D. Rockefeller, who "symbolized" cultural exchanges with Japan, to accompany him to Tokyo. Dulles "wanted it understood in Japan that we were not thinking entirely in military and economic terms but also hoped to strengthen long-range cultural relations between the United States and Japan." Dulles felt that a peace treaty would prove to be insufficient unless most of the people in both countries strongly supported it. As he explained to his staff on January 26, his goal in the negotiations with the Japanese was "a genuine meeting of minds on all important issues."[37] The negotiations, however, did not go as Dulles intended.

Dulles's first encounter with Yoshida had been in June 1950 in Tokyo. The result had been, to quote John Allison, "a dismal failure." Dulles had approached his assignment enthusiastically and had hoped to elicit from Yoshida some suggestions on how to resolve the problem of Japanese security, which had been at the time the major bone of contention between State and Defense. Yoshida, however, had been cautious and evasive, and "particularly reluctant to make any commitment on security matters." The exchange had left Dulles "completely frustrated and almost bitter."[38] Given the hostilities in Korea, this time around Dulles expected Yoshida to be more concerned over security matters and thus more favorable to Japanese rearmament. In fact, Yoshida's confidant, Jiro Shirasu, had told Fearey that Article 9 of the Japanese Constitution "should and can

[36] Dulles to Acheson, January 4, 1951, *FR, 1951*, 6:781–83; Acheson to Marshall, January 9, 1951, enclosure, "Memorandum for the President," and "Draft Letter to Mr. Dulles," ibid., 787–89.

[37] Memorandum by Fearey, "Minutes of Dulles Mission Staff Meeting," January 26, 1951, *FR, 1951*, 6:813–14. On Dulles's view on cultural relations, see editorial note, ibid., 825–27.

[38] John M. Allison, *Ambassador from the Prairie or Allison Wonderland* (Boston, 1973), 148.

without great difficulty be amended at an early date to permit rearmament." Dulles also met his friend Harry F. Kern, senior editor of *Newsweek*, before his departure for Tokyo. Kern advised Dulles that "Japanese protestations about the disarmament clauses of their constitution and their desire for perpetual peace were being made largely for bargaining purposes."[39] No doubt because of such information and advice, and because his primary mission was to obtain Japan's firm commitment to the free world, at the first meeting with Yoshida Dulles chose to divorce the issue of Japanese security from the Pacific pact. Yoshida foiled the tactic, nevertheless, by expressing his determination to resist American requests for a military contribution to any collective security arrangement.

For his part, Yoshida had carefully planned his negotiating strategy. Turning Dulles's perception of the strategic dynamic on its head, he believed that the Korean War and the Chinese intervention considerably strengthened his bargaining hand by virtue of Japan's geographic importance.[40] A paper prepared by the Foreign Ministry for the Dulles visit, which closely reflected Yoshida's views, indicates his basic approach to the negotiations was as follows. To begin with, he would assure Dulles of Japan's unequivocal support for the Western democratic nations and of its pledge to cooperate with them in the maintenance of international peace and stability. He would make clear, nevertheless, that Japan's contributions should be limited to nonmilitary resources such as its industrial potential. Yoshida also intended to agree to conclude a peace treaty with the democratic nations on the basis of the seven-point statement of general principles as proposed by the United States, and, of great importance, he would sign a bilateral security agreement with Washington. But he would continue to resist Japanese rearmament. Yoshida saw no contradiction between Japan's membership in the Western community and its refusal to rearm.[41]

Yoshida never wavered from the conviction that Japan's economic growth should be the prime national goal. For the time being and until Japan could afford the cost, Japan should not rearm and must avoid involvement in international political-strategic issues. Japan would provide bases for the United States. In return Washington

[39] Memorandum by Fearey to Dulles, January 25, 1951, *FR, 1951*, 6:810–11. Harry F. Kern to John Foster Dulles, January 19, 1951, "Kern, Harry F.," DPP.

[40] Kosaka, *Prime Minister Yoshida*, 51; and Yoshitsu, *Japan and the Settlement*, chap. 3.

[41] Akio Watanabe, "Kowamondi to Nihon no Sentaku" [Peace Settlement and Japan's Choice], in A. Watanabe and S. Miyasato, eds., *San Furansisuko Kowa* [The San Francisco Peace] (Tokyo, 1986), 44–47. See also Katsuo Okazaki interview, JFDOHC.

would include Japan in its protective umbrella and cooperate with Tokyo in promoting economic development.[42]

Yoshida correctly predicted that Japanese rearmament would become the central item on Dulles's agenda. He thus ordered two studies on security. One, "Proposals to Promote Peace and Security in the Northern Pacific Area," concentrated on achieving Japanese security through general disarmament in Northeast Asia and the abolition or limitation of armaments in the Western Pacific. He wanted to have these findings for bargaining purposes. The other study was actually a draft bilateral security agreement with the United States. It provided that the UN would be responsible for the security of disarmed Japan, and, by a resolution, delegate this responsibility to the United States. The bilateral security agreement would formalize this arrangement. Prior to Dulles's visit to Tokyo, Yoshida had also consulted with former Japanese generals regarding the size of ground forces necessary for its internal security. The generals replied that approximately two hundred thousand men would be adequate. Once Dulles arrived, the canny prime minister encouraged America's negotiator to meet with Japanese opposition leaders. They favored a total peace with all allied powers and opposed the stationing of U.S. forces in Japan. Yoshida reckoned that posed with a choice between his proposals and the opposition's advocacy of neutralism, Dulles would jump at the offer of a bilateral security agreement and bases.[43]

Dulles tried strenuously to avoid Yoshida's trap. He insisted that Japan should make its due contribution to collective security. As Dulles explained to the foreign ministers of Australia and New Zealand, he lectured Yoshida that "it was necessary for all who expected to benefit by such a [collective security] system to make contributions in accordance with their own means and abilities." He wanted to convey to the Japanese (as he did later in Canberra in the context of the ANZUS pact) "the idea that their [Japanese] security has now become a collective problem and that no nation should any longer have purely national forces." Dulles proposed to "keep Japanese rearmament on a modest basis . . . over a long period." During this interval no effort would be made to balance the naval and air forces with the army. In a later interview with *Newsweek*, Dulles stated that he made clear that Japan "cannot indefinitely get a 'free ride,' " and she was

---

[42] Masataka Kosaka, ed., *Yoshida Shigeru: Sono Haikei to Isan* [Shigeru Yoshida: His Background and Heritage] (Tokyo, 1982), 97.

[43] See Watanabe, "Peace Settlement," 44–47; and Hosoya, *Road to San Francisco*, 161–67.

expected to "contribute armed forces" to collective security. He thus urged Japan to create moderate ground forces that could be used for collective security.[44]

Yoshida in turn argued that rearmament was impossible for Japan. At the most basic level, it could well give rise to the reemergence of militarism. At a minimum Japan's Asian neighbors would "fear the recurrence of Japanese aggression." Of more immediate concern, Japan lacked the basic resources required for modern armament, and the "burden of rearmament would immediately crush our national economy and impoverish our people, breeding social unrest, which is exactly what the Communists want." To Yoshida the economy had to take precedence.

For Dulles, standing with the free world by creating a small collective force within Japan's means was a matter of principle. He surely believed that Yoshida was equivocating. Demonstrating the quality for which he would be known as secretary of state, he stubbornly persisted. His perseverence paid off and Dulles exacted from Yoshida a written promise ("Initial Steps for a Rearmament Program") to establish a fifty-thousand-man national defense force composed of land and sea units. This force would be in addition to, and independent of, the Japanese National Police Reserve (NPRJ), would be armed with superior weapons, and would be a nucleus for a democratically reconstructed military force in Japan. Yoshida also accepted an American request to establish a Ministry of National Security.[45]

Yoshida yielded to Dulles because otherwise the negotiations would have been deadlocked; there would have been no peace treaty. His assumption that the international developments had strengthened his bargaining hand vis-à-vis the United States proved to be incorrect, or Dulles had proven to be a harder bargainer than he had expected. Indeed, for help he had turned to MacArthur. Yoshida told MacArthur on February 6, 1951, that he wanted to avoid explicitly mentioning Japanese rearmament in any treaty or agreements. MacArthur agreed, and the next day Yoshida succeeded in persuading Dulles not to make any reference to the agreement in any document.[46] Thus the Security Treaty, in its preamble, provided that

[44] Memorandum by Fearey, February 16, 1951, *FR, 1951*, 6:161; "Japan's Future: Interview with John Foster Dulles," *Newsweek*, September 10, 1951, "Japanese Peace Treaty and Security Related Material," DPP.

[45] Undated memorandum by Yoshida, "Suggested Agenda," *FR, 1951*, 6:831; Memorandum of conversation, January 29, 1951, ibid., 829–30.

[46] Yoshitsu, *Japan and the Settlement*, 64–65.

Japan will itself increasingly assume responsibility for its own defense against direct and indirect aggression, always avoiding any armament which could be an offensive threat or serve other than to promote peace and security in accordance with the purpose and principles of the United Nations Charter.[47]

During the negotiations Yoshida paid very close attention to all prepared papers. He studied them carefully, and he was often found standing alone in his official residence in the late afternoons, evidently digesting the day's discussions and contemplating his next move. Such preparation and concern for detail were unusual for him. A friend found him after the negotiations physically exhausted. The results exacted an emotional toll as well. Dulles had compelled Yoshida to promise to establish a collective security force, which would surely require an amendment of Article 9. But the prime minister had failed to obtain a U.S. commitment to defend Japan. For Yoshida the lack of this commitment had political ramifications. It became a symbol of inequality for the Japanese. Repeatedly Japan requested that the United States make a formal commitment to defend Japan, but in vain. Not until the revision of the Security Treaty in 1960 did Tokyo gain this objective. By that time Japanese resentment was so manifest that it all but barred President Eisenhower from visiting Japan.

This is not to say that Dulles defined the negotiations as a complete success either. He had hoped to commit the United States to defend Japan, realizing such a solid arrangement would both strengthen their bilateral relationship and enhance Japanese confidence. It would also further deter potential communist aggression. But Dulles understood that no treaty would be useful unless it were acceptable to the Senate. For these purposes Yoshida's mere promise to rearm was insufficient. Until Japan amended its Constitution and put itself in a position formally and publicly to pledge a certain number of divisions to regional security, the Senate would never sanction Washington's commitment to its defense. To do so would be to assume more responsibility than it did for Western Europe. When Colonel C. S. Babcock stated in one of the staff meetings held each day during the negotiations that "the Japanese had shown [a] willingness to assume certain obligations," Dulles argued back, venting his displeasure that "it was not clear what those obligations could at present be." Babcock was referring to Yoshida's promise to establish a fifty-thousand-

[47] United States–Japanese Draft of a Bilateral Security Treaty, July 31, 1951, *FR, 1951*, 6:1233.

man security force. Dulles implied that he was not sure whether Yoshida would carry out this promise. He was confident, nevertheless, that the defense of Japan would be secure. To his way of thinking, "the practical consequences of our keeping troops in Japan would be more important than any paper guarantee."[48]

Perhaps it was for this reason that Dulles did not follow up the promise made by Yoshida. He may well have felt he had achieved as much as was then possible, and to press further would jeopardize his accomplishments. This feeling would be congruent with his general lack of confidence in Yoshida and of the Japanese in general. Dulles told the Australian and New Zealand prime ministers in Canberra that the Japanese attitude on rearmament was "one of extreme pacifism." Though they did not have to worry about a revival of Japanese militarism, the United States could not count on Yoshida to live up to his promise to rearm.[49]

In the event Dulles underestimated Yoshida's internal difficulties. As Kosaka correctly points out, Yoshida feared that some rightist opposition leaders who had been advocating rearmament through constitutional amendment might take advantage of it. Extremely reluctant to provide them with an opportunity to challenge his government, he considered it prudent to postpone his promise indefinitely. Another probable reason for backing off was his fear that the United States might try to use this collective security force abroad. A lot of suspicion remained between the two nations.[50]

In the meantime, the Joint Chiefs of Staff were taking another route to rearm Japan. Soon after the outbreak of the Korean War, MacArthur instructed the Japanese government to establish a seventy-five-thousand-man NPRJ to compensate for the deployment of American troops to Korea. Although this force was ostensibly for internal security, on January 3, 1951, MacArthur requested that the Department of the Army, as a matter of urgency, equip the NPRJ with heavy weapons. The State Department, however, objected to delivering this equipment to the NPRJ before a peace treaty on the grounds that the action would violate Far Eastern countries' opposition to a peace treaty. But it agreed to stockpile weapons in Tokyo so that they could be delivered to the NPRJ immediately after the conclusion of the peace treaty. A detailed analysis of this process of Japanese rearmament would require another chapter. The point here is that the Joint

[48] Undated memorandum by Fearey, *FR, 1951*, 6:850–57.

[49] *FR, 1951*, 6:857; Memorandum by Fearey, February 16, 1951, ibid., 861.

[50] Kosaka, *Prime Minister Yoshida*, 108–9; and J. W. Dower, *Empire and Aftermath: Yoshida Shigeru and the Japanese Experience, 1878–1954* (Cambridge, Mass., 1979), 388–89.

Chiefs were already taking steps for Japanese rearmament quite apart from Yoshida's promise to Dulles to establish a small collective security force.[51]

. . .

I have analyzed Dulles's role in two cases integral to the making of the peace settlement with Japan. The first, resulting in NSC 60/1 of September 1950, brought about a compromise between State and Defense. The second, the negotiations in Tokyo in early 1951, produced the major provisions of the peace treaty. I can now draw some conclusions from the analysis.

First, Dulles adopted the view of the State Department that the United States should seek an early and liberal peace. His perception evolved from his axiom, a product of his Versailles experience, that political, economic, and psychological factors are critical for negotiating lasting agreements and sustaining friendly relationships. In this sense, Dulles must share credit for the treaty with State officials. From the perspective of exercising leadership, however, Dulles's contribution was unique. He was quick to grasp his first opportunity to bring about a compromise between State and Defense over the post-treaty security of Japan, conferred with MacArthur and Johnson separately, and advised MacArthur to produce the June 23 memorandum that met Defense's request. At that time the relationship between the two departments was so tense that Sebald thought that Dulles had not even met with Johnson at all. Dulles's ability to forge a compromise, if not a consensus, was an impressive accomplishment.

Second, in successfully assuming this leadership, Dulles proved to be very pragmatic. Although never one to be easily deflected from a chosen path, in this case he showed surprising flexibility and adaptability. Nsc 60/1 included virtually all the Joint Chiefs' requests. Dulles accepted the compromise to break the deadlock and to proceed with early negotiations. He did so even though, based on his legal as well as diplomatic training, he rejected the JCS's position. As he explained to Dean Rusk long after NSC 60/1 had been written and approved:

> Those who think primarily in legalistic terms, or who feel that their particular duty is to spell out, on paper, United States rights adequate to meet all conceivable contingencies, may seek an agreement which will concede

[51] Marshall to Acheson, February 15, 1951, *FR, 1951*, 6:884–85.

us elaborate extraterritorial privileges, command relationships and prestige positions. Such an approach could be self-defeating.[52]

The demand for "elaborate extraterritorial privileges, command relationships and prestige positions," it should be recalled, was included in NSC 60/1. Yet Dulles agreed to it.

Dulles's negotiations with Prime Minister Yoshida tell us much about his diplomatic style. He prepared for the talks extensively, and by the time he reached Tokyo he had developed a carefully crafted strategy. He knew what he wanted and felt confident that he knew how to get it. He would rely on a hard and persistent approach to the difficult issues (in this case those related to security matters), accepting compromises only when the alternative was to fail to obtain any settlement at all. When the bargaining reached an impasse, he was sure that his understanding of the contemporary international situation, especially with regard to the relationship between the Korean War and the threat to Japan, and his reading of the political, economic, and psychological dynamics influencing Japanese behavior, would tip the balance in America's favor.

To a larger degree Dulles was correct in his assessment. He did bring home a treaty before the resolution of the Korean conflict, and in his face-off with Yoshida over Japanese rearmament he received the prime minister's written pledge to establish a fifty-thousand-man defense force. Yet his success must be qualified. Yoshida never carried out his promise, and as a consequence, Dulles failed to obtain Japan's military participation in a collective security system. In his eyes, therefore, he never induced Tokyo to become a full-fledged member of the free world coalition. Further, Dulles was unable to overcome the mutual suspicion that lingered between the two countries. Considering himself a good judge of Japan's "national character," Dulles doubted that the Japanese would ever live up to their military responsibilities. It was as if World War II had taken all the fight out of them, leaving them with an attitude of "extreme pacifism." For the future secretary of state this attitude had no place in the cold war. As for Yoshida, he surmised that Dulles was not sufficiently sympathetic to his difficulties. Yoshida did strongly support the United States, but his top priority had to be Japan's domestic concerns. Further, he could not guarantee to the Japanese that committing forces to a collective security arrangement would not lead to involvement in another war. In truth Dulles was sensitive to Japan's concerns. But neither he nor Yoshida could resolve the conflict to either side's satisfaction.

[52] Dulles to Rusk, October 22, 1951, *FR, 1951*, 6:1380–81.

Still, Dulles was proud of his accomplishment, and he incorporated it into both his diplomatic and strategic perspectives. Although Dulles had attended conferences among great powers for as long as he could remember, this was the first time that he headed the negotiating team and was singularly responsible for its results. Predictably he derived important lessons from the experience. Because he did gauge the treaty a general success, he would follow similar tactics when negotiating as secretary of state. On the strategic level, moreover, he would always try to guarantee that he was not only bargaining from strength but also could assure that the agreements would be implemented. This approach could be seen, for example, in his diplomatic posture at Panmunjom in 1953 and Geneva in 1954. These talks also demonstrate the extent to which his involvement in the Japanese Peace Treaty influenced his geopolitical design for Asia and the Pacific. Ironically, notwithstanding his reputation as an Atlanticist, even before his appointment as secretary of state John Foster Dulles had emerged as a central actor in the Far East.

CHAPTER 8

"A Good Stout Effort": John Foster Dulles and the Indochina Crisis, 1954–1955

George C. Herring

BETWEEN March 1954 and June 1955, Indochina consumed much of the attention of John Foster Dulles. Fearful that the triumph of communism there might cost the West the remainder of Southeast Asia, the secretary of state struggled to protect a region perceived vital to U.S. security. With the hedgehog determination for which he was famous, he relentlessly promoted what he called "United Action." Plowing determinedly through various diplomatic minefields, he eventually put together a collective security arrangement designed to shield Southeast Asia from communist advances. He also initiated the process of nation-building in newly independent Laos, Cambodia, and southern Vietnam. Against heavy odds, Dulles attained notable short-term successes. But he paid a very high price in terms of relations with America's major allies, and the security arrangement he had so painstakingly constructed barely survived his death.

Indochina posed extremely complex challenges for Dulles. By the time the United States began to focus on the problem, the French position had drastically deteriorated and prospects for success were slim. In addition, the United States, Great Britain, and France viewed the crisis quite differently, and for the United States to achieve its own policy objectives without alienating its allies proved impossible. There were also problems at home. Having exploited the alleged "loss" of China by the Democrats at the polls in 1952, the administration could ill afford to "lose" additional territory to communism. On the other hand, painful memories of Korea placed constraints on the use of military power. Perhaps because of the political delicacy of the crisis, Dulles remained at center stage throughout, formulating and defending the administration's policies, personally conducting many of the negotiations, playing the role of point man and lightning rod.

The Indochina crisis took form in mid-March 1954. Exhausted from nearly eight years of fighting the Vietminh revolutionaries, France in February succeeded in putting the Indochina issue on the agenda of a major international conference to be held in Geneva. In the meantime, General Henri Navarre had placed twelve thousand of his troops in the remote village of Dien Bien Phu in northwestern Vietnam and established a fortress in a broad valley surrounded by hills. The Vietminh laid siege to the French fortress and on March 13 seized two hill outposts established by the French to protect the airfield and fortress below. Vietminh artillery quickly knocked out the airfield, making resupply possible only by parachute drop. Thus on the eve of the Geneva conference, France faced the likelihood of a serious military defeat.

The administration of Dwight D. Eisenhower had accepted without reservation the assessment of the importance of Indochina bequeathed by its precedessor. The fall of China to Mao Tse-tung's Communists in 1949 aroused grave fears for the security of adjoining areas, and the establishment of close ties between the Chinese Communists and the Vietminh significantly increased the threat to Indochina. Top U.S. officials were certain that the loss of Indochina would cause the loss of all of Southeast Asia, depriving the United States and its allies of naval bases, strategic water routes, and vital raw materials. The loss of Southeast Asia, in turn, by depriving Japan of access to indispensable raw materials and markets, would threaten the loss of that crucial nation. "The situation of the Japanese is hard enough with China being commie," Dulles commented in January 1953, and if Southeast Asia were lost, "the Japs would be thinking of how to get on the other side." The loss of Indochina would also have disastrous consequences in Europe. The Laniel government in France, friendly to the European Defense Community, would fall, threatening the keystone of the administration's plans for European security. The loss of Indochina would endanger Malaya, a major source of dollars for Britain, undermining the economic basis of the Western alliance. Top administration officials agreed in March 1953 that Indochina "had probably the top priority in foreign policy, being in some ways more important than Korea because the consequences . . . could not be localized but would spread throughout Asia and Europe."[1]

From the time it took office the administration was also deeply concerned about the way in which France was "muddling along" in Indochina. The main problem, Dulles told a British diplomat, was a lack of "will and resolution." The French had not mobilized their resources for war or formulated an aggressive, offensive strategy. They had refused to make clear and unequivocal promises of indepen-

[1] Record of meeting, January 28, 1953, *FR, 1952–1954*, 13:361–62; Memorandum of conversation by Dulles, March 24, 1953, ibid., 419–20.

dence to the noncommunist Vietnamese and had dragged their feet in building a Vietnamese army. Dulles was certain that the war could be won or reduced to manageable proportions in eighteen months to two years if France pursued it wisely and vigorously. In late 1953 the United States extracted from the French (in return for major commitments of military aid) promises to "perfect" the independence of the Vietnamese, expand and improve the training of the Vietnamese National Army, and conduct offensive operations against the enemy. But the half-hearted way in which the French implemented the so-called Navarre Plan only reinforced long-standing American concerns.[2]

The Dien Bien Phu crisis transformed concern into outright alarm. Dulles had tried to block French efforts to negotiate, even to the point of contemplating a cutoff of aid, but he feared that drastic action might produce an anti-American uproar in Paris that would carry EDC "down the drain." He therefore acquiesced, although he was afraid of a French surrender at Geneva. The threat of a military disaster at Dien Bien Phu underscored his fears. A special committee appointed by the president to review Indochina policy recommended in mid-March that the United States should do everything possible to discourage defeatist tendencies in France and use its influence to block a settlement. If, despite American efforts, the French agreed to an unacceptable settlement, the United States might have to arrange with the Vietnamese or other interested nations to continue the war without France. The Dien Bien Phu crisis thus posed for the first time the possibility of direct U.S. intervention in the Indochina conflict.[3]

Dulles has often been cast as the villain in the Dien Bien Phu crisis. The role probably pleased him, and it was partly of his own making. To deter the Russians and especially the Chinese from intervention in Indochina, he deliberately cultivated an image of aggressiveness, and in a much-quoted *Life* article in 1956 he boasted that the Indochina crisis was one of three times when he had successfully practiced "brinkmanship," taking the United States "perilously close" to war in order to thwart communist aggression. Democratic congressmen reinforced the image, retorting that a reckless Dulles would have taken the United States "over the brink" if they had not applied the brakes. French foreign minister Georges Bidault subsequently claimed that at a critical point in the crisis Dulles had offered to lend him two

[2] Anthony Eden memorandum of conversation with Dulles, February 4, 1953, PRO, FO 371/106765; R. H. Scott to Foreign Office, July 30, 1953, PRO, FO 371/10679.

[3] George Herring and Richard Immerman, "Eisenhower, Dulles, and Dienbienphu: 'The Day We Didn't Go to War' Revisited," *Journal of American History* 71 (September 1984): 352.

atomic bombs. Many writers have thus portrayed Dulles, along with Vice President Richard M. Nixon and Admiral Arthur Radford, chairman of the Joint Chiefs of Staff, as hawkish and reckless, the belligerent foils to Eisenhower, the closet dove. The United States would have gone to war, it has been argued, had it not been for the restraints imposed on Dulles and his fellow hawks by Congress, the British, and Eisenhower.[4]

Dulles's role was much more complex than it is often portrayed. The differences between him and Eisenhower were infrequent and insignificant, and he was far less bellicose than he appeared. He staunchly opposed the sort of air intervention at Dien Bien Phu pushed by Admiral Radford, and he opposed unilateral military intervention in any form. He promoted instead what he called United Action, a plan for possible multilateral military intervention. Whether this was primarily bluff or whether Dulles was committed to some kind of military intervention cannot be determined conclusively. He and Eisenhower obscured their intentions so well that they confused their contemporaries and baffled scholars. Whatever the case, Dulles approached the Dien Bien Phu crisis in a most cautious and calculating way. If he did favor intervention, it was to be carefully circumscribed and, in the case of the United States, limited primarily to air and naval power.

Unwilling to give France a blank check on the use of U.S. military power, Dulles flatly rejected unconditional advance commitments to intervene. When French chief of staff General Paul Ely came to Washington in late March and asked for U.S. intervention if the Chinese sent aircraft to Dien Bien Phu, Dulles responded cautiously. He and Radford agreed that they would make no commitments until they were certain that France would take the steps necessary to win the war. Dulles informed Ely that the United States would not invest its prestige except under conditions where military success was likely, which would require France to extend "a greater degree of partnership" than had prevailed in the past. The discussions produced nothing more than a tightly qualified "agreed minute" directing military officials to begin planning immediately so that no time would be wasted if the two governments decided to oppose Chinese air intervention should it occur.[5]

[4] James Shepley, "How Dulles Averted War," *Life* (January 16, 1956): 70–72. For the Democrats' response, see *New York Times*, January 23–24, 1956. For Bidault's charges, see Georges Bidault, *Resistance: The Political Autobiography of Georges Bidault*, Marianne Sinclair, trans. (London, 1967), 94–96, 170, 191, 196–97. For the portrayal of Dulles as reckless and belligerent, see Bernard Fall, *Hell in a Very Small Place* (Philadelphia, 1967), 297; and David Halberstam, *The Best and the Brightest* (New York, 1972), 141.

[5] Memorandum of conversation, Radford, Ely, and Dulles, March 23, 1954, DSRG 59,

Dulles also opposed Operation Vulture, the plan for air intervention at Dien Bien Phu originally developed by French and American military officials in Saigon and promoted by Radford after Ely left Washington. The secretary was deeply concerned that the Chinese might intervene in Indochina and that France might capitulate, and he was prepared to take risks. Like Eisenhower, however, he appears not to have been convinced that Vulture was either feasible or necessary. Should the Chinese intervene, he speculated, he would prefer such things as "harrassing tactics from Formosa and along the Chinese seacoast," measures that "would be more readily within our natural facilities than actually fighting in Indochina."[6] In part because of the opposition of Dulles, the administration never seriously contemplated the sort of intervention pressed by Radford.

Dulles labeled his preferred response to the Dien Bien Phu crisis United Action. The plan was cautious and flexible, and it was designed to meet the many contingencies of the Indochina crisis. Dulles claimed that United Action was based on the Pacific pact, a regional security program he had proposed when negotiating the Japanese Peace Treaty for Truman. Its keystone was the formation of a coalition composed of the United States, Great Britain, France, Australia, New Zealand, Thailand, the Philippines, and the Associated States of Indochina, and committed to the defense of Indochina and the rest of Southeast Asia. The mere establishment of such a coalition accompanied by stern warnings might be sufficient to deter Chinese intervention in the war, moderate communist demands at Geneva, and bolster the French will to resist, thus making outside intervention unnecessary. It is indeed possible that United Action was all bluff, and that Eisenhower and Dulles never seriously contemplated the possibility of military intervention.[7]

More likely, United Action was designed to ensure that if the United States intervened it would do so under the most favorable circumstances. The administration never committed itself to military intervention during the Dien Bien Phu crisis, but it left that option open to meet the contingencies of Chinese intervention, a French military collapse, or, preferably, a breakdown of the Geneva negotiations and a continuation of the war. Eisenhower and Dulles agreed

---

715G.00/3–2354; Dulles memorandum of conversation with Eisenhower, March 24, 1954, ibid., box 222, lot 64D199.

[6] James Hagerty Diary, March 26, 1954, Eisenhower Library; Dulles memorandum of conversation with Eisenhower, March 24, 1954, DSRG 59, box 222, lot 64D199.

[7] SFRC, 1954, 6:263–64. For representative Dulles descriptions of the purposes of United Action and the way it might work, see memorandum of conversation, April 5, 1954, FR, 1952–1954, 12: pt. 1, 402; and memorandum of conversation, May 2, 1954, ibid., 440.

that the United States should intervene only as part of a genuinely collective effort and that U.S. ground forces must not become bogged down in Asia. United Action would provide a legal basis for collective action. A multilateral effort would remove the taint of a war for French colonialism and would provide additional leverage to force the French to share political and military decision-making. If, on the other hand, France pulled out, United Action would ensure that the United States did not have to fight alone. In keeping with the New Look military doctrine, local and regional forces would bear the brunt of the ground fighting while the Americans, as Dulles put it, would do those things "we can do better": provide naval and air support, furnish money and supplies, and train indigenous troops.[8]

Dulles promoted the plan feverishly after March 29, but he met roadblocks everywhere he turned. Congressional leaders would agree to back a resolution calling for intervention only if "satisfactory commitments" could be obtained from Britain and other allies to go in collectively and from France to "internationalize" the war and grant the Vietnamese independence. Dulles could not secure such commitments. Bidault made clear that his people would not support continuation of the war if ties between the Associated States and France were severed, and he refused to internationalize the war. Most important, the British flatly rejected United Action. Prime Minister Winston Churchill and Foreign Secretary Anthony Eden were reluctant to intervene in a war they felt could not be won. They were convinced that France retained sufficient influence to secure a reasonable settlement at Geneva, and they feared that outside intervention would provoke war with China, possibly precipitating World War III. Eden agreed to discuss with the United States a regional grouping for Southeast Asia; only, however, after the conclusion of the Geneva conference.[9]

British opposition to United Action sealed the fate of Dien Bien Phu. On April 22, Bidault made a last frantic request for U.S. air intervention, even hinting at French willingness to internationalize the war. Dulles pressed Eden to go along, but the British refused to budge and Dulles summarily rejected Bidault's appeal for unilateral U.S. intervention. An air strike might not save Dien Bien Phu, he

---

[8] Dulles telephone conversation with H. Alexander Smith, April 19, 1954, TTS, "March 1–April 30, 1954 (1)," DPEL. For commentary on the form American intervention might have taken, see also Dulles telephone conversation with Alexander Wiley, April 7, 1954, ibid.; SFRC, 1954, 6:263–264; Memorandum of conversation, April 25, 1954, FR, 1952–1954, 16:558.

[9] For a full discussion of these events, see Herring and Immerman, "Eisenhower, Dulles, and Dienbienphu," 353–58.

advised Eisenhower, and the United States could not be certain that if it intervened France would stay in the war. There would not be time to arrange "proper political understandings" with the French, he went on, and "once our prestige is committed in battle, our negotiating position in these matters would be almost negligible." Furious with both the British and French, Eisenhower and Dulles decided to hold up any military action pending developments at Geneva. After fifty-five days of heroic but futile resistance, the hopelessly outnumbered French garrison surrendered on May 7, the day before the Indochina phase of the Geneva conference opened.[10]

Even more than in the Dien Bien Phu crisis, Dulles has been cast in the role of archvillain at Geneva. In the words of biographer Townsend Hoopes, he conducted himself with the "pinched distaste of a puritan in a house of ill repute."[11] Much has been made of his refusal to shake hands with Chinese foreign minister Chou En-lai and his unwillingness to have anything to do with the Chinese delegation. He has been roundly criticized for the general rudeness of his demeanor, and his apparent willingness to wreck the conference. As much as any other single individual, he has been held responsible for the failure of the conference to negotiate a lasting settlement of the Indochina problem.

Such criticism is justified, but to focus on Dulles's behavior at Geneva misses the larger point. As during the Dien Bien Phu crisis, his major objective throughout these months was to establish a collective security mechanism for the future defense of Southeast Asia. During the first phase of the Geneva conference, he appears to have viewed the possible collapse of negotiations with equanimity, and he pressed forward vigorously with plans for a Southeast Asian security pact. Ironically, his efforts may have contributed to the settlement he abhorred. Still, he adapted, finding a way to integrate the prospective settlement into his larger plans for Southeast Asia. Although notably hostile toward the Geneva agreements in public, he and Eisenhower were not entirely displeased, seeing in them the means to accomplish their larger goals.

Geneva presented a baffling array of difficulties. The administration feared that the conference might endorse major communist gains. To be associated with such a result left the Republicans vulnerable to Democratic charges of complicity in another Yalta. Yet to remain aloof would deprive the United States of any means to influence the outcome. Although Congress and the nation would likely oppose

---

[10] Herring and Immerman, "Eisenhower, Dulles, and Dienbienphu," 358–62.
[11] Townsend Hoopes, *The Devil and John Foster Dulles* (Boston, 1973), 222.

military intervention in Indochina, they would also undoubtedly attack the administration if it did nothing. Problems with America's allies were even more acute. Dulles feared that the British, particularly Eden, were inclined to appease the communists, but Britain's cooperation was crucial to European defense and to future plans for collective security in Southeast Asia. Besides, the United States could not afford a break with its closest ally. France posed especially delicate problems. Dulles and Eisenhower feared that to push France too hard risked a collapse in Indochina and defeat of EDC. Conversely, they perceived that continuation of French policy along existing lines would produce a sellout at Geneva. Dulles was nearly obsessed with the suspicion that France would try to put the United States in a position where it could be held responsible for the loss of Indochina and the failure of the Geneva conference.

Not surprisingly, during the first phase of the conference Dulles was both negative and aloof. The fall of Dien Bien Phu on the very eve of the conference reinforced U.S. fears of a French surrender. The communists appeared confident of a major diplomatic victory and seemed unlikely to make concessions. Dulles not only refused to shake hands with Chou; he would not sit at a table with him or indeed near any communist delegation, creating enormous logistical problems for those responsible for protocol.[12] He was outraged when the British and French failed to defend the United States against Chou's verbal tirades. A British diplomat described his demeanor as one of "almost pathological rage and gloom," and observed him sitting at the conference table "not knowing where to look, his mouth drawn down at the corners, and his eyes on the ceiling, sucking on his teeth."[13] To underscore American distaste for and distance from the proceedings, the secretary of state departed Geneva before the Indochina phase of the conference began. He instructed the American delegation that it should participate in the conference only as an "interested nation," not as a "belligerent or a principal in the negotiations," and should not endorse an agreement that in any way impaired the territorial integrity of the Associated States.[14] Given the military position of the Vietminh when the conference opened, Dulles was saying that the United States would approve no settlement at all.

While the conferees struggled to resolve the issues at Geneva, Dulles continued to promote United Action. He toyed with the idea of

---

[12] U. Alexis Johnson, *The Right Hand of Power* (Englewood Cliffs, N.J., 1984), 204.

[13] Evelyn Shuckburgh, *Descent to Suez: Diaries 1951–1956* (London, 1986), 185–86.

[14] Dulles to Walter Bedell Smith, May 12, 1954, U.S. Congress, House, Committee on Armed Services, *United States–Vietnam Relations, 1945–1967: A Study Prepared by the Department of Defense* (Washington, 1971), book 9:457–59.

forming a coalition without Britain, abandoning it only when he could not gain Australian support.[15] He then shifted back to working with Britain, accepting Eden's qualification that no formal arrangement could be consummated until after the completion of the Geneva conference. In the meantime, he worked tirelessly to line up support among other prospective members of the alliance. In late May, as part of the United Action strategy, the United States hosted military staff talks with participants from Britain, France, Australia, and New Zealand in order to map out a long-range strategy. Dulles also felt that the talks might have some impact at Geneva, serving "as window dressing with the Russians, who had no way of knowing what was going on."[16]

In Dulles's view the "only ray of hope" at Geneva was a credible threat of U.S. intervention, and during the first weeks of the conference he sought to keep this possibility alive.[17] Administration officials developed an elaborate scenario for possible intervention, including a draft joint resolution to be submitted to Congress, plans for actual military operations, and proposals for a multilateral command structure and the training of Vietnamese troops. For more than four weeks the United States discussed with France the possibility of internationalizing the war, setting forth in great detail the conditions it would insist upon for its own intervention.[18]

Even more than in the Dien Bien Phu crisis, the intentions of Eisenhower and Dulles are unclear, if indeed they were committed to any specific course of action. They seem to have hoped throughout the crisis that the French would eventually come to their senses and invite the United States into Indochina, as the British had in Greece. Yet the terms they demanded of Paris were so stiff that, as Bidault informed Eden, no French government could accept them. It is possible that they were developed with the idea they would be rejected, thereby eliminating any real likelihood of intervention and comprising yet another stage of Dulles's strategy of bluff.[19] At one point in the negotiations Dulles admitted that the discussions were little more than an "academic exercise" except as they affected "those who are

[15] Gregory Pemberton, "Australia, the United States, and the Indochina Crisis of 1954," *Diplomatic History* 13 (Winter 1989): 61–66.

[16] Memorandum of conversation, May 28, 1954, *FR, 1952–1954*, 12: pt. 1, 526. For the results of the five-power staff talks, see ibid., 555–63.

[17] Memorandum of NSC meeting, May 20, 1954, *FR, 1952–1954*, 13:1590.

[18] The discussions regarding military intervention can be followed in *FR, 1952–1954*, 13:1586–1659.

[19] Eden to Foreign Office, May 16, 1954, PRO, FO 371/112066; and May 17, 1954, ibid., PREM 649.

in Geneva," and he conceded that the administration was trying to create an "impression in the minds of the French and those in Geneva that serious talks are going on."[20] On the other hand, the care with which the plans for intervention were drawn up suggests that the exercise may have been more than a charade, and Dulles on one occasion indicated that if the talks with France succeeded they would comprise the cornerstone of United Action.

If Eisenhower and Dulles were bluffing they soon found they were playing a dangerous game. The French responded with tough conditions of their own, including an advance U.S. commitment to employ ground forces. The haggling over conditions, moreover, aroused concern in Washington that the French were trying to draw the United States into a series of "piecemeal commitments" without the general understanding necessary to make United Action work. Washington also feared that by the time the French got around to agreeing on the terms for U.S. intervention, it would be too late. And Dulles increasingly worried that the French would use the harsh American conditions as an alibi for their surrender to the communists or would try to maneuver the United States into a position where it would have to go to war on their terms. The secretary made clear to French ambassador Henri Bonnet on June 9 that it was "all or nothing." Unless France accepted its conditions the United States would make no commitments.[21] The exercise in futility became irrelevant four days later when the Laniel government fell.

Developments in Geneva in June evoked mixed feelings from Washington. Eisenhower and Dulles remained concerned with both Eden's apparent determination to achieve a settlement at almost any cost and France's pervasive weakness. On several occasions an obviously frustrated Dulles speculated that it would be best if France got out of Indochina entirely, permitting the United States to start from scratch. He even talked of unilateral U.S. intervention, and of matching the communists in a "game of tit for tat"—"when the Commies grab land we grab some from them."[22]

On the other hand, the administration saw reason for hope. Negotiations quickly deadlocked over such issues as the partition of Vietnam, composition of an international body to oversee the cease-fire, and withdrawal of Vietminh troops from Cambodia and Laos. It appeared increasingly likely that the conference might adjourn without any agreement. Perhaps then the British would accept U.S. pro-

[20] Memorandum of NSC meeting, May 20, 1954, *FR, 1952–1954*, 12: pt. 1, 498–99.
[21] Dulles to U.S. Delegation, Geneva, June 9, 1954, *FR, 1952–1954*, 16:1100–1.
[22] Memorandum of NSC meeting, June 17, 1954, *FR, 1952–1954*, 13:1716; Memorandum of meeting, June 30, 1954, ibid., 1768.

posals for collective security in Southeast Asia, Dulles reasoned. Privately, he informed Walter Bedell Smith that final adjournment of the conference might be "in our best interest," provided that France did not conclude that it had been deserted by its allies and surrender to the communists in Europe and Indochina. Dulles publicly accused the communists of sabotaging negotiations, and reaffirmed the need for collective security.[23]

Dulles's diplomatic bluster may have contributed to the outcome he least favored. Threatened with the breakdown of the conference, Eden redoubled his efforts to promote a compromise. Apparently convinced that a cessation of negotiations might lead to U.S. military intervention, the Soviet Union, China, and the Vietminh made major concessions, agreeing to withdraw troops from Laos and Cambodia, accepting a temporary partition of Vietnam, and conceding on the composition of the control commission. In the meantime Pierre Mendès-France replaced Laniel and shocked the delegates by proclaiming that he would resign if a settlement were not reached by July 21. Eden leaped to Mendès-France's support and dashed Dulles's hopes by indicating that Britain would wait until the conclusion of the Geneva conference to move forward on collective security.

These dramatic events forced a change in U.S. policy. Eisenhower and Dulles abandoned hopes of a collapse at Geneva and ended serious talk of military intervention in the Indochina War. Admitting that it would be something they would "gag about," they accepted the inevitability of a compromise settlement.[24] They sought henceforth to exert U.S. influence to promote an agreement on Indochina that could be integrated into the larger framework of a Southeast Asian security pact. The removal of France from the area, they reasoned, would make it possible to salvage something "free of the taint of French colonialism." The United States could take the lead in forming a strong regional grouping "to keep alive freedom" in Southeast Asia. It could draw a line that the communists could not cross; take over from France responsibility for defending Laos, Cambodia, and that part of Vietnam below the partition line; and, ultimately, "hold

[23] Dulles to Smith, June 14, 1954, *FR, 1952–1954*, 16:1146–47. This section draws heavily on Gary R. Hess, "Redefining the American Position in Southeast Asia: The United States and the Geneva Conference 1954," unpublished paper in possession of author.

[24] Hagerty Diary, June 24, 1954, Hagerty Papers, Eisenhower Library. Lloyd C. Gardner, *Approaching Vietnam: From World War II to Dienbienphu, 1941–1954* (New York, 1988), 256–57, suggests that Dulles had hinted at acceptance of partition in a private conversation with Soviet foreign minister Molotov before the Indochina phase of the Geneva conference opened.

this area and fight subversion within it with all the strength we have."[25]

Remarkably, Dulles and Eisenhower won British support for their policy. Churchill and Eden had originally preferred the neutralization of Laos, Cambodia, and the noncommunist part of Vietnam. Apparently to secure American support for a negotiated settlement, they agreed during talks in Washington from June 25 to June 27 to a seven-point plan that permitted the three states to have "stable, non-Communist" governments, maintain military forces, and accept foreign military aid and advisers. This arrangement at least implied a permanent division of Vietnam.[26]

Dulles's stubborn determination to avoid being tainted by negotiations with the communists almost undid his handiwork. Seeking to exploit France's apparent isolation from its allies and Mendès-France's self-imposed deadline, the Vietminh held out for a partition line at the 13th parallel, far below what the Americans and British deemed acceptable. Fearing that Mendès-France might cave in, Eisenhower and Dulles once again began to contemplate how to respond to an unacceptable agreement. Dulles may have been tempted by the renewed possibility that negotiations might break down. At the very least he did not want to be identified with an unsatisfactory settlement. Hence he refused to return to Geneva himself and would not even send Smith back. He made clear that the United States would do no more than "respect" an unacceptable agreement. It would not guarantee or publicly support it.

For the first time during the Indochina crisis, Eisenhower overruled his secretary of state. The president may have been impressed with Mendès-France's plea for a unified Western stand in the final, critical stages of the conference. In any event, he conceded to press secretary James Hagerty, refusal to participate would make America appear "like a little boy sulking in his tent," and participation would give America a chance to influence the settlement. Deferring a decision on participation, Eisenhower sent Dulles to Paris to confer with Mendès-France, probably in hopes that it would bring the secretary of state around.[27]

Eisenhower's ploy appears to have worked. Mendès-France "fought his corner brilliantly," according to Eden, and a "shaken" Dulles acquiesced.[28] The French prime minister persuaded Dulles that a settlement within the framework of the seven-point plan was

[25] Hagerty Diary, June 23, 24, 28, 1954, Hagerty Papers.
[26] Hess, "Redefining the American Position in Southeast Asia," 23–27.
[27] Hagerty Diary, July 8–11, 1954, Hagerty Papers.
[28] Eden to Foreign Office, July 14, 1954, pro, fo 371/112077.

possible, but could only be attained if the Western powers stood together and the United States participated. Mendès-France signed a
statement promising not to hold the United States responsible for
failure at Geneva. Dulles indicated U.S. willingness to respect an
agreement consistent with the seven points, and on July 14 announced that Smith would return to Geneva to head the U.S. delegation. Making the best of his cave-in the secretary claimed a victory
for American diplomacy and, especially, exulted in the way his presence had demonstrated American power. Mendès-France and Eden
had rushed to meet with him, he said, leaving the communists "cool-
ing their heels." When "it really comes down to something important," he told the National Security Council, "the United States is the
key nation."[29]

Mainly as a result of Mendès-France's initiative, the Western allies
attained an agreement consistent with the seven points. Dulles's return to Paris attracted a great deal of publicity, probably raising once
again fears among the communists that a breakdown of negotiations
would lead to American intervention in the war. Moreover, British
and American backing in the last stage of the conference vastly
strengthened the French bargaining position. Bending to pressure
from the Soviet Union and China, the Vietminh compromised on
both the cease-fire line and timing of elections. Dulles and Eisenhower contemplated one more public threat of American military
intervention in case the negotiations stalled. It turned out to be unnecessary. The agreement was completed just hours after Mendès-
France's deadline had expired. The United States, true to Dulles's
pledge, simply "took note" of the Geneva accords and vowed not to
"disturb them" by the "threat or the use of force."[30]

Eisenhower and Dulles viewed the outcome at Geneva with mixed
feelings. They had never looked happily on the negotiations and
deeply regretted losing northern Vietnam—"the keystone to the
arch" of Southeast Asia. They were stung by criticism from Congress
and the public. Still they recognized, as Bedell Smith put it, that "diplomacy has never been able to gain at the conference table what cannot be held on the battlefield," and the agreements were better than
might have been expected in mid-June. The "important thing," Dulles observed, was "not to mourn the past but to seize the future opportunity to prevent the loss in Northern Vietnam from leading to

[29] Memorandum of NSC meeting, July 15, 1954, *FR, 1952–1954*, 13:1834–40.
[30] Statement by Walter Bedell Smith, July 21, 1954, U.S. Congress, Senate, Subcommittee on Public Buildings and Grounds, *The Pentagon Papers (The Senator Gravel Edition)* (4 vols.: Boston, 1971), 1:571–72.

the extension of communism throughout Southeast Asia and the Southwest Pacific."[31]

Dulles immediately set out to construct the security arrangements that had eluded him since March. At a press conference on July 23 he outlined his plans. The free nations must profit from the lessons of the past few months, he insisted. The first lesson was that collective security arrangements had to be made "in advance of aggression, not after it is underway." The United States would therefore take "prompt steps" to put such a mechanism into effect. The second lesson was that resistance to communism required popular support. One of the "good aspects" of Geneva, the secretary went on, was that it advanced the "truly independent status" of Laos, Cambodia, and southern Vietnam, and the "free governments of the area should from now on be able to enlist the loyalty of their people to maintain their independence against communist colonialism." In the aftermath of Geneva, the United States set out to promote the independence of these governments and develop them into bulwarks against further communist advances in Southeast Asia.[32]

Negotiation of a collective security treaty was the first priority. As Dulles saw it, the major purpose of such a treaty was to deter Chinese aggression. The signatories would draw a line across Southeast Asia and make clear to the Chinese that they would retaliate if the line was crossed. Should the pact fail to deter, Dulles vaguely noted, member nations would deal with aggression in "the most feasible and effective way." The administration was especially concerned with subversion in Southeast Asia, and Dulles foresaw for SEATO a role in combating it. The mere existence of the alliance would give member nations more confidence to deal with subversion. The United States could assist in the development of internal security forces, provide economic assistance to help combat the social and economic ills that helped subversion flourish, and give "underground intelligence support." Dulles even speculated that the United States might have highly specialized military forces to dispatch to the scene to help allied nations deal with subversion.[33]

Eisenhower and Dulles approached SEATO with the same caution they had shown in the Dien Bien Phu crisis. They admitted that the

[31] *New York Times*, July 24, 1954; Dulles news conference transcript, July 23, 1954, "Press Conference July 23, 1954," DPP.

[32] *New York Times*, July 24, 1954; Dulles news conference transcript, July 23, 1954, "Press Conference July 23, 1954," DPP.

[33] Minutes of meeting on Southeast Asia, July 24, 1954, *FR, 1952–1954*, 12: pt. 1, 666–71; Memorandum of conversation, July 26, 1954, ibid., 673–75; Dulles to Embassy, United Kingdom, July 28, 1954, ibid., 680–81.

"western colorization" of the pact was "unfortunate," but conceded that it was necessary because of the weakness of the nations in the area. Eisenhower was "frankly puzzled" by the dilemma of trying to combat subversion without turning the United States into an "armed camp." The two men shared concern about assuming major commitments in an area as unpromising as Indochina. They also concluded, however, that they could not surrender the area "without a struggle" and commitment was therefore "the lesser of two evils."

The president and secretary of state did design the alliance to limit the risks. They scrupulously avoided NATO-type arrangements for fear of the expense and danger involved, proposing instead a Monroe Doctrine–type consultative agreement. Indeed, they would have preferred a name other than SEATO because it so closely resembled that of the European alliance. They made clear from the outset that the United States would not support SEATO with specific commitments of troops. Dulles's idea rather was to provide a mobile strike force that could be quickly sent to trouble spots. Wary of eager supplicants, they also made clear the United States would not provide economic assistance for member nations on a scale approaching the Marshall Plan.[34]

The Southeast Asia Treaty Organization was negotiated at Manila in September, and Dulles was generally satisfied with the result. SEATO had obvious weaknesses. Major neutralist nations in the region such as Burma, India, and Indonesia refused to participate, and because of restrictions imposed by the Geneva accords, Laos, Cambodia, and southern Vietnam could not join. Much to Dulles's annoyance, the British and other member nations resisted appeals to specify meeting "*communist* aggression" as the purpose of the treaty. It was as much because of the United States as any other nation, however, that the treaty lacked teeth. Member nations agreed only to "meet common danger" in accordance with their "own constitutional processes" and to "consult." Still, from Dulles's standpoint SEATO was more than satisfactory. It would serve as a deterrent. More important, a separate protocol designated Laos, Cambodia, and southern Vietnam as areas which, if threatened, would "endanger" the "peace and security" of all signatories. The SEATO protocol thus established a legal basis for United Action and gave southern Vietnam a measure of status as an independent nation.[35]

[34] Memorandum of conversation, July 26, 1954, *FR, 1952–1954*, 12: pt. 1, 675; Memorandum of NSC meeting, August 12, 1954, ibid., 729; Memorandum of conversation, Eisenhower and Dulles, August 17, 1954, ibid., 735; Memorandum of NSC meeting, September 12, 1954, ibid., 903.

[35] For Dulles's post-Manila appraisal of the treaty, see memorandum of NSC meeting,

With SEATO in place the administration set out to shore up former French Indochina, the crucial northern tier of the alliance. In the fall of 1954 U.S. officials initiated discussions with Laos and Cambodia for the provision of economic and military aid and for military missions to oversee the organization and training of internal security forces. In Laos Dulles made abundantly clear that no aid would be forthcoming if the Pathet Lao insurgents were admitted to the government.[36] In Cambodia, judged the "soundest and most hopeful" of the former Associated States despite "a disturbing trend of neutralism," the administration encountered major opposition. The British insisted that a massive influx of American men and money would violate the Geneva accords. Long frustrated by having to work with the French, the Joint Chiefs refused to send a military mission to Cambodia until the French had withdrawn all their military personnel. As one U.S. diplomat put it, however, the French, "like their Bourbon kings, never learn and never forget." After Geneva they seemed determined to maintain as much influence as possible in newly independent Cambodia.[37] Nation-building in Indochina thus got off to a very slow start.

The administration viewed southern Vietnam as the key to Indochina and Southeast Asia, and it was there that Dulles focused his attention in late 1954 and early 1955. He overrode military opposition to involvement in Vietnam. He handled the French with considerable finesse, holding off those Americans who wished to force them out of Indochina and appeasing French sensitivities without compromising U.S. objectives. Challenging highly unfavorable odds, he committed U.S. prestige to an independent, noncommunist South Vietnam; firmly backed the premiership of Ngo Dinh Diem; and instituted a major aid program. When French obstructionism finally became too burdensome, Dulles asserted America's independence, leading the French ultimately to remove themselves from South Vietnam.

At the outset the prospects in Vietnam were decidedly unpromising. North Vietnam had at its disposal a large, combat-tested army and a tightly organized party apparatus. Equally important, the Communists had earned broad nationalist backing for winning the war

---

September 12, 1954, *FR, 1952–1954*, 12: pt. 1, 903–8. For an insightful view of Dulles's attitudes toward the alliance, see Richard Bissell interview, JFDOHC.

[36] Dulles to Legation, Laos, December 6, 1954, *FR, 1952–1954*, 13:2345–46.

[37] Kenneth Young memorandum to Herbert Hoover, Jr., December 14, 1954, *FR, 1952–1954*, 13:2373; Memorandum of conversation by Livingston Merchant, December 2, 1954, ibid., 2329; Robert McClintock to Department of State, December 22, 1954, ibid., 2410; McClintock to Department of State, December 24, 1954, ibid., 2423.

against France. In the south, by contrast, chaos was king. The government was a government in name only, a pathetic remnant of the puppet established earlier by France. The major political forces were two feudalistic political-religious sects, the Cao Dai and the Hoa Hao, and a gangster group, the Binh Xuyen, that ran organized gambling and the police force in Saigon. The army, in the words of French general Henri Navarre, was little more than a "rabble." Strong leadership was demanded, but Premier Ngo Dinh Diem appeared to lack the requisite qualities—"a messiah without a message," one U.S. diplomat described him. The French remained, and their presence and uncertain intentions further complicated an already difficult situation. Dulles's most optimistic estimate of the prospects of success was one in three, his most pessimistic one in ten.[38]

Respecting the odds, the Joint Chiefs of Staff and Secretary of Defense Charles E. Wilson vigorously opposed U.S. involvement. The JCS expressed doubt that an effective army could be created in the absence of political stability. They despaired of accomplishing anything as long as France remained and warned that restrictions imposed by the Geneva accords sharply limited their capacity to build a respectable army. Wilson was especially outspoken. The situation in South Vietnam was "utterly hopeless," he admonished, and he could see "nothing but grief" for the United States if it remained. The "only sensible course" was to get out as "completely and as soon as possible," leaving the French and Vietnamese "to stew in their own juice."[39]

Dulles and Eisenhower conceded some of the arguments, but rejected the conclusions. France was a problem, Dulles admitted, but to force her out prematurely would remove a major source of stability and compel the United States to assume full responsibility in an area where the future was highly uncertain. Sensing that time was on the side of the United States, Dulles counseled patience and tolerance. Should it come to a test of wills, he added, the United States held winning cards. The threat to withdraw had left Mendès-France "aghast."[40]

Dulles also feared committing U.S. prestige in an area "where we had little control and where the situation was by no means promis-

[38] For vivid descriptions of post-Geneva South Vietnam, see memorandum by acting special assistant for intelligence, August 10, 1954, *FR, 1952–1954*, 13:1934–35, and National Intelligence Estimate, August 3, 1954, ibid., 1905–14. Dulles's estimates are in James Lawton Collins, *Lightning Joe: An Autobiography* (Baton Rouge, 1983), 379.

[39] Vice Admiral Arthur Davis to Dulles, October 20, 1954, *FR, 1952–1954*, 13:2146; Memorandum of NSC meeting, October 26, 1954, ibid., 2125.

[40] Memorandum of conversation, October 31, 1954, *FR, 1952–1954*, 13:2199.

ing." Yet the United States had to do something. Conceding that he was indulging in the "familiar hen and egg argument," he advised the JCS that building an army in South Vietnam might help promote political stability. And even if the United States could do nothing more than create a situation in which North Vietnam had to resort to "internal violence" to achieve its aims, it would at least pose Hanoi with a "serious dilemma."[41] Explaining the high-risk gamble to the Senate Foreign Relations Committee several months later, Dulles observed that it would be a mistake to act only when there was a "100-percent chance of success." He pinpointed Vietnam as one of those places where it was right to "put up a good stout effort even though it is by no means certain that we will succeed." Referring back to administration success stories of 1953 and 1954, he noted that there had been moments in Iran and Guatemala when the situation seemed hopeless, "but we kept a stout heart, kept our courage up, and then all of a sudden things began to get better, and that is a possibility in Vietnam."[42] Thus the administration in late October endorsed a military aid program of $100 million and the dispatch of a military mission to help the South Vietnamese build an army.

Paying heed to French sensitivities, the United States only gradually eased itself into a position of preeminent influence in South Vietnam. The administration required that its aid go directly to the South Vietnamese. It did agree to coordinate its handling with the French, but insisted upon full responsibility for training Vietnamese troops. When Ambassador J. Lawton Collins tried to force the removal of all French troops from Vietnam, however, Dulles intervened. Should the United States assume full control, he warned, the French might "plaster us with responsibility" and "try to sabotage the result." French cooperation was still necessary to save South Vietnam, and it would be best not to push them too hard. U.S. advisers could gradually replace the French and there was no need for a rigid deadline to eliminate France from the training process.[43]

Over the unrelenting opposition of the French, Dulles also firmly supported Diem. The secretary acknowledged that Diem's govern-

[41] Dulles memorandum of conversation with Eisenhower, August 17, 1954, *FR, 1952–1954*, 13:1953; Dulles to Wilson, August 18, 1954, ibid., 1954–56; Memorandum of NSC meeting, October 22, 1954, ibid., 2125.

[42] Dulles report to Senate Foreign Relations Committee, January 13, 1955, *SFRC, 1955*, 7:7.

[43] George C. Herring, Gary R. Hess, and Richard H. Immerman, "Passage of Empire: The United States, France, and South Vietnam, 1954–1955," in Lawrence Kaplan, Denise Artaud, and Mark Rubin, eds., *From Dienbienphu to Saigon: Atlantic Cooperation and Misunderstanding, 1945–1955* (Wilmington, Del., forthcoming, 1989).

ment needed "more realism, experience and broader geographical representation." It deserved support nonetheless, he said, since Diem had a "better chance of rallying and holding nationalist sentiment than most of the Vietnamese who seem now to be on the scene, or in the wings." The United States did not want to present Diem as its "protege" or appear irrevocably committed to him. "On [the] other hand we do believe [the] kind of thing he stands for is [the] necessary ingredient of success and we do not see it elsewhere." The United States backed Diem against the intrigues of South Vietnamese challengers and against the persistent efforts of France to supplant him.[44]

Even when Collins joined the French in urging Diem's removal in late 1954, Dulles stood firm. Increasingly disillusioned with the prime minister and convinced that his prospects for success were "only fair at best," the ambassador urged that Emperor Bao Dai be brought back or that the United States conduct a "sober reevaluation" of its policy before committing further prestige and money. Dulles refused to budge. If Bao Dai was the alternative, the secretary noted, the United States and France "must indeed be desperate." They must exhaust all means to get Diem to govern more effectively before considering other options.[45]

Dulles wavered momentarily during the climactic "sects crisis" in the spring of 1955. When long-standing conflict between Diem and the sects finally erupted into open warfare, the secretary initially blamed the sects and speculated that if Diem could withstand this latest challenge he would emerge stronger than ever. Collins, conversely, interpreted the crisis as just one more sign of Diem's incapacity to govern and again recommended that he be replaced. After Diem's position seemed to worsen dramatically, Dulles somewhat grudgingly gave in and at Eisenhower's direction drafted a cable authorizing his removal.[46]

Before the order could be implemented Diem, assisted by CIA operatives, saved himself. The premier rallied the Vietnamese National Army to fight the sects, and when the army gained the upper hand Dulles immediately instructed the embassies in Saigon and Paris to put the proposed policy change on hold. The violence might resolve America's dilemma. Diem could emerge a hero, and even if he lost control, the hostilities could get the United States "off the hook." "It is better to make a change in the light of a civil war situation," Director of Central Intelligence Allen Dulles affirmed. Diem in fact stabi-

[44] Ibid., 23–25.
[45] Ibid., 25–26.
[46] Ibid., 27–34.

lized the situation, and by the time Collins returned to Saigon, Washington had instructed him to resist any change in government. Plaintively Collins proposed that the premier be given only a trial period. Dulles retorted that he must not become "another Kerensky" and insisted on an unequivocal endorsement. Diem remained in power, and Collins was removed.[47]

When the French continued to oppose Diem, Dulles asserted himself. During talks in Paris in May the two allies quickly reached a deadlock. Dulles made clear that the United States would not consider a change in government. French premier Edgar Faure insisted that France would no longer "take risks" with Diem. To underline the seriousness of their position, each threatened to withdraw from Vietnam. Responding to Dulles entreaties to remain, Faure agreed to do so and to accept Diem if the premier would broaden his government to include the sects and retain Bao Dai as head of state. Dulles seized this opportunity to eliminate what he finally conceded was a major roadblock to U.S. policy in Indochina. He offered concessions to Faure, but he would not agree to Bao Dai. The French gave up and prepared to depart from Vietnam rather than give in to the United States.[48]

Looking at Southeast Asia from the vantage point of 1956, Dulles could express considerable satisfaction with his handiwork. SEATO was developing in a "slow but healthy way," he told the Senate Foreign Relations Committee, and there was growing recognition that it constituted a "shield" behind which the free institutions and economies of the region could develop. Recent SEATO war games were "extremely impressive," bringing a "surprising amount of power to bear on a selected target area," confirming the notion of a mobile strike force as the primary military instrument of the alliance. The situation in Vietnam was "immensely improved," the secretary went on. "We stuck to Diem at a time when many people, including some in our own Government, felt he should be abandoned." As a result there was now a chance for "really building a strong and effective anti-Communist regime in an area where for a time it looked as though it would be swept away as a result of the French defeat."[49]

Dulles did not note, of course, the damage done to America's relations with its major allies during the Indochina crisis. The United States deeply resented the unwillingness or inability of its allies to take the firm stands required in the face of what seemed obvious dan-

[47] Ibid., 35–37.
[48] Ibid., 37–40.
[49] SFRC, 1956, 8:151, 161.

ger. "The British and French are blocking everything we want to do," Dulles complained in August 1954.[50] For their part the allies deeply resented U.S. actions during the crisis. The British did not appreciate being made "whipping boys" for the failure of United Action. The French were embittered by America's apparent determination to exploit their time of peril. The British and French seethed over the determination of the United States and especially Dulles to run things. Eden surmised early on that the United States wanted to replace France in Indochina. "They want to replace us in Egypt too," he complained. "They want to run the world."[51] Old World diplomats found the "meddling" Americans "tiresome," and protested that they "did at least as much harm" as good by their "ineptitude and total ignorance of the country and people." "The Americans have intervened in Vietnam . . . with a brazenness the French would never have dared to show," a *Le Monde* correspondent complained.[52] The Indochina crisis gravely damaged the Western alliance.

Dulles's assessment of the results in Asia also turned out to be premature. SEATO never became the anchor of regional stability he hoped it would be. Fragile allies from the outset, Laos and Cambodia were incapable of fulfilling the role of anticommunist bulwarks designed for them. Ironically, in large part because of America's "good stout effort," Vietnam, within a short time after Dulles's optimistic statement, was again wracked by conflict. Diem's surprising success in stabilizing the south; his refusal to participate in the elections called for by the Geneva accords; and, with apparent American support, his commitment to permanent partition, all provoked rebellion in South Vietnam, soon supported by the regime in Hanoi. By the time of Dulles's death in May 1959, the second Indochina War was under way, with profound and tragic consequences for Vietnam and for the United States. In the case of Indochina Dulles proved a master tactician who maneuvered skillfully through the most perilous waters to achieve his goal. But his remarkable short-term success laid the basis for America's greatest failure.

[50] Dulles telephone call with Livingston Merchant, August 30, 1954, TTS, "July 1–August 31, 1954," DPEL.

[51] Shuckburgh, *Descent to Suez*, 175, 187.

[52] See, for example, Robert Cloake minutes, October 27, 1954, and December 9, 1954, PRO, FO 371/112118 and FO 371/112112, respectively; and William Gibson memorandum of conversation with Jean Daridan, November 30, 1954, *FR, 1952–1954*, 13:2331–34. Robert Guillain quoted in Philippe Devillers and Jean Lacouture, *End of a War—Indochina, 1954* (New York, 1969), 374.

CHAPTER 9

John Foster Dulles and the Taiwan Roots of the "Two Chinas" Policy

Nancy Bernkopf Tucker

JOHN Foster Dulles brought to his position as secretary of state a background richer in foreign policy expertise than virtually any of his predecessors or successors. Nevertheless he proved ill informed about a number of the issues and problems he would confront during his more than seven years in office. Prime among these was his ignorance of East Asia. In contrast to many around him he felt qualified and he was perceived as an Asian expert. In his youth he served as secretary to the Chinese delegation at the Second Hague Conference on Peace in 1907 and traveled in Asia (he met Chiang Kai-shek initially at Hankow in 1938). Later President Truman named him principal negotiator for the peace treaty with Japan, a responsibility he met successfully in 1951. Yet, in fact, he knew little about Asian affairs.[1]

As was true of Dean Acheson, whom he helped pillory and whose fate haunted him, Dulles was an Atlanticist who saw developments in Europe as of paramount interest and significance. His dominant preoccupation was the Soviet Union and the communist mantle it hoped to impose on a vulnerable world. Beyond the Soviet grasp, Dulles focused on the concerns of France, Germany, and Britain. When Asian issues penetrated his consciousness, it was often because of the colonial connections with European parent states. Thus the Southeast

[1] Eisenhower to Dulles, June 15, 1957, "Eisenhower, Dwight D., 1957," DPP. Dulles's grandfather, John W. Foster, had served as secretary to Li Hung-chang during the negotiation of the Shimonoseki Treaty in 1895. This, the grandson later claimed, predisposed him to an interest in Asia. Prior to his 1938 trip to China and Japan on behalf of his New York law firm he knew T. V. Soong, H. H. Kung, Arthur Young, and Nelson Johnson. See "China and Japan—Trip 1938." DPP. But, as Dulles biographer Ronald Pruessen has written, the 1907 experience at The Hague was remembered largely for the exposure the young Foster Dulles got to Europe rather than to the Chinese. Ronald Pruessen, *John Foster Dulles: The Road to Power* (New York, 1982), 11. See also chapters 4 and 6 regarding the European thrust of his legal career, 58–75, 106–32.

Asia Treaty Organization, which long ranked as one of Dulles's most important accomplishments, grew up in the wake of the dissolution of the French and British colonial empires in Asia.

Dulles's most intense exposure to Asian affairs prior to becoming secretary of state arose out of the months he spent as a special adviser to the department during Dean Acheson's tenure as secretary. Hoping to deflect partisan criticism, President Truman and Acheson sought a prominent Republican party member to work from the inside on an important foreign policy issue. Dulles, having recently lost a senatorial election campaign, was available and had the credentials for the job. As a result the public and many Republicans came to share Dulles's own delusion that he possessed special knowledge about the East. Indeed, Truman sought to name him ambassador to Japan, but Dulles felt so certain that the Republicans would win the 1952 campaign that he turned down the appointment.[2]

What his service in the department under Acheson really taught Dulles was the political parameters within which America's policy toward China could safely be conducted. Dulles became attuned to issues and actions that would send his more right-wing allies into a frenzy. He built a relationship with the China Lobby, collaborating to keep aid flowing to the Chinese Nationalists during the late 1940s and early 1950s. Having worked together with the China Lobby, he recognized the dangers of disregarding their concerns. He labored tirelessly to avoid Acheson's fate, certain that he could navigate between the shoals of foreign communism and anticommunist fanaticism, compromising where necessary to preserve his influence in Congress and the White House. Thus, in the Acheson days he devised a formula whereby neither Communist nor Nationalist China attended the conference or signed the peace treaty ending World War II with Japan. The Japanese would instead negotiate a subsequent and parallel agreement with the China of their choice and Dulles would endure Chiang's anger (although the Japanese were not, in fact, free to choose mainland China) while reconciling the generalissimo's American supporters and America's British allies to the arrangement.[3] Later, when the responsibilities of State rested in his hands, he set aside his book (published in 1950) that talked about the

[2] Memorandum of conversation, Dulles with Truman, October 3, 1951, "Japan 1951," DPP. For details see chapter 7 in this book, by Seigen Miyasato.

[3] Warren I. Cohen, "China as an Issue in Japanese–American Relations, 1950–1972," in Warren I. Cohen and Akira Iriye, eds., *The United States and Japan in the Postwar World* (Lexington, Ky., 1989).

need and fundamental reasonableness of making the Chinese Communists active members of the UN, realizing that a flexible, liberal approach would not serve him well in the partisan struggles of Washington.[4]

Dulles's advocacy of the cause of Chiang Kai-shek did not, however, reflect any special love of the Kuomintang (KMT) or its leader. Early in his dealings with them Dulles recognized and disliked the manipulative and self-interested nature of the Nationalists. He feared their desire to increase U.S. involvement in the Chinese civil war and became ever more convinced that Chiang would not blanch at inciting World War III to accomplish his goals. In 1950 Dulles had collaborated with Dean Rusk on a plan to rid Taiwan of Chiang and protect it against communism by making it a UN trusteeship territory, but the scheme failed to persuade Acheson. The KMT survived and tightened its grip on the island.[5] By the time he became secretary, the Nationalists constituted the only viable alternative to complete Communist domination of the Chinese people; for that reason Dulles considered them palatable. Any inclination he had had to view the Chinese Communists as independent of Soviet control and determined to strengthen their country along nationalist lines disappeared with Chinese intervention in the Korean War. His accession to power over and responsibility for American foreign policy buttressed his conviction. In his eyes the Chinese Communists became virtually irredeemable puppets against whom he seriously considered using atomic weapons.

At the same time Dulles's response to developments in China grew out of the domestic environment in the United States. The secretary was perpetually under siege by the right wing of his own party on a variety of difficult issues.[6] In the case of China, a little-known and

---

[4] John Foster Dulles, *War or Peace* (New York, 1950), 190–91. Prior to election day in 1952 Dulles told Ales Bebler, vice minister for foreign affairs of Yugoslavia, that he thought Yugoslavia "was qualified for economic and military aid as being the only country which, once subject to Soviet Communism, had broken free, and done so peacefully. That peaceful break-away showed a possibility that other countries such as Czechoslovakia, Poland and China, might in due course peacefully resume effective control of their affairs. I said that while Yugoslavia was not symbolic of what Americans like as a form of government, and while we would wish it different, it was symbolic of the possibility of breaking up the Soviet empire without war. . . ." Memorandum of conversation, June 24, 1952, "Eisenhower, Dwight D.," DPP.

[5] Nancy Bernkopf Tucker, *Patterns in the Dust: Chinese-American Relations and the Recognition Controversy, 1949–1950* (New York, 1983), 187.

[6] Dulles worried that his onetime close association with Alger Hiss might mark him for McCarthyite attacks. When coupled with his participation in the Truman adminis-

distant land, Dulles proved willing to practice appeasement. In order to protect himself and policies he considered more central, the secretary blithely issued military threats and implemented economic sanctions, presenting them with rhetorical flourishes that frightened the British and made the Communist Chinese edgy as well.

Dulles's views would, however, not remain constant. During the course of his tenure he came to believe that the Chinese Communists could be engaged in negotiations, might have reasons to suspect and fear both the Nationalists and the Americans, and could slowly be pried away from the Soviets. Dulles persuaded himself that the key to such advances rested in implementation of a "Two Chinas" formula. His dedication to preserving a Nationalist alternative to Peking's rule did not flag. But his critical appraisal of Chiang Kai-shek's regime would only become more pronounced over time. He steadfastly rejected KMT objections to American contacts with the mainland and deftly avoided commitments to the Nationalist government that might precipitate a world war.

The most useful approach to understanding U.S. policy toward China under Dulles's stewardship, then, may well be to examine U.S. intercourse with Taipei. Official diplomatic relations with the PRC did not exist, and American rhetoric remained inflammatory to pacify the Knowlands and their ilk. Thus the parameters of policy might best be measured by analyzing concrete actions taken toward Taiwan. This strategy has been little utilized up to now. The story that emerges reads more like a soap opera script than a happy children's fable.

Dulles knew little and cared little about the inner workings of the KMT but saw Chiang's government as an important symbol for the free world in Asia.[7] That the KMT was a Leninist organization dominating a one-party state that survived by oppressing the Taiwanese people did not unduly alarm Washington.[8] Dulles even recognized

---

tration and close alliance with moderate, internationalist, Republican Thomas Dewey, Dulles had reason to be concerned. Henry W. Brands, *Cold Warriors: Eisenhower's Generation and American Foreign Policy* (New York, 1988), 13. Dulles was troubled enough to try to make amends with China Lobbyist Alfred Kohlberg, writing that "there has been highly organized and formidable Soviet communist penetration into the public and private affairs of our nation." Kohlberg remained unmoved. Pruessen, *John Foster Dulles*, 401.

[7] In November 1952 Dulles reportedly told John Allison that Nationalist Foreign Minister George Yeh "did not seem to amount to much." He also told Yeh that he was not interested in a war against Russia in order to solve problems in Asia. Tomlinson to Scott, November 21, 1952, PRO, FO 371/99259.

[8] Dulles did take the opportunity of Chiang Ching-kuo's 1953 visit to the United

that Chiang was unpopular with the people living on Taiwan.[9] Nevertheless, Chiang and his party were portrayed as preserving ancient Chinese tradition and modern democratic practices, all of which Moscow's minions were trying to eliminate. In the wake of Communist conquest of China, economic dislocation in Japan, war in Korea, and fighting in Indochina, Dulles viewed the region as vulnerable, in need of protection from invasion or subversion. This also led him to an unprecedented concern over the dispersed Chinese populations in each of the Asian nations and the question of where their allegiances lay.

John Foster Dulles, then, found himself in a difficult position. Determined to safeguard a free Asia, he pursued policies that challenged the Communists in China, seeking to contain and perhaps topple their regime. His goal required working with the Nationalists to create a viable alternative government if and when Communist power crumbled. But the process of cooperating with the KMT on a series of problems—including the mutual defense treaty, the first Taiwan Strait crisis, and the evacuation of Nationalist troops from Burma—disillusioned Dulles. He came to realize that Chiang Kai-shek, despite his dependency upon the United States, had an agenda only occasionally congruent with his own. Dulles's opposition to the Chinese Communists moderated as a result of initiatives pursued by Peking. At the same time his annoyance and disenchantment with Chiang contributed to his willingness to accept two coexisting Chinas conducting relations with the United States and the UN.

. . .

The Eisenhower administration commenced its Asia policy with the provocative step of unleashing Chiang Kai-shek. The president and secretary publicly declared that a situation whereby American forces provided protection for communists against the attacks of the Free Chinese could no longer be tolerated. Principles aside, decision mak-

States to urge him to demonstrate more respect for human rights and due process of law in Formosa. Walter McConaughy memorandum for the files, Department of State, November 13, 1953, *FR, 1952–1954*, 14:253. In 1955 M.G.L. Joy reported from the British Embassy in Washington that the ouster of America's favorite, General Sun Li-jen, by Chiang Ching-kuo seemed to State Department officers "yet another sign of the steady degeneration of the political respectibility of the Nationalist regime," because he was one of the few with prodemocratic inclinations. Joy to Crowe, October 17, 1955, PRO, FO 371/114987.

[9] Memorandum of NSC meeting, October 6, 1954, *FR, 1952–1954*, 14:700.

ers hoped that unleashing Chiang would improve morale among the exiled Nationalists and distract the Chinese fighting in Korea. Forces would presumably be diverted from the north to garrison suddenly exposed territories such as Fujian against Nationalist raids.

The new policy, however, carried with it some not entirely welcome implications. Chiang Kai-shek considered it a license to attack the Communists whenever and with whatever strength he could muster. Such Nationalist provocation could incite the Communists, whose reaction in turn might jeopardize Taipei's survival. The fact that this would almost certainly necessitate American intervention produced an international outcry against the policy. U.S. allies, especially in Europe, objected strongly to what they believed to be unwarranted risk-taking.[10]

In actuality the ploy was primarily propagandistic. Raids across the Taiwan Strait had begun in the Truman period and were not escalated significantly under Eisenhower. Moreover, Dulles and the president never intended to approve activity serious enough to threaten PRC sovereignty.

The administration designed the unleashing of Chiang to trouble the Communist rulers of China, but Dulles soon found that efforts to retain American control in such a situation could generate as much if not more friction between Washington and Taipei. In April 1953, a few short months after Chiang's new freedom of action was announced, the secretary told the NSC that he opposed continued deliveries of jet bombers to Taiwan until the generalissimo had pledged not to use them "recklessly." Eisenhower agreed that Chiang must be restrained lest war develop. The American Embassy and the State Department applied pressure and finally elicited a secret understanding that large-scale offensive operations would not be prosecuted without prior approval by the United States. The generalissimo might well have wondered why the "liberationist" Republicans insisted on restraints over military equipment that the unsympathetic Truman administration had not demanded.[11]

Chiang Kai-shek proved less amenable regarding Taiwan's overall relationship with Washington. Endeavoring to solidify and institu-

[10] State Department Study of Reactions to Unleashing, drafted by Ogburn, February 11, 1953, DSRG 59, Records of the Office of Chinese Affairs, "410 Chinese Nationalist Armed Forces" (hereafter cited as DSRG 59, CA Records).

[11] Memorandum of NSC meeting, April 8, 1953, *FR, 1952–1954*, 14:181; Dulles to Rankin, April 16, 1953, ibid., 191. The requisite guarantee was given April 23, 1953. Chargé in the Republic of China (Jones) to Department of State, April 23, 1953, ibid., 193.

tionalize the Taiwan-U.S. connection through a treaty of mutual defense, he demonstrated a stubbornness and disregard for American interests that gave impetus to the distrust with which Dulles viewed his ally. The secretary clearly preferred to maintain his operational flexibility and sought to delay negotiation of a military alliance for as long as possible. The prospect arising from the Quemoy-Matsu crises of 1954–1955 and 1958—that the United States might be plunged into a world war over a handful of islands barely off China's coast—made the rhetorically belligerent secretary pragmatically cautious.[12]

To overcome administration reluctance to sign a pact, Chiang utilized his contacts on the American domestic front. He brought pressure to bear through the conservative Republican adherents of the China Lobby in Congress and the media.[13] His tentacles reached into the halls of the Department of State where various of Dulles's own staff including Walter Robertson, Ambassador Karl Rankin, and Walter McConaughy pushed for the alliance in the face of the secretary's unhappiness.[14] Chiang's ambassador, V. K. Wellington Koo, argued his case more formally to sympathetic figures like Robertson, Vice President Richard Nixon, and Senator William Knowland.[15]

In spite of his own pro-Nationalist inclinations, Dulles objected to the pressure and refused to be rushed into an agreement that could have negative effects on Washington's more important relations in Europe. Several things finally impelled the secretary to authorize initiation of the treaty process: his dispiriting experience at Geneva,

[12] Memorandum of conversation between Koo and Dulles, July 1, 1954, V. K. Wellington Koo Papers, box 191, Manuscript Library, Columbia University. Dulles seriously considered cancelling his trip to Taiwan in September 1954 because the Communist attack on Quemoy meant that Chiang would press him too hard for assistance and a mutual defense pact. Dulles went anyway, largely for domestic political reasons of concern to the president. Sir Robert Scott to Foreign Office, September 7, 1954, PRO, FO 371/110231. For an interpretation that sees Eisenhower and Dulles as belligerent and willing to go to war, see Gordon H. Chang, "To the Nuclear Brink: Eisenhower, Dulles, and the Quemoy-Matsu Crisis," *International Security* 12 (Spring 1988): 96–123.

[13] Memorandum of conversation between Koo and Judd, July 16, 1954, box 191, Koo Papers.

[14] Memorandum of conversation between Koo and Drumright, July 16, 1954, box 191, Koo Papers.

[15] Memorandum of conversation between Koo and Drumright, April 29, 1954, box 191, Koo Papers; Memorandum of conversation between Koo and Knowland, July 14, 1954, and with Nixon, July 15, 1954, ibid. See also Yeh to Nixon, December 18, 1953, DSRG 84, China Post Files, "KMT Troops in Burma"; Rankin to Department of State, November 18, 1953, *FR, 1952–1954*, 14:333.

which produced an Indochina agreement that he deplored; the outbreak of fighting in the Taiwan Strait; and his decision to try to settle that confrontation through the UN. An alliance had become the price for submitting a cease-fire resolution to the Security Council and avoiding a KMT veto. Dulles's attempt to disguise America's role at the UN by convincing New Zealand to submit that resolution in Washington's stead neither fooled nor ultimately deterred the generalissimo. But Dulles dismissed KMT opposition, citing the resolution as Taiwan's best chance to retain the offshore islands.[16]

Moreover, Dulles's acquiescence did not resolve all the differences between the United States and Taipei over treaty language. The Eisenhower administration prevented inclusion of any specific reference to the offshore islands. Foreign Minister George Yeh, however, successfully pushed for an allusion to "such other territories as may be determined by mutual agreement," thereby preserving some possibility of extending the treaty's purview.[17] More acrimony developed regarding the central issue of whether Americans should exercise control over the movements of Nationalist military forces. By insisting on notification prior to the use of KMT troops against the mainland and a veto power over operations, the United States was depriving the Nationalists of their right to recover the mainland. This not only robbed them of their raison d'être but also undermined their credibility in Taiwan. Ambassador Koo cited the indignant words of a Hong Kong editorial to explain his position:

> If this is done the Chinese Nationalist Government and its people on Formosa become merely the instrument of U.S. purposes as a link in the Asian off-shore island defensive chain. . . . The Chinese government should not blindly accept U.S. wishes in this matter. China had followed U.S. policy after World War II and it resulted in the loss of the Mainland. If such restrictions are insisted upon, it would be better not to have a Treaty.[18]

Even Walter Robertson, who stayed in close contact with Dulles during the extended discussions he conducted with the Chinese ambassador, clearly was angered by Koo's attempts to manipulate the United States. Robertson made it painfully clear that the United States had granted the treaty at Chiang's request and the Nationalists

[16] Dulles to Department of State, October 1, 1954, *FR, 1952–1954*, 14:670.
[17] Memorandum of conversation between Yeh, Koo, and Robertson, November 4, 1954, box 192, Koo Papers.
[18] Memorandum of conversation between Koo, Tan, Robertson, and McConaughy, November 12, 1954, *FR, 1952–1954*, 14:889.

were not to try to use the press to dictate American policy.[19] As for Koo's efforts to argue that equity demanded reciprocity regarding control of troop deployments, Dulles's deputy declared that Washington would never allow Chiang any authority over the allocation or deployment of American forces. Moreover, the United States feared being put in a position where the Nationalists had stationed virtually all their forces on the offshore islands and Washington would have to send in its own troops to protect Taiwan.[20] Foreign Minister Yeh pointed out that the United States had not accepted any responsibility for the defense of the islands and had no right, even though it had equipped and trained their forces, to prevent the Nationalists from doing what they deemed necessary.[21] But Robertson, at Dulles's insistence, remained unmoveable. The United States had no interest in an offensive treaty or an agreement that had the potential of involving it in a war.

Chiang Kai-shek's continued emphasis on recovering the mainland became for Dulles not just an annoyance but a potential crisis. The secretary of state did not take seriously the generalissimo's proclamations that his KMT regime would soon return to the mainland to take over from a failing Communist government. In February 1955 he observed to Yeh that "[t]he people [in Taiwan] must be getting a little disillusioned with hearing every year from the Generalissimo and other Government leaders that they would march back to the Mainland in the course of the coming year. When year after year went by without this happening, some cynicism and disbelief must surely be engendered which might tend to discredit the Chinese Government."[22] The Nationalists clearly did not have the strength to carry out the operation without extensive American assistance. But the secretary remained determined not to provide such dangerous aid. In 1954 the United States finally agreed to the signing of a mutual defense treaty. But far from encouraging Chiang's determina-

[19] Apparently the occasion for the Hong Kong *Kung Shan Jih Pao* story was a Yeh briefing for the press at the Chinese Embassy in Washington. Yeh had spoken fairly candidly with reporters and as a result Chalmers Roberts had written a revealing story giving publicity to a still sensitive negotiation at a difficult moment. *FR, 1952–1954*, 14:888–89.

[20] Memorandum of conversation between Koo and Robertson, November 12, 1954, box 192, Koo Papers.

[21] Memorandum of conversation between Yeh, Koo, Tan, Robertson, and McConaughy, November 16, 1954, *FR, 1952–1954*, 14:898.

[22] Memorandum of conversation between Yeh and Koo, and Dulles, Robertson, and McConaughy, February 10, 1955, *FR, 1955–1957*, 2:252.

tion to recover his country, Dulles explicitly (albeit secretly) released Chiang, mandating that all sizable attacks on the mainland had to have prior American authorization.[23]

·   ·   ·

The secretary also waged a concurrent struggle against Chiang's efforts to recover the mainland through China's back or southern door. Dulles was bedeviled by the problem of KMT troops operating in the northern reaches of Burma, a situation inherited from the Truman presidency. These forces, which had been driven from southern China by the Communists, claimed to be a liberation army determined to return to China and rescue their countrymen. The emptiness of their promises, however, had become apparent in 1951 when on two occasions their efforts to penetrate Yunnan province failed miserably. The roughly two-thousand-man contingent, poorly disciplined and factionalized, proved no match for the well-trained, well-provisioned, and well-organized Chinese Communist armies.[24] Thereafter, the KMT remnants, loosely united under the leadership of Li Mi, had much more difficulty justifying their presence and came increasingly under attack as interlopers, threatening Burma's sovereignty and security.

For the Burmese government the situation appeared complex and menacing. Rangoon objected to the lodging of foreign soldiers upon its soil, and its protests became especially insistent after KMT units began attacking Burmese villages and engaging government troops in conjunction with antiregime insurgents. A lucrative trade in arms and opium that enriched the Chinese military leaders also angered Burmese authorities. Further, the possibility that Chinese Communist forces might cross the border to pursue raiding parties or attempt to eliminate the KMT threat entirely remained a constant concern. At the same time, Burma's central government did not exert

[23] Nationalist discomfort with this reality was demonstrated in a CBS "Face the Nation" interview during which the reporter was unable to corner Ambassador Koo into admitting that the United States would have to preapprove any invasion attempt. December 19, 1954, PRO, FO 371/110243.

[24] Sebald to Department of State, September 3, 1952, DSRG 59, 793.551/9-352. The Foreign Ministry later asserted that the first attack, which was premature, had been undertaken because of U.S. urgings. Rankin to Department of State, May 21, 1953, DSRG 84, "10—Troops in Burma 1952–53." A third unsuccessful effort was made in August 1952. Alfred W. McCoy, *The Politics of Heroin in Southeast Asia* (New York, 1972), 129–30.

control over its northern territories within which KMT units functioned; it could neither quell the Chinese troops nor oust them from Burma.

Too weak to act on its own, Rangoon turned to the United States to solve the problem that Burmese officials believed was at least in part of American making. Viewing Chiang Kai-shek as a U.S. puppet, they felt that Nationalist intervention in Burma could not have continued without Washington's approval and assistance. According to the American Embassy in New Delhi, the Indian press had for some months been accusing Washington of complicity in the maintenance of KMT contingents by supplying them with equipment and advisers.[25] The Soviets raised the issue in the UN General Assembly in January 1951, charging Washington with transporting soldiers from Taiwan to Burma.[26] A February 1952 newspaper column by Joseph and Stewart Alsop asserting that the CIA had provided assistance for the disastrous Yunnan incursions provoked still more criticism.[27] (Chiang Kai-shek himself would later contend that outside aid flowing to Li Mi during 1951 must have been clandestinely provided by the United States.) Denials by American officials did not persuade the Burmese government or other cynical observers, especially after Eisenhower unleashed Chiang Kai-shek and Burmese forces began to capture American-made weapons.[28]

The U.S. government, in fact, viewed the developing crisis inside Burma with alarm despite the involvement it had had in subsidizing the Chinese insurgents. Efforts by the CIA to utilize Li Mi's troops had continued until the summer of 1953.[29] The CIA had chartered a Miami-based company known as Sea Supply to provide equipment to the Thai police force whose training was in CIA hands. Lieutenant

---

[25] Drumright to Department of State, January 23, 1952, DSRG 59, 611.93/1-2352.

[26] Draft Statement by Martin, April 15, 1953, DSRG 59, CA Records, "Ex-Chinese National Troops in Burma."

[27] Sebald to Department of State, February 12, 1953, *FR, 1952–1954*, 12: pt. 2, 52, n. 4.

[28] *FR, 1952–1954*, 12: pt. 2, 52, n. 4.; Background paper given to Allen (Australian Embassy), April 7, 1953, DSRG 59, CA Records, "410.1"; Sebald to Department of State, February 13, 1953, *FR, 1952–1954*, 12: pt. 2, 52, n. 2.

[29] According to Li Mi, the final U.S. payment of $25,000 was received in July 1953. Rankin to Department of State, March 3, 1953, *FR, 1952–1954*, 12: pt. 2, 61. Already in March, Assistant Secretary for Far Eastern Affairs John M. Allison assured the British that all agencies of the U.S. government agreed that Li Mi's forces should be evacuated. Makins to Foreign Office, March 6, 1953, PRO, FO 371/106685. Weapons also had been supplied at least in 1951. See Rankin to Department of State, December 2, 1953, *FR, 1952–1954*, 12: pt. 2, 180.

General Phao Sriyanon, director general of the police and head of Thailand's intelligence operations, "a cherub with a Cheshire cat smile," covertly funneled large quantities of modern weapons to the Kuomintang troops in Burma, facilitating mysterious nighttime cargo flights, marketing KMT opium, and preventing outsiders from getting close looks at local activities.[30] Evidence suggests that even after the U.S. government determined that Li Mi's forces would not accomplish America's anticommunist goals and should be evacuated or cut off, private Americans continued supply efforts.[31] Precisely when or if the operation passed from official into freelance hands remains unclear. Activities were so closely held that not only State Department officers, including ambassadors, but also high-ranking CIA officials did not know about it while the agency ran the show.[32]

But as the American ambassador to India observed, although "our skirts are not entirely clean in this matter . . . I do not think we can afford to let fear that our earlier indiscretions will be revealed (as they undoubtedly will be) prevent us from taking those actions which are necessary." Ambassador George Allen contended that the Rangoon authorities' "preoccupation is the KMT troop issue. It permeates their thinking to the point of obsession and vitiates their ability to act on other domestic and foreign matters."[33]

Convinced, then, that without resolution the problem could topple Burma's rulers or force reorganization into a coalition regime with communist participation, the United States tried on several occasions to prompt Chiang Kai-shek into withdrawing the Chinese troops. As early as October 1952 Assistant Secretary of State John Allison traveled to Taiwan to emphasize the problems caused by this presence in

[30] McCoy, *Politics of Heroin*, 126–40; David Wise and Thomas B. Ross, *The Invisible Government* (New York, 1964), 131–35; John Prados, *Presidents' Secret Wars: CIA and Pentagon Covert Operations since World War II* (New York, 1986), 74–76. Unfortunately none of these sources are particularly well documented. Enough corroborating evidence in *FR*, the records of the British Foreign Office, and the *New York Times* is available to lend credibility to the story these authors tell. In PRO see for example: Report by Military Attaché Tonry, 1954, FO 371/111967; Whitteridge to Foreign Office, July 29, 1953, Whitteridge to Marquis of Salisburg, July 30, 1953, both in FO 371/106689; MacDonald to Foreign Office, September 1, 1951, FO 371/92142; and S.O. (I) HK to Admirality (D.N.I.), May 6, 1951, FO 371/92140. In U.S. records see Bowles to Department of State, March 19, 1952, *FR, 1952–1954*, 12: pt. 2, 22–23.

[31] Minute by Clemens, July 23, 1953, PRO, FO 371/106689; Sarell, Rangoon, to Tomlinson, SEA Department, July 25, 1955, ibid., FO 371/106694.

[32] Wise and Ross, *Invisible Government*, 131; Franks to Foreign Office, October 4, 1951, PRO, FO 371/92143.

[33] Allen to Department of State, November 30, 1953, *FR, 1952–1954*, 12: pt. 2, 178–79.

Burma, but Chiang refused to change his policy.[34] The Eisenhower administration early in 1953 approached Chiang to request immediate evacuation. Chiang denied any authority over Li Mi but also argued that by removing him the KMT would forfeit what little influence it could exercise. (Chiang may also have feared that if the Nationalist government ordered an evacuation and Li Mi did not comply, its prestige would be severely damaged.) Chiang insisted that Chinese troops had not interfered in the domestic affairs of Burma and that their existence did not undermine American efforts to win Burma away from the Communist Chinese. As for an invasion from the north, the generalissimo maintained that when the CCP decided to move into Southeast Asia it would do so for reasons other than the presence or absence of Nationalist troops.[35]

Despite the urgency expressed by Dulles, Ambassador Rankin could get no cooperation from Chiang. Indeed, the KMT continued to argue that Nationalist troops in Burma tied down large numbers of Communist soldiers who would otherwise be deployed in Fukien or Korea.[36] When the time finally came to mount an invasion of the mainland from Taiwan, moreover, Li Mi's forces could contribute to a successful operation.[37] KMT intransigence seemed also to be fed by Madame Chiang who, according to Rankin, returned from the United States in March 1953 alleging that American officials had promised additional aid for guerrilla operations on the mainland.[38]

[34] Rankin to Department of State, May 21, 1953, DSRG 84, "10—Troops in Burma 1952–53."

[35] Memorandum of conversation between Chiang, Wang Shih-chieh, and Rankin, February 21, 1953, DSRG 84, "10—Troops in Burma 1952–53." During 1951 and 1952, evidence accumulated that Li Mi's troops did not operate independently but rather received aim from Taipei. During one of many brief stays in Taiwan, Li Mi received the title of governor of Yunnan. Rumors also circulated in Taipei during 1953 that the new Nationalist budget would include funding for Li Mi.

[36] Memorandum of conversation between Chiang Kai-shek, Wang Shih-chieh (Secretary General, Presidential Office), Samson Shen (interpreter), Rankin, and Ewing, February 21, 1953, DSRG 84, "10—Troops in Burma 1952–53." For further denials of Taipei's authority over the troops in Burma that were made by other Kuomintang officials, see Memorandum of conversation between Ouang Hsiao-hsi, Hsueh Yu-ch'i (Director and Deputy Director, Far Eastern Department, Foreign Ministry), and Robert Rindin, DSRG 84, "KMT Troops in Burma." On fears that Li Mi would not comply, see Rankin to Department of State, March 9, 1953, DSRG 84 "10—Troops in Burma 1952–53." Thailand's Prime Minister Pibul told the British that he had willingly agreed to cooperate in helping to supply these forces when asked by an "American clandestine organisation" because this was part of a general Asian defense against communism. Wallinger to Foreign Office, October 13, 1951, PRO, FO 371/92143.

[37] Anderson to Martin, March 9, 1953, DSRG 59, CA Records, "410.1 Ex-Chinese Nationalist Troops in Burma (I)."

[38] Rankin to Department of State, May 21, 1953, DSRG 84, "10—Troops in Burma

The ambassador suggested that KMT officials were not responsive to American requests because Chiang believed that Washington's entreaties were just for the record and did not reflect the real position of the government.[39]

Dulles rejected all efforts by Ambassador Rankin to exonerate the KMT despite onetime American complicity. He insisted that the Chinese Nationalist troops had to be withdrawn lest their presence provoke a Chinese Communist invasion and Burma be lost to the communist bloc. It had become apparent that harassment of the Chinese Communists from north Burma was not effective enough to warrant the threat to Burma or the damage to Burmese-American relations. The secretary believed that Chiang had the power to effect a withdrawal. The Nationalist regime provided monthly subsidies to Li Mi and permitted private funds to be collected in Taiwan and supply expeditions to be raised. Dulles assumed dependency equaled control.[40] Rankin received instructions to offer American assistance in mounting an evacuation in hopes of blunting KMT assertions that it lacked the logistical capability to carry out such a plan.[41] The department also instructed the ambassador to "take all necessary steps" to prevent the continuation of provisioning operations from Taiwan.[42] Moreover, Washington sought to persuade Chiang that the views relayed by Rankin regarding the need to evacuate represented the convictions of the entire American government and, therefore, the generalissimo's customary efforts to use one agency (the military, for example) to deter another (such as the State Department) would not be effective.[43]

Confronted with Chiang's intransigence, Dulles became agitated enough to threaten a reconsideration of the entire American policy supporting Taiwan if the Nationalists refused to accept Washington's injunction. Although a fundamental disruption of the Taipei-Wash-

---

1952–53." Li Mi's contacts reached into the U.S. Congress as well. Representative Charles J. Kersten urged Walter Robertson to consider seriously the benefits of supporting Li. Memorandum of conversation, 1953, DSRG 59, CA Records, "030 Visits and Tours."

[39] Rankin to McConaughy, September 13, 1954, "Chiang Kai-shek," Karl Rankin Papers, Seeley G. Mudd Library, Princeton University.

[40] Rankin to Department of State, March 8, 1953, *FR, 1952–1954*, 12: pt. 2, 66, n. 1, discussed a statement by the foreign minister that acknowledged these contacts.

[41] Rankin to Department of State, March 4, 1953; Dulles to Rankin, March 5, 1953; and another Dulles to Rankin, March 5, 1953, all in DSRG 84, "10—Troops in Burma 1952–53."

[42] Dulles to Rankin, March 7, 1953, *FR, 1952–1954*, 12: pt. 2, 92–93.

[43] Dulles to Rankin, March 23, 1953, DSRG 84, "10—Troops in Burma 1952–53"; CSUSA to General Clark, March 1953, DSRG 59, CA Records, "410.1 (75)."

ington relationship was unlikely, and he instructed Rankin to convey the thrust of his thoughts without being quoted, Dulles urged the ambassador to make clear "that flouting of United States wishes in [a] matter of this importance inevitably would affect [the] climate in which future US/Chinese negotiations [are] conducted."[44]

Conscious of Burma's desperation and growing determination to take the issue to the UN, Dulles also worried about the views of America's allies. Once in the UN the question could unleash a torrent of criticism directed at both Taiwan and the United States. In Great Britain the Labour party contended that Washington had actively supported the Chinese in Burma.[45] A British Embassy official confided that his government feared Washington did not understand the proportions of the brewing crisis.[46] Indeed, the British worried and wondered about American complicity throughout the period and sought repeated assurances from the State Department that the United States was not involved.[47] Nehru, nervous about security in the region, told American officials that India would have to intervene were the Chinese Communists to try to deal directly with the KMT units.[48] Although in March 1953 American pressures finally elicited a KMT agreement in principle to pull Li Mi's troops out, the pledge did not prevent inclusion of the matter on the General Assembly agenda. In April it condemned hostile actions carried out by Nationalist troops in Burma, called on concerned parties not to resupply the units, and proposed ways of removing them from the area. With few alternatives available to them, Nationalist authorities agreed to follow the UN injunction.

The subsequent evacuation program, nevertheless, proved slow and modest—largely a farce.[49] A respected Burmese reporter con-

---

[44] Dulles to Rankin, March 13, 1953, DSRG 84, "10—Troops in Burma 1952–53"; quote from Dulles to Rankin, March 18, 1953, ibid.

[45] Memorandum of telephone conversation of Ringwalt with McConaughy, March 24, 1953, DSRG 59, CA Records, "410.1."

[46] Memorandum of conversation between Francis R. MacGinnis and R. H. Foster, July 27, 1953, DSRG 59, CA Records, "410.1."

[47] See the following extensive PRO files on the issue of Kuomintang troops in Burma: Franks to Foreign Office October 17, 1951, FO 371/92143; Tahourdin minute, February 11, 1953, FO 371/106684; and Scott to Allen, September 25, 1953, FO 371/106690. The British also entertained suspicions that State Department officials were not being entirely candid about what they did and did not know regarding Burma. See Foreign Office, July 26, 1951, FO 371/92140. They attributed some of the American duplicity to pressures from the China Lobby. Minute by MacCleary, April 14, 1955, FO 371/117038.

[48] Bowles to Department of State, March 5, 1952, DSRG 59, 793.5890B/3-552.

[49] "Chinese Nationalists in Burma," *Manchester Guardian*, October 7, 1953.

tended that the men being shipped out included new recruits from the Shan states who would, after training in Taiwan, return to operate as an undercover force within Burma.[50] State Department officer Walter McConaughy noted that most of those withdrawn departed without their weapons and Burmese authorities publicly disparaged the program as a phoney.[51] The department also recognized that re-supply flights from Taiwan had continued despite assurances to the contrary.[52] Late in 1954 the Burmese claimed some five thousand Chinese troops remained active in parts of the country although the evacuation program had ended at the beginning of September.[53]

Officials at the State Department had themselves concluded that the halfhearted effort might have been a "smokescreen for continuation [of] KMT operations in Burma" or that "certain segments [of the] Chinese Government" hoped to use Chinese remnant forces for "nefarious operations . . . including opium smuggling."[54] Intelligence gathering, in fact, unearthed a secret plan (Operation Heaven), involving token compliance with the UN directive, adopted by the Nationalists in June 1953.[55] The American ambassador in Burma lamented:

I read the despatch . . . with a sense of depression brought on by the real-ization that the United States . . . could be so thoroughly hoodwinked by a friendly government. In consequence, its officers were placed in the posi-tion . . . again and again to nurse along, in strong language and with sooth-ing promises, the Burmese and others, and to explain away the Chinese delays and frustrations which . . . were agreed upon in advance and actu-ally carried out according to plan.[56]

The impact of the Burmese crisis not only harmed U.S.-Burmese relations but also, clearly, took its toll on American relations with the

[50] Sebald to Department of State, October–November 1953, DSRG 84, "KMT Troops in Burma."

[51] McConaughy to Robertson, November 24, 1953, DSRG 59, CA Records, "410.1 (I)"; Allen to Department of State, November 30, 1953, FR, 1952–1954, 12: pt. 2, 178; Wallinger to Foreign Office, November 29, 1953, PRO, FO 371/106694.

[52] Dougall through Jenkins to McConaughy and Martin, April 8, 1953, DSRG 59, CA Records, "410.1 (TS)"; Dulles to Embassy in the Republic of China, September 22, 1953, FR, 1952–1954, 12: pt. 2, 147.

[53] Acly to Department of State, September 27, 1954, DSRG 84, "KMT Troops in Burma"; "Note on KMT Forces in Laos–Burma–Thailand Border Area," December 12, 1956, PRO, FO 371/123328.

[54] Sebald to Department of State, November 23, 1953, FR, 1952–1954, 12: pt. 2, 173.

[55] "Some Observations on the Conduct of the First Phase of the Evacuation of Li Mi's Troops from Burma," April 6, 1954, FR, 1952–1954, 12: pt. 2, 220–21, n. 1.

[56] Sebald to Bonsal, April 29, 1954, FR, 1952–1954, 12: pt. 2, 220–21.

KMT. Ambassador Rankin contended that nothing since the infamous China White Paper of 1949 had so severely damaged Taipei-Washington ties. He reported to former oss chief and current ambassador to Thailand William Donovan that "even our best friends among the Chinese are unhappy to see their country now publicly labeled as the sole culprit in a situation which appears to have been developed originally as a Third Force scheme without reference to the Government in Taipei." How, Rankin wondered, could he explain why an anticommunist Republican administration wanted to remove a potentially important fighting force from the mainland of Asia when the long-disparaged Democratic Truman administration had provided it assistance?[57]

. . .

Similar irritations continued to brew between the Nationalists and Dulles in connection with the offshore islands. Dulles counseled the KMT regime to evacuate the Tachen Islands in 1955 even in the face of Chiang's obvious displeasure. Reversing earlier American encouragement for strengthening efforts to hold that island group,[58] the secretary feared any defense would be futile. At an NSC meeting in January 1955, he agreed with Treasury and Defense secretaries Humphrey and Wilson that eventually all the offshore islands would have to return to mainland control. In the short term, nonetheless, Dulles believed that Nationalist morale could not sustain the loss of Quemoy and Matsu as well as the Tachens.[59] Dulles worried about the unreliability of dispirited Nationalist troops on Taiwan whose generals, in what the secretary considered a Chinese tradition, might allow themselves to be bought out by the Communists.[60]

Even so Dulles refused to permit continued KMT objections to Operation Oracle (that is, presentation of the New Zealand resolution) to deter his efforts to inject a UN presence into the Taiwan Strait and thereby deescalate a crisis that he believed Chiang Kai-shek hoped to

[57] Rankin to Donovan, November 25, 1953, DSRG 84, "KMT Troops in Burma."

[58] Memorandum of NSC meeting, July 9, 1953, FR, 1952–1954, 14:227; Rankin to Department of State, July 17, 1953, ibid., 230; Rankin to Department of State, July 24, 1953, summarized in Hope to Drumright, January 29, 1954, DSRG 59, CA Records, "306.11x CINCPAC Directive."

[59] Memorandum of NSC meeting, January 20, 1955, FR, 1955–1957, 2:69–82. Although both Quemoy and Matsu comprise island groups, this book follows the popular convention and refers to each in the singular.

[60] Memorandum of NSC meeting, March 10, 1955, NSCS, "240th Meeting of the NSC, March 10, 1955," AWF.

exploit.[61] He also held out initially against intense pressure from Chiang to include specific mention of Quemoy and Matsu in either his own or the president's public addresses regarding American action in the Taiwan area.[62] Dulles wanted to preserve an escape route for Washington that the generalissimo sought urgently to close. Chiang, infuriated when Eisenhower's January statement made no mention of Quemoy or Matsu, decided that if the United States would not clarify matters his own declaration would be explicit.[63] Dulles, however, in the name of American national interest, warned that he might be compelled publicly to repudiate such an announcement, causing both the Nationalists and the Americans considerable embarrassment.[64]

As the offshore islands crises progressed Dulles changed his assessments of the Nationalists and Communists. Initially he saw the Chinese Communists as aggressors and the Nationalists as victims. His first impulse was to worry about Nationalist morale and recommend American support for KMT resistance should that be militarily feasible.[65] The secretary of state gradually realized, however, that the situation was more complex. Dulles came to believe that Chiang Kai-shek's forces had a role in provoking the confrontations. In the beginning the secretary had hoped to utilize the Nationalist presence on the small islands just off China's coast to harass Communist shipping and to monitor military dispositions from radar installations. NSC 146/2, "United States Objectives and Courses of Action with Respect to Formosa and the Chinese National Government," approved in November 1953, called for encouragement and assistance to the Kuomintang to defend the islands and raid both Communist commerce and territory.[66] In 1954 Dulles and others in Washington, confronted with Communist shelling of the islands, concluded instantly that this very possibly heralded the long anticipated assault and believed that American credibility in Asia and the world depended

[61] Memorandum of conversation of Yeh and Koo with Dulles and Robertson, January 21, 1955, box 195, Koo Papers.

[62] Koo Diary, January 31, 1955, box 220, Koo Papers; Memorandum of conversation between Yeh and Robertson, February 3, 1955, box 195, ibid.; Memorandum of conversation of Yeh and Koo with Dulles, Robertson, and McConaughy, January 28, 1955, *FR, 1955–1957*, 2:156; Rankin to Department of State, January 29 and 30, 1955, ibid., 166–68.

[63] Koo Diary, January 31, 1955, box 220, Koo Papers.

[64] Memorandum of conversation of Yeh and Koo with Dulles, Robertson, and McConaughy, January 28, 1955, *FR, 1955–1957*, 2:156.

[65] Dulles to Department of State, September 4, 1954, *FR, 1952–1954*, 14:560.

[66] NSC 146/2, November 11, 1953, *FR, 1952–1954*, 14:308.

upon U.S. ability to help preserve the Nationalists' hold on Taiwan and any territories vitally linked with the island.

But, although the administration's decision to support Chiang's position in Quemoy and Matsu survived crises in 1954–1955 and 1958, Dulles's enthusiasm for utilizing the offshore islands moderated as he became convinced of the logistical problems of defending these points. That Chiang Kai-shek had garrisoned them with some 50 percent of his best troops and had transferred considerable amounts of American equipment to such vulnerable posts troubled the secretary. The decision, he told the press in September 1958 had been "foolish."[67] Should they be lost the impact upon KMT fortunes and American prestige would be devastating. Efforts by Eisenhower and Dulles to convince Chiang to reduce the significance of the offshore islands by treating them as outposts elicited only resistance. By 1958 Chiang had doubled the number of soldiers on the islands to some one hundred thousand.[68] Dulles raised the question personally during visits to Taipei in the autumns of 1954 and 1958 but could not budge a determined Chiang.[69]

Chiang's unwillingness to compromise regarding the issue of force levels suggested to Dulles (and to many in the State Department, and the military—most especially those in the field) that Chiang Kai-shek viewed confrontation in the strait as a way to entangle Washington further in the KMT's struggle against Mao.[70] The United States would have no choice, Eisenhower complained, but to rescue so large a part of the generalissimo's army.[71]

The likelihood of American involvement would be even higher if the KMT soldiers did not demonstrate a concerted effort to win once under fire. Suspicion regarding the lack of Nationalist determination to fight arose during the first Strait crisis. During the second confrontation Dulles concluded that Chiang bore responsibility for provok-

[67] Dulles press and radio news conference, September 30, 1958, "China, People's Republic of," DPP.

[68] Regarding the problem of Chiang placing too many soldiers on the offshore islands, see JSPC [Joint Strategic Plans Committee] 958/257, July 18, 1955, JCSRG 218, CCS [Combined Chiefs of Staff] 381 Formosa (11-8-48) sec. 28; CHMAAG Formosa to CINCPAC, September 18, 1955, ibid., 180530z, CCS 381 Formosa (11-8-48) sec. 29.

[69] Morton Halperin, "The 1958 Taiwan Straits Crisis: A Documented History," RM 4900-ISA, Rand Corporation, December 1966, p. 529; New York Times, September 30, 1958. In April 1955 word of Dulles's efforts leaked to the press but he denied trying to change Chiang's position. Dulles press and radio news conference, April 5, 1955, "China, People's Republic of," DPP.

[70] Halperin, "1958 Taiwan Straits Crisis," 84 n.; JCS to Adm. Felt, JCSRG 218, September 12, 1958, JCS 9447931, CCS 381 Formosa (11-8-48) sec. 39.

[71] Dwight D. Eisenhower interview, JFDOHC, 22.

ing the Communists but then avoided prosecuting the battle energetically in order to manipulate the United States into taking a larger role. In August Dulles wrote Robertson and Under Secretary Christian Herter:

> I do not feel that we have a case which is altogether defensible. It is one thing to contend that the CHICOMS should keep their hands off the present territorial and political status of Taiwan, the Penghus, Quemoy, and Matsu, and not attempt to change this by violence. . . . It is another thing to contend that they should be quiescent while this area is used by the CHINATS as an active base for attempting to foment civil strife.[72]

Ultimately he felt he had no choice but publicly to attack the idea of reconquest at a press conference.[73]

. . .

Dulles's disaffection from the Nationalists served less to diminish his determination to support them than to confirm his assessment that the United States must eventually deal with two Chinas. The Communists might be the embodiment of evil, in Dulles's view, but it had become clear that they were consolidating their hold on the mainland and would not fall from power in the foreseeable future. The secretary's first instinct had been to try to destabilize the regime, and he remained determined to wage economic warfare even in the face of resistance from America's closest allies, who progressively undermined the trade embargo that he favored.[74] But Dulles also realized that the KMT continued to be too weak to destroy the Peking government and was unlikely to become sufficiently attractive an alternative to catalyze an uprising among the Chinese on the mainland.[75] The features that Dulles deplored in the Nationalist coalition, including

[72] Quoted in Halperin, "1958 Taiwan Straits Crisis," 102.

[73] The press briefing was held September 30, 1958. *New York Times*, October 1, 1958, 1.

[74] See the work of Cohen, "China as an Issue"; Qing Simei, "The Eisenhower Administration and Changes in Western Embargo Policy against China, 1954–1958," in Warren I. Cohen, ed., *The International Relations of East Asia in the Eisenhower Era* (New York, 1990); Nancy Bernkopf Tucker, "Cold War Contacts: America and China, 1952–1956," in Harry Harding and Yuan Ming, eds., *Sino-American Relations, 1945–1955: A Collaborative Reassessment of a Troubled Time* (Wilmington, Del., 1989).

[75] Memorandum of NSC meeting, September 12, 1954, *FR, 1952–1954*, 14:615. Nsc 166/1, approved November 6, 1953, specifically ruled out the use of American forces either directly or by supporting the KMT to oust the Communist government. Ibid., 280–81.

self-interest, unreliability, inefficiency, and corruption, robbed them of the opportunity to amass a broad popular following.

Dulles's interest in a Two Chinas policy belied his public rhetoric about overturning the despotic regime on the mainland. It evidenced his desire to explore a more rational policy toward China than that embodied in the fiction that Chiang's Nationalists could be considered representative of the entire Chinese people. Dulles had written Henry Luce in 1950 that Peking should not be isolated and excluded from the UN on ideological grounds. If the government proved able to exercise effective control over the Chinese people, then it would merit entry.[76] After Korea erupted in war in June, Dulles's assessment seemed to have changed radically. But he had not abandoned entirely the idea that China should be included in the world association.

In the summer of 1954 Dulles twice discussed ways to facilitate the PRC's admission into the UN. Determined to keep Taiwan in the organization, he sought mechanisms for accommodating two Chinese states with equal votes. In July he raised the issue with British Foreign Secretary Anthony Eden and India's Prime Minister Jawaharlal Nehru. India, he thought, might replace China on the Security Council and then the General Assembly could seat two equal Chinese regimes.[77] The following month he approached John Dickey, an international lawyer, regarding a possible amendment to the UN Charter designed to change the composition of the Security Council. Removing China from the council and thereby eliminating the issue of a second Communist veto would make entry of the PRC into the UN a less fearful prospect.[78]

Throughout the debates, moreover, Dulles's State Department took the position that the United States could not exercise its veto in the Security Council to keep the Communist Chinese out. Such a precedent would, it feared, allow the council "indefinitely [to] prevent the seating of representatives of non-permanent members . . . or any changes in the representative of a permanent member." This would make it impossible for it to conduct business while other UN

[76] Dulles to Luce, April 24, 1950, "Luce, Henry," DPP.

[77] Dulles wrote Rusk on June 28, 1953, that he had discussed the UN issue with Nehru during his visit to South Asia. William P. Snyder, "Dean Rusk to John Foster Dulles, May–June 1953: The Office, the First 100 Days, and Red China," *Diplomatic History* 7 (Winter 1983): 85–86. Memorandum of conversation, July 2, 1954, *FR, 1952–1954*, 3: 733–34.

[78] Wang Jisi, "The Origins of America's 'Two China' Policy," paper for the Center for Chinese Studies, University of California, Berkeley, November 11, 1985 (in possession of author).

organs, lacking veto provisions, would admit Peking into their deliberations. It would be far better for the United States to accept the will
of the majority when the time came for such a consensus to emerge.[79]

The test of the administration's posture came not on the question
of admitting China itself but with regard to the controversy over
Outer Mongolia. In 1955, as part of a package deal providing for the
entry of Austria, Italy, Spain, Ireland, and fourteen other countries,
the Mongolian People's Republic applied for a seat in the General
Assembly. Denying the validity of Mongolia's independence, Taipei
insisted upon using its veto. The United States urged Chiang not to
take this course, speaking strongly against the procedure as well as
the specific circumstances of the Nationalist government's vulnerability in the UN. President Eisenhower appealed personally to the generalissimo, observing that the United States would not veto entry of
any nation favored by requisite votes in the Security Council and
General Assembly and cautioning that a veto by Taipei might precipitate an unfavorable vote on its own challenged status. But the Nationalists ignored American entreaties and each side walked away angered at the shortsightedness of the other.[80]

Dulles quite consciously, then, followed the UN policies adopted by
his predecessor Dean Acheson even against impassioned arguments
put forth by UN representative Henry Cabot Lodge (who also took
the Taipei view on Mongolia) and, of course, the KMT.[81] The secretary
further weighed in heavily against Senator William Knowland's
threats to pull the United States out of the UN or to refuse to pay
assessments should the Chinese Communists be admitted.[82]

The Taiwan Strait crisis of September once again provoked consid-

[79] "Views of the Department of State on Certain Questions Relating to China
[1954?]," "China, People's Republic of (1954)," DPP.

[80] Dulles to Chiang, November 22, 1955; Koo and Chiang to Dulles, November 26,
1955; and Eisenhower to Chiang, November 28, 1955, all DHS, "Dulles—November 1955
(1)," AWF; Rankin paraphrase of messages sent to Washington November 28, 1955 and
December 4, 1955, "Chiang Kai-shek, Mme," and "China, Republic of," Rankin Papers;
Rankin to Department of State, December 23, 1955, "Chiang Kai-shek, Mme," ibid.

[81] Lodge to Department of State, June 9, 1953, FR, 1952–1954, 3:661–62; Memorandum of conversation, June 10, 1953, ibid., 663–65; Lodge to Dulles, June 11, 1953,
ibid., 667. Dulles to Lodge, June 19, 1953, ibid., 679–80. It should also be noted that
Lodge independently, in private conversation with Nationalist UN representative T. F.
Tsiang, provided assurances that if necessary he would veto Peking's entry. Telephone
conversation, June 10, 1953, box 187, Koo Papers.

[82] Memorandum of conversation between Dulles and Knowland, July 6, 1954, FR,
1952–1954, 3:735–36. In 1957 Dulles observed to Macmillan that, although congressional opinion was indignant, public opinion polls showed that Americans generally
believed the United States should remain in the UN in any case. Memorandum of
conversation, March 23, 1957, "China, People's Republic of," DPP.

eration of the problem. Explaining his plan to take the emergency to the UN, Dulles acknowledged the likelihood that "a probable *ultimate* outcome of UN intervention . . . would be the independence of Formosa and the Pescadores." Moreover, he wrote, it would mean the end of Nationalist harassment of the mainland, its seizure of ships, and the trade embargo.[83]

Were American policy, inherent in the Mutual Defense Treaty that followed soon thereafter, successful, it promised to yield the same result. An agreement that protected Chiang on Taiwan but refused to allow him to reconquer the mainland, in effect, created a second China. Although he denied such thoughts to reporters in December, Dulles had told Anthony Eden just two months earlier that he saw the treaty as an opportunity to separate Formosa from the mainland and that eventually two Chinas might sit in the UN.[84] Dulles also told the NSC that, whereas nonrecognition of the PRC remained a fundamental principle, he would follow a policy of "dealing with it on a de facto basis when circumstances make this useful."[85]

Dulles railed against the PRC once more during the height of the 1955 Strait crisis and even considered the possibility of a nuclear attack. Still, he had not rejected the attempt to devise a viable Two Chinas formula. Early in the year Dulles had told Foreign Minister Yeh that China—like Germany and Korea—had become a divided nation and the Nationalist regime should begin to behave in a manner consistent with that reality.[86] In 1956 the secretary asked Dean Rusk to discuss the possibility of a new bipartisan policy toward China with Chairman of the Senate Foreign Relations Committee Walter George. Dulles wanted George to sell Congress recognition of two Chinas, but the idea died when the senator decided not to run for reelection.[87]

On the economic front the United States also moved grudgingly toward greater flexibility, for its allies if not for itself, although in this area Dulles pursued a line notably harder than that of the president and others in the administration. Eisenhower insisted repeatedly in

[83] Memorandum prepared by Dulles, September 12, 1954, *FR, 1952–1954*, 14:612–13. Dulles communicated a similar message to Anthony Eden during his September 1954 trip to London and then insisted that minutes of their meeting be cursory and closely held. Merchant to O'Connor, September 19, 1954, ibid., 649–51.

[84] However, Dulles indicated that he had little faith in the possibility of having both Chinas in the UN. Eden to Foreign Office, October 20, 1954, PRO, FO 371/110235; Transcript of press conference, December 1, 1954, "China, People's Republic of," DPP.

[85] Report by the Secretary of State to the NSC, October 28, 1954, *FR, 1952–1954*, 14:810.

[86] Memorandum of conversation of Yeh and Koo with Dulles, February 10, 1955, box 195, Koo Papers.

[87] Warren I. Cohen, *Dean Rusk* (Totowa, N.J., 1980), 85.

the confidential forums of the NSC that the United States ought to be conducting commercial exchanges with the Communist Chinese. He pushed the NSC to study the issue, but it would not go so far as to reverse American policy in the face of opposition from Dulles, the JCS, and the China Lobby.[88] The position articulated by Dulles and the State Department remained staunchly, although not invariably, behind continuation of trade controls. Dulles appeared momentarily more expansive when confronted by Indonesian problems in marketing rubber and tin. He termed Eisenhower's proposal to let the Indonesians sell these materials to any buyer, including China, "constructive" because the United States could not itself meet Indonesian needs.[89] More often, however, he worried about the sensitivity of right-wing Republicans to trade liberalization. Eisenhower, similarly attuned, nonetheless recognized the need to relax efforts to hold Britain, Japan, and others to principles they did not sympathize with. Dulles himself would ultimately accept the reality that America's allies intended to follow what they saw as their own national interests. Although the United States retained its embargo, Washington stopped trying to coerce allied governments into maintaining unwanted restrictions.

Nationalist Chinese reacted with dismay and anger to American flirtation with a Two Chinas policy. They had hailed Eisenhower's election and the appointment of John Foster Dulles,[90] anticipating a far more favorable response to Taiwan's needs from the new Republican administration. But distrust, developed over long association with Americans, made the Nationalists sensitive to the slightest suggestion that American China policy might become more moderate toward the Communists. When Dulles told members of Congress at his confirmation hearings that the heart of the problem with mainland China rested in its subservience to the Soviet Union, Nationalists feared he meant that a rupture between Moscow and Peking would lead to U.S. relations with the Communists.[91] Similarly, determined Nationalist opposition to the New Zealand resolution (Operation Oracle) stemmed from recognition that it would sanctify the existence

[88] Eisenhower even went so far as to disparage controls over rubber, which Director of the Foreign Operations Administration Harold Stassen pointed out was among the most important strategic commodities. Memorandum of NSC meeting November 19, 1953, *FR, 1952–1954*, 12: pt. 2, 389–90.

[89] *FR, 1952–1954*, 12: pt. 2, 392.

[90] Rankin to Department of State, November 1952, DSRG 84, despatch 268.

[91] Rankin to Department of State, January 30, 1954, DSRG 59, 793.00/1-3053. He generated similar distress in November 1953 with remarks along the same lines to the press. David Allen Mayers, *Cracking the Monolith: U.S. Policy against the Sino-Soviet Alliance, 1949–1955* (Baton Rouge, 1986), 128.

of two Chinas.[92] Chiang Kai-shek repeatedly suggested that the Two Chinas scheme was being foisted upon Americans by the British (always Chiang's villains) who saw a UN-imposed cease-fire as the first step in implementing their nefarious policy.[93]

According to American observers in Taipei, morale deteriorated during 1955 because of growing interest among Americans in realization of a Two Chinas policy.[94] Ambassador Rankin wrote fellow KMT sympathizer in the State Department, Walter McConaughy, that

> [t]he Chinese on Taiwan are very much aware that the United States wrote them off once before. . . . They believe, with some justification, that important and influential elements inside and outside our Government would like nothing better than a plausible excuse to sell Free China down the river. These elements include isolationists, Europe-firsters, fellow-travelers and others who . . . continue to hate the guts of Chiang Kai-shek.[95]

The secretary of state did not want to eliminate the Nationalists, but Rankin and Chiang were correct in worrying that the administration had considered opening relations with the Communists and dealing with both regimes at once.

Perhaps the Nationalists' strongest ally in warding off this grim possibility was, ironically, Mao Tse-tung. The Chinese Communists demonstrated every bit as much hostility to the concept of two Chinas.[96] Sensitive to the implications of divorcing the offshore islands from Taiwan, the New China News Agency, speaking on behalf of the government, warned that "the U.S. aggressive clique" wanted to "hoodwink world public opinion by arranging for the traitorous Chiang Kai-shek group to 'quit' the coastal islands."[97] Chou En-lai's denunciations of the Mutual Defense Treaty pinpointed the effort to

[92] Memorandum of conversation of Yeh and Koo with Robertson, January 27, 1955, box 195, Koo Papers; Memorandum of conversation between Yeh and Koo and Dulles and Robertson, January 21, 1955, ibid.

[93] Koo Diary, January 22, 1955, box 220, Koo Papers. Koo also entertained a healthy suspicion regarding the British; see memorandum of conversation between Koo and Herbert Hoover, October 4, 1954, box 191, ibid. The British, who were blamed by Taipei for the "Two Chinas" formula, were, in fact, quite skeptical regarding its viability. June 1955, PRO, FO 371/115050. For additional information consult PRO registers for file FC1041/837.

[94] Paraphrase of telegram Rankin to Department of State, May 6, 1955, "China, People's Republic of," Rankin Papers.

[95] Rankin to McConaughy, November 17, 1954, "China, Republic of," Rankin Papers.

[96] Cumming to Herter, November 29, 1957, FR, 1955–1957, 3:642–43. See also He Di, "The Evolution of the People's Republic of China's Policy toward the Offshore Islands (Quemoy, Matsu)," in Cohen, The International Relations.

[97] Survey of China Mainland Press, #935, November 25, 1954, 7.

create a second China as the intolerable result of America's pledge to protect Taiwan.[98] On July 30, 1955, he sought to exploit visible tensions in Kuomintang-U.S. relations by suggesting talks between Peking and Taipei to resolve the Taiwan problem. In 1958, noting that Chiang Kai-shek had joined all patriotic Chinese in rejecting America's Two China policy, Chou warned the National People's Congress that Washington was pursuing the goal relentlessly through its military presence in Taiwan where it might seek to establish a more submissive regime.[99] Awareness of frictions between Chiang and Eisenhower over the offshore islands, in fact, led Mao precipitously to cut off the attack by the People's Republic upon Quemoy and Matsu. He feared that PRC success would play into American hands by eliminating the remaining stepping stones to Taiwan and creating a less surmountable barrier between Communist and Nationalist forces.[100] Indeed Mao took the moment as an opportunity to demonstrate to Chinese living on Taiwan that they shared important values with their brothers at home.

> There is but one China in the world; there are not two Chinas. On this point, we concur with each other. Americans are using their technique to try to force upon us a Two China policy. All the Chinese people, including you and our overseas Chinese compatriots, will absolutely not let this materialize.[101]

As much as the Chinese Communists deplored the concept of two Chinas, they did not shrink from joining in diplomatic conversations with the Americans at Geneva and Warsaw on these grounds.[102] The talks, which began in the wake of the international conferences in Geneva and Bandung, dealt primarily with the freeing of prisoners held by Peking and students and scientists detained in the United States by Washington. Discussions soon moved on to other subjects, most particularly Washington's demand that the Chinese Communists publicly renounce the use of force to resolve the dispute over Taiwan's status.

The Nationalists found these talks frightening, viewing them as clear evidence of a growing American interest in a Two Chinas pol-

---

[98] Robertson to Dulles, December 8, 1954, DSRG 59, 693.94a/12-854.

[99] He Di, "The Evolution of PRC Policy."

[100] He Di, "The Evolution of PRC Policy."

[101] He Di, "The Evolution of PRC Policy."

[102] America's representative at the talks, however, remembered that Wang Bingnan, China's delegate, accused him of advocating a "Two Chinas doctrine" when the U.S. desire for China's renunciation of force was presented as the primary talking point. U. Alexis Johnson, *The Right Hand of Power* (Englewood Cliffs, N.J., 1984), 254.

icy. Worse yet the meetings threatened to produce a U.S. decision to abandon Taiwan and acknowledge Peking's claims to recognition. The American chargé d'affaires in Taipei, William Cochran, wrote an absent Ambassador Rankin:

> I assume you are also aware of the emotional ferment into which the Chinese public and press were thrown by the announcement of our Ambassadorial talks at Geneva. Under a KMT directive, the vituperation became both shrill and virulent, to the point where [Foreign Minister] George Yeh asked me to hold a press conference to assure the local newspapers and people that American policy had not changed, nor had American Chinese relations. I did so and elicited a savagely bitter editorial [response].[103]

The Nationalists kept up a flow of strident criticism and harsh warnings regarding the impropriety and danger of the talks. Chiang feared that Washington might be gullible enough to believe that the Communists would renounce the use of force in the Strait and then, after Taiwan's protection had been withdrawn, stage a surprise attack or bring the government down through subversion. Foreign Minister Yeh, miscalculating the Communist response to Dulles's formula, warned explicitly that a force renunciation agreement would be the entering wedge toward a general political settlement of Taiwan's status, destroying the regime.[104] When the secretary publicly averred that the Communists need not renounce their claims to Taiwan but only pursue them peacefully, the Nationalists felt even more betrayed.[105] The mere fact that the Americans convened with the Chinese Communists in diplomatic surroundings accorded them far too much prestige and, Chiang reminded Washington, influenced impressionable peoples in vulnerable parts of Asia.[106]

John Foster Dulles understood and sympathized with Chiang's discomfort. But he grew irritated, nonetheless, by the opposition from Taiwan.[107] Dulles believed himself wise enough to avoid PRC traps and considered the continuation of the talks an essential component of a rational American policy toward East Asia.[108] Once again the normally sympathetic Walter Robertson reflected administration an-

[103] Cochran to Rankin, August 8, 1955, "China, Republic of," DPP.

[104] Rankin to Department of State, November 17, 1955, *FR, 1955–1957*, 3:175–76.

[105] Rankin to Department of State, January 26, 1956, *FR, 1955–1957*, 3:279–82; Press and radio news conference, March 15, 1955, and September 30, 1958, "China, People's Republic of," DPP.

[106] Rankin to Department of State, October 21, 1955, *FR, 1955–1957*, 3:140–41.

[107] Regarding the awareness of opposition from Taiwan to the talks, see memorandum of conversation, October 4, 1955, *FR, 1955–1957*, 3:111–12.

[108] Johnson, *Right Hand of Power*, 239.

noyance when Ambassador Koo suggested that he could not rely on Eisenhower's or Dulles's statements that there would be no Chou En-lai meeting with Dulles. Both men had gone on public record, Robertson reminded him. They could not provide any more forceful guarantee; a confidential memo could not compare with putting "the whole world on notice what our position was."[109]

Of course, a Two Chinas strategy would not come to fruition during Dulles's years in office, although his awareness of the need to deal with both Chinas accorded with reality better than his professed determination to isolate and destroy the Communists in Peking. The secretary remained a champion of the right of the "Free Chinese" to control a government on Taiwan. He saw to it that American aid continued to support the economic and military development of the KMT regime. But his dismay at the Nationalists' narrow vision and unreasonable demands that the United States risk prosperity and security to return Chiang to the mainland led him to distance himself from the pro-KMT camp in Washington. He did not share the beliefs of the China Lobby, although his behavior sometimes suggested that he did. Along with the president he served and to whom his foreign policy initiatives were ultimately subordinated, Dulles's goal in Asia was peace and stability that would free him to devote his attention to the complex and (to him) more important problems of Europe. This might necessitate occasionally climbing the ramparts to preserve a free Vietnam or Chinese island redoubt. But despite belligerent rhetoric and anticommunist passion, Dulles generally recognized that the national interest required a more balanced policy regarding China. He would not lead a crusade to restore Chiang to the Middle Kingdom's throne but work with the script as he had inherited it from Acheson, adding touches of drama but not fundamentally altering the lines or the outcome.

[109] Memorandum of conversation, August 9, 1955, *FR, 1955–1957*, 3:25.

Conclusion

Richard H. Immerman

"I walked away from [my last meeting with John Foster Dulles] largely ignorant of the intellectual qualities of the man I had just encountered," George Kennan recalled on the centennial of Dulles's birth. Kennan went on to explain that only with the benefit of extensive new documentation has the "full picture" of these qualities begun to emerge. He quickly added, "[T]hat picture, had I known it then, would certainly have surprised me and puzzled me in a sense, as it does today." What surprises and puzzles Kennan is that this emerging picture is in most respects the "negative" of that projected in the 1950s and in the subsequent literature; the Dulles revealed through the archives bears little resemblance to the one Kennan thought he knew. He is now persuaded that Dulles possessed a "highly sophisticated, politically imaginative intelligence." More than that, the evidence has convinced Kennan that the much-criticized secretary of state was "clearly well ahead of anyone else on the political scene of the day in his understanding of international situations" and in his "critical assessment of the developing problems for American policy that the world of his day provided."[1]

That George Kennan arrived at this conclusion speaks volumes about the ongoing reappraisal of Dulles's tenure in office. Dulles had, after all, fired Kennan from the Foreign Service. The scholar-diplomat continues to bear the scars from that wound and, more generally, to resent what he considers Dulles's shameful treatment of his State Department colleagues during Scott McLeod's reign of terror.[2] Less subjectively, as a founder of the "realist" school of international relations, Kennan expounded the view that Dulles's excessive moralism and legalism were detrimental to the conduct of foreign affairs. The year after Dulles took office Kennan published a scathing attack on the Republican program, zeroing in on the concepts of liberation and massive retaliation for which Dulles was noted. "I see no reason for jitters, for panic, or for melodramatic actions," Kennan implicitly

---

[1] George Kennan commentary, February 25, 1988, Dulles Centennial Conference.

[2] In addition to Kennan's commentary at the Dulles Centennial Conference, see his *Memoirs: 1950–1963* (Boston, 1972), 168–89.

lectured the architect of the administration's foreign policy. "I do see reasons for hard work, for sober thinking, for a great deliberateness of statemanship, for a high degree of national self-discipline, and for the cultivation of an atmosphere of unity and mutual confidence among our own people."[3]

Kennan's low opinion of Dulles's diplomacy reflected the common wisdom. The consensus throughout the scholarly community, not to mention among other realists such as Hans Morgenthau and Norman Graebner, held that Dulles poorly served the interests of the United States and, by extension, international peace and stability.[4] The irony of this orthodoxy lies not in its inaccuracy; notwithstanding Kennan's revised assessment, the contributors to this book still find much to fault in Dulles's approach. Rather, the irony lies in the methodology by which judgments about the secretary of state were reached. Scholars scrutinized—and criticized—Dulles intensively not only because he presented a conspicuous target; they did so also because they were convinced that they had an uncommonly rich data base to draw upon for their investigations. It was almost as if Dulles's reputation suffered in inverse proportion to the massive written record he bequeathed to students of his statecraft.

The studies by Ole Holsti referred to in my introduction epitomize this phenomenon. A pioneer in the "operational code" approach to the study of political leaders, Holsti selected Dulles as his subject because even before his appointment by Eisenhower, Dulles had "attained some distinction for his philosophical inquiries into the nature of politics." These writings, combined with over four hundred press conference transcripts, speeches, congressional testimonies, and similar documents amassed between 1953 and 1959, comprised Holsti's primary evidence for examining Dulles's philosophical and instrumental beliefs. Because, as he put it, collectively these sources "provide a volume of material one rarely finds for a contemporary figure," Holsti had good reason to feel confident about his conclusions.[5]

Suffice it to say Holsti's were the same public sources that had informed more conventional studies and, for that matter, contemporary journalistic accounts. Thus it is no surprise that the political scientist arrived at a belief system for Dulles congruent with the less "clinical" judgments of Kennan, Morgenthau, and like-minded schol-

[3] George F. Kennan, *Realities of American Foreign Policy* (Princeton, 1954), 3–30, 75–90. The quote appears on p. 89.

[4] See my introduction to this book.

[5] Ole Holsti, "The 'Operational Code' Approach to the Study of Political Leaders: John Foster Dulles' Philosophical and Instrumental Beliefs," *Canadian Journal of Political Science* 3 (March 1970): 124.

ars. Holsti's Dulles was the antithesis of the realist. He "explained for-eign policy behavior in spiritual terms," and consequently perceived the cold war as "fundamentally a moral rather than a political con-flict." Accordingly Dulles's "belief number 7" was that "cold war pol-itics are a zero-sum game." It followed from this basic worldview that the causes of war were not to be found in defects of the international system, as the realists suggested, or in human nature. Dulles, accord-ing to Holsti, "identified the source of international conflict in the clash between opposing universalist faiths," positing an irreconcilable division between the good and the evil. This premise all but ruled out negotiation or compromise.[6]

What is more, Dulles's Manichaean perspective produced what Holsti labeled the "inherent bad faith model," the secretary's predis-position to assimilate new information, including that which is discor-dant, into an unshakable preexisting belief: namely, the Kremlin was irredeemable. Assuming implacable hostility, he would interpret any Soviet conciliatory gesture, for example, as a trick or as a sign of weakness that should be exploited. As a result Dulles ran the double risk of either missing opportunities for the peaceful resolution of dif-ferences or seriously underestimating the Soviets' true strength. Hol-sti could excuse Dulles's less-than-perfect knowledge about and fixa-tion with the "enemy." What he could not excuse was the secretary's propensity for "reducing complexities to simplicities, ruling out alter-native sources of information and evaluation, and closing off to scru-tiny and consideration competing views of reality. On these counts Dulles is open to legitimate criticism."[7]

He certainly is, if in fact Holsti's findings are valid. But, as Kennan recognizes and this book affirms, the new documentation suggests that, at a minimum, this one-dimensional characterization of Dulles must be severely qualified. The same consideration that drove Hol-sti's interpretation—the currently available data base—is driving its revision. This is not to imply that the picture emerging from the opening of archival collections is, to use Kennan's word, the "nega-tive" of what Holsti and others drew. Indeed, the picture remains blurred, or perhaps more accurately, fragmented. The preceding chapters cast doubt on the image of Dulles as the inflexible moralist, the bombastic ideologue better suited for the ministry than for the State Department. But they do not shatter it altogether. Nor do they produce a new consensus or synthesis. In 1975 Holsti himself entitled

[6] Holsti, "The 'Operational Code' Approach," 129–48.
[7] Holsti, "Cognitive Dynamics and Images of the Enemy: Dulles and Russia," in David Finlay, Ole Holsti, and Richard Fagen, *Enemies in Politics* (Chicago, 1967), 56–69, 96.

a review essay on Dulles "Will the Real Dulles Please Stand Up?"[8] A decade and a half later we continue to wait, all the while discovering additional dimensions of the "unexpected" Dulles.

To be sure, the contributors agree on a number of fundamental points. Common to all the studies is the proposition that Eisenhower and Dulles held strikingly parallel views in America's foreign and national security policy. In the final analysis, nevertheless, the documents confirm that it was the president who made the decisions. They likewise confirm the recollections of Dulles's associates and the hypotheses of early revisionists that Dulles did not carry the State Department in his hat.[9] He was most assuredly a man of strong convictions who came to Foggy Bottom with a series of interlocking preconceptions. Yet he earnestly consulted with the president, his colleagues in the cabinet and National Security Council, and, perhaps most importantly, his department subordinates. In doing so not only did he show a counterintuitive willingness to accept others' advice, but he demonstrated a capacity to learn. Although this last trait is most prevalent in his attitude toward nuclear weapons, it is apparent in a number of other areas as well, such as his attitude toward the Third World and its leaders.

Just as they underscore that Dulles was neither the fanatic nor even the dogmatist that commentators led us to believe, so the contributors to this book portray the secretary of state as fundamentally pragmatic. What Dulles said and what he did were frequently at odds. He was a devout anticommunist and never doubted that the Kremlin represented values that were more than antithetical to those of the United States; they were devoid of moral foundation. Ultimately, then, America would prevail. But ultimately was a long way off, and for the immediate future the international system had to incorporate—and accommodate—both poles. Defining the cold war primarily in terms of geopolitics and political economy, not spiritual or ideological universalities, Dulles subscribed to balance-of-power theory and formulated his strategic design accordingly. He arrived at his program recommendations through systematic study and deliberation, not by memorizing Stalin's *Problems of Leninism*.

This methodical style translated into a more imaginative, complex—and restrained—strategy than that implied by the "policy of boldness" on which Dulles campaigned. He was acutely aware of the risks inherent in liberation and massive retaliation, and he was more

[8] Ole Holsti, "Will the Real Dulles Please Stand Up?" *International Journal* 30 (Winter 1974–1975): 34–44.

[9] Richard Immerman, "Eisenhower and Dulles: Who Made the Decisions?" *Political Psychology* 1 (Autumn 1979).

cautious when it came to approaching the brink than once was thought.[10] To incorporate nuclear weapons into strategic thinking is not the same as to become a prisoner to them. Morever, Dulles did not equate all negotiated settlements with communists with Faustian bargains, nor did he suffer from ideologically induced blindness when it came to recognizing the defects of allies. He was all too aware that not all anticommunists were democrats, even as he understood that not all those who resisted Washington were communists. Dulles was likewise sensitive to the centrifugal forces within the Soviet bloc; he was even reconciled to the continuation of communist regimes, including those in Peking and Hanoi.

But Dulles revisionists must be careful not to beatify their subject, and the assessments of these studies are far from uncritical. On the less positive side of the preceding equation, Dulles's flexibility and pragmatism were also manifest in the degree to which he pandered, for want of a better word, to what he considered the domestic and international facts of life. Certainly a realistic perception of the environment is essential for mobilizing and maintaining the support effective statesmanship requires. Yet Dulles paid inordinate, indeed obsessive attention to coalition building and protecting his bases of power. Despite the different circumstances under which he served, he seems to have been cognitively incapable of seeing beyond historical precedent, slavishly adhering to the lessons he had derived, especially from the experiences of his uncle Robert Lansing and predecessor Dean Acheson.[11] Accordingly, he would readily compromise rather than hold rigorously to principles that might jeopardize his relationship with patrons and constituents. Thus, with regard to Latin American military assistance, the secretary of state rapidly retreated when his ideas conflicted with Eisenhower's. Or in virtually all dimensions of Dulles's Far Eastern policy, he catered to congressional opinion, that of the Democratic opposition as well as the Republican right wing, despite his own considered judgment. Examples abound, but it is enough to argue that on too many occasions Dulles appeared more prone to appease than to lead. Perhaps Dulles's awareness of

[10] Several of the studies point this out; nevertheless, although not trigger-happy, Dulles was not gun-shy either. For a recent indictment of Dulles's brinkmanship, see Gordon H. Chang, "To the Nuclear Brink: Eisenhower, Dulles, and the Quemoy-Matsu Crisis," *International Security* 12 (Spring 1988): 96–123.

[11] For the influence of personal experiences on policymakers' cognitions, see Robert Jervis, *Perception and Misperception in International Politics* (Princeton, 1976), 239–71. See also Susan Fiske and Shelly Taylor, *Social Cognition* (Reading, Mass., 1984), 373–75; and Richard Nisbett and Lee Ross, *Human Inference: Strategies and Shortcomings of Social Judgment* (Englewood Cliffs, N.J., 1980), 45–50.

the political factors that influenced his selection to negotiate the Japanese Peace Treaty, or for that matter the rewards he received from orchestrating his appeal to both wings of the Republican party, impaired his ability to distinguish between pragmatism and opportunism. He followed political currents as carefully as he did international ones.

The pragmatic, even malleable component of Dulles's nature poses severe problems to students of his diplomacy. Relying on the public record, analysts like Holsti assumed a fundamental consistency in the secretary of state's beliefs and behavior.[12] Yet rarely does an individual exhibit such consistency; because personal values are hierarchically ordered, situational variables can prove decisive.[13] Judging from the contributors' conclusions in this book, Dulles was no exception. Whereas Nancy Bernkopf Tucker shows he sought to distance the United States from recalcitrant clients such as Chiang Kai-shek, in Vietnam and Latin America a government's anticommunism seemed to be the only criterion Dulles considered. Wm. Roger Louis reveals that throughout the Suez crisis the secretary of state expressed passionately anticolonialist and anti-imperialist sentiments. With equal passion he repeatedly upheld the inviolability of international law. Yet, as Stephen Rabe explains, in Guatemala Dulles reflexively advocated intervention to overthrow the constitutionally elected government, sanctioned an illegal blockade, and sabotaged efforts to bring Guatemala's complaint before the UN Security Council.

When negotiating the Japanese Peace Treaty, to provide an illustration from Seigen Miyasato's study, Dulles skillfully reconciled opposing positions, planned for contingencies, and maintained his sights on long-range objectives. Despite an enthnocentric perspective, he sought to account for cultural differences, and he placed a premium on promoting and managing allied harmony. In all these areas, however, he was singularly ineffective during the EDC talks. Perhaps no one—at least no American—could have salvaged EDC. According to Hans-Jürgen Grabbe, Dulles's conduct was more adroit than his critics contend. And, Ronald Pruessen points out, Dulles did enthusiastically embrace the NATO solution, which after all, approximated his original criteria. Yet his single-track approach, Rolf Steininger suggests, left the United States without a fall-back position, thereby abrogating its leadership role to the British. Similarly, at Geneva in 1954, Dulles's narrow-mindedness and shortsightedness may well

12 Holsti, "The 'Operational Code' Approach," 126.
13 Walter Mischel, "Convergences and Challenges in the Search for Consistency," *American Psychologist* 39 (April 1984), 351–64.

have contributed to precisely the settlement he abhorred. Could the same man who developed, in John Gaddis's view, "a sophisticated long-term strategy for encouraging fragmentation within the communist bloc that . . . [may] even have contributed to the break-up of the Sino-Soviet alliance," have also, to quote George Herring on Vietnam, "proved [to be] a master tactician" whose "remarkable short-term success laid the basis for America's greatest failure?" The documents suggest that he could.

The evidence is perhaps most contradictory, and thus subject to the most widely divergent interpretations, on the question of Dulles's attitude toward nuclear weapons and the Peoples' Republic of China. These attitudes can be treated in tandem because they converged with such potential explosiveness during the offshore islands crises. Consequently over the years scholars have used the crises as a barometer by which to gauge Dulles's diplomacy, and they remain a source of profound controversy.[14] For this reason Dulles's posture toward Quemoy and Matsu figures prominently in several of the chapters, each of which characterizes his intent, objectives, and strategy differently.

Pruessen maintains that the new documentation does not alter earlier interpretations that challenged the wisdom of the administration's policies. He argues that despite perceiving little intrinsic interest in defending the offshore islands, Dulles, reflecting several predicaments of power, succumbed to domestic pressure, a crisis orientation, Chiang Kai-shek's obduracy, and, most fundamentally, ambitions disproportionate to resources. As a result the secretary of state helped to devise a convoluted course of action that combined the most dangerous options. He thereby risked a nuclear conflagration over insignificant real estate.

Looking at much the same evidence, Gaddis arrives at a substantively contrasting conclusion. Unlike Pruessen he does not depict Dulles as guilty of overextension. Rather, while agreeing that political

---

[14] See O. Edmund Clubb, "Formosa and the Offshore Islands in American Foreign Policy," *Political Science Quarterly* 74 (December 1959): 517–31; Morton Halperin and Tang Tsou, "United States Policy toward the Offshore Islands," *Public Policy* 15 (1966): 119–38; Alexander George and Richard Smoke, *Deterrence in American Foreign Policy* (New York, 1971), 266–94. The recent literature includes Bennett Rushkoff, "Eisenhower, Dulles and the Quemoy-Matsu Crisis, 1954–1955," *Political Science Quarterly* 96 (Fall 1981): 465–80; Leonard H. D. Gordon, "United States Opposition to Use of Force in the Taiwan Strait, 1954–1962," *Journal of American History* 72 (December 1985): 637–60; Chang, "To the Nuclear Brink," 96–123; and H. W. Brands, Jr., "Testing Massive Retaliation: Credibility and Crisis Management in the Taiwan Strait," *International Security* 12 (Spring 1988): 124–51. Because of the continued classification of documents on the 1958 crisis, scholars have concentrated on the 1954–1955 episode.

considerations influenced the shape of the administration's reaction, Gaddis contends that the secretary of state seized the opportunity of the offshore islands crises to further his objective of exacerbating divisions within the communist bloc. Certainly there were inherent dangers, but hardball diplomacy is rarely risk-free. Besides, Dulles did exercise caution, the crises did pass, and Sino-Soviet tension did produce a rift.

Tucker portrays Dulles more as a victim of circumstances than either a misguided brinkman or shrewd strategist. Consistently pursuing a policy to promote a Two Chinas solution, he was frustrated at every turn by Chiang Kai-shek. In 1953–1954 Dulles sought to defuse the crisis, but the generalissimo was determined to involve the United States in hostilities with the PRC. After initially playing into the KMT's hand, Dulles caught onto Chiang's game plan. Paradoxically, then, Dulles's anticommunist sympathies and concern for America's credibility in Asia contributed to the escalating crisis. This escalation reinforced his conviction that unequivocal support for Taiwan did not serve the national interest, and that Washington must not permit itself to be manipulated by adventurous clients.

Scholars may never achieve a consensus concerning Dulles's and Eisenhower's behavior toward Quemoy and Matsu. Documents, no matter how extensive and accessible, do not reveal all; history is an imprecise science. Indeed, in terms of reappraising Dulles's diplomacy the existence of such diversity of opinion on an issue that was once considered clear-cut is instructive. Like Eisenhower, Dulles believed that effective diplomacy required holding one's cards close to one's chest; he disclosed as little as possible about his true beliefs and intentions. To do otherwise, he was convinced, would foreclose options and allow adversaries to predict behavior. Further, navigating the international rapids required intricate maneuvering and even subterfuge that could not be explained to an uninformed, normatively uninterested public. Just to try would run the risk of raising the level of discourse to where it would be more perplexing—and paralyzing—than educational. As Richard Nixon, who observed Dulles closely and is an expert in these matters, remarked, Dulles's "mind worked deviously and his tactics were devious." To Nixon, this was a positive attribute. "Anybody who's been a great successful Wall Street lawyer, as he was," he explained, "had to have, shall we say, many roads to the end. . . . [T]his is another side of his character which those of us who knew him well came to admire him for—his political generalship."[15]

---

[15] Richard Nixon interview, JFDOHC.

The archives suggest that Dulles succeeded in confusing, or misleading, contemporary observers and a generation of scholars. Even now, with access to an unprecedented corpus of documentary material, analysts dispute his intentions and strategies. They argue over the components and nature of Dulles's belief system, whether there was an "inner" and "outer" Dulles, and, ironically, whether in truth the secretary of state was guided by a firm core of values at all.[16] In the academic arena such controversies generate exciting debates and promote imaginative research. They will generate a new body of literature that demonstrates increased skepticism toward the traditional stereotypes and results in a greater sense of Dulles's complexities as a diplomatist and as a person.

But in the international arena ambiguity may be counterproductive—and dangerous. The dichotomy between Dulles's public rhetoric and private policy, his hidden hand or consciously deceptive approach to diplomacy, was, one could argue, inappropriate for the nuclear age. This reappraisal provides persuasive evidence that Dulles was no Dr. Strangelove. However, he *appeared* so: to the Washington community, to the attentive public, to allied leaders. Even those with whom he worked closely in the State Department suspected him of being too much the nuclear enthusiast.[17] Thus one can only imagine the signals he sent to the Soviets, Chinese Communists, and other adversaries. There is much to be said for keeping one's enemies guessing as to one's intentions. Still, if that enemy has a history of insecurity, has recently been devastated by a foreign invader, and considers itself vulnerable to attack, it is likely to interpret ambiguous actions as aggressive.[18] The distinction between offensive and defensive behavior—or strategies—can be obscure. Dulles was convinced that the United States would not initiate hostilities—but was the Kremlin leadership? This security dilemma is conducive to wars of miscalculation, precisely what Dulles sought to avoid.[19] His diplomatic style, nevertheless, may well have exacerbated it. Similarly, as indicated by the confusion over United Action's intent and the Suez

[16] For the variety of views on Dulles's beliefs, see the exchange among the scholars at the "Roundtable on Contemporary Implications and Future Research," February 27, 1988, Dulles Centennial Conference.

[17] For example see Gerard Smith Commentary, February 26, 1954, Dulles Centennial Conference.

[18] For an insight into the extent to which Soviet insecurity affected its perceptions as well as policies, see the exchanges between Dulles and Molotov at the Berlin Conference, January 25–February 18, 1954, *FR, 1952–1954*, 7:601–1233.

[19] Robert Jervis, "Corporation under the Security Dilemma," *World Politics* 30 (January 1978): 167–214. See also the conclusion by Richard Ned Lebow in Jervis, Lebow, and Janice Gross Stein, *Psychology and Deterrence* (Baltimore, 1985), 203–32.

imbroglio, Dulles's oblique communications could be equally perplexing for America's friends.

The question of whether or not Dulles's approach fed a spiral of misperception that heightened cold war and interallied tensions tops the agenda for future research. The next generation of scholarship must determine the overall significance of Dulles's "inner" beliefs considering that outwardly they exerted little, or unintelligible, influence on his behavior. Without the availability of foreign—most notably Soviet—archives, however, one cannot with confidence arrive at firm conclusions. Moreover, to distinguish Dulles's theory-driven from data-driven analyses, it will be necessary to gain access to additional American material, especially the intelligence on which Dulles drew. As the prototype for the inherent bad-faith model, Dulles, according to Holsti and others sympathetic to his interpretation, was a poor consumer of intelligence. The evidence suggests, however, that the problem went beyond his ability to process information, discordant or otherwise. When briefing the NSC early in the administration on "the general subject of the adequacy and accuracy of intelligence relative to the Soviet Union," CIA director Allen Dulles "freely admitted shortcomings of a serious nature."[20] It is possible, then, that the secretary of state felt that he lacked the quality of information required to develop innovative and coherent policies. Prudence dictated that he be conservative: avoid planning too far ahead; take few chances; and rely on amorphous strategies that allow for abrupt tactical shifts that changing circumstances often warrant. If this was the case, the dichotomy between the private and public Dulles in truth reflected a fundamental, less sui generis ambivalence and uncertainty.

It follows, therefore, that future scholarship on Dulles must pay closer attention to his grand strategy and the process by which he formulated—and implemented—it. Probably the only common denominator between Dulles's critics and champions is that he was a strategist.[21] But as indicated above, the new documentation opens even this "truism" to debate. The inconsistency of his policies suggests more of a tactical than strategic orientation. In this regard the relationship of his tactics to strategy is at times tenuous. Again, the offshore islands crisis serves as a revealing example. Dulles's recom-

[20] Memorandum of special NSC meeting March 31, 1953, *FR, 1952–1954*, 2: 268.

[21] Liberation and "massive retaliation," of course, are strategies. In addition to John Gaddis's contribution to this book (chapter 2), for a positive appraisal of Dulles's strategic thinking see Gaddis's *Strategies of Containment: A Critical Appraisal of Postwar American National Security Policy* (New York, 1982), 127–63, and the Douglas Dillon and Andrew Goodpaster commentaries, February 26, 1988, Dulles Centennial Conference.

mended courses of action provide little indication of his strategic objectives in the Far East. Were they intended to shore up American credibility and the line of containment, to drive a wedge between Soviets and Communist Chinese, or to promote a Two China solution that would institutionalize the status quo? Dulles's concerns appear to have been predominantly geopolitical. Indeed, given the reputation he achieved from his work on German reparations and his success as a corporate lawyer, he evinced surprisingly little interest in economic questions. Witness his approach to Latin America and the Middle East.[22] Yet Dulles may not have differentiated between geopolitical and economic considerations or, for that matter, psychological, cultural, and ideological ones. Scholars must endeavor to establish his scale of priorities and expertise. Put more generally, they must establish how Dulles defined America's interests: did he have a clear vision of his objectives, and, if so, were these objectives in proper proportion to his proposed means of achieving them?

These are critical questions, and raising them does not imply criticism of the secretary. Rather, it points toward the avenues that subsequent research must follow. With the benefit of additional declassification, particularly the records of the State Department Policy Planning Staff and the NSC Planning Board, scholars, one would hope, will be able explore the foundations of Dulles's strategic thought. And in doing so they will also be able to determine what other options were discussed—and considered available. The chapters in this book demonstrate what rich material can be culled from the deliberations of the NSC and other top-level forums. But for Dulles's inner thoughts it is necessary to look at the next level of the process, where the position papers and policy statements that Dulles influenced and, in turn, influenced him, were hammered out. To these documents the researcher must turn to assess, for example, what if any impact the death of Stalin had on policy planning, or to what extent Dulles considered recognizing the PRC. By examining the grist that went into the policy mill, analysts can evaluate the role negotiations played in his national security outlook, and, other than the axiomatic negotiating from strength, what constituted his strategies. Would Dulles adhere only to strict reciprocal bargaining, or did he ever seriously contemplate taking the initiative and proposing ma-

---

[22] This argument is developed most persuasively in Diane B. Kunz, *The Economic Diplomacy of the Suez Crisis* (Chapel Hill, forthcoming). See also Burton I. Kaufman, *Trade and Aid: Eisenhower's Foreign Economic Policy, 1953–1961* (Baltimore, 1982), and Thomas Zoumaris, "Eisenhower's Foreign Economic Policy: The Case of Latin America," in Richard Melanson and David Mayers, eds., *Reevaluating Eisenhower: American Foreign Policy in the Fifties* (Urbana, 1987).

jor concessions to the Soviets with the purpose of fostering trust and cooperation?[23] The documents reveal that he ruminated about major initiatives, but they do not indicate whether these musings represented anything more than thinking out loud. The bottom line, after all, is that under Dulles's stewardship the administration made little progress toward arms control agreements or the like. Was this inertia due simply to the Soviets? Or was it also a function of Dulles's beliefs and his behavior?

The above inventory of unanswered questions is not comprehensive. Indeed, it is but symptomatic of the profound dimensions of Dulles's diplomacy that can be examined thoroughly only with increased access to archival sources. Admittedly scholars will still have to infer from these sources what was truly on Dulles's mind. But without them they can probe just so far. More than that, only by peering into the inner sanctums of the policymaking process can the secretary of state's personal influence on policy be evaluated. Students of the administration's diplomacy have understandably focused on Eisenhower and Dulles, although recently other actors in the process have received attention.[24] Yet at issue is not just who participated, but how these participants interacted to produce strategy. And if strategy is defined in the "grand" sense—the integration of the diplomatic, military, political, economic, psychological, and related spheres—one realizes how misleading it is to refer to "Dulles's strategy."

The process itself placed constraints on Dulles's direct input. He may not even have played a substantial role in "Project Solarium," a seminal component of the New Look security policy, and his contribution to America's military posture is likewise problematic.[25] As a

[23] See Robert Axelrod, *The Evolution of Cooperation* (New York, 1984), and Charles Osgood, *Alternative to War or Surrender* (Urbana, 1962). Deborah Welch Larson has examined Dulles's negotiating style with regard to the Austrian State Treaty: "Crisis Prevention and the Austrian State Treaty," *International Organization* 41 (Winter 1987): 27–60. See also Richard H. Immerman, "The United States and the Geneva Conference of 1954: A New Look," *Diplomatic History* 14 (forthcoming, 1990).

[24] See, for examples, H. W. Brands, Jr., *Cold Warriors: Eisenhower's Generation and American Foreign Policy* (New York, 1988); and Nancy Bernkopf Tucker, "A House Divided: The United States, the Department of State, and China," in Warren I. Cohen, ed., *The International Relations of East Asia in the Eisenhower Era* (New York, forthcoming, 1990).

[25] Although the Solarium reports have been declassified, there is no documentation in the public domain that indicates Dulles was directly involved in the exercise, or that he participated in the integration of the reports into the "New Look" policy statement, NSC 162/2. He did take part, of course, in the NSC discussions of Solarium and NSC 162/2. *FR, 1952–1954*, 2:323–596. See also "Project Solarium: A Collective Oral History," February 27, 1988, Dulles Centennial Conference. As for the view that Dulles was out

matter of fact, to a large degree America's nuclear posture appears to have evolved independently of either the White House or the State Department.[26] Dulles insisted on his primacy in foreign affairs, and particularly when juxtaposed with the infighting that characterized the policymaking apparatus during subsequent administrations, the chain of command under Eisenhower has much to commend it. Bureaucratic rivalries and end-runs, nevertheless, were very much in evidence throughout Dulles's tenure. Because such considerations bore directly on his diplomacy, the secretary's relationship not just to Eisenhower but to the entire constellation of national security managers must be examined.

One of the relationships that warrants close scrutiny is that of the two Dulles brothers. Of course no scholar of cold war diplomacy during the 1950s would think of dismissing their successive appointments as secretary of state and CIA director as curious coincidences. Foster probably was not the determining variable in Eisenhower's selection of Allen as director of central intelligence (DCI), as some writers have speculated.[27] Doubtless, however, the president was aware of his secretary of state–designate's preference, and once in office Foster may well have protected his brother from Eisenhower's displeasure over the CIA's administrative and analytical failings.[28] Moreover, the intimacy between the two brothers, the archives make clear, carried over to their institutional interactions. This connection is of supreme interest to students of the period; even though incomplete, the evidence on Eisenhower's enthusiasm for clandestine interventions suggests that covert operations were central, not supplemental, to his administration's national security strategy.[29]

---

of his element in military matters, see Douglas Kinnard, *President Eisenhower and Strategy Management: A Study in Defense Politics* (Lexington, Ky., 1977), 19.

[26] David Rosenberg, " 'A Smoking Radiating Ruin at the End of Two Hours'," *International Security* 6 (Winter 1981–82), 2–38; Rosenberg, "The Origins of Overkill: Nuclear Weapons and American Strategy," in Norman Graebner, ed., *The National Security: Its Theory and Practice, 1945–1960* (New York, 1986), 123–95; McGeorge Bundy, *Danger and Survival: Choices about the Bomb in the First Fifty Years* (New York, 1988), 319–25.

[27] Leonard Mosley, *Dulles: A Biography of Eleanor, Allen, and John Foster Dulles and Their Family Network* (New York, 1978), 293–97.

[28] Stephen Ambrose with Richard Immerman, *Ike's Spies: Eisenhower and the Espionage Establishment* (Garden City, N.Y., 1981), 242–44.

[29] Already the literature on CIA activities during the 1950s is too extensive to list. Recent surveys with extensive notes and bibliographies include John Ranelagh, *The Agency: The Rise and Decline of the CIA* (New York, 1986), 229–348, and John Prados, *Presidents' Secret Wars: CIA and Pentagon Covert Operations since World War II* (New York, 1986), 91–171. See also William Blum, *The CIA: A Forgotten History: U.S. Global Interventions since World War II* (London and New Jersey, 1986), 59–165. In a particularly

This book does not attempt a comprehensive investigation of CIA activities during the 1950s because of insufficient documentation. Nevertheless, several chapters do refer to covert projects, and this arena must command attention as primary material becomes progressively available. How important was the unique relationship of the two Dulles brothers to the formulation and implementation of Eisenhower's global policies? Do the ends justify the means, and can the CIA's behavior be reconciled with Dulles's—indeed the administration's—professed veneration for international law and order? For that matter, can it be reconciled with the principles of an open and democratic society that meant so much to Dulles? Keep in mind that in his day congressional oversight was nonexistent. Most fundamentally of all, in terms of evaluating Dulles's overall record, does a reliance on low-profile, "secret wars" warrant more criticism than the revisionists concede or more praise than the critics acknowledge?[30] At present these and related questions cannot be answered. They must be.

On the other hand, in concentrating on Dulles's intra-administration relations, especially those concerning brother Allen and the CIA, future scholars must be careful not to take an overly narrow, too Washington-centered tack. As is the case with much of the historiography of U.S. foreign policy, studies of Eisenhower–Dulles diplomacy have focused on internal policymaking, coordination, and implementation. Dulles's lengthy career in the private sector, however, his many influential former clients, and his intimate involvement with extragovernmental bodies such as the Council on Foreign Relations, suggest that a corporatist approach should prove fruitful.[31]

Further, the evolution of the CIA's legend of omnipotence during this period, juxtaposed with portrayals of an international system in which the wishes of allies and Third World nations were not thought to count for very much, accentuated the enthnocentric bias common to American diplomatic history. Yet the preceding chapters demonstrate how distorting this oversimplification is. Not only is it clear that even supposedly weak clients—Juscelino Kubitschek and Shigeru

insightful analysis, Gregory Treverton argues that the Eisenhower administration established a "political culture" of covert operation that "set the mold" for subsequent actions. Treverton, *Covert Operations: The Limits of Intervention in the Postwar World* (New York, 1986), 12–88.

[30] Robert Divine's flattering portrait of Eisenhower's diplomacy explicity excludes covert operations. Divine, *Eisenhower and the Cold War* (New York, 1981), ix. For a damning indictment, see Blum, *CIA*, 59–165.

[31] See Thomas McCormick, "Drift or Mastery? A Corporatist Synthesis for American Diplomatic History," *Reviews in American History* 10 (December 1982): 318–30.

Yoshida as well as notorious ones like Chiang Kai-shek and Ngo Dinh Diem—exercised substantial influence over the direction of American policy, but also leaders of the neutral and nonaligned nations were of prime concern to Dulles and his associates. Of this group Nasser may have been the most conspicuous—witness Dulles throughout the Suez affair. Nehru, Sukarno, Tito, and others, nevertheless, were on balance no less significant. Indeed, considering that Julius Raab and Leopold Figl in Austria were also "neutrals," notwithstanding Dulles's rhetoric concerning the "immorality" of those who sought not to choose poles, his relations toward these nations is a fertile area for research.[32] Before one begins, however, one must define precisely what Dulles meant by "neutrality" and "nonalignment" within the framework of bipolarism.

As the chapters by Rolf Steininger and Hans-Jürgen Grabbe, appropriately, make especially clear, examinations of Dulles's policies toward Europe similarly demonstrate how misleading it is to exaggerate Washington's responsibility for the evolving international system. Dulles's objective was the promotion of European integration: strategic, economic, even political. What progress was made, however, appears to have depended essentially on the Europeans themselves. In these chapters the roles of Adenauer, Eden, and an aged Churchill emerge in the boldest relief. Further forays into the archives will illuminate the contributions of Jean Monnet, Alcide De Gasperi, Paul-Henri Spaak, and a host of others. Dulles's relations with the foreign dignitaries in several cases anteceded his relations with his administration colleagues, and in certain respects they were arguably of more consequence for whatever "successes" his policies toward Europe produced. In international affairs, knowing when to follow is as important as knowing when to lead, not that Dulles always had a choice. From this perspective what Eisenhower called the personal equation must not be minimized. Imagine, for example, German-American relations without Dulles and Adenauer, or Anglo-American relations without Dulles and Eden.

Raising the issue of personalities, however, forces one to examine

[32] Early efforts in this direction include Henry William Brands, Jr., "The Specter of Neutralism: Eisenhower, India, and the Problem of Non-Alignment," in Joann P. Krieg, ed., *Dwight D. Eisenhower: Soldier, President, Statesman* (Westport, Conn., 1987), 197–205; Robert McMahon, "United States Cold War Strategy in South Asia: Making a Military Commitment to Pakistan, 1947–1954," *Journal of American History* 75 (December 1988): 812–40; Günther Bischof, "John Foster Dulles and Austrian Neutrality," Proceedings of the John Foster Dulles Centennial Conference, Seeley G. Mudd Library, Princeton University. See also the commentaries by Bischof and Wolfgang Danspeckgruber, "Roundtable on Contemporary Implications and Future Research," February 27, 1988, Dulles Centennial Conference.

the validity, or utility, of this level of analysis. Put another way, have historians and social scientists erred by the attention they pay to specific leaders, problems of perception and misperception, the dynamics of the decision-making process, and other individual-oriented concerns? Perhaps, as many leading theorists of international relations maintain, particularly when characterized by bipolarism, the global system determines state behavior. Though each state arrives at policies according to internal processes, "its decisions are shaped by the very presence of other states as well as by interactions with them." Those responsible for the conduct of their nation's foreign affairs, then, are little more than "automatons lacking all freedom of choice."[33] By this logic, therefore, it mattered little whether Eisenhower or Dulles made the decisions, whether the secretary of state was a moralist or a realist, whether his brother ran the CIA, whether he believed in monolithic communism or was sensitive to its pluralistic nature, or whether he held immature or sophisticated views on nuclear weapons. The United States behaved as any other great power in the same circumstances would have behaved.

None of the contributors to this book subscribe to such reductionism.[34] Nevertheless, they all recognize that there were systemic as well as domestic influences—and constraints—on Dulles's actions. At the time of Dulles's appointment as secretary of state the recovery from global depression and war was far from complete. The UN had not proven itself capable of overcoming international anarchy, and, because alliances—and allegiances—remained fluid, so did the balance of power. Within this threatening, unstable environment states tend to balance,[35] and indeed, throughout Dulles's years in office he witnessed the progressive division of the globe into two competing blocs, all but institutionalizing the cold war. The authors of these chapters shed light on this process and Dulles's contribution to it. Subsequent studies must examine what alternatives were available. What actions might Dulles have taken toward reversing this tide, and had he taken them, would they have been successful? And would they have been beneficial? Was the nuclear Armageddon averted because neither the United States nor Soviet Union thought the stakes high enough to risk precipitating war? Or perhaps world peace required the division

[33] Kenneth Waltz, *Theory of International Politics* (Reading, Mass., 1979), 65; Arnold Wolfers, *Discord and Collaboration: Essays on International Politics* (Baltimore, 1961), 13. For a rigorous analysis of the distinction between "reductionist" and systemic approaches to international relations, see Waltz, *Theory of International Politics*, 18–78.

[34] Reductionism in this sense should not be confused with Waltz's use: those theories that concentrate on individual and national explanations for state behavior.

[35] See Stephen Walt, *The Origins of Alliances* (Ithaca, 1987).

of Germany, the deterrent effect of both superpowers squared off against each other with their respective nuclear arsenals and military pacts, and an international system that left as little room as possible for "vacuums" and "windows of opportunity." If so, was Dulles prescient enough to understand these systemic sources of stability? Or was he, and the world's population, just lucky?

The evidence presented in this reappraisal, incomplete and contradictory as it is, suggests that more than luck was involved. A summary evaluation of Dulles's conduct in office at this stage of the revisionist process would rate him higher than those historians who included him among the five worst secretaries of state in UN history. Indeed, George Kennan may prove to be close to the mark in his assessment. From an intellectual perspective—or what Eisenhower referred to as "technical competence"[36]—Dulles did demonstrate an uncommon understanding of the global configuration; he was an astute student of what one might label international geometry. Time and again he revealed a capacity to see beyond the immediate problem. Systematically he would break it down into its components, analyzing the factors bearing on it and the likely consequences of various contingencies. To Dulles the map of the world resembled an intricate mosaic. If he could apply the proper pressure at the correct points, the pieces would fit together—albeit imprecisely.

Predictably, Dulles was particularly adept at drawing geopolitical and strategic connections. His sensitivity to the interrelatedness and interdependence of the world evolved from his Wilsonian outlook, an outlook reinforced by his experiences at Versailles and during the interwar years. Following his return to public service after World War II these principles shaped his approach to negotiating the Japanese Peace Treaty. Dulles never lost sight of the relationship between the treaty and America's strategic posture in the Far East, the reintegration of Japan into the free world community, its political complexion, its rearmament and the problems that might present for nearby countries, the promotion of symbiotic commercial relations between Japan and especially Southeast Asia, and what that would mean for regional stability and security, and so on. Once Dulles became secretary of state, parallel considerations governed his policies toward China and Indochina, Latin America, and even the Middle East before, during, and after the Suez crisis.

But Dulles was at his best when he addressed the centerpiece of his strategic construct—Europe. Only a man with a reservoir of knowl-

[36] Entry for January 10, 1956, in Robert Ferrell, ed., *The Eisenhower Diaries* (New York, 1981), 306.

edge, a sophisticated intellect, boundless energy, and a great deal of self-confidence would attempt to juggle European integration, German reunification and rearmament, French insecurity and intransigence, British ambitions and Victorianism, and more, all against the backdrop of a fluid military balance, escalating nuclear terror, and declining colonial systems. That Dulles fumbled more than once is not as surprising as his overall record of achievement. After all, NATO admitted the Federal Republic, the European Coal and Steel Community begat the Common Market and EURATOM, and, most generally, the Western alliance not only survived EDC, Indochina, Suez, and Berlin, but it became progressively stronger.

Yet Dulles's attributes and worldview were a two-edged sword. Much like Woodrow Wilson himself, Dulles believed he could manage the changing international environment by diagnosing its ills and prescribing the remedies necessary to guide the world toward a new, stable, and prosperous order. Like Wilson, Dulles based his diagnoses and prescriptions on the American Way; for someone reknowned for his globetrotting propensities he was remarkably ethnocentric and parochial. As a consequence, he displayed an inability to empathize with the peoples who comprised the international system that he studied so intently. He could not comprehend how others perceived *their* world and defined *their* interests. This deficiency was of less consequence to Dulles's European policies because, notwithstanding the many misunderstandings, miscommunications, and personality clashes, there existed a common denominator of beliefs, values, and objectives. And for every Anthony Eden there was a Jean Monnet plus a Konrad Adenauer.

But this was not the case beyond the Atlantic Community, particularly in the Third World. There Dulles floundered in an alien sea. In this context one must distinguish between his passionate anticolonialism and the advocacy of nationalism. Dulles promoted the end of empires because he was convinced that American interests, the global system, and cold war politics, which were inextricably intertwined, demanded it—not because he sympathized with struggles for liberation or the aspirations of newly emergent nations. Although he deserves praise for his position during the Suez crisis, Dulles could not comprehend the attitudes and motives of the Europeans, Egyptians, or Israelis. It is difficult to find much at all to praise in his handling of affairs in Latin America or Asia. As for the Kremlin leadership, Dulles appeared insensitive to its fears and sense of vulnerability, while conversely remaining wedded to the axiom that Soviets were dispositionally inclined toward aggression. The evidence suggests that Dulles's lack of empathy contributed significantly to his frequent confusion of nationalism and communism. This confusion undercut his ability to manage change and impeded the construction of the new, stable world order he so fervently sought. In fact, it laid the foundation for the volatile structure and derivative crises that preoccupied his successors.

How well these generalizations will withstand further investigation remains to be seen. Moreover, the historian must resist treating Dulles as exceptional and judging him according to twenty-twenty hindsight. Although, as Kennan observed, in his "understanding of international situations" and "critical assessment of the developing problems for American policy," Dulles may have been "well ahead of anyone else on the political scene of the day,"[37] his perceptions and recommendations reflected the beliefs, axioms, and political culture that pervaded his era. In this regard, before one singles Dulles out for criticism—or for that matter praise—one must consider the other factors influencing his policies: the views of Eisenhower; others in and out of the administration, and allied leaders; congressional opinion and the domestic context; the frequently ambiguous behavior of other international actors and the concomitant problem of intelligence gathering and analysis; and the complementary considerations outlined in this chapter.

Some readers may find it disconcerting that this reappraisal raises as many questions as it provides answers. Yet such is the state of the historiography on John Foster Dulles's diplomacy, and why it is so exciting. To reiterate what I wrote in the introduction, this book does not purport to be definitive. Relatively few documents from Eisenhower's second term are in the public domain, and the record for the first one is riddled with holes. These chapters do, nevertheless, demonstrate the great strides that have been made toward coming to grips with a complex, controversial, and influential public official. As a result they highlight those features of Dulles the individual and Dulles the policymaker that appear uncommon if not unique. This collection therefore provides important insights into the qualities one should look for—and avoid—in a secretary of state.

In establishing an agenda for future scholarship, the authors have exploited the archival material recently made available in order to explore anew the traditional dimensions of Dulles's policies and postures and illuminate additional ones. In doing so they have reinforced certain notions, shed doubts on some, and even exploded others. No longer can students of the 1950s, and of U.S. diplomatic history, be content with the caricatures of Herblock, or for that mat-

[37] George Kennan commentary, February 25, 1988, Dulles Centennial Conference.

ter the operational codes of Ole Holsti. They must strive to produce a new synthesis based on the disparate elements of Dulles's personality and behavior that are only now coming to the surface. In doing so they will have the opportunity to incorporate the interdisciplinary and internationalist perspectives and methodologies that have generated such excitement among historians of U.S. foreign relations.

No matter how exciting, however, the task of producing this synthesis will tax the most prodigious researcher and thoughtful conceptualist. Yet for policy-related as well as academic reasons, the effort must be made. Applying the lessons of history to contemporary problems is a perilous enterprise.[38] In toto this book nonetheless underscores that the manner by which Dulles traversed the international landscape holds vast significance for our own era, and the contributors provide perspective on much of the current national agenda. Among the salient items are regional issues such as U.S. policy toward Central America and the Middle and Far East. They also include perceptions and definitions of the international communist movement, responses to changes in Soviet leadership, and "peace offensives"; the nexus between deterrence, arms limitation and control, summitry, and superpower relations; alliance management; the projection of U.S. power in the Pacific; and America's relations with and attitude toward the movement for European integration, which now, as during the 1950s, incorporates political, economic, and strategic dimensions. Overshadowing all is the tension between the crusading spirit inherent in America's acceptance of the title "leader of the free world" and the realpolitik—pragmatic concerns—on which it bases its international conduct. As a schooled diplomatist, veteran attorney, and religious enthusiast, Dulles embodied this tension.

Likewise both historians and contemporary observers will profit from the authors' attention to the domestic influences on Dulles's secretaryship. The institutional relations he established with such fledgling organs as the NSC, the unified Department of Defense (DOD), and the CIA, as well as his personal relations with President Eisenhower, the White House assistant for national security affairs, the chairman of the JCS, and other officials were without precise precedent and had long-range consequences. So did the posture he assumed toward Congress, the public, the political opposition, and his own bureaucracy. The preceding list, though not exhaustive, suggests that this

---

[38] David Hackett Fischer, *Historians' Fallacies: Toward a Logic of Historical Thought* (New York, 1970); Richard Neustadt and Ernest May, *Thinking in Time: The Uses of History for Decision-Makers* (New York, 1986).

book represents more than an academic exercise. To study what Dulles did then tells us much about what we do today. During a time when America's international relations—especially with the Soviet Union—may again be undergoing a fundamental transformation, and the capacity of its foreign policymaking community to demonstrate sufficient flexibility and creativity is in question, this reappraisal of Dulles may prove prescriptive as well as illuminating.

A Note on the Contributors

JOHN LEWIS GADDIS is Distinguished Professor of History and director of the Contemporary History Institute at Ohio University. He received his Ph.D. from the University of Texas, Austin, and has been a visiting professor of politics at Princeton University, a visiting professor of strategy at the U.S. Naval War College, and Bicentennial Professor of American Studies at the University of Helsinki. The recipient of the Bancroft and Stuart Bernath Prizes for *The United States and the Origins of the Cold War, 1941–1947* (1972), Professor Gaddis's most recent books are *Strategies of Containment: A Critical Appraisal of Postwar American National Security Policy* (1982) and *The Long Peace* (1987).

HANS-JÜRGEN GRABBE is assistant professor of North American history at the University of Hamburg, where he earned his Ph.D. He spent a year at the University of Pennsylvania as an American Council of Learned Societies' American Studies Fellow, and is one of the Federal Republic of Germany's leading experts on the United States. His publications include *Union Parties, Social Democrats, and the United States, 1945–1966* (1983), and "How Konrad Adenauer Saw America," *Amerikastudien/American Studies* (1986).

GEORGE C. HERRING received his Ph.D. from the University of Virginia. Having taught at Ohio University, he is currently professor of history at the University of Kentucky, where he has been selected Hallam Professor of History, University Research Professor, and Distinguished Professor, Arts and Sciences. Professor Herring was elected president of the Society for Historians of American Foreign Relations for 1989, and among his many books are *Aid to Russia, 1941* (1973), *America's Longest War* (rev. ed., 1985), and *The Central American Crisis* (ed. with Kenneth Coleman, 1985).

RICHARD H. IMMERMAN was a visiting fellow at Princeton University's Woodrow Wilson School from 1987 to 1989. A Boston College Ph.D., he is associate professor of history at the University of Hawaii, where he has received the Regents' Excellence in Research Award. The author of many studies of the Eisenhower administration's foreign policies, Professor Immerman won the Stuart Bernath Book Prize for

The CIA in Guatemala (1982), and, with Stephen Ambrose, he has written a biography of Dwight Eisenhower's brother, *Milton S. Eisenhower* (1983). In 1989, he was awarded the Stuart Bernath Lecture Prize. Professor Immerman edited this book while an ssrc/MacArthur Foundation Fellow in International Peace and Security Studies.

WM. ROGER LOUIS holds the Kerr Professorship of English History and Culture at the University of Texas, Austin, and is a fellow of St. Antony's College, Oxford University. In 1979 Oxford awarded him a D.Litt. in recognition of his published work on the history of the British Empire and Commonwealth. His books include *Imperialism at Bay* (1977) and *The British Empire in the Middle East* (1984), which won the George Louis Beer Prize of the American Historical Association. With Hedly Bull Louis he edited *The Special Relationship: Anglo-American Relations since 1945* (1986), and, with Roger Owen, *Suez 1956: The Crisis and Its Consequences* (1989).

SEIGEN MIYASATO is professor and dean of the Graduate School of International Relations at the International University of Japan. He earned his Ph.D. from Ohio State University, and he has been a visiting scholar at Johns Hopkins University's School of Advanced International Studies, the Brookings Institution, Harvard University, and Princeton's Center of International Study. Professor Miyasato has concentrated on U.S. relations with Japan, and his latest writings include *The San Francisco Peace Settlement* (edited with Akio Watanabe, 1986), "Making the Administrative Agreement between the United States and Japan," in a special issue of Japan's *International Relations* (1987), and *American Policy towards Okinawa* (1986).

RONALD W. PRUESSEN is professor of history at Erindale College, University of Toronto, which he came to after having taught at Temple University. He began studying John Foster Dulles while completing his Ph.D. at the University of Pennsylvania. He published the first volume of his biography, *John Foster Dulles: The Road to Power, 1882–1952* in 1982, and he hopes to complete the second volume in 1990. The author of many articles, with Lynn H. Miller he edited *Reflections on the Cold War* (1974).

STEPHEN G. RABE is professor of history at the University of Texas at Dallas. A specialist in both the history of U.S. foreign policy and Latin American history, his Ph.D. is from the University of Connecticut. Rabe's *Road to OPEC: United States Relations with Venezuela, 1919–1976* (1982) won the scolas Book Award, and with Richard Brown he wrote *Slavery in American Society* (1976). In 1989, he received the Stuart Bernath Book Prize for *Eisenhower in Latin America: The Foreign Policy of Anticommunism* (1988). Rabe also won the 1988 Stuart Bernath Lecture Prize, awarded by the Society for Historians of American Foreign Relations.

ROLF STEININGER is director of the Institute for Contemporary History at the University of Innsbruck, Austria. Originally from the Federal Republic of Germany, he received his Ph.D. and Habilitation at the University of Hannover. Steininger has been recognized for his films and television documentaries as well as his many articles, and ten books in both German and English. Best known for his writings on the "Stalin Note" of March 1952 (Columbia University Press is preparing an English translation), and the two-volume *History of Germany, 1945–1961* (4th ed., 1988), Steininger has recently published *The Division of Germany* (1988) and *The Ruhr Question 1945–46 and the Founding of the State of Nordrhein-Westfalen* (1988).

NANCY BERNKOPF TUCKER is associate professor in the School of Foreign Service and the History Department at Georgetown University, having moved from Colgate University in 1987. She received her Ph.D. from Columbia University, along with a Certificate of the East Asian Institute. Her many publications on U.S. relations with China include *Patterns in the Dust: Chinese-American Relations and the Recognition Controversy, 1948–1950* (1983) and "Alone in the Policy Jungle: An Academic Braves the Department of State" (1987). From 1988 to 1989 Professor Tucker was a fellow at Harvard University's Charles Warren Center, and she is the recipient of the Stuart Bernath Lecture Prize and a Council on Foreign Relations International Affairs Fellowship.

Index